AF887795

SOTHIS PRESS

Sothis Press aims to completely reimagine the public domain book with an emphasis on universal access to captivatingly designed print editions. We believe that technology will enable every single book ever published to be perpetually accessible in beautiful print form. Sothis is beauty in ubiquity.

www.sothis.press
1 Waterhouse Square, London, ECIN 2ST

Cost Accounting

Principles and Practice

John Packard Jordan

SOTHIS PRESS

ISBN 978-1-0365-0548-6

Cost Accounting is in
the public domain.

This edition is published by
Sothis Press © 2023. The company
is registered in England and Wales.
The Company Number is 14900389.

COST ACCOUNTING

PRINCIPLES AND PRACTICE

By

J. P. JORDAN

Consulting Management Engineer; Member of the firm of Stevenson, Harrison & Jordan, Management Engineers; Member of American Society of Mechanical Engineers, American Management Association, Society of Industrial Engineers; formerly President National Association of Cost Accountants.

And

GOULD L. HARRIS, A. M.

Assistant Professor of Management, School of Commerce, Accounts and Finance, New York University.

SECOND EDITION

REVISED

THE RONALD PRESS COMPANY

NEW YORK

Copyright, 1920, by
The Ronald Press Company

Copyright 1925, by
The Ronald Press Company

All Rights Reserved

PREFACE

This work presents a comprehensive treatment of the subject of Cost Accounting, with emphasis upon the relation of Cost Accounting to Management. There has been kept in mind throughout not only the viewpoint of the accountant but those of the executive and engineer as well. The cost records and the accounting procedure described are designed to assure accuracy through rigid control accounts, to furnish the cost information to executives at the time the operations are taking place, and to provide statements of direct and indirect costs, a profit and loss account, and a balance sheet, wherein the executive may at a glance read a true story to guide him and his responsible department heads in conducting the business to a higher plane of profits.

The usefulness for students also of the management approach here followed, as well as of the method of illustrating principles and procedure at every step with details of actual practice, would seem indicated by the wide use of the earlier edition as a text-book in university classes. In this edition the entire work has been revised in detail, to adjust it still further to class room conditions. There has been considerable change in the order of presentation, and the scope of the work has been broadened both as to the treatment of individual topics and as to the range of subjects covered. Chapters I to XXVIII present the flow of cost procedure in a connected sequence of operations. Chapters XXIX to XXXV deal with special points not part of the regular flow of cost procedure but met with in everyday business life, such as Budgetary Control, Uses of Cost Records by Executives and Department Heads, Interest as a Cost, Joint and By-Products Costs, etc. The Chapters on Interest and on Joint and By-Products are entirely new, as well as those on Sales and Distribution Costs, Administrative Costs, and Working Plans for Specifications of Products.

In the Appendix will be found a series of questions and problems based on each chapter. These are designed to provide an opportunity for the student to grasp the subject matter step by step.

Following the chapter problems is a general problem by Professor H. H. Baily of the University of Illinois, which brings into action the entire procedure as specified in the book, including the working up of all statements, expense, burden, profit and loss, and balance sheet.

In the treatment of the new matter, as well as in the revision of the old, the purpose of the original edition has been steadily kept in mind, namely, that of concentration upon the basic principles which must be observed in all plans of cost accounting. Whatever special adaptations of cost procedure or methods, such as Standard Costs, Complete Machine Rates, etc., may be developed by the cost accountant for individual situations, the basic controls must still remain those which are outlined in this volume.

J. P. Jordan
Gould L. Harris

New York City,
August 1, 1925.

CONTENTS

FORMS

COST ACCOUNTING
PRINCIPLES AND PRACTICE

CHAPTER I

WHAT COST ACCOUNTING IS

The Purpose of Cost Accounting.—Cost Accounting is the accounting for all value entering into the manufacture or carrying of product or goods for sale, the selling and distribution of the product or goods, the administration of the business and the interpretation of such costs in such a manner that:

1. The management may know the extent of and be able to fully control expenditures of every description.
2. The management may know the cost of all products for the purpose of control of lines of product sold.
3. The management may have complete and accurate statements of conditions at reasonably short intervals.

It should be noted particularly that the first object of cost accounting is to provide data for the *control* of the business.

Originally, if a small business man found his bank account keeping up, he knew everything was going along all right. The growth of business required this same man to have some books, but he accounted for as little as he could. About all his accounting amounted to was an accounting of cash paid out and a record of what was owed him, kept on account of fear that he would forget it. He did not worry about what he owed as the other fellow would remind him of it. Once a year or so, perhaps not so soon, he would list up what bills he found, count his stock and see how he stood.

As business grew, the business man was obliged by banks and because of the fact that he could no longer handle all affairs himself, to install better accounting methods. Therefore, he had a scheme of double entry bookkeeping installed and accounted for everything in so far as it concerned his relations with *outside* interests.

This created a condition as illustrated in Figure 1. Note particularly that no accounting took place between the original entries of everything purchased and the point where the manufactured goods left his plant as "sales."

The Beginning of Cost Accounting.—Then came the stage when progressive general accountants realized the difficulty of setting selling prices for products manufactured, and thereupon started to develop internal accounting methods to supply some knowledge as to what the products cost. Compared with present day methods, the methods used were crude. But nevertheless, great credit is due these early accountants who started cost accounting, and it undoubtedly is true that what they developed was entirely sufficient for the purposes at that time.

From an entirely separate direction came another and different development. This development was of an engineering nature whereby intensive research and study was made of the disposition of the time of workers paid for as shown by the pay-roll account. Note that this development was in regard to the *disposition* of the *time* paid for—not just what was *paid* for the time. In other words, the "Accounting" angle developed simply history; the "Engineering" angle developed knowledge of a tangible and profitable nature.

Unfortunately, however, the engineering approach concerned itself almost wholly with the development of the standardizing, planning and routing of direct operations of manufacture, and concerned itself very little with the indirect costs of the business commonly called "overhead." In other words, the engineer concerned himself with efforts to control and lower costs which were directly measurable and apparent. Such efforts were of advantage to industry.

It may be asked: Why was no attention paid to the overhead by the engineer? The answer is simple. The accountant had failed to arrange the accounts in such a manner that they could serve any particular purpose for usable control and the engineer had no figures to work with.

At this point, with competition increasing rapidly, with the pressure of necessity for curtailing costs, cost accounting received the attention of minds other than accountants, or in some cases of accountants who had opinions other than those along the line of orthodox accounting. And while it is inevitable that cost accounting always will be known as such (and should be as it is in reality a process of accounting), the approach to its problems and its place in industry *must* be from an entirely different angle than that to orthodox accounting. The handling of accounts as such in the books is one thing, and here is required accounting knowledge as it is generally regarded; but in cost accounting the knowledge of accounts in the books is the least consideration. If a bulk cost of generating electric power is required, simply a control account is necessary in the accounting scheme; but the setting up of a usable power cost requires a knowledge of the actual factors entering into the manufacture of power—the grouping of the items of cost whereby they will be worth something to the head of the power department and the management, and a knowledge of how this power should be distributed on the basis of actual consumption. The same is true with respect to all other expense and manufacturing operations of the plant. In other words, there must be a knowledge of the manufacturing and sales problems to properly set up the costs in a manner to be either accurate or in any way useful. Figure 2 shows where the Mystery Section of Figure 1 has been replaced by cost knowledge, and this represents the field of cost accounting.

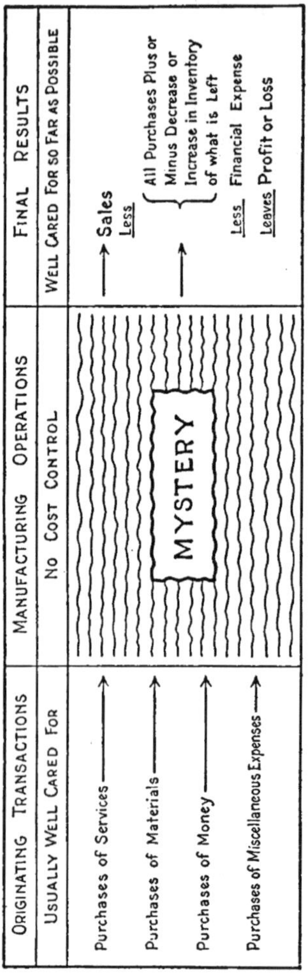

Figure 1.—Manufacturing Flow in a Concern Without Cost Control

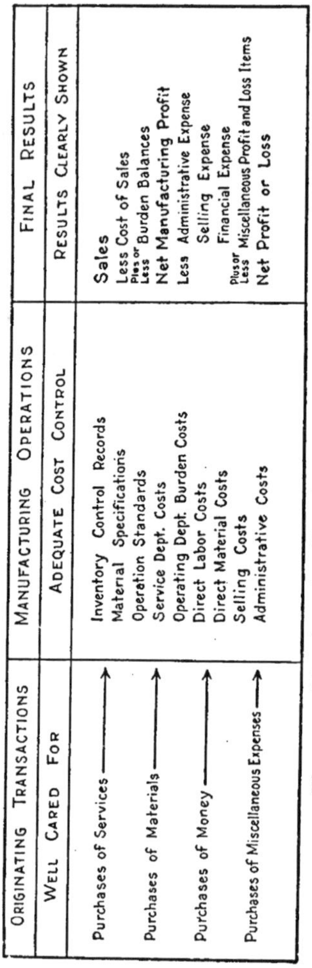

Figure 2.—Manufacturing Flow in a Concern Having Cost Control

This, however, is *not* accounting as orthodox accounting is understood today and always will be. Neither is the ability to carry out proper cost accounting procedure a function of engineering. In reality it is a science by itself—the science of *Cost Accounting.* This fact has been very clearly demonstrated because the engineer stopped at the overhead for want of figures, and the orthodox accountant stopped at the same point as he could go no further through lack of operating knowledge.

Relation of Cost Accounting to Management, Engineering and General Accounting.—Cost accounting, therefore, stands somewhat apart from, but is closely allied to the work of

1. The Manager
2. The Engineer
3. The General Accountant

Taking these three points in succession they may be elaborated upon as follows:

1. The cost accounting accounts for the internal disposition of every dollar used in the manufacture and sale of the product. If there had been no need of such accounting, the first efforts in that direction by the general accountants would never have been made. But the problems of management require a different viewpoint than is held by the orthodox accountant, and, in turn, still a different viewpoint than is held by the engineer. The attitude of co-operation and co-ordination so valuable to management must be predominant in the cost accountant, as he is essentially a staff man. He prepares, presents and interprets the most intimate figures of the business. He must be sympathetic and helpful to everyone and on equally good terms with all—that is to say on the very best of terms, irrespective of varying individualities. He must always remember that the accurate interpretation of departmental results means much to the department heads and to the rest of the management. The cost accountant's degree of tact, diplomacy, vision and help-

fulness measures his standing with the management and all others in the organization. With a good basic knowledge of the manufacturing and selling operations, a scheme of cost figuring that tells a real story and is of tangible use, and with an ability *to interpret* the figures for the entire organization, the cost accountant is invaluable to the management.

2. The cost accountant should work as close as he possibly can to the engineer. It is the engineer on whom he must rely for the correctness and value of much of his data. It is the engineer, who not only helps the cost accountant, but also whom the cost accountant wants to help. The engineer is also a staff man for the service of the organization. Many of the problems brought up for solution by the cost accountant fall to the engineer for solution in the same way as many problems of the management assigned to the engineer require the co-operation of the cost accountant for solution. Therefore, the cost accountant and the engineer should work just as closely as two functional heads can possibly work. The engineer should rely on the cost accountant for all records whether concerning cost, production or any other like work. The cost accountant should rely on the engineer for co-operation in the task of accounting for the many intricate details of plant operation. This combination of efforts is absolutely invaluable to the management.

3. The cost accountant must also work in close harmony with the general accountant, as in the general books of account lie the accounts which control the cost accounts. The accuracy of the cost accounts, as far as being certain of accounting for every dollar, depends on a correct balancing with the general books. Beyond this the responsibility for the accuracy of costs lies with the members of the organization throughout plant, sales and office. All original figures as to purchases and obligations of every sort must come to the cost accountant from the general accountant. The cost accountant must return to the general accountant proper journal entries for the transferring of amounts from the original to the subsequent accounts

which represent and control the progressive operations of the business. Accordingly, there must be a very close relationship between the cost accountant and the general accountant, even though this relationship is less immediately important than the relationship of the cost accountant to the engineer and departmental heads.

Cost Accounting as a Managerial Control.—Reference has already been made to the relation of cost accounting to the management, but this feature is too important to pass without particular reference to this very valuable phase of cost accounting.

Has the reader ever tried to assume a responsibility without having figures and facts to guide him? Has the reader ever sat through a baseball or football game without knowing how the score stood? It would be a dry game indeed if no score were kept.

Cost and production accounting furnishes the score to those who are playing a game far more vital than either baseball or football, in which are tied up ambitions, hopes and loyal work. Yet many a department head goes without proper figure guidance either because the management fails to appreciate its necessity, or because the cost accountant has not proven equal to the task of preparing something that is worthy of use. In the second case, of course, the management cannot be blamed, except for its failure to get a better and more useful cost accountant.

Even today, however, many executives are not enough familiar with cost accounting methods and their possibilities to appreciate or understand the great value to management of properly departmentalized costs as a backing and guide for each responsible department head in the organization. "Costs" are too often regarded as being the cost of the completed product and *nothing else,* which is far from true. Departmental costs are far from complete product costs, and many costs may be expressed in terms other than dollars and cents when used at the time an operation takes place, as is explained in Chapter XXXI where the follow-up of direct operations is described.

Under properly designed cost methods, costs are figured at strategic points in many ways. Each department, whether direct (or producing), or service, should have cost figures for the guidance of its head. For instance, a plant restaurant may simply be represented by an account in the ledger charged with all purchases of material and labor and credited with what may be received for meals—the balance to be distributed as an expense to some other accounts. This of course is a method of accounting for the restaurant expense, but to what purpose? Instead of this method, the head of the restaurant should be provided with a statement of the complete cost, the number of meals served, and a unit cost per meal irrespective of whether they were paid for or not. How else can such expense be controlled by either the management or the head of the department? This same reasoning applies to such departments as Electric Power Generation, Steam, Teaming, Timekeeping, Pay-Roll, General Superintendent's Office and every other kind of indirect or service departments.

The producing departments will have a control of direct labor by comparison with standards (see Chapter XXXI). The indirect expense or burden of each producing department will be itemized and figured on the unit basis of the direct time of the department. Is not this information valuable to the department head? Can or should the department head be held responsible to any extent unless such purely departmental costs are furnished him? The answer is naturally not with any degree of fairness or good management.

The psychological effect of furnishing such costs to the department heads is found to be an element of unlimited value. Giving to department heads the current results of their departments in figures immediately places them on an entirely different plane of responsibility. Greater interest is taken as they have something tangible to work with. Progress is evidenced by the reduction of the costs from month to month, which could not be brought about without the definite and usable knowledge which the cost figures bring to them.

Therefore, cost accounting is a managerial control which could not be replaced. While product costs, it is true, are simply history and of absolutely no value for management purposes, current departmental costs are a guide to better management and lower costs.

Product Costs of Comparatively Little Value.—Cost accounting is of course indispensable in its relation to product costs, although its value in this respect is far less than in its use for the support and backing of current operations.

The theory has been that product costs constitute:

1. The basis of selling prices.
2. The means of detecting unprofitable lines in order that they may be eliminated.
3. Part of the means of obtaining frequent statements of profit and loss and of balance sheets.

Actually, with the majority of businesses, neither of the first two statements is true.

1. Selling prices are largely controlled by economic and trade conditions. Exceptions to this exist, but they are rare. In jobbing businesses where time and material are charged, the cost of the product naturally is used in establishing the selling price, but in all staple lines such as steel, iron, textiles, oils, rubber, together with those businesses which use those staples in manufacturing fabricated products such as machinery, garments, tires, etc., competition and trade conditions determine more selling prices than do the product costs. Repair parts for such fabricated products may of course be priced upon costs as a basis because competition counts for less, but even here, in many cases, the effect of competition and trade requirements is felt.

2. As for detecting unprofitable lines, here again we deal with trade and competition conditions. It is usually quite necessary to sell some unprofitable items to hold customers, and this will continue as long as business exists. It is true, however, that where and when it is known that some items are unprofitable, the knowledge may hold back the sales department from undue pressure of selling effort on each item, simply selling such goods where the good-will of customers so demands.

3. There is no question but that product costs are necessary in completing the knowledge required for the preparation of frequent profit and loss statements and balance sheets.

Summarizing the relation of cost accounting to the business so far as product costs are concerned, we can but conclude that while product costs are necessary and valuable, this feature of cost accounting is far less valuable than the intermediate or departmental costs which control the expenditure of the money at the time and in the place where the expenditure is made. By the time product costs are reached, the profit has long since been made, or the loss has been suffered.

The Necessity for Cost Accounting.—The vastness of industry and commerce today permits of no guesswork. Competition is keen, not only in domestic affairs but far more in foreign. The rehabilitation of foreign countries assures keen competition between nations for many years to come and a natural result will be that our internal competition will accordingly become more intense.

Cost accounting as just an accounting operation is simply a mechanism. The need of industry and commerce for cost accounting as a purely accounting function is no greater than its need for many other mechanisms which can be bought and paid for. But business needs more than that. It needs cost accounting as a guide—an *interpreter* of facts and conditions; and it is hoped that the study of cost accounting will be approached with this point of view clearly and constantly in mind. Mechanism? To properly account for costs in order to have dependable figures, it is surely necessary to study and understand the mechanism of how it is done. But do not let the study or thought of mechanism obscure or becloud the one great objective of cost accounting—i.e., to so account for costs by responsible departments and products whereby the management may have dependable guidance and support, where those who are responsible for the expenditure of the money may work intelligently, and where the business may prosper through the use of actual knowledge.

CHAPTER II

RELATION OF COST ACCOUNTING TO MANAGEMENT

The Position of Cost Accounting.—It will be well for the reader before he reaches the technical chapters to fully realize the relation of cost accounting to the management. The method of approach to any subject greatly affects the viewpoint as the details are taken up.

Cost Accounting and cost accountants are rapidly coming into their own in industry and general business. But in all cases where cost accountants have risen to positions of large responsibility, it has been due far more to their vision and their ability to "put things across" than to their knowledge merely of the technic of cost accounting. To be sure the cost man must know his technic, but this is simply of high grade clerical value unless he has the ability to promote the use of cost figures for the guidance of management.

Need of Co-ordination.—Comparatively little actual use of cost data has been as yet made by industry. That fact is largely responsible for the more or less sharp distinction which exists between the plant organization and the executive management. Particularly in cases where the executive management is segregated from the plant, either in a distant city or in another part of the city, this condition has been apparent. It is natural enough for such a feeling to exist, as lack of actual knowledge of conditions causes more or less competition between the operating departments and the office departments. Too often, however, most unfortunate and regrettable relations between the plant and office have resulted. This is the worst possible condition that can exist in a manufacturing institution, where, in order that the greatest benefits may be reached by both the plant and the executive management, full co-ordination and co-operation must prevail.

The cost department of a manufacturing institution which is sometimes connected chiefly with the executive branch, is in other cases still chiefly connected with the operating branch. Just as surely as there is a closer affiliation with one than with the other, just so surely this lamentable misunderstanding is bound to develop.

As a matter of fact, need of entire co-ordination between the executive management and the management of the operating departments cannot be emphasized too strongly. It is only when the executives are fully alive to all the problems of the operating department, particularly those which the operating department has to contend with every day, that they are in the best position to perform the service which they, in their managerial capacity, are bound to perform. Likewise, those in charge of the operating branch should be more closely in touch with the problems of the executive branch, in order that they may intelligently handle their own work.

The logical department of the plant to effect this co-ordination is the cost department. That department has at its command all figures in connection with all operations, and should be thoroughly in touch with all the circumstances which bring about the results set forth in the cost statements.

Strategic Position of the Cost Department.—The cost department is therefore in the most strategic position in the plant to effect co-ordination and bring about reforms and improvements which may mean the success of the company. It is in a position to know in money or other unit value the efficiency not only of each operating department, but of nearly every superintendent, foreman, and any other department head. Thus it possesses more valuable information than any other routine department of the organization.

All members of the cost department, therefore, should bear in mind constantly that they carry a responsibility which is very great and very grave. The information which they possess is confidential, except for those who are entitled to receive it. Its use is far-reaching with respect to the management as well as to the departments affected. Because of their unique position great care must be taken by the members of the cost department as to their conduct in their relations with executive managers and those responsible for the operation of any department. The work of the department must be conducted along dignified and absolutely unbiased lines. In many cases, cost department men have been known to discuss results of one department with someone connected with another department, and in a manner more like gossip than necessary business discussion. Such conduct is most unfortunate; it is an abuse of privilege. Every member of the department must be most careful to use such information as he possesses only in a manner that makes for assistance and co-operation—never for personal criticism or condemnation.

Responsibility of Cost Department's Head.—The head of the cost department has the greatest responsibility in connection with not only the conduct of the department and the excellence of the cost figures secured, but also with the interpretation and use of the knowledge collected by the cost department, in furthering the co-ordination between the executive management and the operating departments.

Like all others in the department, the department head has confidential information which must be used only in proper ways. He will be consulted by the executive management in connection with many problems which arise, and in his answers he must always hold to absolute straightforwardness and accuracy. He must be of a firm and yet considerate nature. He must exhibit no likes and dislikes so far as personalities are concerned—as it will be difficult if not impossible for him to construe correctly the figures relating to the departments in charge of persons whom he dislikes.

He must maintain a position of co-operation at all times, and must use every endeavor to cull from successful departments the points which may be used in assisting a department not so successful.

In this connection, an instance may be related of the head of the cost department in a large manufacturing institution. A visitor was sitting in the office of a department head when the head of the cost department walked into the room. There was a smile on the face of the cost man, but in about two minutes a battle royal was on between the two men.

After the cost man had left the office, the department head remarked that he had very little use for the cost man. He went on to say that every time the cost man came into his office with a smile on, he knew that his department was in trouble—that it seemed almost a diabolical pleasure for the cost man to be able to come into his office with bad news. On the contrary, whenever the cost man came into the office with a long face, he knew that his department must have turned out some good results.

That is exactly the wrong way for a cost man to conduct himself. His own efficiency is absolutely crippled where a man in the plant regards him in such a way, as he can expect no assistance or co-operation when such a feeling is in existence.

When he goes into an operating office he should feel just as he would if he were in charge of the operations. Only when he has this feeling towards operations in the plant, or towards the sales or any other departments, can he expect to make the proper headway in the work with which he is charged.

Relation Between Cost Man and Executives.—In dealing with executives, the cost man must be guarded in everything he says, not evasive by any means, but absolutely fair and free from bias in any opinions expressed as a result of the figures produced. This does not mean that he is to act as a shield for anyone who is not producing the right results in any particular department, but he must be absolutely certain of his knowledge of all conditions before either bringing up any bad situation for action, or expressing—even on request—any opinion in regard to a condition.

A cost man is in somewhat the position of a judge. The evidence consists of the data collected by his department in relation to conditions affecting the various departments involved in the plant. He is called in by the executive management, and very often what he says may swing one way or the other any proposition which is up for consideration. When he is certain of his ground he must take a decided stand and stick to it. But his attitude must be entirely fair and unbiased; he must eliminate all personal feelings and confine himself always to the evidence. By the evidence is meant here the actual results accomplished by the department, or rather the procedure which is in question—not mere opinion.

The cost man is often called into conferences with the executives to assist in deciding as to new departments, new equipment, or the like. Here again, he should make it an invariable rule to confine his evidence to objective facts, deduced from the past experiences of the business, and to eliminate personal opinions based on anything else.

He should be very careful, also, as to what he calls to the special attention of the executive management. He should always be sure that he understands all the underlying circumstances in connection with the figures. The figures alone, even when apparently unfavorable, do not always prove that a given department is at fault. For instance, when the rate per hour or the percentage on labor of the operating burden goes up, it may be found that the trouble is not due to the operating departments, but to the failure of the employment department to supply the necessary workers. Countless other illustrations might be given. For the cost man to be in a thoroughly tenable position in respect to various problems which continually arise is a most responsible and difficult task.

In any event, the principal point regarding the attitude of the cost man to the management is that he must be absolutely square. If he is, his own sound sense will lead him into very careful investigation of any matter before he influences the judgment of the executive one way or the other.

The Relation of Cost Men to Budgets.—More and more the responsibility of budgets is devolving on the cost department. This is exactly as it should be. Budgets are simply forecasts of the future based upon the experience of the past tempered by judgment of the conditions ahead in the light of improvements which are expected to be made.

As budgets come into more general use the cost man finds his field—a field of great usefulness. With increasingly effective co-operation with executive management and department heads a surer and truer forecast of the future will develop. The surer and safer the forecast the more accurately the department heads can adjust their expenses, and thus greater profits will result.

It is obvious, therefore, that the cost and budget work should be inseparably linked together. But to be most effective, the cost man must constantly broaden his vision, his knowledge and his research. The field is his for the taking; but it means hard work and intense and prolonged study.

Importance of Cost Men's Position.—To repeat—the head of the cost department and all members of the department are in a most important position in connection with the operation of an industrial plant. Those who are in a position to know the operations in such intimate detail are bound to become—unless they neglect their own opportunities—a power in the organization. Whether the department rises to a rank of trust and importance, or its work remains in the class of clerical routine, depends wholly upon the mental attitude of the department head towards his duties. Unfortunately, many men who have entered the field of cost accounting relegated themselves to positions of simply high-class clerks by their own actions. They have made out of the cost department no more than a figuring machine for assembling routine items—a position without dignity or standing.

It should be borne in mind at all times that the guiding features in all cost accounting work should be not only accurate knowledge and sound judgment but also, and primarily, honesty and fairness.

CHAPTER III

DEPARTMENTALIZATION

The Need of Departmentalization.—It is obvious that an industrial plant must be organized properly in order to operate well. Proper organization involves intelligent departmentalization. For successful operation it is sometimes necessary to provide not only for main departments but also for minor or subsidiary departments. Intelligent departmentalization is also an indispensable prerequisite to the successful application of cost methods.

In fact, organization, management and cost accounting are so intimately related that it is almost impossible to consider them separately. However, the subject of departmentalization is treated in this chapter mainly from the point of view of the cost accountant.

If the cost accountant finds that the concern is not properly departmentalized for his needs, he must see to it that the organization is rearranged or he cannot do his own work satisfactorily. Therefore, the successful cost accountant must be familiar with the principles and practice of management in a good organization, as well as the principles and practice of cost accounting, and—what is probably even more important—he must know how to correlate or tie up cost accounting with management.

As the cost accountant works with the factory executives in deciding what is the most effective way of grouping departments from the viewpoint both of management and of cost accounting, he begins to visualize in a general way the kind of records necessary to reflect the costs of the material, labor, and burden as they are applied to each individual department.

For example, the character of departments influences in

large measure the selection of suitable cost methods. At this point the objectives of managerial control as well as costing requirements must be considered. Elements of this problem are:

1. What definite grouping of service or indirect departments should be made from the standpoint of good organization and also from the standpoint of proper costing?
2. What definite grouping of direct producing departments should be made for the same reasons?

Matters to be Considered in Departmentalization.—The factors to be considered in departmentalizing a concern are:

1. Division of responsibility.
2. Nature of operations:
   - (a) With respect to physical movements.
   - (b) With respect to costing.
3. Location of operations.

Division of Responsibility.—The assignment of definite responsibility is absolutely necessary from the point of view alike of the management and of the cost accountant. The definite assignment of physical and financial responsibility constitutes indeed the essential basis of departmentalization. Coupled with the assignment of definite responsibility is the necessity of providing the means of reflecting the results of this responsibility in figures.

Thus a foreman or department head is appointed to take charge of each department, perhaps with the aid of one or more assistant foremen. He should then be furnished with a monthly statement of the burden cost of his department. In some departments he should also get statements of direct material, and direct labor costs as incurred in his departments. Thus he is in a position to control his costs and thereby discharge his responsibility properly.

Nature of Operations.—The second important factor to consider in departmentalization is the nature of the operations for which each department head is responsible. In many cases it is necessary to unite, under one responsible head, two departments which have dissimilar operations. A case in point would be a small machine shop which manufactures special machine tools with a force of fifty mechanics. Assume that forty of this number work on individual parts with machine tools, that the other ten do bench and assembly work, and that one foreman supervises the work of the entire number. In this case the two branches of work in the shop must be treated as two departments, in order to gauge results properly and to obtain accurate costs.

An additional reason for this division of work exists in this particular case inasmuch as the plant sells two products: individual parts for repairs, and assembled units. The manufacturing cost per hour for the individual parts is far greater than the manufacturing cost per hour for the assemblies, because the depreciation, the power cost of operating machine tools, the maintenance cost of equipment, etc., are higher for individual parts than for assemblies. Since as a matter of fact these items do not constitute a part of the assembly burden, the assembly burden is a comparatively low figure per hour. Under a single rate of overhead, proper costs could not be obtained for either individual parts or assemblies. As a result, losses would be suffered on sales of repair parts because of insufficient selling prices based on costs which are too low. Thus a firm using the single overhead rate would be doubly unfortunate because one of the essential objects of a business of this nature is to sell as many machine units as possible in order to secure the repair part business which naturally follows.

The nature of operations must likewise be considered in determining what service or indirect departments are necessary. Obviously, the method of determining the cost of steam generation is entirely different in principle and detail from that of determining the cost of electric power generation. The nature of teaming service in every respect differs from the restaurant. This is true also of all other service departments. Not only does the responsibility lie with different men in every case, but the costs must be handled in a considerably different manner for each service or indirect department.

Location of Operations.—The location of operations is the third important factor to consider in departmentalization. Heavy work may best be done on the lower floors of the factory and lighter work on the upper floors. For certain operations more light is required than for others. Operations of a like character may be grouped, although this is not always done. The factor of location of operations is influenced very materially both by the assignment of responsibility and by the nature of operations, already discussed.

In the case of two similar departments—such as two machine shops or two assembly departments—which are in separate locations, even though one person is actually responsible for both of them, the mere fact of similarity should be no justification for combining either the two machine shops or the two assembly departments into a single department. A similar department in a separate location should be treated as a separate department.

Subsidiary Departmentalization.—Reference has been made to the fact that it is frequently necessary to provide for subsidiary or minor departments as well as for main departments. These minor departments are sometimes called cost centers. For example, the process of hardening certain parts may not warrant the maintenance of a whole department for hardening alone. In this case a minor departmentalization is effected in order properly to collect and distribute the cost to the parts. Another case of minor or subsidiary departmentalization occurs in a small foundry where one foreman is in charge of all operations. In this case, if proper costs are to be kept, it is necessary to have the following minor departments: melting, core-making, moulding, finishing, and pattern. In all cases, however, a great deal of thought and planning is necessary to arrange the most efficient divisions to produce the necessary results.

Classes of Departments.—Regardless of the nature of the factory, its departments may be divided into two main classes: Direct or producing departments, and indirect or non-producing departments—usually called service departments. To a limited extent, however, producing departments may perform service, and service departments may produce.

Producing Departments.—Producing departments are those which actually make the product.

While some work for the maintenance of the plant may be done in producing departments, this fact does not in any way alter their status as producing departments, as such maintenance work may properly be classed as production as far as these departments are concerned.

Service Departments.—Service departments are those which are not directly engaged in the manufacturing of the product, but which render services for the benefit of the producing departments. The expenses of service departments are closed into the producing departmental burden accounts so that they may be applied to the product.

Examples of service departments are stores, tool and machine maintenance, electric power, steam, teaming, process inspection, final inspection, and shipping departments.

Departments Partly for Production and Partly for Service.—The work of some departments is of a hybrid or mixed character, i.e., partly for production and partly for service. For example, the tool design department may manufacture tools for individual parts on a job, which are chargeable thereto, or it may make small tools which are serviceable for a variety of jobs, the cost of the tools being treated as a part of the manufacturing burden. Other examples of departments whose work is partly productive and partly of a service character are the blacksmith shop, the machine shop, and the pattern department. The costs of such departments, like those of service departments, are closed into the departmental burden accounts kept for productive departments.

Inasmuch as burden cannot be controlled like direct labor and material by production control records, the importance of ascertaining correct departmental burden rates is evident. The department is the only unit which affords the proper basis for the calculation and application of such rates.

Planning a Cost Structure.—After the departments have been organized in a new concern, or rearranged in a going concern, greater attention can be given to the details of the cost methods. The kind of original and detailed records as well as summary records must be kept in mind. In other words, the use to be made of cost figures summarized in reports, returns, and statements for foremen, managers, and executives should never be lost sight of in devising detailed records, as the managerial use of cost figures is the most important feature to keep in mind.

One important step in planning the cost structure is to recognize and control the manufacturing branches of the plant on the one hand and the selling and administrative branches on the other. There may be, of course, only one selling and administrative unit for the entire organization, or there may be separate units for each division.

Secret of Correct Costing.—One of the most important elements in accurate cost-keeping is to charge as many items as possible to their final resting place in the accounts. In a well-regulated cost system, therefore, as many items as possible should be charged directly to productive or standing orders of productive departments. Items such as division expense, division labor, general expense, steam expense, electric power expense, compressed air expense, and trucking expense, are entered first in collecting accounts for the above items. Then these accounts are distributed to expense accounts and departmental burden accounts, and later applied to cost units.

If a concern has been departmentalized along the lines that have been explained in this chapter, a sound foundation is provided on which to erect the superstructure of a cost system, for the various departments so organized afford a convenient basis for the assembling of cost data. In fact, one of the most important advantages in departmentalization is that a basis is thereby provided for the calculation and application of departmental burden rates. (See Chapter XXII.)

CHAPTER IV

COST COMPONENTS

Purposes of Chapter.—The purposes of this chapter are to convey a definite idea of the broad classes of components or elements of costs; to show the reasons of cost classification; and particularly to stress the fact that many diverse elements make up the overhead or burden—one of the major cost components—thus emphasizing the necessity of properly recording and summarizing the overhead for presentation to the management. The chart on page 31 shows graphically the cost components that make up the cost of a unit of product. Do not study the chart, however, until you have read further in this chapter. The cost man must know the elements of cost and how to classify them before he can hope to build a cost structure that can be successfully operated and intelligently used.

Classification of Costs Upon Basis of Function or Activity.—Costs may first be classified upon the basis of function or activity. Accordingly, costs may be divided finally into three groups

1. Manufacturing or production
2. Selling
3. Administrative

One purpose of the classification just given is to enable the costs of the primary divisions of a business to be ascertained separately. Responsibility for production, for selling and for administration should not, under any form of management, be assumed by one and the same individual. The need of this separation of responsibility is particularly in evidence when the factory and general offices are not in the same locality. If divided responsibility exists, means should be provided to control it. Control is dependent on information with regard to all branches of the business—the manufacturing, the selling and the administrative work. The information necessary for control is found in the cost data. Hence, cost methods should be so planned as to maintain a distinct separation between factory accounts, selling, and administrative accounts. This fundamental of cost accounting has been emphasized in cost literature only within recent years, although the principle has been known and observed for some time.

Costs Classified According to Requirements for Accurate Construction.—After costs have been classified in such a way as to separate those pertaining to manufacturing, selling, and administration, they must be further classified in a manner to permit the accurate construction of the final cost of product. This requires the division into the following three elements or components of cost:

1. *Direct or Productive Material,* that is, material directly entering into the manufactured product—such as the felt, silk, ribbon, leather band and thread in a hat.

2. *Direct or Productive Labor,* that is, the wages paid for work applied directly to the product—such as the labor of actually forming and finishing the hat.

3. *Factory Burden or Overhead,* that is, all other cost in the factory which cannot be directly applied to the product. Reference to Figure 3 graphically illustrates that this burden is a composite figure arrived at through the apportionment of (a) many expense accounts which serve all productive departments, (b) reserve accounts through which come periodical "fixed" charges such as insurance, taxes, etc., and (c) those charges for material and labor incurred directly by each burden account such as for supervision, clerical work, handling material

and repairs. While this chart seems to indicate that the burden or overhead is a complicated matter, the reverse is actually the case when the steps are taken care of as shown, that is to say where enough expense accounts are provided to permit scientific measurement of the efficiency of each expense account for managerial purpose, and where intelligent distribution to the producing departments which use the service may be effected.

Common practice has established the terminology that

Prime Cost is the sum of the direct material and direct labor and

Manufacturing, Factory or Production Cost is the sum of all costs in the manufacturing department, including Direct Material, Direct Labor and the Burden or Overhead.

4. *Selling Expense,* that is, all costs incident to distributing and selling the product, such as salaries, rents of branches, advertising, etc. This cost is added to the manufacturing cost according to some ratio consistent with the circumstances in each business—most companies using a flat percentage. A discussion of this point will be found in Chapter XXVII.

5. *Administrative Expense,* that is, the expense of the general functions of the business, such as general administrative officers and offices. This cost, like selling expense, is most often added by flat percentage to manufacturing cost, and is also discussed in Chapter XXVI.

The total of these five major components is called *Total Cost.*

Manufacturing Cost.—Thus Manufacturing Cost may be considered, as the term is used in cost accounting, as follows: the aggregate payments or charges for direct material, direct labor, or overhead, the purpose of which is to create marketable assets—finished product. Various combinations of the components of cost arise in the creation of marketable assets.

It is important to point out that capital expenditures (expenditures for assets) and exchanges of certain assets for other assets are not costs within the meaning of this definition of cost. While the purchase of a machine, for example, in the non-technical sense "costs" money, it is not a cost as the term is used in cost accounting.

The mere statement of the elements that make up the aggregate cost of an article, with single illustrations, however, does not give a clear idea of the real nature of cost components. The reader probably already knows fairly well what is meant by the terms *direct material* and *direct labor,* but may not be so clear as to what is meant by *overhead* or *burden.* Just what differentiates direct material from indirect material, direct labor from indirect labor; and why these indirect costs are classified as burden instead of direct material and direct labor, respectively, these and other questions are apt to puzzle the reader who is beginning a study of cost accounting. These questions should be cleared up before proceeding further.

Direct and Indirect Costs.—Costs are therefore further divided into direct costs and indirect costs.

Direct costs are payments or charges for labor and material expended upon a definitely determined unit of product. It follows, therefore, that indirect costs are those which cannot be charged directly to the product. An example of a direct cost is the cost of the raw material in a chair. Indirect costs arise from the following sources:

1. Indirect material—for instance, those materials used in repairs, rags and waste, fuel.
2. Indirect labor—for instance, wages of foremen, inspectors, laborers handling materials.
3. Prorated charges—for instance, heat, light, power and other service charges.
4. Fixed charges—for instance, depreciation, taxes and insurance.

Adherence to the above cost classification adds to the accuracy of the records for this reason: By charging all possible items directly to the cost units, the remaining costs (indirect costs) are reduced to the minimum. Indirect costs are distributed over the product in various ways as accurately as possible, but such charging is less accurate than direct charging. For instance, while raw material can be accurately measured and charged directly against a chair, the depreciation of the equipment used in manufacturing the chair cannot be determined with any measuring device. It must be prorated as equitably as possible. Any charging, therefore, which reduces the distributable costs, thereby increases automatically the accuracy of the cost records. The growing observance of the principle of direct—that is to say correct—charging has done much to improve the exactness of cost accounting.

The exercise of judgment in correct allocation of costs as they are incurred more than pays for the effort expended. The salary of a foreman, for example, who works only in department A should be charged only to A. But his pay very often is grouped with others and treated as a group supervision cost, the total being apportioned to several departments, none of which, except A, received any benefit from the foreman's services, and consequently should not be charged with any portion of his salary. In other words, every expenditure of material or labor should be charged where it belongs at the start.

If different costs are to be controlled, their amounts must be known and compared with past costs and with standard costs. Costs cannot be subjected to the highest degree of control unless they are definitely known, and then compared with standard costs.

Chart of Elements of Cost.—We are now ready to present a composite picture, so to speak, of the components or elements that enter into the *manufacturing cost* of any individual unit of

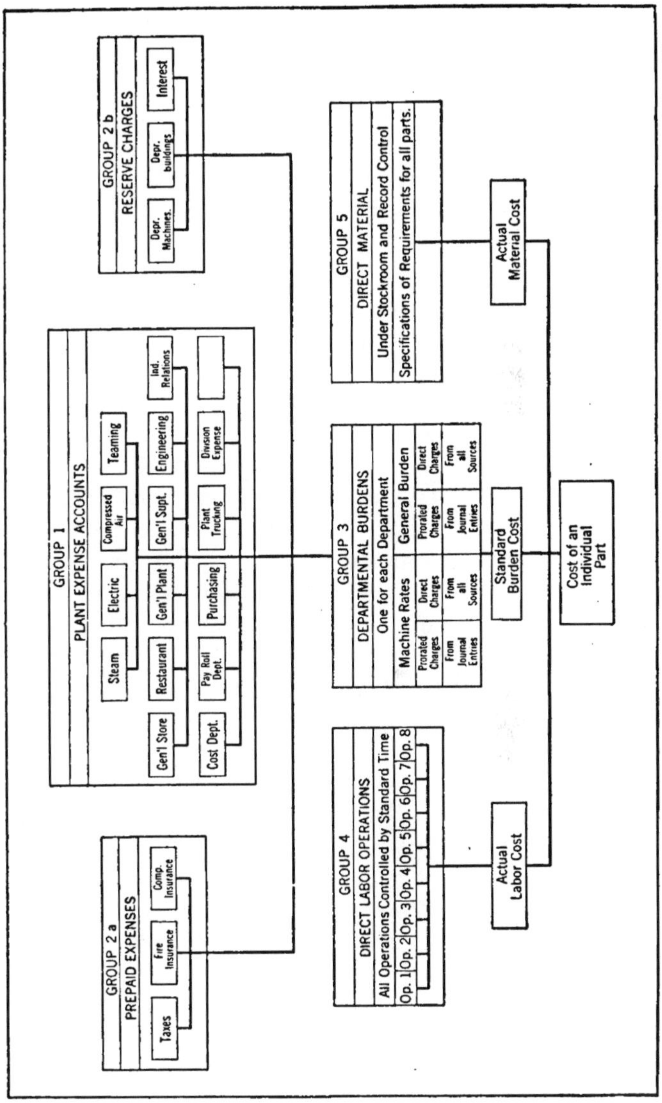

Figure 3.—Illustration of What Enters into Cost of Product Either Directly or Indirectly. This is not a Flow Chart

product. This picture is shown graphically in Figure 3, page 31.

It should be noted particularly how large a portion of the final or total cost of an article is made up of the manufacturing cost of the product shown in Groups 1, 2 and 3, which has to be controlled entirely separately from any consideration of the final or complete manufacturing cost.

By reference to this chart it may be clearly seen that:

Group 1 is a collection of service or indirect departments. Over these the head of any direct or producing department has no control at the time the service charges are incurred, yet each of these service departments is established for the purpose of rendering service entirely for the benefit of the direct or producing departments.

Furthermore, the cost of operating these service departments is eventually charged to the direct departments. Therefore, it is absolutely necessary to have a cost statement, usually termed an expense statement, for *each* of these service departments. By so doing the head of each service department has figures by which to control his department and furthermore the cost department is able to charge the direct departments benefited according to the volume of service rendered by each service department.

The expenses incurred in operating the service departments, together with the rest of the burden cost, ultimately appear in burden statements. The expenses of the service departments are listed in the "Prorated" or "Apportioned" section of each burden statement. A burden statement is prepared for each direct or producing department.

Group 2 on the chart represents the fixed charges which are prorated to the direct or producing departments according to bases which as correctly as possible measure the benefits received.

Group 3 on the chart stands for the burden of each direct or producing department.

The burden of each direct department consists of three major classes of items:

(a) The department's *own* expenditures for indirect costs (burden) such as supervision, clerical, inspection, repairs and supplies.
(b) Charges prorated from Group 1 (service charges).
(c) Charges prorated from Group 2 (fixed charges).

The head of each direct department is *wholly responsible* for costs under "a"; *partially responsible* for costs under "b"; and *not responsible* for costs under "c."

The costs in Group 3 are figured into the product by various methods described in Chapter XXII. These methods do not at the present concern the reader.

Group 4 represents the direct labor operations on the product. The cost of these operations is for labor *directly* applied to the article manufactured such as turning, milling, boring, etc., in a machine shop. If the time of the direct labor operations is carefully recorded, it is comparatively easy to calculate with precision the costs of the operations.

The efficiency of the operations may be determined by comparing the actual time taken on the operations with the standard time required as established by time studies or observance of many past runs of product.

Group 5 on the chart represents the direct material cost of the article, which is determined from material requisitions drawn on stores in stock rooms, and is effectively controlled by means of standard specifications of exact amounts of material required to make the individual product.

Chief Purpose of Chapter.—The chief purpose of this chapter is to impress on the reader that the preponderant problem in cost accounting is in the component known as "overhead" as represented in Groups 1, 2 and 3. It can readily be seen that many responsibilities are involved before the final cost of an individual product is reached. It may also be realized readily that for proper "cost control" there must be an intelligent analysis of departments, both direct or producing and indirect or service departments; not only for accurate costing purposes, but for the still greater purpose of effective managerial control.

As stated before, it is not assumed that the reader will understand at this point the technic involved in the proper accounting of all the components shown in Figure 3. But if the mind has been influenced as to the extent and necessity of the problem, the technic will be easy to understand as it is covered step by step in the succeeding chapters.

It may be stated at this point that no mention has yet been made of the administrative and selling costs, as this portion of the "overhead" is treated entirely separately from the factory or manufacturing overhead.

Final Manufacturing Cost of Product.—The final or complete manufacturing cost of the product is but an assembly of the components. The technic of assembling final costs in all its details will be explained in other chapters.

The use of complete costs in actual practice is of small value as compared to the use of the intermediate or component costs by the management for the purpose of cost reduction.

The principal uses of complete product costs are:

1. To permit the completion of frequent profit and loss statements by furnishing the cost of goods sold.
2. To assist in the setting of selling prices, particularly of "repair parts" and in jobbing plants where work is sold on a "time and material basis." In general, however, selling prices are set by competition and trade conditions and not determined by costs.
3. To indicate unprofitable goods. Although this seldom means dropping these goods from the line, it does, however, guide the sales department in its sales campaigns

restricting pressure for sales, in such articles, and increasing pressure on the profitable lines.

This enumeration of the comparatively restricted use of complete product costs is quite opposed to past claims for the value of cost accounting to manufacturing businesses. The value of the uses of costs—by departments and at their source for the purposes of the control of costs, the stimulation of cost reduction, and the guidance of the men who are responsible for the various departments has so far over-shadowed the possible uses of the product costs that there remains hardly a comparison. Obviously, complete product costs are historical, being available too long after they are incurred to be of any use whatever to the management for betterment purposes. On the contrary, properly departmentalized costs are of the utmost value for managerial purposes and for the increasing of the profits of the business.

CHAPTER V

ESTABLISHING THE BASES OF COSTS

Necessities for Proper Bases of Costs.—Before the detailed recording, accumulation and presentation of costs can be accomplished and intelligent uses made of cost figures by the management, proper *cost bases* must be established not only for building up completed product costs but also departmental operating costs.

As the technical procedure of the various steps of cost accounting is explained in subsequent chapters it will frequently be noted by the reader that the establishment of cost bases is extremely important; in fact, absolutely necessary. Particularly, is this so when you stop to consider the uses of costs that may be made by the executives and departmental heads.

The principal reasons for accurate cost bases are as follows:

1. To make as certain as possible the accurate calculation and accumulation of operating departmental costs, and final or completed product costs.
2. To provide a means of cost measurement whereby the executives and departmental heads may have reliable cost figures to intelligently direct and control the business.

Definition of Cost Bases.—A cost basis is the natural point of focus for expressing cost in quantitative measurement.

In the manufacture of an automobile tire, this principle is apparent from the following major operations:

Operation 1	– Gathering and weighing the ingredients for the rubber compound	– Basis, per batch
Operation 2	– Milling the rubber	– Basis, per pound
Operation 3	– Calendering the fabric	– Basis, per yard
Operation 4	– Building the tire	– Basis, per tire

If a cost basis in a given instance is wrong—and it may be remarked parenthetically that it is easy to select a wrong basis if careful attention is not paid to the matter—the cost calculated on the basis will be incorrect as far as getting the most use out of it is concerned. As a matter of fact, the most prevalent cause of failure of cost methods to operate satisfactorily is lack of understanding as to proper bases on which to figure costs in the first place; and then the problem exists of definitely settling the combination of several cost bases, often as many as five or six, to use in building up the final cost of the product. In short there must be a wise choice and use of cost bases.

The problem of selecting the best cost basis arises at various stages in the cost procedure and in every department, whether sales, production or service.

Control Through Cost Bases.—Far more important than securing final costs of product is the control and use of costs *at the source* or *at the time* the work is being performed. Generally speaking, an example of what is meant by *use* in this respect is the comparison of *actual costs* of a department with the *standard costs* previously determined for that department. (See Chapters XXXI and XXXVII.) Thus an idea of the operating efficiency of the department can be gained and measures instituted to increase the efficiency, thereby saving time and money. Costs, therefore, must be used to measure or gauge results. Otherwise, they will be of comparatively little value, except as mere business history. Business men today are more interested in the future of their concerns than in the past or current accomplishments.

Before the final or completed unit cost of an article is determined, a number of cost bases must be used, often as many as five or six. The management then must have the cost of the various service departments, and the costs of the product at different stages as it moves through the plant.

After the total cost of any service department has been obtained, it is divided by some unit basis to get the unit cost of rendering the service (such as kilowatt-hours in the Electric Power Plant) ; and the total cost of a product in a given direct or producing department is divided by some *unit of measurement,* such as the piece, hundred pieces, pound, hundred pounds, ton, dozen, or gross. The selection of what units of measurement are to be used as cost bases should be carefully considered in order to have the best one in each given instance.

Cost Bases in a Restaurant.—Let us consider some illustrations of cost bases. Suppose a factory has a restaurant. The *net cost* of operating the restaurant might be distributed to all direct departments on the basis of the respective number of persons in each department. In other words the restaurant cost might be calculated on a per person basis for each day, week, month or some other unit of time. There is justification for using this basis on the theory that the restaurant is maintained for the benefit of all departments and that the employees in each department have the opportunity to buy meals in the restaurant. It might be contended that the management can get a line on the efficiency of the restaurant by ascertaining whether the restaurant cost on a per capita basis is increasing or decreasing. But such a basis is practically of no value as a measure of the efficiency in operating the restaurant, because not all employees will use it, and those who patronize it may not do so regularly. Consequently, a more accurate cost basis in this case is in the *meal.* The cost per meal served should be determined. The *total costs* of operating the restaurant divided by the *total meals served* will give the cost per meal, irrespective of whether a total profit or loss is made or suffered in running the restaurant.

Cost Basis of an Electric Power Department.—As another illustration of a cost basis consider the generation of electric power. Departments may be charged a fixed service charge, plus a charge for the cost of actual power consumed. But the correct basis for measuring the efficiency of the power department is the kilowatt-hour. The total cost of generating electric power, or the total cost of power bought, or the sum of both, is divided by the total kilowatt-hours delivered, to give an electric power cost per kilowatt-hour.

Electric power costs are distributed to departments according to the respective kilowatt-hours consumed by each department.

The restaurant and the electric power cases just mentioned illustrate cost bases for two service departments, and all other service departments are treated in a similar manner, but with bases which fit each case.

Direct Cost Bases.—To illustrate the matter of cost bases in connection with producing or direct departments. Consider a paper box factory which is making cigarette boxes of various sizes. In this case it is absolutely impossible to arrive at the cost per box directly; and even if it were possible no advantage would be gained.

1. Many parts of a cigarette box are common to various boxes used for packing different brands of cigarettes, such as tops, sides, bottoms, etc. Such parts are manufactured in common strawboard in large quantities, in many cases a million at one time, irrespective of what box they will be used for. The cost basis in this case, therefore, is *per thousand.*
2. The scoring of the board as well as other operations are common to many styles and sizes of boxes, and therefore have a definite relation to the *measurement of scoring* accomplished or the *number of sheets* scored.
3. The cost of assembling boxes even of different sizes within a reasonable range of sizes is figured on a basis of *per box* or *per hundred boxes* and is the same regardless of the size within the given range.

4. The coating of strawboard is calculated on a *square foot basis of board coated.*

It is obvious, therefore that both for control of efficiency and for accurate costing, the basic cost units differ. The final cost of product is a built up combination of the various component parts of the box at the cost of each part.

Gray Iron Foundry Industry.—In a gray iron foundry of average size the bases of cost used are as follows:

1. *Metal Cost.* The metal cost is arrived at on the basis of the total weight in pounds of liquid metal delivered from the spout of the cupola. Two items make up this cost: conversion or melting cost, and cost of metals.

From this it is possible to arrive at a cost per pound of the metal as it is poured into the moulds, irrespective as to whether it is later accounted for in the shape of good castings, bad castings, or "sprue" which includes the metal in the runners for pouring the casting. That is to say the basis of this section of cost is the pound.

2. *Moulding Department Cost.* In the Moulding Department, three separate and distinct bases of cost are involved:

(a) Direct moulding labor
(b) Moulding department burden
(c) Moulding machine burden

These three items involve the use of three different bases, as follows: The first item involves the direct time of making the mould, which is invariably on a per mould or per piece basis. Even though first regarded on the per mould basis, it is considered eventually on the basis of the number of pieces per day which the moulder can produce and the rate per piece for the direct moulding cost.

The second item, the general burden of the moulding department, should be on the basis of the direct-labor hours applied to each job. However, it may also be figured on the direct-labor cost, the difference between the two being explained in subsequent chapters. In any event, the general overhead of the moulding department must be applicable to the job on the basis of the direct hours applied to the job, or the direct-labor cost of the job.

The third item is used when a special rate on account of moulding machines is applied to the cost of a job. In this case the basis is expressed in the number of hours that any particular machine was used in producing the order.

3. *Core Department Cost.* The bases used for the core department are the same as for the moulding department, involving, similarly, the direct labor, the general department overhead, and special charges on account of machines used.

4. *Finishing Department Cost.* The finishing department cost in the usual gray iron foundry is handled on the basis of the combined moulding and core-making direct-labor hours, or the combined moulding and core-making direct-labor cost. In other words, the entire cost, including direct and indirect costs, of the finishing department is carried into the cost sheet on the bases stated above. Exceptions to this rule occur, however, in any gray iron plant where the direct labor may be applied to the orders which pass through the department. For instance, in plants where there is a large amount of repeat work, and where it is possible to charge to each casting the amount of grinding, chipping, etc., the direct labor is applied to the product itself, and the indirect cost of the department is applied in the cost sheet on the basis of the direct-labor hours involved, or the direct-labor cost.

From the foregoing, it will be seen that the cost sheet of a casting is made up of the cost of pounds of metal, direct-labor charges, indirect expenses on the basis of the direct-labor hours or cost, and finally the finishing cost on the basis of a combination of the moulding and core-making direct costs.

Wood Box Industry.—The procedure in the wood box industry with respect to bases of cost may be illustrated as follows:

1. *Dry Kiln Cost.* The cost of kiln-drying is established on the basis of thousand feet. This holds true irrespective of the kind of lumber which goes into the kiln, although it is necessary, if various grades of lumber are used, to keep the various kinds separate in order to arrive at true costs.

2. *Planing Cost.* As the planing of lumber is an operation which applies to all product which goes through a mill, the cost of planing lumber should be found on the basis per thousand feet. Irrespective of the final disposition of the lumber which goes through the planers—as a particular lot of lumber going through is usually divided up later among many orders—it is impossible to consider this cost on any other basis than straight per thousand feet.

3. *Rip Sawing Cost.* After the lumber has been planed, the next operation is to run it through the rip saws. In this operation the final disposition of the material which is being worked on is not known. Therefore, in order to establish any accurate cost basis, it is necessary to adjust the cost on the basis of the operation, as in the case of planing.

In this case, however, the width of the material sawed is immaterial; the main point of consideration is the lineal feet of material passed through the saws. In this operation, therefore, a basic figure of the lineal feet passed through the saws should be collected, and the cost of the operation computed on this basis.

4. *Cross-Cutting Cost.* In this simple illustration it is doubtful as to whether the cost of cross-cutting can be applied to some particular order for goods, or whether the basis of an operation cost must be continued, somewhat as in the case of rip sawing.

Reference to a common practice will illustrate the difficulty in establishing a proper distribution of this particular item of cost. A lot of lumber may be running through, intended for three kinds of boxes. The specification for the first box calls for absolutely clear lumber, that for the second box permits of one knot in each side or end, and that for the third box permits any number of knots in either side or end. The length of the sides and ends in each of these three boxes varies. The sawyer, therefore, may have six gauges to work to.

In drawing through the lumber, he first squares off the end and finds that he can get a full piece of clear lumber for the first specification. He cuts this off to the proper length. He then finds that one knot hole is so close to the end that it is necessary for him to cut the next piece to the gauge representing the end of the box which will permit of one knot hole; this is an entirely different box from the one for which he cut the first piece. The next strip of lumber has three or four knots in it, and he therefore cuts a side for the third box. This procedure continues throughout the entire run.

It would be manifestly impossible for the sawyer to distribute his time as between the three kinds of boxes being produced. One thing, however, is common to all of them, namely, the time required to make the cut. Therefore, in a business where large runs of boxes are being put through, it is obvious that the only practical way would be to establish an operation cost based on the cost per cut for the various widths of the sizes involved in the boxes being manufactured. This cost per cut could then be used in compiling the cost of the boxes so far as the direct labor is concerned.

5. *Other Operations.* We can now readily imagine that all other operations in connection with the manufacture of the boxes are peculiar to the particular box being manufactured, permitting no special consideration as to operation costs. This would then involve the charging of the direct labor to the particular order covering the goods.

6. *Burden Charges.* In each of the preceding operations there is involved at least one consideration, and very likely two, in connection with the distribution of the burden. The general burden of the department is distributed on the basis of the direct-labor hours, or the direct-labor cost. In the case of special machines which require the establishment of a special machine rate, this burden will be charged on the basis of the machine hours applied to the particular work in question.

In any woodworking plant of this description there are of course many other problems relating to the basis of cost which are not here mentioned. Enough material has been presented, however, to bring out the fact that the building up of the final cost involves the use of a number of separate and distinct bases.

Pipe-Rolling Industry.—Illustrations of bases of still different kinds may be found in a pipe-rolling industry, starting from sheets of metal cut to the required size for the various sizes of pipe.

1. *Bending and Welding Costs.* In this particular department of a tubemill, the bending and welding is a very large and entirely continuous operation. The sheets of metal are heated, passed through bending rolls, reheated, passed through welding and straightening rolls, and the crop ends cut off—leaving a blank which awaits the further operations in connection with threading and finishing. After the sheet metal has started on the initial heating there is no stop until the actual pipe has cooled down and the crop ends are cut off.

In such a case a *gang cost* is found which includes all costs actually applied to working the pipe and to the maintenance of the equipment used. This cost is reduced to a *cost per hour of the running time of the gang.*

A tally is kept of the lineal feet of pipe put through in each particular run of a certain size. The charge to this run is on the *basis of the hours actually used* in making the run. This charge is then divided by either the *number of lengths of pipe, the pounds of pipe produced,* or the *lineal feet of pipe produced,* resulting in giving a cost per pound or per foot, up to the point where it is ready for the finishing operations. This cost involves both direct and indirect charges.

2. *Finishing Cost.* After any one particular size of pipe has been welded and cut off there is the possibility of its being treated in many different ways. It will be remembered that up to this point the cost per foot or per pound has been determined. This cost now becomes the material cost of the orders which call for the various kinds of finishing, and the finishing costs are found on the order basis, which in turn may be subdivided to give the cost per piece, or, so far as the threading is concerned, to give the cost per thread or hundred threads.

For each particular order, the cost per piece will, of course, be the main object. This cost per piece is calculated on the basis of the individual piece of pipe, or better still, on the number of ends threaded. It is determined by charging to the order the direct time of the workers in threading and finishing the pipe.

It is possible, of course, that the pieces of pipe may vary in length, so that the cost per lineal foot of many runs of the same pipe may have to be recapitulated to arrive at a flat average per lineal foot covering lengths. In computing the individual order, however, it is necessary to take into consideration, for comparative and actual purposes, the number of ends threaded. In addition, it may be found of value to assemble figures from various runs of like thread to arrive at the cost per hundred threads for estimating purposes.

Another feature of the finishing cost is that of testing the pipe, which for comparative purposes should be figured on the basis per piece of pipe. It makes no difference in testing the pipe what the length of each piece may be.

As in all other departments of this nature, the burden of the department is figured on the basis of the applied direct-labor hours or direct-labor cost, so far as the general burden is concerned, with the addition of special machine charges based on the number of hours each machine may be used on each particular run.

Rubber Tire Industry.—In the manufacture of rubber tires the various bases involved in arriving at a final cost per tire are:

1. *Milling Cost.* The various compounds which are involved in the manufacture require different lengths of time for the milling process. Therefore, it is necessary to find the cost of the milled compound on a pound basis.

2. *Calendering Cost.* The fabric is usually purchased on a pound basis, and in finding the cost of frictioned fabric the material cost enters the records on the basis of pounds for the fabric and also for the milled stock.

The direct time of the operators of the calenders is kept for the particular run of material which is passed through as well as the machine time involved. These charges are made to the run on the basis of the value of the direct labor—as shown by the time cards—for all the labor involved, with its burden on the particular basis which may be used, and for the number of hours of the machine equipment involved. A tally is kept of the lineal feet of fabric passed through the machine, together with its width. All the elements of cost above mentioned are brought together and divided by the square yards of the product finished by the calenders. The basic unit, therefore, in this case is the square yard.

3. *Bias Cutting Cost.* As the bias cutter operates at a constant speed, the labor and burden cost of this operation is on the per piece basis. For comparative purposes, therefore,

the cost of the direct labor with its dependent overhead is figured on the piece.

4. *Other Operations.* Without going further into detail it may be said that the other major operations are largely on an order basis, particularly the building of the tires. In this case, the direct labor with its burden is charged to the orders for each particular size of tire as a result of which the cost per tire is arrived at.

Building Up the Basic Plan of Costs.—While the foregoing illustrations by no means are intended to indicate all that is involved in any one kind of industry, they *will* give an idea of what is meant by establishing the basis of cost.

There is probably no industry in which it is possible to arrive at the final cost of the product without establishing a series of many basic cost figures, the various combinations of which in time will produce the final cost. The accuracy of the final cost depends on the intelligence with which the various bases of figuring are established.

But far more important than the securing of the cost of the product is the matter of so fixing the bases of costs as to give a real, usable and effective control of all the operations necessary to produce the goods. With such costs it is then possible and exceedingly profitable to *use* the cost figures *at the source* or in other words at the time the work is being performed. By comparing to standards of how and in what time the work should be done, the operating foreman and other department heads will be in a position to produce actual savings in cost and prevent losses of time and money.

CHAPTER VI

CONTROLLING COST RECORDS

The Necessity for Control Accounts.—If cost records are to be useful to the management, they should be kept in considerable detail. The necessary detail, however, is too great to be recorded in any ledger, either the general ledger, or even in a subsidiary ledger.

Suppose a machine shop (regarded as simply one department) is working on two hundred orders. The cost of the time taken and the material used on each order is charged to the order by means of time cards and material requisitions, respectively. It is obviously impracticable, however, to keep an account in the general ledger for each order. Instead, two control accounts are set up in the general ledger, namely:

1. Direct Labor
2. Work in Process Material

Control of Direct Labor and Material.—At the end of each pay-roll period, say a week, the total pay-roll of the machine shop is determined. It is entered in the Voucher Register where Vouchers Payable account is credited and Pay-Roll account is debited. Each weekly pay-roll is automatically analyzed as explained in Chapter XIX, and from this analysis it is found that the direct labor charge to production orders for the full month (May, for instance) was $22,000. This part of the labor journal entry for May would therefore be:

Dr. Machine Shop Direct Labor Account..........	$22,000.00	
Cr. Pay-Roll Account		$22,000.00

The amount of $22,000 is then posted to the Machine Shop Direct Labor account shown below.

Machine Shop Direct Labor
(Controlling Account in Ledger)

Debit		Credit	
Balance from April......	$14,822.00	Direct Labor on Production Orders Completed for May per Journal Entry	$26,850.00
Direct Labor Applied to Production Orders for May per Pay-Roll Journal Entry	22,000.00	Balance down	9,972.00
	$36,822.00		$36,822.00
Balance	$ 9,972.00		

Note—If the direct labor charges on all production orders uncompleted on May 31st were accumulated, the total should equal this balance of $9,972.00.

All these charges in detail are filed against each production order on which work was done, and are available at any time for accumulation when orders are completed or when it is desired to verify the control account.

At the same time as the labor is being expended on these production orders, material on which to work is drawn by material requisitions from the store rooms. These requisitions are summarized daily as explained in Chapter XXIV, and at the close of the month this summary gives the total amount for material used on the production orders of the machine shop: This portion of the journal entry distributing the material requisitions for the month would be

Dr. Machine Shop Work in Process Material Account	$20,560.00	
Cr. Stores Accounts (specify)...........		$20,560.00

This amount of $20,560 is then posted to the Machine Shop Work in Process Material account, shown below.

All these charges in detail are filed against each production order as in the case of labor, and are available at any time for accumulation when orders are completed or when it is desired to verify the control account.

MACHINE SHOP IN PROCESS MATERIAL
(Controlling Account in Ledger)

DEBIT		CREDIT	
Balance from April......	$ 6,250.00	Material on Production Orders Completed for May per Journal Entry	$19,800.00
Material Charged to Production Orders for May per Distribution of Requisitions Journal Entry	20,560.00	Balance Down	7,010.00
	$26,810.00		$26,810.00
Balance	$ 7,010.00		

NOTE—If the material charges on all production orders uncompleted on May 31st were accumulated, the total should equal $7,010.00.

As orders are completed, the time cards and material requisitions charged to each order are accumulated, and the cost of the order found. An accumulation is made of all orders completed for the month and this furnishes the total direct labor and material which is to be taken out of work in process and transferred to the next logical account which we will assume is the Finished Stock account. We will assume the direct labor amount to be $26,850, and the material to be $19,800. The portion of the journal entry affecting the direct labor and material would be

Dr. Finished Stock Account........................	$46,650.00	
Cr. Machine Shop Direct Labor Account..		$26,850.00
Machine Shop Work in Process Material Account		19,800.00

These credits will be posted to their respective control accounts as shown in the illustrations of these accounts just preceding.

Consummation of Control of Direct Labor and Material.—The Direct Labor and Work in Process Material accounts now show balances of $9,972 and $7,010, respectively, and they each represent in the general ledger the inventory value of this particular work in process. Those amounts, therefore, form part of the inventory balances which will be used in the balance sheet, and which permit a periodical set of statements to indicate the position of the business.

The ledger balances represent the total of all charges on incomplete orders, and can be verified at any time by accumulating the time cards and requisitions remaining in the files.

The principles and procedure up to this point apply to *all* work in process accounts of direct labor and material. It is always desirable if possible to have such a control account for each shop or manufacturing unit, as the verification of control accounts is much more readily accomplished if they are kept in easily handled units.

Control of Burdens.—Thus far we have discussed only the control accounts for direct labor and work in process material. The control of the third major component or element of cost, namely overhead or burden, is handled in a different manner by means of Expense, and Burden (control) accounts, although the principle of control is the same.

All expense and burden accounts are built up by the use of a code of standing orders as shown in Chapters X and XXV.

Expense accounts differ from Burden accounts only in that the Expense accounts (such as electric power, etc.) are closed out to the Burden accounts each month, and the Burden accounts become the final recapitulation of operating department indirect cost.

Expense and burdens must be kept in great detail in order to provide, automatically, necessary and specific information as to what money for overhead is being spent for. Because of the volume of this detail, it would be impracticable to have a separate account in the general ledger for each item making up each expense and burden account. It will be remembered that the same point was made above in describing the control of direct labor and work in process material.

The aggregate of the actual burden incurred by the machine shop, to continue our illustration, is recorded in a controlling account, called the "Burden Account," maintained in the general ledger. The debits to this account come from various sources:

1. Labor from the pay-roll distribution.
2. Material from the entry distributing material requisitions drawn from stores.
3. Items charged directly from the voucher register, known technically as Expense Ledger Items. (See Chapter VII for explanation of details in handling such items.)
4. Prorated charges from the journal entry which distributes the proportion of expenses, originally charged to service departments, into the Machine Shop Burden account.
5. Fixed charges from journal entry distributing such items.

Reference may be made to the control account called "Electric Power" which is explained in greater detail in the following pages. As the operation of the debit side of the account is exactly the same in principle as all other expense and burden accounts it will serve here to illustrate the Burden account of the machine shop.

The journal entry which gives the analysis of the pay-roll for the month gives not only the direct labor for each department, but also the *total* labor charged to each departmental burden account. The same is true of the journal entry of the materials drawn from stores, and also of the journal entry distributing the direct charges from the voucher through the "Expense Ledger" (see Chapter XXIV).

Standard journal entries for Depreciation, Taxes, Insurance, etc., all contribute charges to all burden and expense accounts, and the monthly journal entries distributing other expense accounts also contribute.

From whatever source the various charges come, the control account for each departmental burden is charged with the *total amount* of each class of cost, as for instance the *total labor* charged to the Machine Shop Burden account. The *detail* of each class of cost (labor, material, etc.) is shown by the many standing orders which make up the detailed burden account. This is exactly similar to the case of the production orders, where each order is charged with a certain amount of labor, or labor and material, the total only showing in the control account.

It is obvious, therefore, that the total shown by the control account must and will be the same as the total shown by the detailed burden statement for this particular account. In the control account the total is arrived at by accumulation of entries in accordance with their sources, while in the burden statement the entries are in accordance with the use of the charges, many items thereon receiving charges of labor, material, direct debits from the voucher register and charges from other departments. (Reference to the "Electric Power" description following will make this clear.)

The credits to burden accounts are described in Chapter XXII and need not be considered here. The debit side of Departmental Burden accounts is allowed to accumulate through the year in order to give control figures. Expense accounts are not accumulated through the year but are closed out to the burden accounts each month.

Control of Expenses.—A complete and typical control of both Expense and Burden accounts will now be given. The illustration chosen is that of the Electric Power Expense in a large plant.

Assume that a manufacturing concern purchases 60% of its electric power at high voltage, and that in order to render this power serviceable and to produce the remaining 40%, the following equipment is necessary:

1. Transformers to transfer or step down power bought.
2. Two gas engines to generate balance of normal load.
3. Gas producers to make gas for engines.

4. Two steam engines to take peak loads.
5. Steam from steam plant for engines.
6. Storage battery for safety factor.

In this case the general ledger would have a control account known as Electric Power account as shown below. To this account would be charged through journal entries the total amounts for labor, material, and all other charges as in the case of the burden accounts just described and as shown on the debit side of the illustration given below.

ELECTRIC POWER
(Controlling Account in Ledger)

DEBIT		CREDIT	
Labor for May per Pay-Roll Journal Entry.....	$1,950.00	By Journal Entry for May Distributing Expense to Departments That Used Power	$6,350.00
Material for May per Distribution of Requisition Journal Entry	1,315.00		
Expense Ledger Charges per Distribution of Debit Slips Journal Entry....	2,150.00		
Depreciation per Journal Entry	450.00		
Taxes per Journal Entry..	50.00		
Liability Ins. per Journal Entry	60.00		
Gen. Plant Ex. per Journal Entry	350.00		
Teaming per Journal Entry	25.00		
	$6,350.00		$6,350.00

NOTE—This and all other expense accounts closed out by distribution each month.

In this illustration the Electric Power account is shown as having been charged from all sources a total of $6,350. This information alone is of no managerial use whatever, even though it would be perfectly possible to divide this amount by what the switchboard has recorded as the total kilowatts of power produced and find the cost per kilowatt. But if the cost is high or low, what is the reason? The accounting for lump sum charges as they appear in the control account will never answer this question. Therefore, an analyzed Electric Power Expense account is necessary whereby through a code of standing orders the disposition of all charges to the electric power account is accounted for. This expense account follows:

ELECTRIC POWER EXPENSE:	
Purchased Power	
1001 Invoice of Power for Month	$2,150.00
1002 Labor Transforming	250.00
1003 Maintenance of Transformers	125.00
1004 Maintenance of Transformers Building	10.00
1005 Miscellaneous Supplies	65.00
Gas Engine Power	
1021 Gas Engine Labor	350.00
1022 Maintenance of Gas Engines	150.00
1023 Maintenance of Building	25.00
1024 Maintenance of Switchboard, etc.	80.00
1025 Miscellaneous Supplies Engine House	60.00
1031 Gas House Labor	125.00
1032 Maintenance of Gas Producers	50.00
1033 Maintenance Gas Producers Building	10.00
1034 Maintenance Coal and Ash Handling Equipment	10.00
1035 Coal	600.00
1036 Miscellaneous Producers' Supplies	50.00
Steam Power	
1041 Steam Power Labor	250.00
1042 Maintenance Steam Engines	25.00
1043 Maintenance Steam Engines Building	15.00
1044 Maintenance Switchboard and Other Apparatus	25.00
1045 Miscellaneous Supplies	40.00
1046 Steam Charge from Steam Plant	125.00
Storage Battery	
1051 Maintenance of Batteries	180.00
1052 Maintenance of Other Battery Equipment	15.00
1053 Maintenance of Building	10.00
1054 Miscellaneous Supplies	20.00
General Power Expense	
1061 Administrative Salaries	400.00
1062 Maintenance General Electric Lines	125.00
1063 Maintenance General Switchboard	50.00
1064 Miscellaneous—General	25.00

Apportioned Expenses	
Depreciation	450.00
Taxes	50.00
Liability Insurance	60.00
General Plant Expense	350.00
Trucking	25.00
	$6,350.00
Total Electric Power Expense This must equal the amount shown by the control account.	

A comparative cost table of kilowatt-hours produced may be drawn up as follows:

Month	Kilowatt-Hours		Cost		Cost per Kilowatt-Hour	
	For Month	Total to Date	For Month	Total to Date	For Month	Average to Date
January						
February						
March						
April						
May	181.430		$6,350.00		$.0350	
June	190.000	371.430	6,180.00	$12,530.00	.0328	$ 0338
July						
August						
September						
October						
November						
December						

It will now be clearly seen how the control account and the detail cost account of each department work together. One is useless without the other. One controls and the other analyzes in great detail. The analysis afforded by the code of standing orders gives the management and the department head actual knowledge as to *where* the money goes. Where it came from is immaterial.

This same principle should be applied to each expense and burden account.

Classification of Control Accounts.—The various control accounts may be divided into two classes according to their function:

1. Accounts that control data collected for the purpose of analyzing profit and loss and which therefore are of a transitory nature (such as burden and expense accounts).
2. Accounts that control the various asset and liability accounts, to some one of which all other accounts lead (including work in process accounts).

Accounts Controlling Burden and Expense.—The first class of control accounts involves the greater detail, and from a managerial standpoint is the more important of the two, for the reason that the business either makes or loses money according to the way in which transitory operating costs are incurred. It is therefore of the greatest necessity to have the accounts in which data of a transitory nature are recorded so planned and arranged that an accurate and usable set of figures is available for managerial purposes.

It is evident, in view of the material presented in the previous chapters, that the arrangement and assignment of these accounts depend entirely on the nature and organization of the business.

Accounts Controlling Assets and Liabilities.—Control accounts of the second class, the function of which is to control assets and liabilities, differ from those of the first class mainly in that the analysis of them is made from more permanent records than are used for the first class of controls which as already stated are of a transitory nature. Controls of the second class are made largely from stock records, machine records, tool records, and the perhaps slightly less permanent record of the Work in Process accounts for production orders.

In the case of a Raw Material account, the analysis of the control account is entered on a stock record. As explained in Chapter XIII the stock record may consist either of sheets in book form or of cards. Each item of material has its own individual record, showing receipts and disbursements, etc., which of course indicate the balance on hand. If the balances of all individual items were footed at the close of the month, the total should equal the balance shown in the control account, Raw Material.

Various asset control accounts are opened according to the requirements of the business. For instance, many control accounts may be needed for raw materials alone. It may be desirable to control separate stockrooms, or the magnitude of an individual item may warrant a separate control account, such as Pig Iron in a large steel plant, or Bar Steel in a forge plant.

When stockrooms are controlled by a separate control account, a set of stock records will be set up for each stockroom unit in order that the entire stock may be properly analyzed.

It may not be necessary to have more than one work in process account for the work of each department, but it is usually best to have a control for each component of the cost, i.e., material, labor, and burden.

Another Classification of Control Accounts.—Control accounts may also be considered as divided into three specific groups according to their degree of permanency.

1. Accounts with permanent balances, representing inventories and like data.
2. Accounts with accumulating balances through the year which control the operating burden accounts.
3. Accounts used each month for the sole purpose of collecting the charges to expense accounts which, after collection, are distributed to burden accounts in the same month.

The accounts in the first group consist of those kept for raw material, supplies, finished stock, work in process, and all such accounts as hold the value of the various material assets of the company. These accounts are debited with purchases and all new acquisitions, either from the outside, or through changes in the form of product inside the plant; and are credited with records which show the disposition of whatever is represented by the accounts. In the case of materials in stock and finished product, the records of disposition are requisitions, and sales or shipping orders, respectively.

The accounts in the second group consist of the operating burden accounts, which are carried in the books—as explained later in this volume—in such form as to produce an accumulative balance and thus give a figure at the end of the month which represents the total of the analytical statement of each burden account as it is made up.

The accounts of the third group represent the controls of all such monthly expense accounts as Electric Power, Teaming, etc. These are collected in order to show what each expense amounts to for the month, giving a total figure to be accounted for on the detail statement of each expense. As these accounts, after all charges thereto are in, are immediately split up and charged to the various operating burden accounts, they become simply verifying accounts to assure the exactness of the distribution to the operating accounts.

Flow of Data Through Control Accounts.—The use of control accounts is in reality very simple. Once they are understood, their uses are readily appreciated, first because of the assurance they give of the accuracy of all expense and burden accounts; secondly, because they so simplify the work of cost procedure through the checks which they afford.

A brief statement of the flow of cost data through the control accounts may be helpful at this point. All obligations assumed by the company, such as for raw materials, supplies, labor, and all other plant items, pass through the voucher register and are charged to some originating control account—a material account, a pay-roll account, or a charge direct to some expense account.

The object of the controls is to insure the accounting for

all moneys paid out. Material purchases to go into stock, subject to requisitions, are charged to the material accounts. This material goes into a stockroom and cannot be issued until a requisition is received for it. The requisitions are credited to the material accounts at the end of the month, and debited to the control accounts affected by the charges made on the requisitions. Material which enters directly into a product is charged to Work in Process Material accounts. Material used on expense orders, i.e., for service departments and direct or producing departments, is charged to the control accounts representing the expense or burden receiving the benefit.

Labor is originally charged, when paid out, to the Pay-Roll account. How this labor is used is shown on the time cards, and at the end of the month the labor is credited to the Pay-Roll account, and debited to the control account which receives the benefit. Labor on direct orders is charged to a Work in Process Labor account. If the labor is expended on an expense account order, or an operating burden account order, it is charged to the control account affected.

Materials, services, or other purchases directly for the benefit of an expense or burden account, are charged directly to such control account from the voucher register through the intermediate account called an "Expense Ledger" account. This account is nothing more or less than a vehicle account to assist in the transfer to the proper expense account.

The control accounts representing expenses such as Electric Power, Trucking, etc., are themselves closed out at the end of the month and journalized to the burden accounts which receive the benefit of the expense.

Burden at standard rates is credited to the various operating Burden Credit accounts, and charged to the Work in Process Burden accounts in ratio to the number of direct-labor hours or direct-labor cost represented by the work performed during the month.

The direct material, direct labor, and work in process burden now rest in the control accounts as representing the value of the material in process; they are further represented as to details in the files by the material requisitions and time cards.

When a production order is completed, these three accounts are credited, and the cost of the order represented by the one figure is then charged to the control account of finished stock or of the cost of sales.

In considering the flow of data through control accounts as explained above, and in all the following chapters which deal with technical procedure, constant reference should be made to the chart entitled "Graphic Illustration of Flow of Cost Procedure," which accompanies this volume and which is not bound in the book for the express purpose of permitting the chart to be spread out for constant reference at all times. Students of cost accounting will find that one of the greatest difficulties is consistently to visualize the flow of procedure. This chart will materially aid in a full understanding of the text if it is constantly used in connection therewith.

CHAPTER VII

MECHANISM OF COST CONTROL

Need of Mechanism.—After a knowledge of cost components and the methods of controlling cost records has been gained, it is next necessary to consider briefly the mechanism of securing correct data and figures which represent those components and which go to make up the controlling accounts. As an outline of this important subject requires considerable space, this chapter is designed as an index to subsequent chapters in which detailed explanations are given.

Orders.—The first requisite for adequate cost records is the control of all movements and transactions through the medium of orders. There may be classified into four main classes:

1. Purchase orders, controlling incoming materials or service. (See Chapter X.)
2. Production orders, controlling what is to be made and how, and the medium for direct costs. (See Chapter X.)
3. Standing expense orders, controlling all indirect costs. (See Chapter X.)
4. Sales or shipping orders, controlling outgoing movements of goods. (See Chapter X.)

Voucher Payable Register or Purchase Journal.—At this point it is best to bring out the fact that the voucher payable register, or purchase journal as it is often called (see Figure 4), is probably the most important pivotal record in the accounting system—no matter how deeply the methods run into cost-figuring. It is through this record that the initial distribution of all expenditures should be made. By so doing, the necessity of providing general distribution facilities is removed

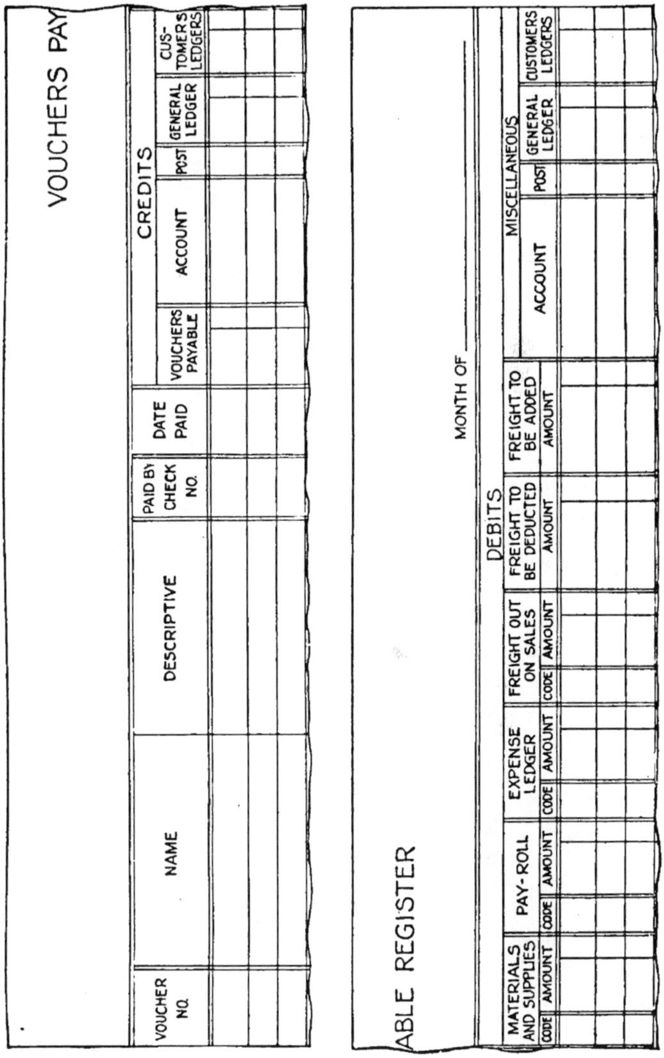

Figure 4.—Vouchers Payable Register. (Size, 24 x 16.)

from all other books of entry, and the function of distribution to proper control accounts is centered in the one record.

Moreover, when one distributing record is used, efforts to make it as efficient a medium as possible can be concentrated upon it; and when the rule is strictly enforced that all expenditures must be vouchered—as should be the case—the fact that a positive channel of distribution exists is perfectly well known.

In small plants this distribution may be accomplished by columnar methods alone; but in the majority of plants it will be found best to condense the book to a few columns, to code the control accounts, and to enter the vouchers in accordance with a method of temporary class control. A detailed analysis of each class should be compiled on a separate analysis sheet. Charges to each individual account can be ascertained for posting purposes at the end of the month from this analysis sheet.

The advantages of this method of entering and distributing vouchers or purchases are:

1. Accuracy. Wide columnar books are very difficult to handle and the danger of entering data in wrong columns is great. Not even the so-called "slip-leaf books" obviate this possibility.
2. Economy. By the method shown, the greatest possible use is made of the stationery investment consistent with necessary control of work.
3. Speed. While this method may at first appear to entail more labor than the columnar method the fact has been clearly demonstrated that it is actually faster than the method of locating the one little spot to enter the distribution on a voucher register with numerous columns.

Distribution Columns of the Voucher Register.—The distribution columns of the debit side of the voucher register (Figure 4) are listed below.

Materials and Supplies. All charges to control accounts of materials and supplies which go into stock, subject to withdrawal by requisitions, are entered in this column. Entries are analyzed and recorded on the analysis sheet.

Pay-Roll. This column provides for all entries of pay-roll. Each department must have its own pay-roll account for proper control of the cost figures, as explained in Chapter XIV. This is later analyzed by departments.

Expense Ledger Charges. All entries of charges to standing expense orders are recorded here. No special analysis is necessary, as these charges are cared for by the use of the expense debit slip (Figure 5).

HOLDEN MANUFACTURING COMPANY

EXPENSE DEBIT SLIP

Date ....

Charge ....

Description of Charge.. ....

....

....

....

Date of Invoice...................

Voucher Payable No. ....

Issued by .... Amount ....

Figure 5.—Expense Debit Slip. (Size, 6 x 4.)

Freight Out on Sales. Freight charges paid for the delivery of goods sold are entered in this column. Charges are analyzed by sales accounts. (See also Chapter XII.)

Freight to be Deducted. Entries of freight paid on incoming goods when purchase terms are "delivered buyer's works," are recorded here and are analyzed in accordance with the methods explained in Chapter XII.

Freight to be Added. This column provides for entries of freight paid on goods sold when the charge is to be added to the invoice for the goods. For details of handling see Chapter XII.

Miscellaneous. Charges which cannot be entered under other headings are recorded in this column. A great many items, while important, appear very seldom, such as Insurance, Taxes, Telephone and Telegraph Bills, Water, Gas, Power, etc. All these are posted directly to the control account specified.

Under each control column on the voucher register there are two items of information called for—the code number and the amount to be charged. Every control account should, therefore, be assigned a code symbol for the purpose of distribution. The symbols should be in numerical code so that they can be used in connection with electric tabulating machines whenever the occasion demands. Even a small business should always code and plan all points so that future growth will not necessitate many changes thus hindering and interrupting routine.

Analysis of Voucher Register.—The following columns of the voucher register (Figure 4) require analysis.

Materials and Supplies. The analysis is recorded in a column on the analysis sheet for each material or supply account, such as Pig Iron, Sand, Coal, Bar Iron, Blank Stock, Trimmings, Fabrics, Crude Rubber, General Stores, Store No. 1, or any other control account desired, each with its code number.

Pay-Roll. A column is provided for each pay-roll account. In a foundry, for instance, examples of these accounts might be Melting Department, Moulding Department, Core Department, Finishing Department, and General Pay-Roll. Each has its own designating number.

Freight Out on Sales. A column is reserved for each sales division when it is desirable or possible to get a distribution of the delivery freight. This may be by products, such as Complete Machine Sales, Repair Part Sales, or a more detailed distribution, as, in a lace curtain plant, Window Curtains, Bed Sets, Panels, etc. Each sales account has its own number.

Closing the Voucher Register.—At the end of the month the most satisfactory method of closing the voucher register operated as outlined above is as follows: Each analysis sheet should be closed up and proved to balance with the class control total in the voucher register. Then a compound journal entry should be prepared and entered in the distribution journal as follows:

Debits:

Material and Supplies Accounts. All the accounts shown on the analysis under this heading should be debited. The actual names of accounts should be shown.

Expense Ledger Account. The amount to be debited should be the total of the control column. This account is credited as described in Chapter XXIV.

Department (No. ....) Pay-Roll Account. All accounts of this nature should be debited and the actual name of each shown.

(Name of Sales Account) Freight Out on Sales. Each sales account of this nature should be debited.

Freight to be Deducted. The total of the column in the analysis under this heading should be posted to this account.

Freight to be Added. The amount with which the account should be debited is the total of the analysis column under this heading.

Miscellaneous. The total of the miscellaneous column should be shown in this entry, but all postings should be made direct from the entries in the voucher register.

Credit:

Vouchers Payable Account. This account should be credited with the total of all vouchers shown in the control column.

Importance of the Voucher Register.—Too much stress cannot be laid on the importance of the voucher register, inasmuch as it is the start of the scheme of controlling all features of cost accounting procedure. Through this medium is obtained the first distribution to the control accounts—where the values lie until used and passed on to some other control account. This, therefore, is the start, and the whole structure of control depends on the intelligence, care, and accuracy displayed in the distributions to the various accounts, as just explained.

Expense Ledger Accounts.—In all attempts to tie up cost procedure thoroughly, the disposition of intangible items of expense has continually led to confusion and error. Examples of such items are charges for repairs by outsiders, charges for all outside service, and charges for special repair materials never regularly carried in stock.

Some illustrations will make this clear. For instance, a gas engine breaks down, and a specialist is called from outside to repair it. He sends his bill. Nothing is received in the receiving room, nothing goes into stock, and no "inventory" account can be charged with this item to be requisitioned, which means that there is nothing to enter on a stock record. Again, an accident happens to a machine tool and a part is broken which is never carried in stock as a repair part. The part is ordered by express for this particular case, and on receipt is immediately snatched by the master mechanic and rushed to the machine. When these parts are charged to stores, experience has shown that in about 50% of all cases no requisition is made out. The part will be carried on the stock ledger until a check up discloses the fact that it is missing, and then it will become a part of an "adjustment."

Treatment of Direct Charges to Expense Codes.—Hundreds of such illustrations could be given to bring out the reason for the rule that—

When any material or service is known at the time of making out the request for purchase to be for a special use in connection with a standing expense order and is not likely ever to be a stock matter, subject to requisition, the request for purchase shall show the standing order number to be charged with the material or service; the purchase order shall show its charge, as "Expense Ledger Account—Standing Order No. . . . ."

When the item is material—not service—the receiving clerk shall certify as to receipt as usual, and secure the receipt of the department to which destined. This closes the transaction so far as the plant is concerned. When service is rendered, the office must get the proper plant authority to certify that the service was satisfactory. Nothing more is required of the plant.

The invoice is then vouchered. The entry of the vouchers charged to Expense Ledger account is made in the column of this name. The standing expense order shown in the charge is entered in the code column under the same general heading. Then, either in lots or by individual vouchers entered under this heading, an expense debit slip is made out giving all the information called for on the form. It must be made sure, through checking back, that the entries absolutely agree with the entries in the voucher register.

Advantages of this Method.—Note the result of this method. As a matter of fact, the Expense Ledger account becomes a sort of reservoir for "intangible charges." The expense debit slip acts as a requisition for them, and affords a means of charging the various standing expense orders. In fact, the expense debit slip is exactly the same size as a requisition, and is filed with the requisitions as if it were one.

The great advantages of this method are:

1. Absolute accuracy—nothing can get away.
2. Saving of confusion—such items are always the most difficult to handle.
3. Economy of clerical labor—the method makes a clear course to follow, and no indecision, "chasing up," or check ups are necessary.

Forms for Handling Details of Control.—Having discussed the method of control accounts, we will now consider the forms necessary to handle the details to maintain the controls. It is always best to have as few forms and records as possible, but some of them are absolutely necessary and certain cases call for more forms and records than others.

Forms of Original Control.—The first step is to provide the means of knowing how the product manufactured is made, both as relates to materials and the labor operations necessary to transform this material into the salable product. The forms used are as follows:

1. *Specification of Product.* On this form the bills of material for all product are prepared by units as actually manufactured.

2. *Specification of Operations.* On this form the operations of manufacture necessary to produce each unit are assembled.

The next step is that of procurement—receiving and accounting for incoming items. The forms used are as follows:

1. *Request for Purchases.* On this form some authority requests the purchasing department to purchase goods or services. This slip should show the charge to be made. (See Chapter XI.)

2. *Purchase Order.* This is the order sent to the vendor for goods or services. This order should show what account is to be charged. (See Chapter XI.)

3. *Receiving Record.* Receipt of material is certified on this slip. (See Chapter XI.)

4. *Receipt of Material Record.* This record is to bring together on the copy of the purchase order all data as to actual receipts of material, invoices received, freights, etc. (See Chapter XI.)

5. *Purchasing Department Shipping Order.* This is an order for the use of the purchasing department to facilitate the returning of rejected material. (See Chapter XI.)

6. *Purchasing Department Debit and Credit Memos:* These forms are to get into action a quick record of what may be shipped back on the purchase order, or any adjustments which are necessary to be made. (See Chapter XI.)

7. *Record of Purchases.* This is a record of prices and sources of supply kept for the convenience of the purchasing department. (See Chapter XI.)

8. *Invoice Stamp.* The data called for by this stamp should be entered on each invoice in order that all terms and freight in connection with the material can be entered intelligently. (See Chapters XI and XII.)

9. *Voucher.* This is the enclosure form (see Figure 6) for all invoices and shows data as to distribution, approvals, etc. This form is of vital importance.

10. *Voucher Register.* Vouchers are entered in this book for permanent record and for accumulating the distribution data.

11. *Stock Record.* This subsidiary analytical record of material control accounts shows quantities and values of all

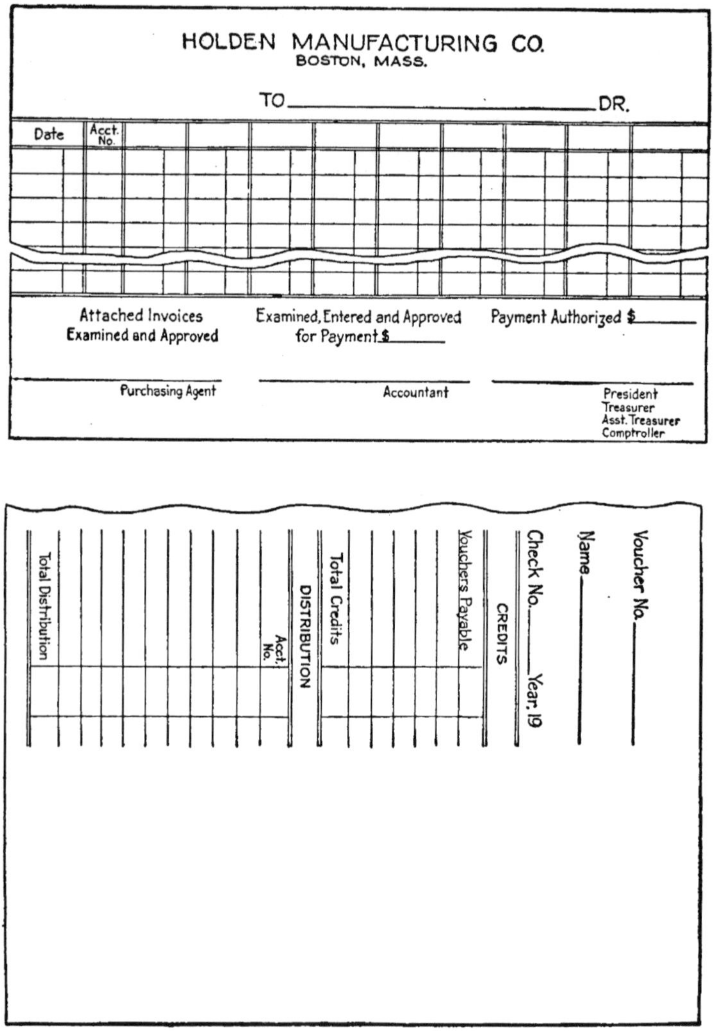

HOLDEN MANUFACTURING CO.
BOSTON, MASS.

TO ______________________ DR.

Date	Acct. No.								

Attached Invoices Examined and Approved

Examined, Entered and Approved for Payment $______

Payment Authorized $______

Purchasing Agent

Accountant

President
Treasurer
Asst. Treasurer
Comptroller

Voucher No.______

Name______

Check No.______ Year, 19

CREDITS

Vouchers Payable

Total Credits

DISTRIBUTION

Acct. No.

Total Distribution

Figure 6.—Voucher (face and reverse). (Size, 8½ x 11.)

transactions in connection with each individual item of stock. (See Chapter XIII.)

Forms Used to Record the Flow of Material.—After incoming materials are entered on stock records, a great deal of care is necessary to keep track of them, owing to the varied nature of their movements. To facilitate a strict accounting, the following forms have been devised:

1. *Material Requisitions.* Stock requisitions are made out on this form. Either a production or a standing expense order is charged. (See Chapter XIII.)

2. *Material Credit Slip.* When excess or unused material is returned to stock the slip is filled out so that the account to which the original requisition was charged may be credited. (See Chapter XIII.)

3. *Scrap Tickets.* This ticket is used to account for spoiled or otherwise useless material. (See Chapter XIII.)

4. *Inspector's Report.* The inspector certifies as to quality and quantity of materials on this form.

5. *Identification and Move Card.* The routing of materials through the various operations is indicated on this card which accompanies the material through the various processes. (See Chapter X.)

6. *Salvage Tag.* Tags are used to identify defective pieces and to specify the work required to salvage. The standing order to be charged should also be given.

7. *Forwarding Slip.* All lots of goods when sent by one department to another—or to stores—should be accompanied by a forwarding slip. (See Chapter VIII.)

8. *Expense Debit Slip.* Direct charges to standing expense orders are entered upon the slip, as explained earlier in this chapter.

9. *Inventory Tags for Physical Inventories.* One of these tags is for material and supplies, and one for work in process, and are used in the taking of actual physical inventories. (See Chapter XVI.)

10. *Inventory Sheets for Physical Inventories.* One of these sheets is for material, supplies, and finished stock, and another is for work in process. These sheets are used for the recording of information from the inventory tags. (See Chapter XVI.)

11. *Inventory Test Sheet.* A sheet for recording periodical tests of inventories by items. (Chapter XVI.)

Forms Used in Accounting for Labor.—All the forms used in accounting for labor are listed and briefly described below. In Chapters XVIII and XIX full explanation of these forms and their application to other cost records is given.

1. *In-and-Out Clock Card.* A card is assigned each employee in order that he may record his own going and coming. (See Chapter XVIII.)

2. *Time Cards.* On these cards are recorded the employee's time against the specific work performed. (See Chapter XVIII.)

3. *Pay-Roll Sheet.* Labor costs are entered on this record from time cards. (See Chapter XIX.)

4. *Overtime Report.* This is used for the daily recording of overtime. (See Chapter XIX.)

5. *Late and Absent Report.* This form is used for the recording of tardiness or absence of employees. (See Chapter XIX.)

6. *Labor Transfer Record.* Temporary loans of employees by one department to another are accounted for on this record. (See Chapter XIX.)

7. *O. D. S. O. Transfer Record.* To be used for the transfers of work done by one department for another. (See Chapter XIX.)

Accumulations for Journal Entries.—Transfers between control accounts are effected by means of journal entries. Figures to be entered come from various sources—some from actual record sheets, and some from special accumulation sheets. The order in which reference is made below to the various accumulation sheets is the normal order in which they would be considered by the cost accountant in actual practice. In the following tabulation, the special accumulation sheets from which the figures for journal entries are obtained are listed before the direct cost sheets.

1. *Inventory Accounts—Credits.* Before requisitions on stockrooms are filed under their proper order numbers, they are sorted daily into the various accounts to be credited. These totals are entered on an accumulation sheet. Monthly totals provide the figures for the journal entry. (See Chapter XXIV.)

2. *Work in Process Material Accounts—Debits.* In the same way, before filing the requisitions those which are charged to production orders are sorted according to the departments as called for by the controls, and the total for the day charged to each is entered on this accumulation sheet. The total for the month provides the figures for the journal entry. (See Chapter XXIV.)

3. *Burden and Expense Accounts—Material Debits.* Similarly as with Work in Process Material accounts, the remaining requisitions should be sorted according to controls of the expense and burden accounts, added and entered daily on an accumulation sheet. These figures will complete the debit side of the material distribution journal entry. All requisitions will be filed under their proper order numbers. (See Chapter XXIV.)

4. *Expense Debit Slips—Accumulation of.* The expense debit slips will be sorted daily by the controls of all expense and burden accounts. The total for each control will be entered on an accumulation sheet to run for a month. This can be proved daily with the total of the expense ledger column in the voucher register, and at the close of the month will give the figures for the journal entry crediting out the entire Expense Ledger account and debiting the various expense and burden accounts. (See Chapter XXIV.)

5. *Accumulation of Material Credit Slips.* The procedure as specified for requisitions is simply reversed in caring for the material credit slips. (See Chapter XXIV.)

6. *Accumulation of Scrap Tickets.* An accumulation sheet is necessary for caring for scrap tickets. Because of the varying accounts affected, it is usually best to have a columnar sheet with blank headings, where the debit and credit headings can be written in. (See Chapter XIII.)

7. *Journal Entries.* The detail treatment of journal entries will be found in Chapter XXIV as well as in many other chapters.

Direct Cost Sheets.—Upon completion of production orders, or upon completion of runs, schedules, or months, the following cost sheets are necessary:

1. *For Individual Parts.* This cost sheet should show all the operations, losses by operations, and the burden by operations, as well as material and labor costs. (See Chapter VIII.)

2. *For Assembled Units.* This cost sheet differs from the individual part sheet because labor operations are few, whereas material items are many. (See Chapter VIII.)

3. *For Specific Processes.* Cost sheets for processes vary almost in proportion to the number of processes, as in most

cases it is necessary to specify many divisions. They are entirely different, moreover, from those noted under points 1 and 2 above. (See Chapter VIII.)

4. *For Operations.* This sheet is somewhat like the process sheets, but far simpler, as it usually deals with one kind of direct labor on one kind of operation. (See Chapter VIII.)

5. *Comparative Cost Sheets.* While not entering into the financial cycle, the comparative cost sheets are of the greatest value in cost procedure from the standpoint of actual beneficial use. (See Chapter VIII.)

6. *Production and Cost Record.* This is a form for process costs. (See Chapter VIII.)

Monthly Statements.—The great object of cost procedure is, of course, to get costs; but to use these costs to real advantage they must be presented properly. Therefore, the monthly statements must be accurate, on time, and well presented.

Overhead is divided into two clear divisions:

1. *Expense Accounts.* Certain expenses are collected in this account, and at the close of the month are distributed to the operating burden accounts through which they enter the cost of the product, as with the plant accounts (See Chapters XX and XXV) and the administrative and selling expense accounts which are treated as an addition to manufacturing cost. (See Chapters XXVI and XXVII.)

2. *Burden Accounts.* These are the real indirect cost accounts. Detailed indirect costs are entered on production cost sheets on a standard burden rate basis. (See Chapter XXV.)

Both of these classes of accounts must be included in monthly statements. The principal monthly statements follow:

1. *Statements of Plant Expense Accounts.* These are collecting accounts which are distributed to the burden accounts

according to the use which each department makes of the expense item controlled, such as Electric Power, Steam, etc. (See Chapters XX and XXV.)

2. *Statements of Administrative and Selling Expenses.* There are collecting accounts for expenses other than for manufacturing. (See Chapters XXVI and XXVII.)

3. *Statement of Burdens.* A separate statement of its actual burden and cost to date for the year is prepared for each department. This statement should show the credit for applied burden at the standard rate. (See Chapter XXV.)

4. *Expense and Burden Account Collating Sheet.* This is to be used as a figuring sheet in assembling expense and burden statements. (See Chapter XXV.)

5. *Statement of Profit and Loss.* This shows the results for the month. (See Chapter XXVIII.)

6. *Various Schedules Subsidiary to Main Profit and Loss Statement.* Sales analysis including sales, freight out on sales, and sales cost for each classification, when too voluminous for the regular profit and loss statement, and the recapitulation of over- and under-absorbed burden balances, when too detailed for regular profit and loss statement, should be entered on subsidiary schedules. (See Chapter XXVIII.)

7. *Balance Sheet.* This shows the financial status of the business at the close of the month under consideration. (See Chapter XXVIII.)

8. *Various Schedules Subsidiary to Balance Sheet.* Inventories, real estate accounts, bills receivable, bills payable, sundry general ledger accounts both receivable and payable, detailed analysis of surplus accounts, and many other details are best shown on special schedule statements keyed to the figures to be explained. (See Chapter XXVIII.)

Using Cost Data.—A few forms which are employed in using cost data in specific cases are as follows:

1. *Cost Analysis Sheet.* This form is used for compiling analyses of burdens when preparing for budgets. (See Chapter XXIX.)

2. *Comparison of Monthly Burdens.* This form is for comparing six months of actual burdens, and is used in connection with the various department heads. (See Chapter XXXI.)

3. *Production Record.* This form is for the purpose of maintaining a daily control of production as compared to standards. (See Chapter XXXI.)

4. *Foundry Scrap Report.* This form illustrates a means of reporting scrap or defective work for the benefit of department heads. (See Chapter XXXII.)

5. *Idle Machine Card.* This time card is for the purpose of keeping time of idle equipment, showing causes of idleness. (See Chapter XXXIII.)

6. *Idle Machine Report.* This form is for tabulating all idle time of machines and the causes of all idleness. (See Chap. ter XXXIII).

CHAPTER VIII

PREVAILING METHODS OF COSTING THE PRODUCT

The Problem of Costing the Product.—In Chapter V the necessity of establishing proper cost bases, and several examples of cost bases were discussed. It was pointed out that a number of bases, often as many as five or six, must be established before the completed cost of product is arrived at. If costs are not determined at different stages of the manufacture of the product, the cost figures are liable to be so bunched that they do not show sufficient detail to be used by the management in directing and controlling the business—a most exasperating situation.

The method of costing as a whole, as well as certain well-defined sections of it, are given distinctive names. The costing method is sometimes called a type of cost system, a cost plan or a cost scheme. In this chapter we shall use the term, *method of costing*. The names of the prevailing methods of costing are:

1. Job or Special Order Method
2. Class Method
3. Operation Method
4. Process Method

The method of costing which prevails in a given plant may be identified according to the preponderance of one or another kind of base. It should be emphasized, however, that seldom does one method of costing prevail throughout the entire plant, because it cannot be used advantageously in all departments of a given concern.

Thus serious consideration should be given to selecting the methods of costing which are best suited to different conditions in a particular instance. Such consideration is often not given. Too many cost men assume that the method of costing which they have inherited or devised themselves is necessarily best fitted to existing conditions. By accepting the *status quo*, irreparable harm may be done through decreasing the usefulness of the cost method to the management.

Methods of Costing.—The essential and distinctive features of each method of costing will be considered in turn.

1. Job or Special Order Method.—When all the various items of cost are charged up to the particular order embracing a specific quantity of a specific unit, the method is known as the "job cost method."

By this method any kind of labor or other direct cost is charged to a particular order number and all the charges against a particular order number constitute the cost of the order when it is figured up.

An illustration of the job or special order method would be the costing of an order for a shaft in a machine-shop. The forging for the shaft is received from another plant and is drawn from the stockroom on requisition, this order being charged with the number of pieces involved. All the machine operations, such as cutting off, turning, and key-seating, are charged against the particular order number for this shaft. The figuring of the total cost of the order would involve computing the time and cost of each operation, the burden, and the material cost. Dividing this total by the total number of pieces produced gives the cost for producing each unit of the material called for by the order.

The job or special order method of costing is still, without doubt, the most common method of costing product, and hence the best known. Fortunately, however, it is being widely supplanted. It is the natural method to use for costing assembly operations and its use is practically universal for this class of work. But for other than assembly operations, the job or special order method of costing is often unsuitable; where more than one operation in turning out work is involved, there is a loss of control. Control, as has been repeatedly emphasized, is one of the most valuable results of cost accounting. At the same time many cases exist where the benefits of comparison of actual time and cost with standard time and cost can be secured, even though all the work on any individual part of a product is being manufactured under one production order number. This benefit is secured by requiring that the time and cost of the work be reported *by operations,* the production order number being simply an identification of one particular run of the part. In this way, operation control is assured.

2. **Class Cost Method.**—In many lines of manufacture it is possible to save much detail by disregarding individual order numbers, and instead of compiling the labor directly for these order numbers, grouping all order numbers—so far as the material they represent permits of such combination—into one large statement of costs.

A very clear example of this may be noted in a foundry. It is often the case that articles up to one pound in weight constitute a convenient class. The cost of all castings produced within this range of weight are accordingly bunched into one cost sheet, thereby saving the necessity of making out an individual cost sheet for each separate casting. Further classes are made up, covering castings from one to two pounds, from two to five, or from five to ten, and so on. In addition to the weight distinction, of course, these classes may be subdivided, for greater accuracy, into perhaps three subclasses, designated as A, B, and C, which vary according to the classified difficulty of coring and moulding.

Some foundries have a total of fifty classes only, to which

all material, labor, and burden are charged, necessitating but fifty cost sheets per month. The cost of any particular casting is determined by the class to which it belongs.

It might be stated, however, that in nearly every foundry using class costs, the moulding and core-making items for each casting are reported separately, so that in case more detailed information is desired it is possible at any time to compute the cost of any individual casting. The regular costing, however, is confined to the classes of product.

This method is similar to the Job Cost Method in that orders are issued for each casting, and likewise the time expended on each casting or the cores therefor is reported for each specific order number. It differs from the Job Cost Method in assembling or compilation of the costs in that *all orders* falling, for instance, in the class of up to one pound would be compiled in bulk by operations, thereby giving the cost of all the one pound class in one figure. As stated before, if one particular casting requires a separate cost it may be so costed by the Job Cost Method.

3. Operation Cost Method.—The method of costing known as Operation Cost Method is in the main quite different from class or job costs. The operation type of cost figuring deals principally with the computing of the cost of a certain operation in plants where this operation is common to a large amount of product.

In the manufacture of storage batteries, for example, the cost of forming is in direct ratio to the square inches of surface formed. One forming row may consist of many different kinds of plates, but the electrical energy used is in direct ratio to the square inches of plate exposed. Therefore, the cost of current, of setting and taking out the rows, and all other costs, are kept for each run, and a tally is prepared of the square inches of plate surface formed. These records are kept in continuous forms so as to provide a monthly cost per square inch for the formation of plates, which cost is used both for estimating and for actual costing.

In a planing-mill, the rip saws may best be regulated if the cost of this operation is kept, figuring it on the basis of lineal feet of work performed.

In a hat business, the operation of sewing in sweatbands is an operation that is the same for any hat made. This cost may best be figured accordingly on the basis of a single hat as a unit.

A distinct advantage of the operation cost is the valuable control made possible by the method. Furthermore, it is a most valuable method because of the data it gives for estimating new work.

An example of this may be cited in the garment industry: The machine work for various types of seams, buttonholes, affixing of decorations, etc., is easily reduced to an operation standard. Plain hemmings should be done on a particular machine at a certain fixed standard number of inches or feet per hour. And so on with practically all other operations.

It should be clearly seen, therefore, that this not only gives very useful and accurate cost data, but it also automatically gives a control on production which is of great value to the operating foreman.

The costing by this method is exceedingly simple, and the actual cost of any product may be found or the cost of a new product be estimated at any time and with despatch.

This method differs entirely from the Job Cost or Class Method as may be clearly seen from the description. The assembly of the final complete cost of product is accomplished simply by listing the operations at the operation unit cost.

4. **Process Cost Method.**—In many lines of work, particularly in industries of the chemical type, the process method of cost prevails.

The production of a chemical plant is almost entirely of

the process nature; many of the steps which might be regarded as operations are not clearly enough defined to permit each operation to be checked at its conclusion.

For instance, in a phenol plant the first operation, strictly speaking, is sulphonating the benzol. The resulting product of this operation, however, is blown over at once to the lime vats, from here through the filters, and so on through every operation until it reaches the drum dryer, where the production reaches a measurable point in the form of the salt. Therefore the operations, from the start to the taking of the dry salt from the drum dryer, have to be treated as one process, and as no cost can be found on the individual operation through lack of the proper basis for figuring, the result is a process cost including all the operations thus far. The process of manufacture of phenol continues in somewhat the same way, until the phenol itself results from the final operation of distillation.

The process cost, therefore, may be defined as a combination of operation costs, usually brought about by the inability to arrive at any basic weight or measure for gauging the intermediate operations involved.

The Process Cost Method differs very materially from the three preceding methods as it deals with no specified order quantity as in the case of the Job Order Method; it is not a combination of different items into a class as in the Class Cost Method; nor is it the cost of any individual operation on the basis of a measured quantity produced as in the case of the Operation Cost Method. It is a combination into a group or process of a number of physical operations, none of which is measurable. The process stops for cost and measurement purposes at the first point where measurement is possible.

Another illustration of the process method is found in an open hearth steel furnace. Here the men perform various operations, but it is necessary to group the operations as no bases can be established for the many individual moves. The metal melted and run into the ladle gives us the basis of cost for the process.

Process Costs usually involve the feature of what are called "yields." For instance, in the phenol plant a certain quantity of benzol is sulphonated and there are used for process purposes sulphuric acid, lime and soda ash. The result of the process is a salt, which, at a given moisture should be in a certain ratio to the benzol. This is called the yield. The pounds of steel finally run into the ladle should be in a certain ratio to the metals charged into the furnace, some being lost in the process.

Choice of a Cost Method.—It is always necessary to settle at the start on the type of costing methods to be installed in a plant. This is sometimes a most difficult task. In making a survey of a plant for the purpose of deciding upon the best type to be used, it is necessary to investigate very carefully the equipment of the plant and the methods actually used in producing the goods.

It is often the case that all methods are used in one plant—even all methods in any one department. The operation and process methods, for instance, are often used extensively in the same plant, largely because they are so nearly alike. It is necessary to study carefully all the product and keep constantly in mind—

1. How to control the efficiency through the records.
2. How to get an accurate cost.

In many plants will be found automatic machines known as "special purpose machines" for performing certain operations which cover a very short range. As these operations are highly specialized and largely automatic, it is easy to see that the operation method should be used in figuring their cost.

The term operation need not be limited to work on one kind or piece of material only, provided it is possible to figure the cost per stroke, per lineal inch, per piece, etc. An example of this appears in the case of the punch press. This machine runs at a constant speed, and the most usable cost record that can be assembled for this operation is on the basis of the number of strokes per hour productively employed. The record of strokes gives a direct line on the efficiency with which the machine is being operated. The case would be the same with any class of machine which maintains a steady stroke per minute.

In a boiler-shop, the cost of shearing is often figured on the basis of the lineal feet sheared per hour. The number of feet varies, of course, according to the size of the material handled, but in the main the method gives a very good basis for controlling the efficiency with which the machine runs. It also gives a very accurate line on the cost, as the number of lineal feet sheared per hour will come much nearer to a standard than would the size or shape of the pieces being sheared, even though the shapes cause a variance in lineal costs.

Combinations of Various Types of Cost Systems.—In most plants, as has been stated, it is necessary to employ to some extent at least two methods of costing, namely: the job cost, and the operation cost methods. Frequently a third method must be employed also—the process method—and in the case of a foundry probably a fourth method—class method—as well.

In plants manufacturing such products as rubber, textiles, or paper, and in rolling mills, it is of the utmost advantage to use the operation cost method, as the comparisons which it constantly presents reveal the efficiency with which the equipment is being used. At the same time, excepting in plants where the product is sold just as it comes from an individual operation, assembly costs usually necessitate some use also of the job cost method.

This may be especially noted in tire-manufacturing, where after the individual operations have been performed the final operation of building the tire is purely an assembly proposition. Even in this case, however, the several operations of building and finishing the tire may be segregated, thereby carrying the entire process through on the operation basis.

The highly specialized operations in connection with the manufacture of clothing have put this industry into the class of operation costs, although in this case some combination with the job cost system is often necessary.

Jobbing machine shops almost invariably are obliged to use the Job Cost Method. On the other hand, machine shops running on standard work will use operation costs to a great extent.

A candy plant generally uses the system of operation costs, although process costs may be used to some extent. Even the packing, though it might be construed as assembly, can be treated as an operation.

A power plant uses the process method of cost, and in a manufacturing plant many of the indirect operations involving steam, electric power, compressed air, etc., may be treated somewhat similarly.

Stocking Points.—Whatever type of cost system is used, careful thought must be given as to where individual and assembled parts should be stocked.

To attain the best results, individual parts which enter into assemblies must on completion be actually placed in a finished parts stockroom. This is necessary for two reasons: (1) to control the recording of the completion of the parts; and (2) to control the parts after being completed, with sufficient supporting data on the stock records to regulate properly the material for assemblies or shipment purposes.

To make this clear, a simple example is given. In the manufacture of any assembled article, the procedure is as follows:

1. Manufacture individual parts.
2. Assemble two or more individual parts into a minor or sub-assembly.
3. Assemble two or more sub-assembled parts, or one sub-assembled part with one or more individual parts and thereby produce another assembled part. This can continne for an indefinite number of assemblies until the completely assembled shipping point is reached.

Two main factors determine these assembly points:

1. Economic Production, not only from the point of the assembly operation itself, but from consideration of how this particular assembly is best used in the next stage of complete assembly.
2. Sales Requirements, that is, what sub or minor assembled parts are necessary to be in stock for shipment as repair parts. The steering knuckle of an automobile is an example of this.

After establishing the standard plan of manufacture, the individual parts when completed should be sent to stockroom and there accumulated for combination with other parts when these arrive. To leave them loose in the shop is bad practice, as production cannot properly be scheduled. The same principle applies to sub-assemblies when completed, as they then assume the same character as individual parts so far as stocking is concerned. By returning everything to the stockroom on completion, the stock records will form the true basis of production planning. By this method, also, we can arrive at proper costs for the individual and assembled parts, which cost is necessary for inventory, sales cost and all other purposes.

Furthermore, it is the only way to use floor space economically, for material can be placed on shelves and stacked up, perhaps ten or twelve deep, instead of in a single layer as when left on the floor or stacked on benches in the operating department. The floors and benches of an operating department should not be a storage place nor a place in which to accumulate material awaiting a different kind of procedure, such as assembly. This applies equally to the sub-assemblies as they are produced—in the automobile industry, for example, to the carburetors, generators, and other small units which eventually enter into the final assembly of the complete automobile. All sub-assemblies should be stocked in a stockroom subject to requisition, and should be issued only on specifications of further assemblies. Accurate specifications of product as to assemblies are entirely impossible of accomplishment in actual practice unless the material is properly stocked. It is economy in every way to put this material in stock.

A great many plants have attempted a method of "theoretical stocking," regarding parts as theoretically going into stock at the conclusion of certain operations, the idea being that it is useless work actually to transport the parts to a stockroom. The reasoning is fallacious. Actual stocking of the parts is of the utmost importance for accounting purposes as explained above.

Theoretical stocking might be followed providing every part which goes into an assembly came through at exactly the same time and reached the assembly floor in company with its companion parts. In actual practice, however, this is never the case. Under the very best methods, parts will straggle along, although with production control they come very much closer together than when there is no accurate method of scheduling.

Forwarding Slip.—In connection with the matter of stocking material, and also that of delivering material from one department to another, when the operations are continuous, a forwarding slip (Figure 7) is an absolute necessity.

This form is simply a record of forwarding from one department to another or to a stockroom, with a description of the material and signature of the person receiving the material. It is prepared in triplicate; the original copy, which may be salmon in color, goes with the goods; the duplicate copy, which may be yellow, goes direct to the stock record department, where it is held until the original comes in properly receipted as a check on the receiving of same; the triplicate, usually a white tissue copy, remains in the hands of the person who forwarded the goods.

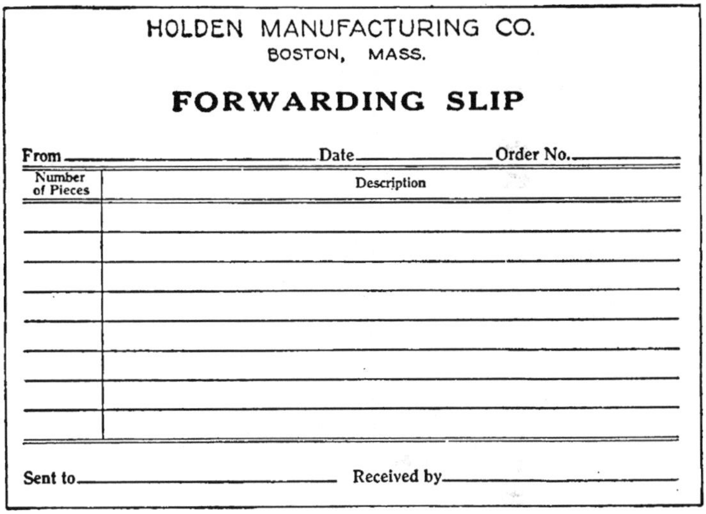

HOLDEN MANUFACTURING CO.
BOSTON, MASS.

FORWARDING SLIP

From ______ Date ______ Order No. ______

Number of Pieces	Description

Sent to ______ Received by ______

Figure 7.—Forwarding Slip. (Size, 6 x 4.)

Job Order Cost Sheets.—Figures 8 and 9 show two cost sheets commonly used with the job order cost system.

Figure 8 shows a cost sheet used for individual parts. In this case the information desired concerns the operations required to make the parts with a minimum of data, usually not more than one line regarding the material cost.

Figure 9 on the other hand, shows the cost sheet for assembled parts. In this case the information regarding material takes up the bulk of the sheet, while the labor operations are of less account.

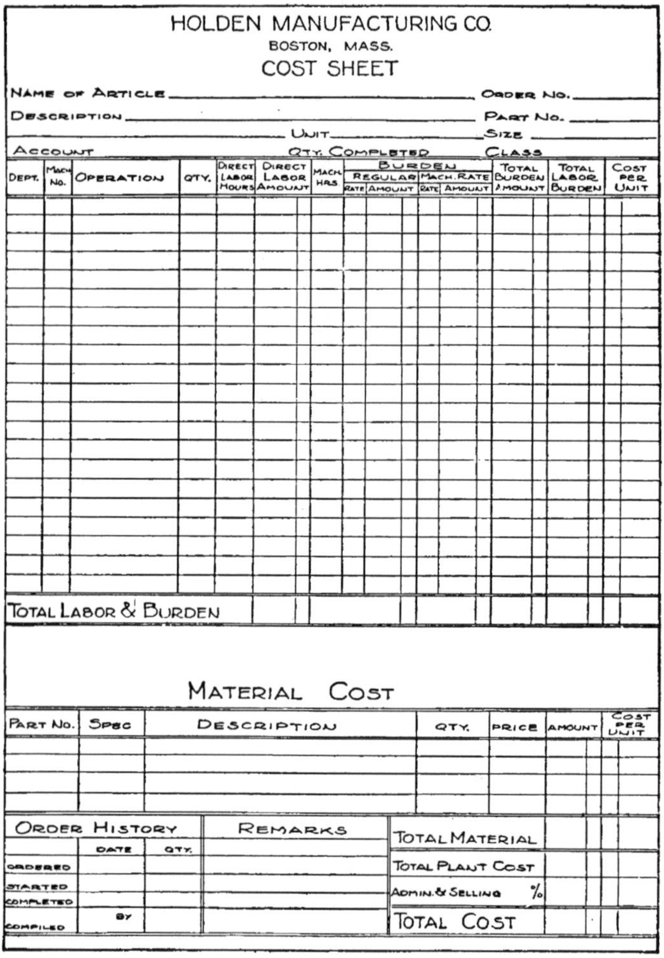

HOLDEN MANUFACTURING CO.
BOSTON, MASS.
COST SHEET

Name of Article ______ Order No. ______
Description ______ Part No. ______
______ Unit ______ Size ______
Account ______ Qty. Completed ______ Class ______

Dept.	Mach. No.	Operation	Qty.	Direct Labor Hours	Direct Labor Amount	Mach. Hrs.	Burden: Regular Rate	Burden: Regular Amount	Burden: Mach. Rate Rate	Burden: Mach. Rate Amount	Total Burden Amount	Total Labor Burden	Cost per Unit
Total Labor & Burden													

Material Cost

Part No.	Spec	Description	Qty.	Price	Amount	Cost per Unit

Order History	Date	Qty.	Remarks		
Ordered				Total Material	
Started				Total Plant Cost	
Completed				Admin. & Selling %	
Compiled	By			Total Cost	

Figure 8.—Individual Part Cost Sheet. (Size, 9½ x 12.)

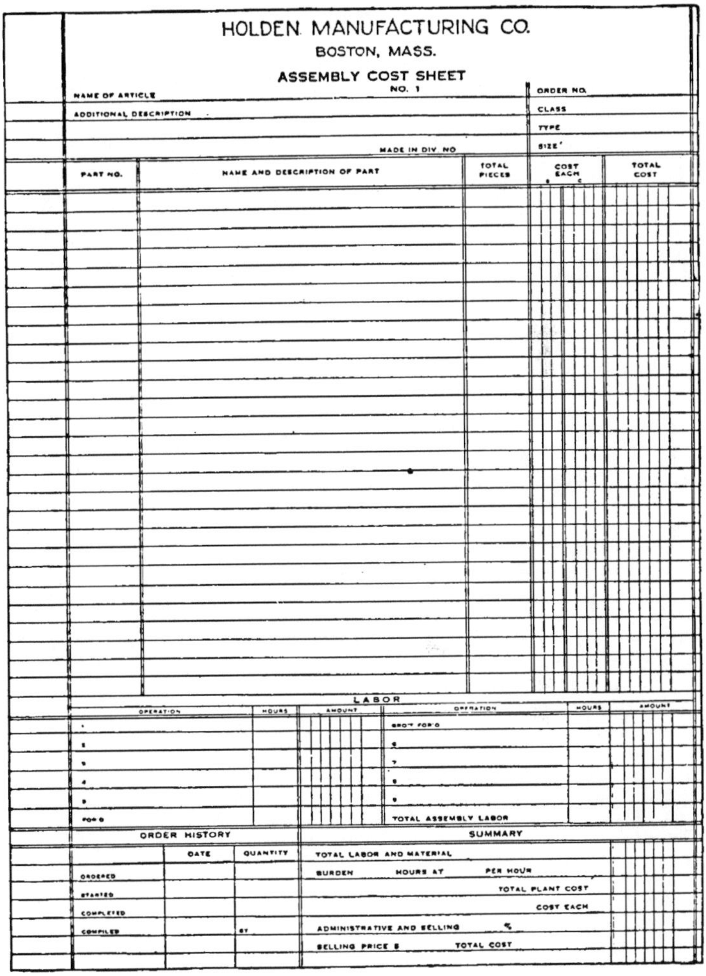
HOLDEN MANUFACTURING CO.
BOSTON, MASS.
ASSEMBLY COST SHEET
NO. 1
NAME OF ARTICLE
ORDER NO.
ADDITIONAL DESCRIPTION
CLASS
TYPE
MADE IN DIV. NO
SIZE
PART NO.
NAME AND DESCRIPTION OF PART
TOTAL PIECES
COST EACH
TOTAL COST
LABOR
OPERATION
HOURS
AMOUNT
OPERATION
HOURS
AMOUNT
1
2
3
4
5
FOR'D
BRO'T FOR'D
6
7
8
9
TOTAL ASSEMBLY LABOR
ORDER HISTORY
DATE
QUANTITY
ORDERED
STARTED
COMPLETED
COMPILED
BY
SUMMARY
TOTAL LABOR AND MATERIAL
BURDEN HOURS AT PER HOUR
TOTAL PLANT COST
COST EACH
ADMINISTRATIVE AND SELLING %
SELLING PRICE $ TOTAL COST

Figure 9.—Assembly Cost Sheet. (Size, 8½ x 11.)

These forms are self-explanatory, though attention may be called to the fact that in Figure 8 provision is made for the direct-labor hours and direct-labor cost as well as for the machine hours, with spaces for both the regular burden and the machine burden.

Figure 10 shows a comparative cost sheet on which is to be entered the information in connection with all the runs made on any one particular individual part. It should be noted that

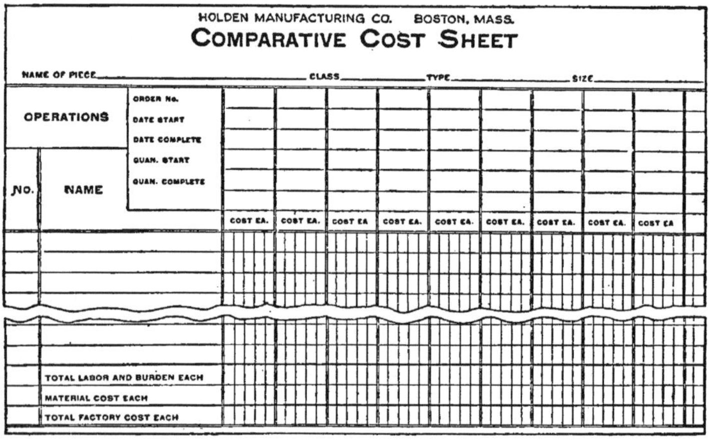

HOLDEN MANUFACTURING CO. BOSTON, MASS.

COMPARATIVE COST SHEET

NAME OF PIECE ________ CLASS ________ TYPE ________ SIZE ________

OPERATIONS

ORDER No.

DATE START

DATE COMPLETE

QUAN. START

QUAN. COMPLETE

NO. NAME

COST EA. COST EA. COST EA. COST EA. COST EA. COST EA. COST EA. COST EA. COST EA.

TOTAL LABOR AND BURDEN EACH

MATERIAL COST EACH

TOTAL FACTORY COST EACH

Figure 10.—Comparative Cost Sheet. (Size, 8½ x 11.)

there are nine columns on each sheet, which will give the comparison, operation by operation, of nine separate runs. It should also be noted that the information called for is the cost of each run, which is obtained from the last column of the cost sheet shown in Figure 8.

The use of this sheet will give the variations in the cost of running each operation on each piece and is of the greatest value in showing the actual cost of production. It should be inspected at regular intervals by the foremen for all the product which comes under their particular control.

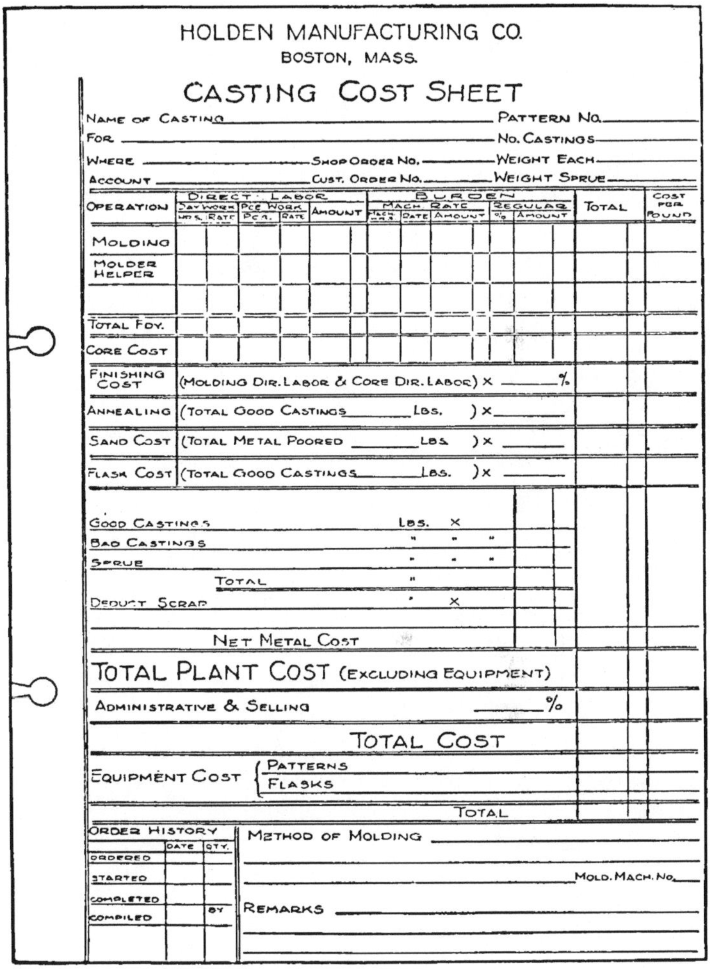

HOLDEN MANUFACTURING CO.
BOSTON, MASS.

CASTING COST SHEET

Name of Casting ____ Pattern No. ____
For ____ No. Castings ____
Where ____ Shop Order No. ____ Weight Each ____
Account ____ Cust. Order No. ____ Weight Sprue ____

Operation	Direct Labor: Daywork Hrs.	Rate	Pce Work Pcs.	Rate	Amount	Burden: Mach. Rate Mach. Hrs.	Rate	Amount	Regular %	Amount	Total	Cost per Pound
Molding												
Molder Helper												
Total Fdy.												
Core Cost												
Finishing Cost	(Molding Dir. Labor & Core Dir. Labor) × ____%											
Annealing	(Total Good Castings ____ Lbs.) × ____											
Sand Cost	(Total Metal Poured ____ Lbs.) × ____											
Flask Cost	(Total Good Castings ____ Lbs.) × ____											

Good Castings Lbs. ×
Bad Castings " " "
Sprue " " "
Total "
Deduct Scrap " ×
Net Metal Cost

TOTAL PLANT COST (Excluding Equipment)
Administrative & Selling ____%
TOTAL COST
Equipment Cost { Patterns / Flasks
Total

Order History	Date	Qty.
Ordered		
Started		
Completed		
Compiled		By

Method of Molding ____
Mold. Mach. No. ____
Remarks ____

Figure 11.—Foundry Individual Piece and Class Cost Sheet.
(Size, 8½ x 11.)

Foundry Individual Piece and Class Cost Sheets.—Figure 11 illustrates a cost sheet to be used for figuring the cost of individual castings and classes of castings, the method of figuring being identically the same in each case.

In this cost sheet the total metal poured is first entered, with credit given for the bad castings and sprue at scrap price, which leaves the net cost of the metal used in the casting or class. Next follow the details in regard to the moulding and core-making, together with their burden, and any machine time and machine rates which may be employed on the job. Next comes the finishing cost by percentage on the moulding and core labor, together with the annealing cost at a price per pound.

The sheet is by no means intended to be represented as fitting all cases, but simply illustrates a cost sheet as used for a medium-sized foundry for both individual patterns and classes.

Operation Cost Sheets.—In compiling costs under the operation method, it is necessary to pay particular attention to two very distinct phases:

1. Setting up a code of operations, the costs of which are to be kept.
2. Providing a sheet for recapitulating the quantities produced each day under each operation.

How these two items are taken care of is shown in Figure 12, a production and cost record of tubes. One of these sheets is used for each size of tube.

The total production for each day is entered on this sheet. The total of the labor charged up against each operation code number as shown under operation is ascertained from the time cards at the close of the month and entered under the heading "Total Labor Cost." It is then simply a matter of routine to fill in the cost per 100 tubes. The burden applicable to all operations in this department is entered below the total cost, thus arriving at the total labor and burden cost of each size of

HOLDEN MANUFACTURING CO.
BOSTON, MASS.

PRODUCTION & COST RECORD

TUBES Month..............................
Description ....
....

Date	Total Production	OPERATION No.	OPERATION Name	Total Labor Cost	Cost Per 100 Tubes
		1100	Making		
		1101	Covering Air Bags		
		1102	Wrapping		
		1103	Curing		
		1104	Tagging		
		1105	Buffing		
		1106	Joining		
		1107	Inserting Valves		
		1108	Cementing		
		1109	Splicing		
		1110	Taking Down		
		1111	Assembling Valves		
		1112	Inspecting		
		1113	Testing		
		1114	Deflating Tubes		
		1115	Deflating Air Bags		
		1116	Tightening Nuts		
		1117	Boxing		
			TOTAL		
			Burden @ %		
			Total Labor and Burden Cost		
		Material Cost			
TOTAL			Lbs. @ Per Lb		
		Credit			
			Lbs Rubber Scrap @ Per Lb		
			Net Material Cost		
			Total Plant Cost		

Figure 12.—Production and Cost Record. (Size, 8½ x 11.)

tube for the month. The material cost is entered on the bottom of the sheet, together with the credits for rubber scrap. As a result of the previous calculations, the net material and total manufacturing cost is shown.

Process Cost Sheets.—No illustration of the process cost sheet is shown, because it is almost exactly the same as an operation cost sheet, differing only in the titles on the sheet. Each operation would be a process in itself, the total of the entire list completing a major process which brings the material up to a point where it is measurable for cost purposes.

CHAPTER IX

SPECIFICATIONS OF PRODUCT AND OPERATIONS

The Necessity for Specifications.—If you start on a motor tour the first thing you think of is your road map. If you start on a rail trip you think of your timetable. If you consider the purchase of a new machine you ask for the blue prints.

In a manufacturing plant the course of engineering, purchasing, manufacturing and selling is along fixed lines of detail. This detail concerns itself with what materials, parts and assemblies must be manufactured; how many and how much are required and of what material. The shops need to know all this and in addition to know how the product is manufactured, what machines are best used, what manufacturing operations are involved, and how long each operation should require.

In other words, every successful manufacturing institution must have basic specifications of its product in complete detail of parts, the raw material required for each part, the parts that enter into each sub-assembly and the individual parts and sub-assemblies that enter into the finally assembled product to be shipped. Likewise, there must be a specification of the machine or process operations necessary to produce each individual part or lot, the equipment and tools best suited for each operation and the standard time which should be taken for each operation or group of operations.

Nomenclature of Specifications.—The specifications of materials are known by various terms. Specifications of parts entering into the product are variously known as specifications, parts lists, material lists, bills of material, product lists, etc.

The specifications of manufacturing operations are known as operation lists, sequence of operations, standard operations, etc.

For our discussion we will call the material section "Specifications of Product," and the manufacturing section "Specifications of Operations."

SPECIFICATION OF PRODUCT

APPROVED BY_________ DATE_____________ PART OR GROUP NO.____________

SUPERSEDES SPEC. DATED______________ BLUE PRINT NO.____________

NAME OF PART______________________________

Part No.	Quan. Each	Name of Parts	Blue Print	Figuring Space

Figure 13.—Specification of Product
(Size 11 x 8½.)

Specifications of Product.—Specifications of product are made up on forms similar to Figure 13, which needs no general description. As to the specifications, however, it must be continually borne in mind that each should represent some group of parts just as it is to be assembled in the plant and finally, just as is to be shipped out to customers. For instance, the receiver of a telephone is a complete unit of manufacture, and may even be shipped out as such. Therefore this unit would have its specification sheet showing the parts that make it up. But in addition there would be the final specification of the completed telephone, where the receiver would appear as an assembled part, together with all the other individual and assembled parts making up the complete telephone.

This same procedure when carried on with respect to the entire product will provide a basic specification for all transactions. It is the basis of stockroom arrangement and location of material therein. It forms the basis for issuing production orders, and is the standard pattern or layout for the figuring of costs.

Uses of Specifications of Product.—The principal uses of specifications of product are as follows:

Ordering Production. When it is desired to run some product, as for instance 500 of a certain style of bicycle, the set of specifications of product applying to this style will indicate exactly what to order. Working back from the final assembly, individual part and sub-assembly orders will be made out as they appear, and for the proper quantities.

Ordering Raw Material. As the production orders for parts require certain raw material, the entry of such parts on the stock records both as "ordered" on the record of the part itself and as "appropriated" on the record of the raw material sheet required for the part will provide the signal for the ordering of the said material necessary for making the part.

Costing the Product. It is obvious that there must be a cost sheet for each individual part. It is also obvious that the specification of product will give an absolutely trustworthy basis of just what parts appear as a material cost in each assembly order. Therefore it may readily be seen that the specifications of product are the bases for the costing of each assembly order, and that if they did *not* exist, there could be no check as far as the cost department is concerned as to whether the requisitions for parts for any assembly order were correct or not.

Issuing of Manufactured Parts. The specifications of product, form a bases for issuing the parts for assemblies in accurate manner and with very little clerical work. For instance, a foreman of the production department in ordering the parts for a telephone receiver, which might be Specification No. 285, would write a requisition calling for 50 sets Specification No. 285 and that is all. The storekeeper would fill the order from his copy of the specification, the foreman would check and assemble as per his copy which, of course, is the same, the stock record clerk would price the requisition at what the total amounted to for all parts, or would submit a list in detail fully costed to the cost department, and the cost department would enter the material cost of the specification being costed with assurance of its correctness.

Storing of Parts. It is obvious that specifications of product furnish an ideal plan for the arrangement of the individual part and assembled part bins in the stockroom. To a great extent this arrangement almost permits a physical specification whereby the stockkeeper can see that he is prepared with parts for any assembly desired. This of course is but auxiliary to the use of the stock records in being sure that required parts are in stock before any assembly is ordered into production.

The foregoing is sufficient to establish the necessity and value of specifications of product. While costs may be figured without such a basic guide, they are more costly and always are subject to doubt as to accuracy. With specifications of product which accurately list exactly what goes into the product, there can be no confusion or error in assembly, price lists and shipping orders may be accurately specified and there can be no errors in the cost of the product so far as the accuracy of items is concerned.

Specifications of Operations.—Specifications of operations are illustrated by Figure 14. A sheet of this nature is made up for each individual part. In some cases where there may be more than one operation concerned in the assembly the same sheet could be used to specify these operations.

This sheet gives complete data concerning each part, all headings on which will probably be clear to the reader except the following:

Best Run means the ideal or lowest quantity of this part that should be run in order to get the lowest cost.

Minimum Run indicates the lowest possible quantity to run without incurring a very distinct loss in unit cost.

Kind of Raw Material, Standard Raw Size and Quantity Raw Per Finished Piece means the kind of material as "Machine Steel," its size as 3 inches round, and the quantity required per finished piece as 4⅛ inches. The latter includes cutting waste per finished piece.

The column headings may best be described in a narrative manner. From past history and by mutual decision of the production department and the foreman, the operations necessary to produce the part will be settled, and listed in their proper sequence, numbered consecutively. The consecutive sequence of operations may take the part to different departments, and therefore the department to do the work will be noted in the proper column.

Each operation is best done on some particular machine. There may be many of this type of machine, and therefore the machine number or the designating number of a group or battery of like machines will be noted as the best method of performing the operation.

From past records or from estimates (which from time to

SPECIFICATION OF OPERATIONS

APPROVED	NAME AND DESCRIPTION OF PART	PART OR GROUP NO.____
BY____ DATE____		BLUE PRINT____
SUPERSEDING SHEET DATED____		SHEET NO.____ OF____
BEST RUN____	KIND OF RAW MATERIAL____	
MINIMUM RUN____	STAND. RAW SIZE____ QUAN. RAW PER FIN. PCE.____	

Oper. No.	Operation Name	Dept.	Best Mch. or Group	Standard Rate		Tools Used
				Running	Set-up	

Figure 14.—Specification of Operations. (Size, 8½ x 11.)

time must be corrected as a result of actual experience) the standard rate of production for each operation should be entered. This may be expressed in different ways as may best fit the circumstances. It may be expressed as units per day, units per hour, hours per unit or any other way. The units per hour is a very satisfactory plan to use, as for instance 3.75 pieces per hour. If the total order should be 75 pieces, the standard time required would be 20 hours. This is known as standard hourly rate of production.

The standard set up time should also be entered, as this time will be necessary in each run cost irrespective of the quantity run. This cost is often the basis of a loss when through bad planning an economical run is not made on each set up.

Where special tools are required for any operation, as for instance special milling cutters, boring bars, etc., the designating number of such tools should appear opposite the operation.

Field for Use of Specifications of Operations.—The field for the use of the specification of operations is as broad as industry itself. While the detailed description just given may apply to machining operations more particularly, the same principle applies to any industry and the form may be adapted accordingly. A rubber tire after being built goes through a series of finishing operations as an individual part.

In the chemical industry a certain quantity of a number of ingredients goes through a series of operations as if an individual part. So also in the textile industry, brick, tile and many others.

Summary of Objectives of Specifications.—No business can possibly operate successfully without basic specifications of what is to be done and how it should be done. It is absolutely impossible to carry minimum inventories, safeguard sufficient materials for production and sale or know what and how to buy without systematic knowledge as to the product.

It is absolutely impossible to reach any degree of control of manufacturing operations unless they are scheduled as to nature and sequence and unless there is a standard of time on which to plan and compare performance.

It is absolutely impossible to arrive at accurate costs unless such basic standard specifications are in existence to serve as a guide and plan whereby it is positively known that each cost covers all material and labor used and no more.

Most important of all is the use of the specifications as the basic means of betterment of manufacture, the constant slogan of the management being to "beat the best time" in every run that is made. This brings us again to the main objective of this book, i.e., costs for cost reduction and actual use by the entire organization for the bettering and increasing of the profits, not just to find out what the profits (or losses) are for statement purposes.

CHAPTER X

ORDERS AND SYMBOLS

Orders as the Basis of Action.—Modern business is an intricate and sensitive mechanism. Its activities must be controlled and synchronized. No goods should be shipped, no work performed nor should any expense be incurred except through a system of orders carefully and definitely planned to control every movement of labor, material and other purchased expense.

Orders become the basis of action; the authority to spend money, and the means of properly accounting for cost. They release goods for shipment and incur liabilities when used for purchases. They are, therefore, the means of communicating authority for the many and varying activities of the business, and thus should be designed to safeguard each of these activities.

Insufficiency of Oral Orders.—Oral orders should be eliminated because they produce mistakes, delays, and an irregular flow of production. Furthermore, oral orders more than any other factor are responsible for the prevalence in industry of the great American game of "passing the buck." The greatest disadvantage of oral orders, however, is the lack of a systematized basis for the collection of data necessary for the control of production and for the preparation of cost reports for executives, managers, and foremen. The factory management has no assurance that oral orders will be carried out. If any oral orders are issued, they should be regarded as "advance notices," and should be confirmed later by written orders. It is astonishing how many factory managers do not even yet realize the inadequacy of oral orders.

Classes of Orders.—The written orders of an industrial plant are divided into five main classes:

1. Purchase orders
2. Production orders
   (a) Special
   (b) Standing
3. Standing expense orders
4. Shipping and sales orders
5. Plant orders

1. *Purchase Orders.* Purchase orders are so generally understood that no reference need be made to them here. (See Chapter XI.)

2. *Production Orders.* The main interest in this chapter centers in those orders which authorize production and expenses, because they provide the means of regulating costs—both direct and indirect. All notifications for the actual manufacture of parts, sub-assemblies, and final assemblies, are made on production orders (see Figure 15). These orders must state clearly just what is to be made, the number to be made, the necessary specifications, blue-prints, etc., to govern the manufacture of the product specified. When occasion demands, production orders may consist of two types:

(a) Special
(b) Standing

Special production orders are the regular production orders for specific quantities of whatever is being ordered. When the quantity ordered is produced, the order is complete.

Standing production orders—or blanket orders as they are sometimes called—may be used wherever there is mass or continuous production. For instance, in a bolt factory there may be standing orders for certain sizes of bolts to be in continuous production.

One general rule to observe in connection with production

orders is to have only *one item on one order.* In other words, one order should cover one run of one item only. This rule is absolutely necessary in order to be able to control positively all production, both as to physical movements and costs. Partly for this reason shipping orders can never be safely used as production orders in a manufacturing plant, because in the great majority of cases the shipping order calls for goods which require from one to many production orders to make.

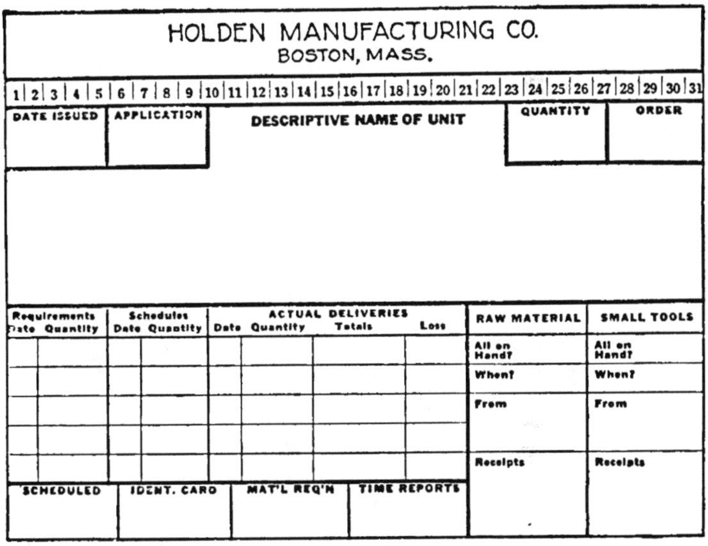

HOLDEN MANUFACTURING CO.
BOSTON, MASS.

1 | 2 | 3 | 4 | 5 | 6 | 7 | 8 | 9 | 10 | 11 | 12 | 13 | 14 | 15 | 16 | 17 | 18 | 19 | 20 | 21 | 22 | 23 | 24 | 25 | 26 | 27 | 28 | 29 | 30 | 31

DATE ISSUED	APPLICATION	DESCRIPTIVE NAME OF UNIT	QUANTITY	ORDER

Requirements Date	Quantity	Schedules Date	Quantity	ACTUAL DELIVERIES Date	Quantity	Totals	Loss	RAW MATERIAL	SMALL TOOLS
								All on Hand?	All on Hand?
								When?	When?
								From	From
								Receipts	Receipts

SCHEDULED	IDENT. CARD	MAT'L REQ'N	TIME REPORTS

Figure 15.—Production Order. (Size, 6 x 4.)

Exceptions to this rule may be made if using the part number in conjunction with the order number can safely be relied on. For instance, if an order covers a fabricated machine and all its parts are special; and further, if each part is numbered, one order number may cover the job. But in all cases, the part number *must* be shown in conjunction with the order number, otherwise no part cost could be known. This exception should be avoided where possible.

Production orders should only authorize the manufacture of work. They should not be combined with cost sheets. Costs should appear on separate records known as cost sheets, which

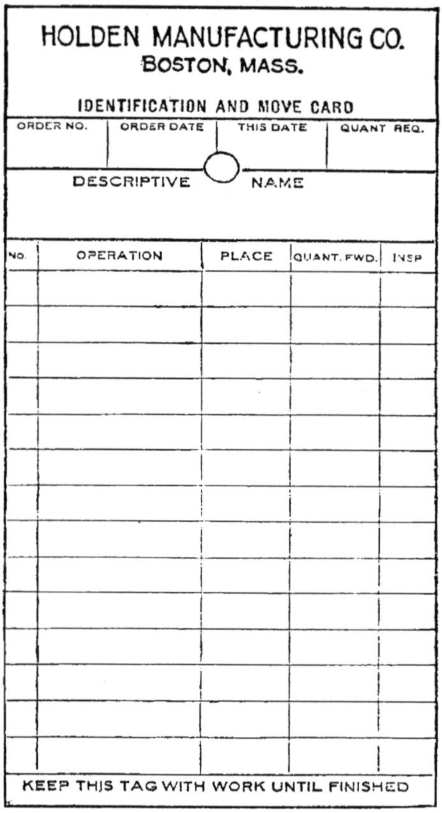
HOLDEN MANUFACTURING CO.
BOSTON, MASS.

IDENTIFICATION AND MOVE CARD

ORDER NO.	ORDER DATE	THIS DATE	QUANT REQ.

DESCRIPTIVE NAME

NO.	OPERATION	PLACE	QUANT. FWD.	INSP

KEEP THIS TAG WITH WORK UNTIL FINISHED

Figure 16.—Identification and Move Card.
(Size, 3 x 5.)

show, however, the number of the production order to which they apply.

In a large plant, production orders are prepared by the

production order department of the general superintendent's office or some other special department, according to the nature of the organization. The number of copies filled out varies according to the type of business and the internal organization of the business.

An adjunct of the production order is the identification and move card as shown in Figure 16. Each lot of material should be accompanied by one of these tags which specifies the order number and the sequence of operations through which the material is to pass. The headings on the tag are self-explanatory. A word might be said, however, concerning the importance of this tag. Since it indicates the proper sequence of operations, guarantees the identity of the material, and shows the proper order number to be entered on the time cards, the tag is the means by which the cost records are safeguarded.

3. *Standing Expense Orders.* The indirect costs of maintaining the organization, such as the costs of executive offices, sales departments, and the so-called "service" departments, are chargeable to a set of orders known as service or standing orders. Examples of service departments in the clerical and administrative part of the organization are the purchasing, payroll, cost, statistical, filing, stenographic, billing, credits and collections, general accounting, and general office departments. In the plant the expenses of trucking, steam, dining-rooms, as well as the regular burden costs of each productive department, are also charged to standing expense orders. As a matter of fact, the term "service department," is broad enough to apply to all indirect departments in a plant.

The reason for calling the class of orders under discussion standing expense orders, is their element of permanence; that is, the orders stand permanently, although the charges to each order are cleared each month. Through them the indirect costs are controlled. In fact the assigning of the standing expense orders can only follow a most exhaustive study of the items of expense which are important to know for the purposes of intelligent guidance of the management and departmental heads.

The construction of a code of standing expense orders should involve everyone who is interested in their use. Every department head is directly interested, as the information he will get each month will be exactly in accordance with the code. It is important, for instance, to know the amount of money spent in each department for supervision, clerical, store or tool keeping, inspection and such other like charges. It is important in a plant with bad floors and no up-to-date way of handling the materials about the place to have a standing order to show the cost of handling materials in each department. Subsequently, when the costs have been operated long enough to give reliable figures, it will be possible to accurately figure the results of laying new floors, purchasing lift trucks and platforms and thereby reduce the handling cost.

Not until the indirect cost or overhead is automatically analyzed each month by such standing orders is it possible for the department heads or the management to realize where to look for opportunities of cutting costs and keeping them cut. Such analysis gives opportunity for research and endeavor that otherwise would be impossible. It becomes the basis for the control of the indirect costs which have always been and always will be the bane of industry.

Objection has been raised here and there to the apparent extra cost of time keeping entailed through having so many places to charge time. The objection has little weight. While a little more time may be needed it should be remembered that no live cost cutting endeavor can possibly be carried on without actual facts as a guide. It pays, therefore, to analyze the indirect costs by the medium of standing orders to the smallest item that has any possibility of savings through careful study of labor saving and material saving devices.

Every item of labor or material that can possibly be measured in its relation to goods produced should be charged directly to product. The indirect cost is often cluttered up with items which should be charged as a direct cost of product, but which are slid into indirect cost on account of the difficulty of doing otherwise. To obviate this fault, methods of caring for small material and labor charges are explained in Chapters XIV and XVIII.

As every indirect expense or burden account has a definite basis for cost figuring (such as kilowatt-hours for electric generation) the unit cost for each item in each expense account gives a monthly comparison of great value. This feature is clearly explained as the uses of costs are taken up.

4. *Shipping and Sales Orders.* Orders of the fourth class—shipping and sales—are so frequently used in general accounting that their description here is unnecessary. They should, however, be adequately provided for.

5. *Plant Orders.* In order to keep the ordering of plant improvements or major repairs separate from either the production or standing expense orders, it is advisable to have a special series of orders for such work. For instance, the orders for the building or installation of a new machine would come in this series.

The Charging of Production and Expense Orders.—Various means are used in plants for ascertaining the time spent by workers on the production and expense orders. Time recorders, traveling timekeepers, foremen or inspectors keep this time as discussed in Chapter XVIII. The principal point to bring out here is that some adequate method of arriving at the actual time spent on both classes of orders must be employed, and be reported through the medium of time cards to the pay-roll and cost department. Great care must be taken in reporting time, as the value of the costs would be entirely nullified by careless attention to this most important detail.

Material is regulated by stockrooms and drawn out by requisitiou. This forms a safe and sure method of getting accurate material charges to both classes of orders. Where material is not in stockrooms, the greatest care must be exercised in arriving at amounts used and charged to either class of orders, otherwise, as in careless accounting of labor, the value of the costs will be nullified. Many charges to expense accounts or to department burden accounts come directly through the voucher register, as explained in Chapter VII.

The Identification of Orders, Accounts, Departments, Machines, etc.—Aside from the matter of cost accounting alone, it is of great advantage to have a method of numerical identification of all factors which in any way enter into the accounting field. Numerical identification is mentioned on account of the rapidly increasing use of electric punched card devices which require numbers for sorting and tabulating purposes. If it were not for this reason, letters could be used in any approved identification scheme.

It is important that departments be identified by number for recording purposes. All machinery, tools and equipment should be so identified for purposes of convenience in accounting, both from the repair and maintenance standpoint and from the inventory standpoint. Every individual part and assembly of the product should be identified by a number as well as each operation necessary to produce them. Each ledger account should also be numbered.

Needless to say we still have the necessity of assigning numbers for our production and standing expense orders, and here great care should be used, as in assigning blocks of numbers it is necessary to assure against conflict of numbers on account of tabulations which are to be made.

Advantages of Coding.—The advantages of code numbers are many. For instance:

1. They aid the memory.
2. They reduce the clerical work involved in writing up

material requisitions, time tickets, expense debit slips, production orders, and standing expense orders.

3. They facilitate the mechanical sorting and tabulating of records in connection with the compilation and presentation of material, labor, and burden costs.

Assignment of Numbers.—To illustrate the setting aside of numbers for order and account purposes, the following schedule is shown:

1 – 1,000	reserved for ledger accounts
1,001 – 30,000	reserved for standing expense and burden orders
30,001 – 100,000	reserved for production orders for individual parts
100,001 – 200,000	reserved for production orders for assembled parts
200,001 – 300,000	reserved for plant orders

Each ledger account should be numbered in the allotment of numbers reserved for this purpose, and the numbers assigned should remain permanent. The standing expense orders, production and plant orders will be assigned within their several groups of numbers.

Standing Expense Orders for Works Accounts.—After careful analysis of items desired has been made, a tabular code of orders should be made as shown in Figure 17. The expense items appear on the left and are identified by numbers from 01 up, as shown. The departments are shown across the top, and each department is identified with a number as shown. The combination of these two numbers, always placing the department number first, forms the order number for the expense item for each department. Each expense order, therefore, will *always* consist of four numbers, the first two digits representing the department, the second two digits representing the expense item.

This method of assigning orders is very elastic as it will be noted that in assigning the numbers to the expense items a generous allowance has been made to permit additional numbers to be assigned at the end of each section. Likewise, the blank vertical columns may be assigned to other departments.

Standing Order Code—Plant

	Expense Orders	General Depts.						Plant Service Depts.						Producing Depts.				
		General	Accounting	Purchasing	Stores	Shipping	Engineering	Electric Power	Steam Power	Compressed Air	Teaming	Maintenance	Personnel	Dept. A	Dept. B	Dept. C	Dept. D	Dept. E
		10	11	12	13	14	15	21	22	23	24	25	26	31	32	33	34	35
	Labor																	
01	Supervision	1001			1301	1401	1501	2101	2201	2301	2401	2501	2601	3101	3201	3301	3401	3501
02	Clerical	1002	1102	1202	1302	1402	1502				2402	2502	2602	3102	3202	3302	3402	3502
03	Inspectors				1303									3103	3203	3303	3403	3503
04	Cleaning and Sweeping	1004												3104	3204	3304	3404	3504
05	Handling Materials													3105	3205	3305	3405	3505
06	Expense a/c Shop Error													3106	3206	3306	3406	3506
07	Idle Time													3107	3207	3307	3407	3507
08	General Labor	1008			1308	1408					2408	2508		3108	3208	3308	3408	3508
09	Watchmen	1009																
10																		
	Maintenance and Improvement																	
21	Machinery	1021						2121	2221	2321	2421	2521		3121	3221	3321	3421	3521
22	Tools													3122	3222	3322	3422	3522

23	Dies, Jigs and Templates																3123	3223	3323	3423	3523	
24	Buildings and Grounds	1024							2124	2224	2324	2424					3124	3224	3324	3424	3524	
25	Fixtures	1025	1125	1225	1325	1425	1525					2425	2525	2625			3125	3225	3325	3425	3525	
26	Pipe and Power Lines	1026							2126	2226	2326						3126	3226	3326	3426	3526	
27	Electrical Apparatus	1027							2127		2327	2427					3127	3227	3327	3427	3527	
28	Other Equipment	1028															3128	3228	3328	3428	3528	
29	Experimental	1029																				
30	Rearrangement																3130	3230	3330	3430	3530	
31																						
41	Expense Material and Service Small Tools																3141	3241	3341	3441	3541	
42	Lights	1042	1142	1242	1342	1442	1542		2142	2242	2342	2442	2542	2642			3142	3242	3342	3442	3542	
43	Oils and Waste	1043							2143	2243	2343	2443	2543				3143	3243	3343	3443	3543	
44	Emery Wheels																3144	3244	3344	3444	3544	
45	Fuel									2245		2445										
46	Miscellaneous	1046	1146	1246	1346	1446	1546		2146	2246	2346	2446	2546	2646			3146	3246	3346	3446	3546	
47	Purchased Electric Current								2147													
48	Office Supplies	1048	1148	1248	1348	1448	1548										3148	3248	3348	3448	3548	
49	Postage	1049																				
50	Telephone and Telegraph	1050																				
51	Dining and Welfare													2651								
52	Sundry Expense	1052																				
53	Inventory Expense	1053			1353	1453											3153	3253	3353	3453	3553	

Figure 17.—Standing Order Code—Plant

Standing Order Code—

	EXPENSE ORDERS	ADMINISTRATION									
		General Administrative	Treasury	Credits and Collections	General Accounting	Billing	Stenographic	General Office	Statistical	Filing	
		101	102	103	104	105	106	107	108	109	
01	Salaries—Office	10101	10201	10301	10401	10501	10601	10701	10801	10901	
02	Salaries—Salesmen										
03	Commissions										
04	Traveling and Entertainment	10104	10204	10304							
05	Office Supplies		10205	10305	10405	10505	10605	10705	10805	10905	
06	Sundries	10106	10206	10306	10406	10506	10606	10706	10806	10906	
07	Telephone and Telegraph	10107	10207	10307							
08	Postage							10708			
09	Rent										
10	Repairs							10710			
11	Grounds Expense							10711			
12	Dues, Subscriptions, Gratuities							10712			
13	Tabulating Rentals								10813		
14	Legal	10114									
15											
16	Advertising—Space										
17	Advertising—Miscel.										
18	Cuts, Electros, Etc.										
19	Catalogs and Circulars										
20	Exhibits										
21											
22	Warehouse Wages										
23	Warehouse Expense										
24											
25											

Figure 18.—Standing Order Code—

Administrative and Selling

SELLING											
General Sales Office	Branch A	Branch B	Branch C	Branch D	Branch E		Sales Promotion	Advertising—General	Distribution	
121	122	123	124	125	126		141	142	143	
12101	12201	12301	12401	12501	12601		14101	14201	14301	
12102	12202	12302	12402	12502	12602					
12103	12202	12303	12403	12503	12603					
12104	12204	12304	12404	12504	12604		14104		14304	
12105	12205	12305	12405	12505	12605		14105	14205	14305	
12106	12206	12306	12406	12506	12606		14106	14206	14306	
12107	12207	12307	12407	12507	12607				14307	
12108	12208	12308	12408	12508	12608		14108			
	12209	12309	12409	12509	12609					
12110	12210	12310	12410	12510	12610					
12112	12212	12312	12412	12512	12612					
12116	12216	12316	12416	12516	12616					
12117	12217	12317	12417	12517	12617					
12118										
12119										
12120	12220	12320	12420	12520	12620					
12122	12222	12322	12422	12522	12622					
12123	12223	12323	12423	12523	12623					

Administrative and Selling

In charging labor and material to these orders in the detailed daily routine, it is obvious that one should be fully acquainted with the various items of this code. For instance, a man is at work repairing a machine in the Pattern Shop. His time and any material he needs will be charged to Order 4542. Repairs to a table for the Engineering Department will be charged to Order 4047. The salary of an inspector in the Moulding Department of the Brass Foundry will be charged to Order 5203, and so on.

Standing Orders for Administrative, Sales and General Office Expenses.—In the same manner as with the works expense orders, a code of standing orders is fixed for the administrative, sales and general office expenses. Such a code is shown in Figure 18. As it is used in exactly the same manner as the code for the plant expenses and burden accounts, no further explanation is needed. Here also the detail of expense items is easily understood without further comment.

CHAPTER XI

PURCHASE AND RECEIVING RECORDS

Importance of Purchase and Receiving Records.—Too much stress cannot be laid on the importance of the records which have to do with the request for, and the actual purchase and receiving of, new materials.

The old methods of ordering materials or services, without consideration as to the accounts to which they were to be charged, or as to the ultimate representation of their costs in the records, have been the cause of endless confusion and inaccuracy not only in the general accounting of the company, but particularly in the cost accounts. It should be distinctly known at the time when the need for any material or service arises, exactly why it is required and where it is to be charged.

An important advantage which accrues from this method is that in many cases the consideration of the ultimate disposition of the costs to be incurred prevents the spending of money for what is after all unnecessary. This applies not only to materials, but also to various services performed which often turn out to be unnecessary.

Obviously, all the records which have to do with purchasing and receiving have a close bearing on the business as a whole, and the mechanism instituted in these departments should be designed and operated, not only with a view to the efficiency of the departments themselves, but with full thought for the assistance which can be given to other departments.

Nature of Purchases.—As there are many kinds of purchases, it is to be expected that they will originate in a number of different ways. Not all of the obligations assumed by a manufacturing institution are by any means handled entirely by the purchasing department, although the methods of handling obligations must be the same throughout the plant in order that methods of control may be standardized.

Purchases may be grouped in the following principal classes:

1. Materials necessary to maintain the regular stocks of raw materials, supplies, and all other merchandise handled by regular stock methods.
2. Items of material which are necessary for purposes of repair, but which are not regular stock items, and which are not represented on stock records at the time of order, and are not likely ever to be.
3. Services of various nature, such as boiler and pipe line repairing, or any work of repair and maintenance which may be requisitioned from outside the organization. This would include also services by outside accountants, engineers, etc.
4. All items, such as advertising, etc., which may be arranged through the publicity division of a company as separate from the purchasing department.
5. All miscellaneous services not covered by any of the above—including telephone and telegraph service, purchased electric power, etc.

Mechanism of Purchasing and Receiving.—As an aid in further discussion, it is important to understand clearly the mechanism involved in the purchasing and receiving department, and particularly the various forms used and their functions and application. The principal ones are:

1. Request for purchase
2. Purchase order
3. Record of receipt of material
4. Purchasing department shipping order
5. Purchasing department debit and credit memos
6. Receiving report
7. Record of purchases
8. Distribution stamp for invoices

1. Request for Purchase.—Figure 19 shows a request for purchase. This term is considered preferable to Purchase Requisition because then there can be no confusion with the term Material Requisition. It is prepared in duplicate, each copy being in a different color. One copy is retained in the department which originates the request, the other being sent to the purchasing department. This form is used to notify the purchasing department of what is desired or, in case arrangements have already been made, to notify the purchasing department to issue a purchase order to cover the item.

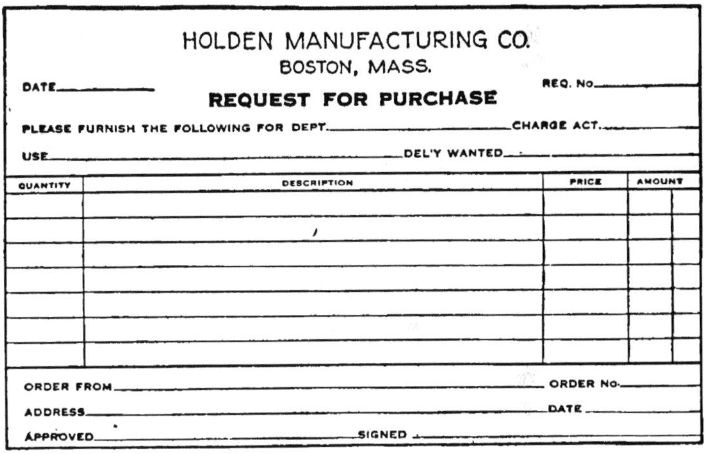

HOLDEN MANUFACTURING CO.
BOSTON, MASS.
DATE ______ REQ. NO. ______
REQUEST FOR PURCHASE
PLEASE FURNISH THE FOLLOWING FOR DEPT. ______ CHARGE ACT. ______
USE ______ DEL'Y WANTED ______

QUANTITY	DESCRIPTION	PRICE	AMOUNT

ORDER FROM ______ ORDER NO. ______
ADDRESS ______ DATE ______
APPROVED ______ SIGNED ______

Figure 19.—Request for Purchase. (Size, 8 x 4.)

These forms should be serially numbered and should show the department for which the material or service is desired, the use to be made of whatever is ordered, and all other essential descriptive data. The form may show also from whom the material or service is to be obtained.

There are two points of prime importance in connection with this form: (1) The request must be approved by some-one in authority other than the one signing the request. (2)

The requisition must show the account which is to be charged with the material ordered; this item is of the utmost importance, as will be shown later.

2. **Purchase Order.**—The purchase order—here illustrated in Figure 20—may be of almost any design, provided it shows clearly all references, such as order number, request for pur-

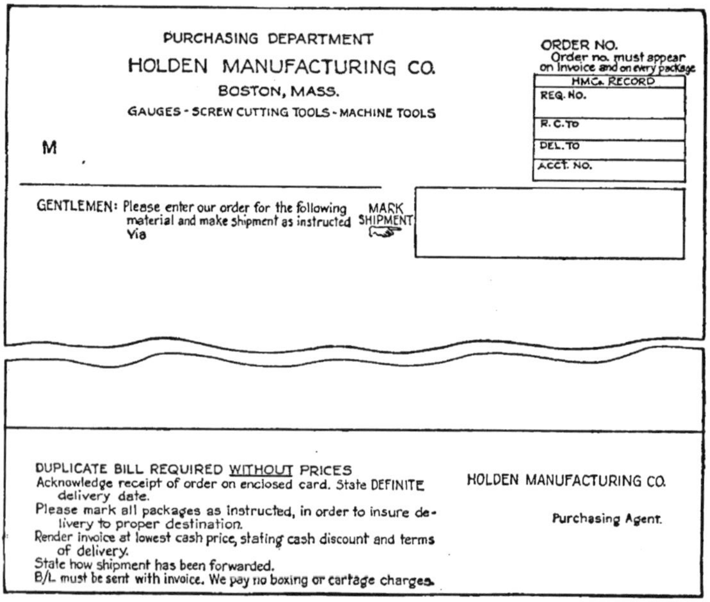
PURCHASING DEPARTMENT
HOLDEN MANUFACTURING CO.
BOSTON, MASS.
GAUGES - SCREW CUTTING TOOLS - MACHINE TOOLS

ORDER NO.
Order no. must appear on Invoice and on every package

HMCo. RECORD
REQ. NO.
R. C. TO
DEL. TO
ACCT. NO.

M

GENTLEMEN: Please enter our order for the following material and make shipment as instructed Via

MARK SHIPMENT

DUPLICATE BILL REQUIRED WITHOUT PRICES
Acknowledge receipt of order on enclosed card. State DEFINITE delivery date.
Please mark all packages as instructed, in order to insure delivery to proper destination.
Render invoice at lowest cash price, stating cash discount and terms of delivery.
State how shipment has been forwarded.
B/L must be sent with invoice. We pay no boxing or cartage charges.

HOLDEN MANUFACTURING CO.

Purchasing Agent.

Figure 20.—Purchase Order. (Size, 8½ x 11.)

chase number, and all other data in connection with what the material should be and from whom it should come. As purchase orders are common, special explanation is hardly necessary. One point, however, demands strong emphasis, namely, that the accounting of the material must be shown *in every case,* and must agree with the charge shown on the request for purchase.

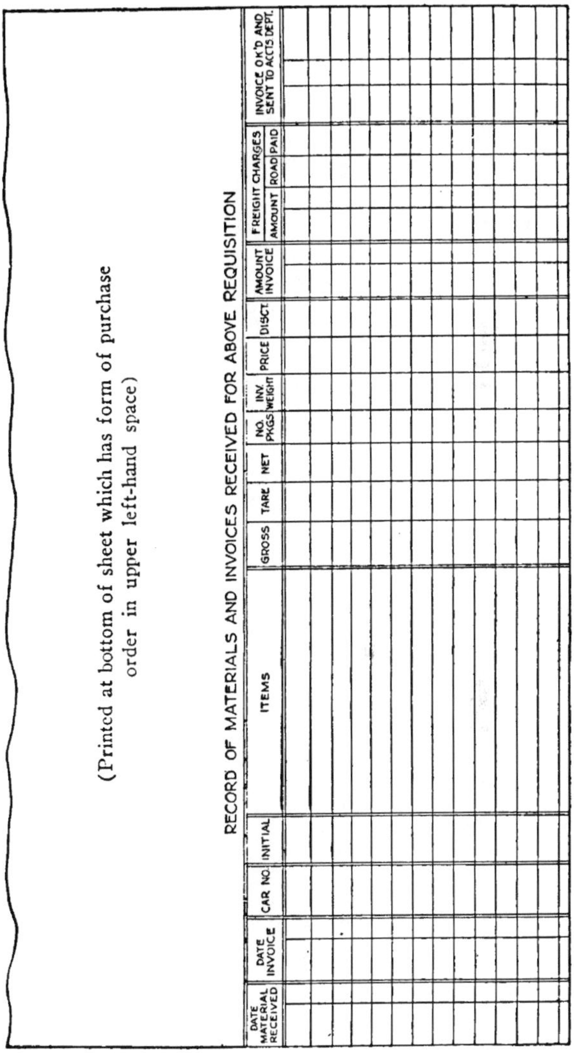

(Printed at bottom of sheet which has form of purchase order in upper left-hand space)

RECORD OF MATERIALS AND INVOICES RECEIVED FOR ABOVE REQUISITION

DATE MATERIAL RECEIVED	DATE INVOICE	CAR NO.	INITIAL	ITEMS	GROSS	TARE	NET	NO. PKGS	INV. WEIGHT	PRICE	DISCT.	AMOUNT INVOICE	FREIGHT CHARGES			INVOICE OK'D AND SENT TO ACCTS DEPT.
													AMOUNT	ROAD	PAID	

Figure 21.—Receipt of Material Record. (Size, 13¾ x 13½.)

3. Receipt of Material Record.—It is important to have a record of all receipts on each purchasing order which will show not only the receipts of items, but also all essential facts connected with each item, such as the date of invoice, car numbers, weights, and freight bills. This is of the utmost importance in properly handling the transportation charges, for when this master record is properly filled out, it hooks together the invoices and the freight bills. This record (Figure 21) is a copy of the purchase order, and is the last carbon when a purchase order is written, the excess edges being folded under at time of writing. The sheets are filed in a multiple ring binder in sequence of purchase order numbers. This record should not be confused with the receiving report discussed later.

4. Purchasing Department Shipping Order.—In many cases material is rejected upon inspection as not complying with the purchase order in the matter of quality or other points. It is therefore necessary to provide some means to authorize shipping such material back to the vendor. As the matter is entirely in the province of the purchasing department, it has been found useful to have purchasing department shipping orders, as shown in Figure 22. These provide a very simple and effective method of quickly handling rejected material, while holding strictly to the rules that nothing should leave the plant without a shipping order. No special comment on the form is needed, except for the caution that here—as with all other transactions in connection with the purchasing department—great care must be taken to give full detail regarding the material.

5. Purchasing Department Debit and Credit Memos.—Figure 23 shows a purchasing department debit memo. The credit memo is identically the same with the exception that the main heading will read "Credit Memo" and further that all the item headings will be reversed as to their meaning, such as "Credit Memo by" in place of "Debit Memo by." These two

HOLDEN MANUFACTURING CO.
BOSTON, MASS.

PURCHASING DEPT. SHIPPING ORDER

SHIP TO ____ P.D. SHIPPING ORDER ____
CARE OF ____ OUR PURCHASE REQ. NO. ____
WHERE ____ DATE THIS ORDER ____
VIA ____ THEIR ORDER NO. ____ DATE THEIR INVOICE ____
ORDER DICTATED BY ____ WRITTEN BY ____ CHECKED BY ____

DESCRIPTIVE	PRICE	AMOUNT

FREIGHT ____ CHARGE ____ AMOUNT ____
REASON FOR ABOVE ____

SHIPPING CLERK'S CERTIFICATE
THE ABOVE WAS SHIPPED AS ABOVE ON ____
CAR INITIAL ____ NUMBER ____ WEIGHT ____
PACKED AS FOLLOWS ____
(SIGNED) ____

DEBIT MEMO. NO. ____ MADE BY ____ DATE ____ CHECKED BY ____

Figure 22.—Purchasing Department Shipping Order. (Size, 8½ x 11.)

memos are designed to speed up the work of adjustments by the purchasing department on incoming materials.

The debit memo, the form of which is self-explanatory, is useful in keeping the accounts of the plant up to date. The issuing of this debit memo immediately upon the shipping out

HOLDEN MANUFACTURING CO.
BOSTON, MASS.

Purchasing Dept. Debit Memo. No.__________

Debit________________ Date__________
Care of________________ P. D. Shipping Order__________
Where________________ Our Purchase Req. No.__________
Via__________ Their Order No.__________ Date Their Invoice__________
Car Initial__________ Number__________ Packed__________
Debit Memo. By________________ Checked By__________

DESCRIPTIVE	WEIGHT	PRICE	AMOUNT
Freight			

Reason for Above__________ Our Purchase A/C__________
E'T'D Stock Record By__________
Prices, Etc. O.K.__________

Figure 23.—Purchasing Department Debit Memo. (Size, 11 x 7.)

of any material on a purchasing department shipping order obviates the necessity of waiting for the credit memo of the vendor to arrive before completing the records. In many cases this is of utmost importance on account of the delay of vendors in issuing credit memos—in some cases many weeks elapse before the credit memos are returned. In the meantime, however, the debit memo issued by the purchasing department is put through the records in regular form, a copy being sent to the vendor.

These purchasing department debit and credit memos may be used for other purposes, such as the adjustment of vendors' prices one way or the other. The principal use of the credit memo is in adjusting prices when some error has been made in the original invoice. Occasionally also the credit memo is used in the case of overshipment by a vendor when the material is acceptable.

With both of these forms, great care must be taken to fill in full data, particularly the accounting references, in order to facilitate the complete accounting procedure of the company.

6. **Receiving Report.**—Figure 24, which is self-explanatory, is a simple type of receiving report.

HOLDEN MANUFACTURING CO.
BOSTON, MASS.
RECEIVING REPORT

No.

Shipper Date 19

CAR LOAD REPORT	LESS THAN CAR LOAD REPORT
Car Initial and No.	Received via:
Invoice Date 19	
Reported Date 19	Date Received 19
Gross Weight	
Tare Weight	
Net Weight	

PURCHASE ORDER NO.	DESCRIPTION OF MATERIAL	PART OR PATTERN NO. OR DIMENSIONS	STYLE OF PACKING	WEIGHT	QUANTITY	✓	STORED	
							SECTION	BIN

Quantities checked by Checker
Quantities approved by Storekeeper
Remarks

Quality approved by Inspector

CAR RECORD
Book
Page
Line

Figure 24.—Receiving Report. (Size, 8½ x 7¼.)

7. Record of Purchases by Items.—It is usually best for the purchasing department to maintain a card or book record (Figure 25) to show the data in connection with the purchasing of all items of sufficient importance to be recorded. Nearly every up-to-date concern maintains some record of this sort in order to furnish full knowledge of what has been done before in relation to each item and as a guide in current purchases. This form is of particular use in connection with items whose

HOLDEN MANUFACTURING CO.
Boston, Mass.
RECORD OF PURCHASES

Article No. Size

Date	Order No.	Name and Address	Quantity	List	Discount	Net	Freight	Unit Cost

Figure 25.—Record of Purchases. (Size, 8 x 5.)

source of supply is more or less restricted and as to which it is necessary to know exactly with whom to deal in connection with the purchase.

For much of the material handled by a manufacturing institution, the stock record (Figure 27) will be found of great value in connection with, or in place of, the record of purchases. This applies particularly to staple articles, such as bolts, nuts, nails, and steel, purchased from vendors whose names are not of great importance, and to all supplies which have to be drawn from many sources.

8. Distribution Stamp for Invoices.—Figure 26 shows a form of rubber stamp which may be used in connection with the approval and distribution of invoices.

It is especially important that all the information shown on this stamp should be given for each invoice. While the

HOLDEN MANUFACTURING CO.
Boston, Mass.

Pch'se. Order No.__________
Terms__________
Freight Charges__________
Material Received - Date__________
Rec. Rep. No.__________
Prices O. K. by__________
Ext'd O. K. by__________
E't'd { Purchase Order by__________
Stock Record by__________
Exp. Lgr. by__________ }

ACCOUNT	AMOUNT	

Figure 26.—Invoice Stamp. (Size, 2½ x 3½.)

stamp is quite large, there is really nothing on it which can be dispensed with.

Other Forms.—There are many other forms which might be shown in connection with the discussion of the work of the purchasing department. In fact, those here shown represent the smallest number with which a purchasing department can operate accurately. It is, of course, necessary for a purchasing department to maintain follow-up files for incoming material, quotation files for the various materials required, and many other detailed records which are important, but which have no direct bearing on the subject of this book.

Origin of Purchases

The origin of purchases has a close bearing on all the procedure which follows. To take up some items in detail will given an idea of how such matters should be handled.

Purchases of Material for Stock.—In the case of the material covered by stock records, the request for purchase is made out by the stock record clerk. Therefore, raw materials, supplies, and in some institutions certain materials purchased from the outside for use in assemblies and for direct shipment, which are in stock, should be covered by stock records.

Before making out the request for purchase, the stock record clerk carefully considers the maximum and minimum limits discussed in Chapter XIII. In addition to these factors, the requirements columns of the stock record sheet show when it is necessary to order material and the quantities needed.

The request for material must receive the approval of the general storekeeper and perhaps of some other official. It is then passed on to the purchasing department for action. The purchasing department returns a copy of the purchasing order to the stock record department, so that an entry may be made on the stock record sheet of the date of order, the purchase order number, and the quantity ordered.

Each stock record sheet should show the material inventory account which covers the material to be ordered, and the number of that account must be placed on the request for purchase.

Items of Material Necessary for Purposes of Repair.—In many instances purchases are made of repair parts which are never carried in stock, nor is it desirable to carry them. Such is the case, for instance, when a piece of material drops into a machine, strips the gears, and necessitates a special order for parts which under ordinary circumstances would never need replacement. In all such cases the request for purchase should originate with the master mechanic and should have the approval of the general superintendent.

A full explanation must be given on the request for purchase of the use to which the material is to be put, not only as a matter of record but also to assist the receiving department in quickly disposing of the material when it is received.

Another important point is that of settling the account to which this material will be charged. Material of this nature should not be charged to an inventory account; instead it should be charged direct to the standing expense order affected by the purchase. On each request for purchase of this nature the entry for charging the account should give the standing expense order covering repairs on the particular piece of equipment for which the material is desired. The accounting department should enter this invoice as a debit against the expense ledger account, and make out an expense debit slip chargeable to the standing order number (see Chapter VII).

Too much stress cannot be laid on the importance of settling at the time of the purchase the destination of a repair charge, as purchases of this nature have probably caused more trouble in cost accounting than any other class. If the procedure here outlined is followed, it is not difficult to account properly for all the incoming material, so far as the records are concerned. In addition, the receiving clerk is given information which will enable him to deliver immediately these repair parts to the master mechanic's department in order to get the crippled equipment into operation.

Services of Various Natures.—In a manufacturing institution of any size there is a constant need for outside services.

Structural workers, boilermakers, special mechanics, various contractors, etc., are called upon to perform work of specialized nature or to undertake work which the organization of the plant is not able to handle.

The request for a purchase of this nature originates with the master mechanic, except in such cases as when the accounting department sends for auditors, or the general superintendent for consulting engineers, etc. Regardless of who makes out a request for purchase, exactly the same explanations should be given as required for special material purchased for repairs. In fact, the procedure is almost identical—particularly in respect to giving the exact charge to be made for the services performed. The only difference which enters into the procedure is that services of this nature are naturally not received in the receiving room, but are certified to by the one who is in touch with the service performed and who is in position to make affidavit that full value was received.

Advertising, etc.—It is quite rare that the purchasing department arranges for such matters as advertising and other publicity features of the selling department. In cases where such contracts are arranged, the department or official arranging the obligation should, upon conclusion of the agreement, fill out a request for purchase, giving all data and particularly the account to be charged, in order that the purchasing department may cover the obligation with a proper confirming order.

In many cases this confirming order is made out purely for the purpose of record, the original of the purchasing order not being sent to the one in whose favor drawn. These orders are sometimes known as "dummy orders," and are placed on record merely to make sure that the invoices are properly O. K'd when they come in—a step which is absolutely necessary.

Miscellaneous Purchases.—In nearly every manufacturing plant many miscellaneous deals are consummated, such as telephone contracts, telegraph arrangements, power contracts, etc., which may or may not be handled by the purchasing department. These purchases are in the same class as advertising, etc., and should be handled in identically the same way. In such cases it should be understood that a request for purchase is to be made out immediately upon the consummation of any arrangement.

Importance of Accounting at Source.—Repeated mention has been made of the importance of settling the accounting at the origin of each purchase. If the account to which each purchase is to be charged is decided upon at the source, and the account number placed on the request for purchase, the account number can be entered on each purchase order. It then becomes possible by automatic means to place this information on each invoice as it is received and approved. This is the simplest and most approved procedure. The receiving clerks know exactly what to do with the material when it is received, to what stockroom it should be sent, or, in the case of charges to standing orders, to what department it should be delivered. This method has its bearing also on the handling of the invoices in the stock record division and in the cost department.

Failure to decide at the source upon the account to which a purchase should finally be charged has been the cause of more work and lost time than any other one point in connection with the handling of cost records, and therefore it is urged that this point be given the most careful attention by anyone who may be attempting the installation of cost records.

Receiving Material.—Much discussion has been given in the past to the methods of receiving material upon its arrival at the plant. The discussion has been principally in connection with whether or not a copy of the purchase order with quantities and all data should be given to the receiving clerk or whether the receiving department should report what is received without any guide. In deciding this particular point the size of the plant and the nature of the organization must be taken into consideration. The proximity of the purchasing to the receiving department has a large bearing upon the question.

For example, if the plant in question is a very large one, the position of the receiving clerk becomes of such importance that there is no question but that he should be furnished with a copy of every purchasing order with full information thereon. Moreover, in such a case the receiving clerk has none of the actual checking and counting to do, and accordingly will not be influenced through his knowledge of the quantities or prices which may appear on the purchase order.

Unquestionably, those who actually open and check the packages should be working on a blind basis in order that they will give a proper report of the nature and count of the material. If the individual opening packages has before him a list of what is supposed to be in the package, with the quantities specified, he is liable to be more or less influenced by the information which he holds. If the plant is so small that the man who actually opens the goods is the receiving clerk, he should certainly not have a copy of the purchasing order with quantities thereon.

If, on the other hand, the plant is of sufficient size to maintain a number of checkers, it is apparent that as the receiving clerk himself is elevated above the point of being influenced by the count, and in fact becomes the intermediary to verify the accomplishment of the actual counters or checkers, he should be given the records in order to be sure that a proper count is made of the incoming material. He can detail his subordinates to open and count the material, giving a blind report thereon. He can then check this report with what was supposed to have been received, and act accordingly.

Inspection of Incoming Material.—Another very important feature of the receiving end of the business is the verification of the quality of the material received. Sometimes material is opened and counted by receiving clerks and then passed on to the inspection department, where it is again taken from the packages and inspected for quality. It is then necessary for the inspection department to count the goods again in order to give a complete record of the number of good and defective pieces received in the shipment. It seems needless to have two separate and distinct counting operations when they might just as well be combined into one, particularly when it has been proved that it can be accomplished without confusion. The receiving clerk should therefore be given full physical control over all the men who are actually doing the work, but the method of inspection and the equipment to be used during inspection should be entirely under the *functional* control of the inspection department. The standards of quality should be set and supervised by the inspection department, the receiving department being furnished with all necessary drawings, gauges, etc., in order that proper inspection may be made.

This method of operating is economical, in that it saves space and has the effect of effectually speeding up the work of disposing of incoming material.

CHAPTER XII

TRANSPORTATION CHARGES

Problems Connected with Transportation Charges.—There is probably no other part of the cost accountant's work regarding which there is so much question as the handling of freight, express, postage, and all other forms of transportation charges. In many concerns the practice has been very erroneously followed of charging all incoming freight to a factory expense account and of charging outgoing freight as a sales expense, for no other reason than the assumption that material coming in is used in manufacture and material going out is sold. The problem of the correct distribution of transportation charges is most important; a full and satisfactory solution must be found if the business is to show cost figures which are at all accurate.

The fact that the material enters the plant is no proof whatever that all incoming transportation charges are a factory expense, as will be explained later. Further than this, even supposing that all the incoming charges were to apply to material which was to be used in manufacture, the ratio of transportation charges on some material to the price paid to the vendor for the material might be two to one, whereas with some other material the transportation charges might be only one-twentieth of the price paid to the vendor for the material. This fact alone will show that for any industrial institution to throw all incoming transportation charges into an expense account is a procedure that is almost ridiculous.

The situation is similar as regards outgoing transportation charges. While some of them may have to do with sales; others may be for raw material returned as defective, or for many other items which have nothing whatever to do with sales expense.

This chapter deals with the various types of transportation charges. In order to exhibit all these types in compact form, the various kinds of transportation charges commonly used have been listed below. This tabulation is followed by a detailed discussion of each kind of charge.

Throughout this chapter, the following terminology is used:

Company means the company whose accounts we are discussing, that is, "ourselves."

Vendors refers to those from whom we, the company, are buying goods.

Customers mean those to whom the company is selling goods.

Incoming Transportation

Incoming transportation charges are incurred on the following classes of goods:

1. Purchased goods.
2. Goods returned by customers.
3. Samples, etc., not covered by a purchase order; this case sometimes occurs though it is bad practice.
4. Goods refused or condemned by company.
5. Receipts of miscellaneous nature.

1. Purchased Goods.—

F.o.b. Works of Company. The charges are either prepaid by the vendor or paid by the company and deducted when settlement is made for the goods. In such cases the straight invoice value is the correct cost of the goods.

F.o.b. Works of Vendor—Freight Allowed. The accounting of the charges is identical with that for "f.o.b. works of company," but the traffic department has the responsibility of pushing all claims for damage with transportation companies, as by the terms the goods belong to the purchaser immediately upon shipment.

F.o.b. Works of Vendor. The company pays all charges, in addition to the invoiced price of the goods. This means that in entering the cost of the materials in question on the price books or stock records, the cost will be the invoice price plus the freight charges. This method places all transportation risk with the company.

2. Goods Returned by Customers.—

Goods returned on Account Company Error. The charges are entered either against a special expense account to show the exact cost of such errors, or against "Miscellaneous Expense Freight."

Goods Returned—Miscellaneous. Many times goods are returned when ordered in error by customers. Charges on goods returned for this or similar reasons should be recovered from customers when possible, but when for selling or other reasons it is thought best to absorb the charges, they may be charged to Miscellaneous Expense Freight.

3. Samples, etc.—Vendors often send samples without notice or authority. In such cases the transportation for such goods should be charged to the expense account receiving the benefit.

4. Goods Refused or Condemned by Company.—Great care should be taken that all transportation charges on goods refused because of error, or because condemned, are charged to the vendors. In any case of the fault of the company, or of doubt, when the company finally has to pay charges, the charge should be made, *not to the material accounts,* but to *Miscellaneous Expense Freight.* (See case 7.)

5. Receipts of Miscellaneous Nature.—There are quite often receipts of various materials not otherwise specified.

These may consist of traveling men's equipment, exhibits returned from conventions, transfers between offices and plant, and many other items.

In all cases of this nature, either a specially designated Miscellaneous Expense Freight account, or some other expense account, should be charged with cost of transportation. For example, suppose an exhibit is returned from a convention. The freight charges on this should be charged either to an expense heading under selling expense called "Convention Expense," or an account called "Selling Miscellaneous Expense Freight."

The main point to bear in mind is that it is of no use to throw all charges into one account, but that it is far more valuable to charge all such transportation cost to the expense account which receives the benefit, and which should be increased by the cost of such transportation. (See also 9.)

Outgoing Transportation

Transportation on outgoing goods covers:

6. Shipments of sales.
7. Shipments of returned purchased goods.
8. Shipments of samples.
9. Shipments of miscellaneous nature.

6. Shipments of Sales.—

F.o.b. Works of Customer. In this case either charges may be prepaid or shipment may be made collect, allowance being made for the freight when the customer pays the invoice.

F.o.b. Works of Company. In this case the usual procedure is the prepayment of charges to any prepay stations on railroads or express lines and the payment of parcel post charges, adding the same to invoices or shipping goods charges collect.

F.o.b. Works of Company—Freight Allowed. This case is treated like that of "shipment f.o.b. works of customer," except that the customer has full responsibility for goods immediately on shipment.

7. Shipments of Returned Purchased Goods.—

Goods Refused or Condemned by Company. (See case 4.) Outgoing charges are treated like incoming charges.

Goods Returned Account Company's Error. The charge should be made to Miscellaneous Expense Freight.

8. Shipments of Samples.—In most cases of shipments of samples the charges should be made to "Miscellaneous Expense" of the selling department. This does not always hold, however, as in the case of the purchasing department sending out samples of material for duplication. In such instances the charge should be made to *Miscellaneous Expense Freight.*

9. Shipments of Miscellaneous Nature.—There are many shipments of miscellaneous nature the transportation charges of which should be charged against various expense accounts. For instance, the charges for a bundle of advertising material sent out by express should go to "Advertising Miscellaneous Expense." In the case of a typewriter shipped for repairs, the charges should go to "Office Sundry Expense," etc. (See 5.)

Accounting for Transportation.—Before applying specifically the directions just outlined for handling freight of various kinds, it is necessary to discuss briefly the actual ledger accounts which are affected by the various charges, with a description comprehensive enough to permit of clearly outlining the procedure which should be followed in connection with each class of charges. Almost every control account of any importance in the ledger may at some time or other be charged with some form of transportation. This is especially true in the case of material inventory accounts and expense accounts.

Transportation charges consist of five main divisions, as follows:

1. Charges to be deducted from payment of invoices of vendors, covering freight charges of any nature which are paid by the company, but are to be deducted from the settlement for the goods in accordance with the terms of the purchase.
2. Charges to be added to invoices for goods sold to customers, consisting of whatever may be expended in prepayment of outgoing shipments, by freight, express, postage, etc., which is to be added to the invoices for the outgoing goods.
3. Charges to be absorbed in cost of goods, including payment on incoming goods, which have to be added to the invoice cost of the goods in order to determine the real cost delivered at the plant.
4. Charges on delivery of sales, covering transportation charges which have been included in the sales price of goods shipped to customers. These charges are not to be added to the invoice.
5. Charges of an expense nature, covering a multitude of cases, both incoming and outgoing, in which the transportation paid is a direct charge to some one of many expense accounts; these expense accounts may be of any nature, perhaps bearing the name of transportation charges, perhaps appearing in one of the expense accounts as shown in the standing order code.

To make clear the handling of the charges in these various types of accounts, each class will be taken up separately with reference to the tabulated statement of the various kinds of transportation charges.

1. Charges to Deduct when Paying Invoices of Vendors. —The charges to be deducted from payment of invoices of vendors are of a troublesome nature so far as the accounts are concerned, because of the danger of paying a large volume of incoming freights and failing to deduct the payment from the settlement of the vendor's invoices for the goods on which the charges were paid. If accuracy is to be assured, it is neces-

sary to create a holding account for such charges in order to maintain an adequate check and insure that all deductions are properly made.

In this connection it will be well to refer to Figure 26, the rubber distribution stamp placed on all invoices at the time they are received. This form, which is self-explanatory, should be constantly borne in mind in the description which follows.

Freight bills often have to be passed through and paid a long time before the invoices for the goods arrive. With all freight bills the following method should be used:

A ledger account should be established called "Freight to be Deducted." This account should be charged with incoming freight which is to be deducted from the vendors' invoices, and credited with all deductions made in the cash disbursements book in settlement of these invoices.

A subsidiary book should be kept in which should be entered the detail of each debit made to the Freight to be Deducted account—one item to a line, with space alongside each detail entry to permit of a corresponding detail entry made from the cash disbursements book at the time this freight is deducted in settlements.

This procedure, although detailed, has proved many times to be a most profitable feature, bringing about a saving far in excess of the extra cost. When the freight bill comes to the purchasing department for accounting, it is identified as to the purchase order to which it applies. If the goods were purchased "f.o.b. works of company," the freight bill is charged to the Freight to be Deducted account, that fact being so noted on the bill. The name of the vendor is written alongside the rubber stamp. This freight is then entered in the record of material received on the purchase order (see Figure 21), and when the invoice is received the terms and the amount of freight paid are filled in on the rubber stamp. This gives the accounting department the full details so that when the settlement is made for invoices of this nature, the proper deductions may be made.

It can now be readily seen that on the subsidiary record of the items in connection with the Freight to be Deducted account, the debit entries which have no credit against them are shown very clearly, and it is possible to make sure that all freight payments of this nature are recovered from the vendors.

In actual practice, this account proves useful in taking care of the transportation charges involved when purchase terms are "f.o.b. works of Company" and "f.o.b. works of vendor—freight allowed."

2. **Charges to be Added to Invoices.**—An equally important procedure is involved in connection with items of transportation paid on outgoing shipments, when the charges are to be added to the customer's invoice. In lines of business in which heavy transportation charges are paid on outgoing shipments, a method similar to that in the case of freight to be deducted should be used. The method of handling is almost identical with the exception of the fact that the credits to the account—called "Freight to be Added" account—come through the medium of the sales journal, rather than the cash disbursements book.

The parcel post, however, is now so largely used that in many plants almost every shipment involves the payment of parcel post charges, with the further complication of adding these charges to the invoice. To carry out the detail as specified for the Freight to be Added account would be altogether too great.

In such a case it would be advantageous to create a ledger account called "Outgoing Parcel Post" account, without keeping the detail of each charge in any subsidiary record. The detail should, however, be provided for by small charge slips, or by some method of noting this information on the shipping order, in order that the invoice department may receive the information necessary to bill the customer properly. In entering the sales the amount of parcel post paid out should be credited to the Outgoing Parcel Post account.

The comments in this section apply to shipments "f.o.b. works of Company."

3. Charges to be Absorbed in Cost of Goods.—In all cases when purchases are made with the transportation terms "f.o.b. works of vendor," this means that one of two methods prevails:

1. The charges have been prepaid by the shipper and added to the invoice.
2. The company pays the freight charges.

In the first case the accounting is quite simple, as the entire invoice, including the freight, is charged to the account shown by the purchase order.

In the second case the invoice comes in simply billing the goods, and there is in addition a bill for the transportation charges entirely separate from the invoice. In this case the transportation bill is charged to the same account to which the material is charged, the amount of freight being shown on the invoice in the rubber stamp. The result is that the stock record department must combine the invoice cost and the transportation cost, and compute therefrom the unit price to be used in charging out the material, which thus represents the cost of the material delivered at the plant.

This covers goods purchased "f.o.b. works of vendor."

4. Charges on Delivery of Sales.—Probably there are more errors made in the entry of transportation charges paid out on the delivery of sales to customers than in any other item in connection with transportation charges.

It is unfortunately the custom in many industrial institutions to treat the delivery cost of sales as a selling expense. This is entirely erroneous. The cost of delivering goods to purchasers is one which may vary from the cost of trucking the goods next door to paying the transportation charges for delivering the goods across the continent.

Every argument is in favor of treating the delivery cost of sales as an item which will appear in the profit and loss statement as a deduction from the sales, the resulting figure being the exact amount received for goods at the plant of the shipper.

The objection may be urged that the price for many goods is fixed, and the selling price of the goods must be the same in all localities—at least for a district bounded by the Atlantic Coast and the Mississippi River. Within this district, however, the actual transportation charges will vary greatly.

The majority of industrial institutions have a fixed price for large territories, and for those plants the amount of delivery cost is of extreme importance. It should be clear that including delivery charges in the selling expense, or any other expense, creates a cost to be added to the manufacturing cost, which may result in a loss of near-by business.

If a company were in competition with another company whose operations did not extend very far from the locality in which the plants were operating, and the manufacturing costs were identical, the company whose operations extended into a large area would lose all local business because of having the selling expense loaded with the cost of long-range transportation. The result would inevitably be a falling off in the near-by trade with an increase in the long-distance trade, inasmuch as the selling prices would be too high near-by and too low for far-away points.

Even though the nature of business demands selling prices which are the same throughout the country, there still remains for each individual company the necessity of knowing the truth as to how far away from its factory it may sell at a profit. A company with a plant on the Atlantic seaboard only is at a great disadvantage with a competitor whose plant is at Chicago, and much more so with a competitor who has plants on both the Atlantic and Pacific seaboards and also at Chicago. To safeguard this feature and to know the exact facts, sales should be classified by geographical divisions and the freight cost of delivering these sales should be kept by the same divisions of territory, otherwise there can be no definite knowledge as to how far away from home it pays to do business.

The procedure in this case is to create for each selling account a companion account to hold the cost of delivery of such sales. This account should be called "Freight Out on Sales" prefixed by the title of the particular sales account to which it belongs. It would be charged with all freights connected with the delivery of sales, whether prepaid or whether deducted by the customer in settling for the goods. In the latter case the entry would come through the cash receipts book.

In any event, the transportation charges connected with the delivery of sales should be a *direct deduction from the gross sales* through the medium of the Freight Out on Sales account, and in no cases should be treated as a selling account.

This provides for shipment "f.o.b. works of customer" and "f.o.b. works of company—freight allowed."

5. **Charges of Expense Nature.**—Charges of an expense nature are very inclusive, embracing all the items in the tabulated statement of freight charges not already discussed.

It is best not to try to specify in absolute detail every type of charge, since the tabulated statement gives a sufficient clue to the various entries of incoming and outgoing transactions involving transportation charges. The point to observe is that very particular attention should be paid to the distribution of the transportation charges which affect the various expense accounts. If that is done, the problem is merely one of determining carefully which accounts should rightfully be penalized with the charge.

A few instances will illustrate the consideration which

should be given to the individual case in order to find the line of least resistance and discontinue bunching freight charges into one or two large accounts that give no clue as to their analytical nature.

A machine tool may break down and have to be returned to the works of the maker for repair. The charge for transporting this machine back and forth is as much a cost of the repairs to this machine as the actual invoice which is later issued by the company making the repairs. These charges accordingly should be made to the standing order number covering the repairs of this machine.

A company may have branch offices necessitating the shipping of samples or supplies of various natures. Most certainly the transportation charges on this material should be charged to the branch office expense if an accurate line is to be kept on the cost of operating the branch.

Material which a company may have shipped out and which the customer rejects as defective is returned. The charges for transporting this material to the customer—which he will probably bill back—together with the cost of getting the material back to its starting point, should most certainly be charged to the account which holds the cost of defective material.

The transportation charges on samples shipped to customers are undeniably chargeable either to a "Samples" account or a "Miscellaneous Expense" account of the selling department.

Illustrations without number could be given to bring out the fact that there is every argument against bunching transportation charges into one big account, or into two accounts, such as "Incoming Transportation" and "Outgoing Transportation." Such bunching of freights results from a failure properly to analyze the cost of the business and such laxity should be corrected.

CHAPTER XIII

STOCK RECORD ACCOUNTING

What Stock Records Are.—The accounting for material up to the time it reaches the storeroom has been described. How it is accounted for there and subsequently will be explained in this and later chapters.

Material, from the general point of view, includes raw stock, supplies such as oils, waste, bolts, repair parts and the like; finished individual parts, sub-assemblies, major or final assemblies or finished stock or completed product. Unless otherwise designated, the term material will be used in its general sense in the chapters that deal with material accounting. Proper material accounting is one of the prime requirements in any business.

Stock records constitute the clearing house through which all material transactions flow. The most prominent uses of stock records follow:

1. They furnish a continuous or perpetual inventory of material on hand, supported and controlled by properly arranged ledger accounts.
2. They furnish a means of recording the prices of each unit of material on hand whereby it is possible to properly price material used, not only for accurate costing purposes but also for furnishing accurate clearance of total value of materials used, thereby keeping the ledger inventory accounts in correct balance as representing the values of inventories.
3. They form the basis for the purchasing of raw material and supplies and for the ordering of production in the plant.
4. They furnish the basis for planning production in that

no orders are put into process until it is known that the material required to make them is on hand.

5. They furnish a safeguard against losses of valuable material.

Before considering the operation of stock records and other records used in material accounting, the organization of the stores department will be briefly described.

Organization of the Stores Department.—After material and product have been received and recorded in the receiving room, and the proper reports have been sent to the departments entitled to receive them, the material is turned over to the storeroom to which it is consigned. The storeroom should be properly arranged with bins or spaces to take systematic care of the material, and should be well equipped with pans, racks, drawers, boxes, etc., according to the most approved storeroom practice.

While the organization of the storeroom will naturally depend on the size and nature of the general organization, certain features should be kept in mind in considering the placing of the stores organization in the general organization.

Every plant, if of sufficient size, should have a general storekeeper, or material supervisor, who has jurisdiction over all storerooms. Each individual storeroom should be in charge of a storekeeper who has entire control of all necessary assistants in the storeroom. Clerical work in the storeroom should be reduced to the absolute minimum, and should consist only of such work as is necessary to follow out the rules in connection with the reporting of receipts and disposition of the material in the storeroom, and of all detail in connection with the requisitions or bills of material which act as vouchers for the material which is issued from the storeroom.

In plants where a comprehensive method of production control is in effect, the control of the storeroom should be vested in the planning department, as the control of all material movements is one of the most important functions of production control. Where there is no planning department, the jurisdiction of the storerooms would best be vested in the general superintendent. He is the official particularly interested in what scheduling and production take place and, therefore, should have control of the movements of material which so vitally affect the efficiency of the production departments.

The storerooms should not be under the control of the purchasing department. Purchasing is an art by itself, and the purchasing agent should have no interest in the details involved in the storing and issuing of material. Such details only detract his attention from the markets.

On the other hand, the stock records should not be under the jurisdiction of the storekeeper, as it is easy to observe that the records of the materials on hand are a constant check on the operations of the stores force.

Use of Stock Records.—Stock records should be used for raw materials, supplies, individual parts, subassemblies, major assemblies, and finished product. It is impossible to cost product if individual parts and assemblies are not accounted for by stock records, because the parts for assemblies may be taken from a mass of parts in a department, the costs of which, though varying individually, are not differentiated on stock records.

Names for Stock Records.—A variety of terms synonymous with the term "stock record" are in use, merely: Stores record; balance of stores record; book, running, going, continuous, or perpetual inventory; stock card; and stock record sheet. The latter term is coming into usage more and more.

Stock Record Forms.—Four different kinds of records are used in accounting for stock, namely:

1. Bound books
2. Visible index cards

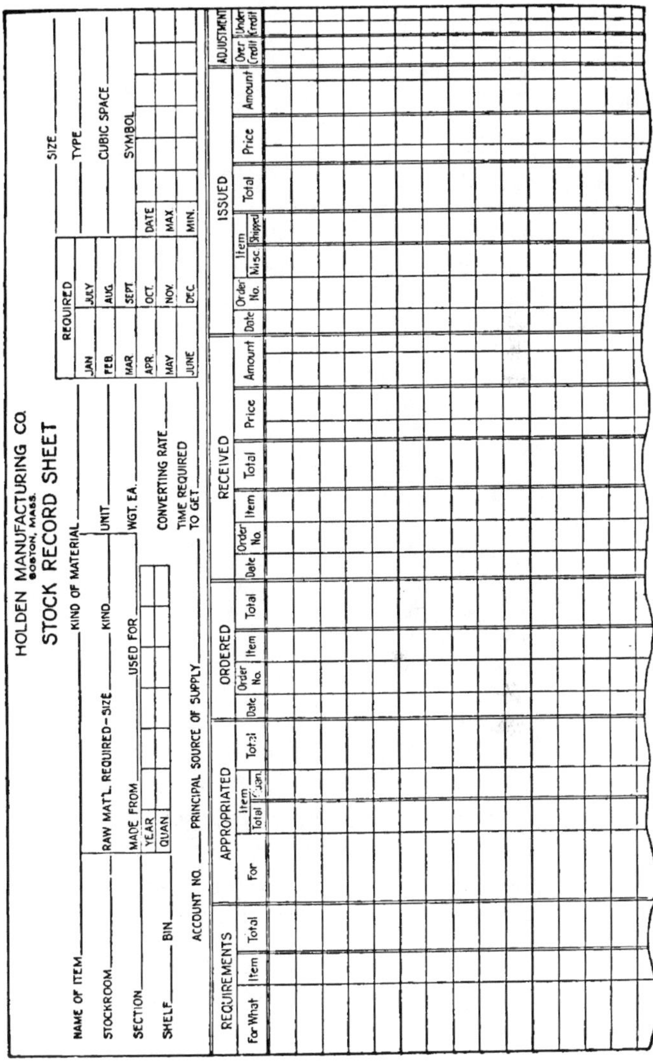
HOLDEN MANUFACTURING CO.
BOSTON, MASS.
STOCK RECORD SHEET

NAME OF ITEM ____ KIND OF MATERIAL ____ SIZE ____
STOCKROOM ____ RAW MAT'L REQUIRED—SIZE ____ KIND ____ UNIT ____ TYPE ____
SECTION ____ MADE FROM ____ USED FOR ____ WGT. EA. ____ CUBIC SPACE ____
SHELF ____ BIN ____ YEAR / QUAN. ____ CONVERTING RATE ____ SYMBOL ____
ACCOUNT NO. ____ PRINCIPAL SOURCE OF SUPPLY ____ TIME REQUIRED TO GET ____

REQUIRED			
JAN.	JULY		
FEB.	AUG.		
MAR.	SEPT.		
APR.	OCT.	DATE	
MAY	NOV.	MAX.	
JUNE	DEC.	MIN.	

REQUIREMENTS			APPROPRIATED				ORDERED				RECEIVED						ISSUED								ADJUSTMENT	
For What	Item	Total	For	Item Total	Item Quan.	Total	Date	Order No.	Item	Total	Date	Order No.	Item	Total	Price	Amount	Date	Order No.	Item Misc.	Item Shipped	Total	Price	Amount		Over Credit	Under Credit

Figure 27.—Stock Record Sheet. (Size, 17 x 14.)

3. Stock cards
4. Stock record sheets

Bound books for stock records without doubt are obsolete.

The development of visible index cards for stock records has been such in recent years that they are large enough to show all the necessary data. A visible index for stock records will prove of great advantage when their use is economical.

Stock cards are probably used more than any other class of stock records, but are being supplanted more and more by stock record sheets with linen-backed separating sheets, which permit greater speed and permanency.

Sections of a Modern Stock Record Sheet.—The following sections of the stock record sheet (Figure 27) will be considered in turn:

1. Heading
2. Requirements columns
3. Appropriated columns
4. Ordered columns
5. Received columns
6. Issued columns
7. Adjustment columns

This stock record sheet is inclusive enough to fit all possible needs of a firm. If a given firm does not wish all the data provided for, the columnarization, etc., can easily be revised. It is usually easier to reduce than to enlarge a stock record sheet. The form here shown eliminates the need for a balance column by providing running total columns which will be explained in due course. Most stock records, however, still show a balance column.

1. Heading.—The heading of a stock sheet may show:

The name of the item (material, individual part, or assembly), as a front axle.

The kind of material in the item, as steel.

The size, type, and symbol of the item, as Type T.

The cubic space block is filled out whenever material, etc., is shipped on the basis of cubic feet, or when cubic feet should be known in order to provide sufficient storage space.

The name of the stockroom where the item is stored and its location (section, shelf, bin) therein.

The size and kind of raw material required for the item, if it is an individual part or an assembly, etc.

The name and weight of a unit of the item, whether the pound, gallon, barrel, foot, yard, or piece.

The unit of purchase is not always the unit of consumption. For example, steel is bought by the pound but may be used by the foot. In order to get the consumption unit, a "covering rate" is applied to the unit of purchase.

The "Made From" memo indicates the kind of material from which a finished or semi-finished part, etc., was made. The "Used For" item shows the kind of product into which the item of material or finished part goes.

In the year and quantity blocks the consumption of material, etc., is shown by years.

The account number is the number of the material controlling account for the item of stock indicated on the sheet.

The time required to get an item after a purchase order is placed is shown.

The principal source of supply is noted, if most of the purchases of the item are made in one place. This is apt to be more common in the case of specialties than staples. Not all sources of supply are entered on the sheet.

The monthly quantities of the item required, as indicated by the production schedule prepared by the control or planning department, are entered in the "Required" table.

The maximum and minimum quantities by months are shown, if the consumption of material varies.

2. **Requirements Columns.**—The quantity of each class of raw material or finished parts needed for production or sale is entered in the Requirements column. The quantities appear in the Item column. Each item required is added to preceding requirements and the sum is extended to the Total column, which is a column of running totals. The requirements are ascertained by the stock record clerk from the planning department as they appear necessary to satisfy shipping requirements.

3. **Appropriated Columns.**—The Appropriated—or Reserve—columns show the quantities of material and parts, etc., which are allocated to certain orders that are given priority over other orders.

An illustration which shows how the Appropriated columns are used is as follows:

Appropriated			
For Order No.	Item		Total
	Total	Quantity	
200	400	400	400
150	300	300	700
200	600	200	900
150	900	600	1,500
300	700	700	2,200
200	1,000	400	2,600

This illustration shows how an order may have material reserved for it more than once. Under "Item" the Total column at the left of the Quantity column accumulates the total appropriated to each order. For instance, Order 200 appears three times, on the first, third and last lines. The first appropriation was 400, making the total for the item the same. On the third line 200 was appropriated, bringing the item total to

600. The 400 in the last line brings the item total to 1,000. The main total at the right is the grand accumulative total of all orders for which appropriations have been made. In short the Quantity column shows single appropriations of material for individual orders; the Total column under the Item column, the total appropriations to date for each order; and the Total column at the right, the total appropriations to date for all orders, irrespective of the order numbers.

4. **Ordered Columns.**—The Ordered columns show purchase order dates and numbers, detailed quantities ordered, and cumulative totals.

5. **Received Columns.**—In all cases entries are made in the Received columns from receiving reports which accompany the stock into the storerooms. The prices are recorded later when invoices arrive. Stock records should be kept up to date and should not be held up because of non-arrival of invoices, as it is vitally necessary to know the moment material arrives in order to properly schedule production. The price may be entered when the invoice arrives.

The "price" is the cost of each unit of each quantity received. This unit cost should include inward transportation charges like freight, express, cartage, parcels post, etc. If an invoice covers more than one class of material the transportation charges in connection therewith should be distributed to the various stock records concerned, in proportion to the respective "rough invoice" costs of the classes of material received or to the weight of the material. In extreme cases inward charges are treated as an overhead item. This is not good practice, however, because it does not produce accurate costs. In cases where the stock record sheet shows the movements of parts and assemblies, the price would be their unit manufacturing cost up to the time of storage. The received section has a running total column.

6. Issued Columns.—The issued section is the credit part of a stock record. Entries are made in the Issued columns from material requisitions and shipping orders. The latter are used when the finished product accounted for by the stock record is sold. The former cover materials, parts, etc., issued to operating departments.

7. Adjustment Columns.—Physical inventories often differ from book inventories. The latter, strange as the fact might appear, are usually more accurate than the physical inventories. The causes of differences are many, some of them being errors and omissions in recording; waste; shrinkage; change in moisture content, inaccurate weighing, measuring, or counting, etc. Differences should be run down, if possible, and corrected or adjusted as the case may be.

The stock record sheet illustrated in Figure 27 shows an Adjustment column with two sub-columns captioned Over Credit and Under Credit, respectively. It is convenient to have these columns, although it is entirely possible to make these adjustments in the other columns affected. If no Adjustment column were used, however, it would be necessary to provide a special record sheet termed "inventory adjustment sheet" in order to accumulate the adjustments for journalizing at regular intervals, usually monthly.

Total adjustments are recorded in the journal so that the Material Controlling account, stock record sheets, and physical inventories may be kept in agreement. Adjustments are debited or credited, as the case may be to an Inventory Adjustment account or Over, Short and Damage account; and credited or debited, correspondingly, to the material inventory controlling accounts. After the details are adjusted on the various stock record sheets, the controlling accounts will "tie up" with the subsidiary records—the stock record sheets.

Material Requisitions.—Materials, parts, etc., requisitioned from storerooms are originally recorded on material requisitions prepared in duplicate and signed by foremen, or by the planning or control department, or by some other originating authority, according to the organization of the plant.

A form of material requisition is shown as Figure 28.

The originating authority fills out the main body of the requisition up to the "Stop Here" space, and also the "Charge" and "For" spaces on the bottom part of the form. Opposite

HOLDEN MANUFACTURING CO.
BOSTON, MASS.

Requisition for Material
Which Is in Stock

Date ....

QUANTITY	SIZE or NUMBER	DESCRIPTION	WEIGHT	Stop Here	PRICE	AMOUNT

Charge .... For ....

Filled from .... Filled by ....

Ent. Stock Book by .... Ext'd by .... Dist. by ....

Signed ....

Figure 28.—Material Requisition. (Size, 6 x 4.)

"Charge" is written the code order number to which the requisition is chargeable, and opposite "For" the use to be made of the material. The originating authority retains for his records the duplicate copies of requisitions in date sequence. The original requisition is presented to the storekeeper in charge of the storeroom where the desired material is located. The storekeeper fills the requisition and writes the name of the storeroom and his initials in the "Filled From" and "Filled By" spaces, respectively.

The storekeeper should keep a loose-leaf book indexed with the names of the persons who have the authority to prepare requisitions, and should absolutely refuse to honor a requisition unless it is properly filled out and signed by a person who has the authority to sign. Neither should a requisition be honored if it calls for the issuance of more than *one class of material* or carries or charges more than *one order.*

The stock record clerk enters each requisition in the Issued columns of the proper stock record sheet, and prices each item. In no case should the stock record clerk make these extensions. A calculating machine operator now makes the extension of prices and amounts after the "Stop Here" space, and initials the requisition on the "Extended By" line.

The original requisitions are forwarded to the cost department, where the material credits and work in process debits are accumulated, as explained in Chapter XXIV. Each requisition is initialed by the clerk who makes the distribution. All requisitions are then filed under their proper order numbers.

Material Credit Slips.—Material returned to the storeroom for any reason is first recorded on a material credit slip (see

MATERIAL CREDIT SLIP

HOLDEN MANUFACTURING CO.
BOSTON, MASS.

Date........................

QUANTITY	SIZE or NUMBER	DESCRIPTION	WEIGHT	Stop Here	PRICE	AMOUNT

Credit........................ For........................

Returned to Room........................ Received by........................

Ent. Stock Book by.................. Extended by.................. Distributed by..................

Signed........................

Figure 29.—Material Credit Slip. (Size, 6 x 4.)

Figure 29). The account or order number which was formerly charged with the material requisitioned and which is now to be credited, is entered on the credit line. The name of the storeroom and of the storekeeper in charge are written on the next line. The rest of the procedure with reference to the form is self-explanatory in view of the description of the handling of a material requisition. In short, the material credit slip reverses the accounting made when a material requisition is filled. Data on material credit slips are entered in the received columns of the stock record sheets.

Accounting for Scrap Parts.—In the manufacture of any article there is always present the necessity of accounting for units of material which are spoiled and which have to be accounted for. For this purpose a scrap ticket (Figure 30) may be put in general use in any industry. The methods of using the form, however, may differ according to the circumstances in each case.

It is to be noted that the scrap ticket calls for the order and piece number, and is designed so that only one kind of piece shall appear on one ticket. The quantity of the same kind of pieces of scrap will appear under the heading "Number of Pieces," followed by its description, kind of material, and weight. On the lower part of the ticket a line is provided for a notation of the exact condition of the piece—that is, a description of the extent to which the piece was manufactured. When the operations are well defined, a notation of the last operation performed is sufficient. If operations are not well defined, it is necessary to indicate what has been done to the piece. The reason for scrapping the piece is then entered and notation made as to what point the material was delivered. The person who receives the material places his initials on the line marked "Received by."

The accounting in connection with scrap materials consists

of two phases, a fact which explains the number of lines left under the debit and credit headings.

The cost of the piece, up to the time of scrapping, should be found from the records, and an entry made in the credit column whereby work in process material, labor, and overhead will receive credit up to the point where the material was spoiled. The

HOLDEN MANUFACTURING CO.
BOSTON, MASS.
SCRAP TICKET

Date________

Order No.________ Piece No.________

NO. PIECES	DESCRIPTION	MATERIAL	WEIGHT

DEBIT			CREDIT		

Condition of Piece________

Reason for Scrapping________

Returned to________ Rec'd by________

Approved________ Signed________

Figure 30.—Scrap Ticket. (Size, 6 x 4.)

total of these three costs will be disposed of as the circumstances require and as illustrated in the following examples:

1. The procedure where work is found to be defective, and the original piece of material worked on is returnable to the vendor when the defect is discovered.
2. The accounting method for a piece of defective work, not returnable to the vendor, which is scrapped immediately after the defect is discovered.
3. The accounting steps taken where a possibility of salvaging or reclaiming defective work exists.

In each case the scrap ticket shows the last operation performed on the defective piece of work and by reference to the proper cost sheet, the cost up to that point may be determined. In each case the accounting treatment of a defective casting will be considered so as to make the illustration uniform. This procedure is typical irrespective of the nature of the material.

Examples of Journalizing Scrap Tickets.—*Example 1:* Suppose a steel casting when about three-quarters done is found defective. The casting cost $25. The total labor performed as found charged to the production order is $14. The burden on this labor at the standard rate is $12. All defective steel castings are charged to an account called "Returnable Scrap," which account is credited as the castings are charged to the vendor who furnished them. All cost in labor and burden put on defective castings is lost, as the manufacturer of castings is liable only for the casting itself.

Dr. Returnable Scrap account	$25.00	
Bad Returnable Castings Loss account	26.00	
Cr. Work in Process Material account		$25.00
Machine Shop Direct Labor account		14.00
Machine Shop Work in Process Burden account		12.00

Example 2: If the same steel casting was spoiled in machining instead of proving defective, and the cost as found from the records were the same, the journal entry would be different. In this case the journal entry is shown, for clarity, in full detail. The full cost spoiled is charged to Spoiled Work account. As the casting has now but a scrap value, say $2, the Spoiled Work account receives credit at once on this ticket for the scrap value at current rate for scrap, Scrap account being charged.

Dr. Spoiled Work account	$51.00	
Scrap account	2.00	
Cr. Work in Process Material account		$25.00
Machine Shop Direct Labor account		14.00
Machine Shop Work in Process Burden account		12.00
Spoiled Work Account		2.00

Example 3: Where a possibility exists of salvaging something of value from material on which defective work has taken place, a Material to Be Salvaged account is opened up. This account is a control account. It is first charged with the value of material, labor and burden that have gone into it up to the time the material was spoiled. The credits to this account depend upon the disposition of the material, but in any event the credits are made at standard or average costs, for the material reclaimed.

All of the cost up to the time of spoilage, plus the total cost of salvaging the material, less the value of reclaimed material, is eventually charged to spoilage loss but not on the scrap ticket, as the reclamation or salvaging work is done later.

The entry to be made to cover the circumstances in this third example is:

Dr. Material to Be Salvaged	$51.00	
Cr. Work in Process Material		$25.00
Machine Shop Direct Labor		14.00
Machine Shop Work in Process Burden		12.00

A recapitulation of all the scrap tickets for the month will give the data for the monthly journal entry, the details of which are shown on each scrap ticket.

It may be well to mention at this point that when a piece is issued for assembly and found defective at the time it is to be used, it should be returned to the storeroom in exchange for a new piece. The storekeeper will then make out all the scrap tickets in connection with such material. Under this method the responsibility is centralized, rather than scattered throughout the assembly department. Scrap tickets for individual parts should be made out, as to original data, by the inspectors and approved by the chief inspector.

Simple Stock Record.—Figure 31 shows a stock record of simpler design than the stock record sheet of Figure 27. This record is kept in the same general way as the stock record sheet just described. The only columns in this record which are not found on the modern stock record as the Due and Balance columns. The Due column shows amounts not delivered on purchase or production orders placed. The Balance columns provide for the differences between receipts and requisitions.

Running total columns have to a large extent taken the place of the Balance columns in modern stock record sheets.

In addition to showing the balance on hand almost as well as the Balance column, running total columns give the up-to-date accumulation of amounts used for any period. As a

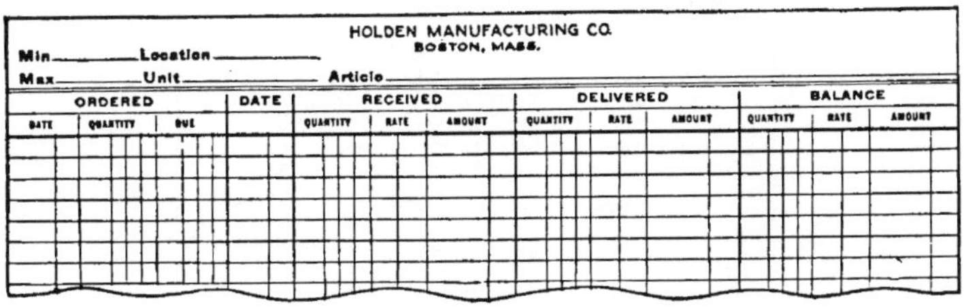

Figure 31.—Stock Record Card. (Size, 8 x 5.)

result, a large saving is made in the clerical work involved in keeping the stock records.

The use of this stock record of simple design is not recommended, as it does not carry the essential information required.

Maximum, Minimum and Quantity to Order.—The protection of adequate stocks of material without inflating the inventories is a consideration of great importance.

If well-seasoned planning methods are in use, and if the business is operating under a budget plan with quotas, the maintenance of stocks becomes more or less automatic. But otherwise, and even when quota methods prevail, there always should be:

1. A minimum limit for each item of stock.
2. An established economical quantity to order.
3. An established maximum.

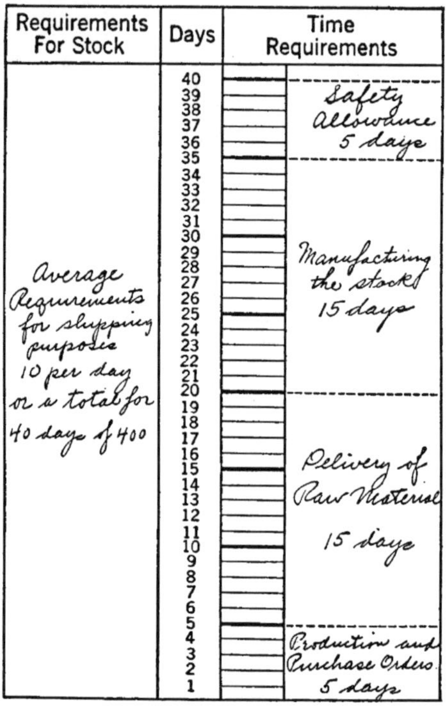

Figure 32.—How Minimum Stock Quantity is Ascertained

These three points may be discussed briefly as follows:

1. Minimum Limit.—This limit requires the consideration of many factors, the element of time being the greatest. Figure 32 graphically illustrates in a simple manner the principal factors involved in considering the minimum stock.

These principal points are:

(a) The time required to issue production and purchase orders for the manufacture of the goods and the procurement of raw material.
(b) The time required for the delivery of the raw materials.
(c) The time required for manufacture.
(d) The time which should be allowed as a factor of safety.

It may be deduced from this illustration that if 400 units were ordered when the stock records showed a balance of 400 on hand, the new 400 would come into stock on the 35th day. On this day the balance on hand would be 50, and with the new parts the total would then be 450. Five days later the stock would again be 400 and a new order would be issued.

If, however, 400 is too small a number to run with economy, and 1,000 is the smallest quantity that pays, 500 may be set as the minimum, and the quantity to order as 1,000.

2. **Quantity to Order.**—The quantity to order depends on the operations involved in the manufacture. or on the circumstances surrounding the purchase of the raw materials.

In connection with the manufacture, consideration must be given to:

(a) The set-up expense.
(b) The quantity necessary to secure the lowest production cost.

In connection with the purchasing of the raw materials, consideration must be given to:

(a) The quantity which permits of economical buying.
(b) The quantity which permits of lowest freight cost.

The cost records furnish the answer to the manufacturing costs, and the purchasing department can answer for the best buying conditions.

3. **Maximum Quantity.**—The maximum quantity is established entirely on the following points:

(a) Storage conditions.
(b) Financial ability of the company to carry stocks that permit of lowest cost on account of large quantity runs or purchases.

CHAPTER XIV

SECURING DATA ON MATERIAL CONSUMPTION

The Problem of Securing Data.—While the medium of reporting the consumption of material is the material requisition or a modification of it, the securing of the data for entry on the requisitions is sometimes a difficult matter. A number of these difficulties will be brought out in this chapter, together with an explanation of methods of surmounting the difficulties.

Where Material is Used on Assembly Orders.—The effort involved in listing all of the individual or sub-assembly parts which enter into a major assembly makes such a procedure not only a burden but also very dangerous from the standpoint of inaccuracy. Furthermore, the cost of such a procedure in time is prohibitive.

The use of specifications of product in connection with requisitioning the material for assembly orders was explained in Chapter IX. If this procedure is followed, the difficulty and possible errors in listing all items on each requisition for assembly orders will be successfully obviated.

Where Material Used is Impossible to Measure.—It is a temptation succumbed to by many to charge to burden or overhead certain materials which actually enter into the completed product when the quantity used in a product is small and difficult of measurement. This is a very bad practice, as in many cases this particular material may not enter into all articles produced in a given department and if charged to burden the unavoidable result is a general distribution over all articles produced in that department.

There is no necessity for such general distribution as with a small amount of careful planning all such material may easily be charged directly to the product which uses it. Illustrations of the class of material referred to may be cited in the use of glue and paint. These items are used to typify those materials which are impossible of measurement for individual units of production.

In the case of glue, suppose a test run of 100 chairs in a chair manufacturing plant is put through the necessary operations. The glue pot, as well as its contents, is weighed before work on the run is started. The total cost of the glue is charged to the run. The run is credited with the cost of the glue left in the pot when work on the run is completed. From the data recorded in connection with this particular run, a standard weight and cost of the glue used per 100 chairs, per chair, or whatever the unit is, plus a small percentage to cover loss or possible error, would be used as the basis in charging future orders of chairs manufactured. The results of tests are preserved on specification sheets, and through this medium become the basis for charging the product.

Tests on the amount of paint used on any product may be made in a similar manner and a standard specification set up for use in charging each run of the product.

From these two illustrations, the method to be pursued where material used in small quantities cannot be measured exactly should be clear. Under this method the material is directly charged to the product.

Where Material Used is Impractical to Measure.—Unlike the case of glue, paint and all other such materials, there is a class of material which could be counted or weighed, but such attempts would be impracticable. Examples of this class are:

1. Rivets used in boiler shops or steel fabrication.
2. Nails used in box or other manufacture.

Rivets are subject to defects and to spoilage as a result of burning. Nails are to some extent defective and in use, whether in nailing machines or by hand, are bent and spoiled.

For such classes of material it is necessary to fix a percentage of waste through the medium of tests. The percentage is added to all charges for the net quantity of the material which appears in the product. For instance, suppose a steel barrel when complete has 20 rivets. If 10% has been found to be the proper waste allowance, the standard charge to this barrel would be 22 rivets. The same principle would apply to nails whenever used in the product.

In such cases two methods, however, are followed:

1. To charge the net quantity of rivets, for instance, *plus* the waste allowance shown as a separate item.
2. To charge the gross quantity (net plus waste) as one charge, the specifications for the product (see Chapter IX) giving this standard quantity. In this case the specifications would show how the amount to be charged is arrived at.

Where the Same Material is Used for Different Products.—Particularly in the wood-working industry and the leather industry, a raw material may go into different products in accordance with what may be cut from the original material.

As referred to in Chapter V in a box plant a quantity of lumber of a fairly good grade is delivered to the sawyer and that four grades of boxes are being manufactured. The lumber which is used for the manufacture of boxes of the first grade must be entirely without knots; the second grade must have not more than two knots per unit; the third grade not more than four knots; and the fourth grade may have any number of knots above four. In cutting the lumber the sawyer keeps in mind this classification of grades. He sets his gauges on his saw and then cuts as much of the first grade as he can. If while cutting he comes to a stretch of lumber that has two knots in it, he does not treat these knots as waste but cuts the full side of lumber which is serviceable in the manufacture of the second grade of boxes. He follows the same general practice in cutting lumber for the third and fourth grades of boxes. By so doing there is little waste, so far as knots are concerned.

In order to get the specifications of material for the boxes to be made, test runs are put through. The quantity and cost of each unit of each class of boxes made is indicated on the specifications which are referred to in costing future orders put through the technical processes. A sample specification might read as follows: "The cost of the material in the first grade of boxes should be charged on the basis of the cost of lumber (free of knots), plus the cost of the normal waste in using the first grade of lumber." The specifications for the other grades of lumber would be worded in the same general way.

This principle of charging material applies equally in the leather or any other industry where the cutting of materials presents similar problems.

Controlling Special Material Situations.—In all such cases of special treatment of material charges it is necessary to employ the use of intermediate controlling accounts. In each case it is clearly impossible to requisition such material as glue, paint, rivets, nails and lumber directly from the stores or whatever other inventory account may hold the main stock.

An intermediate account is therefore assigned, and where it is desired to follow each material mentioned, one such account is provided for each material of this nature handled. For example, in the case of glue an account called "Shop Glue" account will be charged with glue drawn from the storeroom in barrel lots. Each order completed will be charged with the standard or predetermined charge for glue as has already been explained. The requisitions charging these orders will credit the Shop Glue account. This brings into the work in process the proper charges for the glue used on each order, and credits the Shop Glue account. Therefore, the transactions of one such shop material controlling account would be in the following form:

SHOP GLUE ACCOUNT

Inventory June 1	$ 205.00
Withdrawals from stores	1,058.00
(Credit Stores and debit Shop Glue account)	
Total	$1,263.00
Inventory June 30	182.00
Amount used	$1,081.00
Credits by charges to orders at standard specification rates	1,126.00
(Debit work-in-process material and credit Shop Glue account.)	
Amount overcharged	$ 45.00

In this illustration it is apparent that the condition is healthy and that the standard charges have been well established, as a balance of $45 to the good is shown.

The same procedure is followed in *all* cases of like nature, including the previous illustrations of glue, paint, rivets, nails, lumber, leather, etc.

It might be well to mention that the Shop Lumber account is a very important one in wood-working industries. Rarely can lumber be bought to go into some one specific product, nor is it advisable. This kind of treatment permits of an elastic handling of the problem of charging lumber. In the charging of lumber, keep it in mind to charge a product requiring a high grade of lumber with the cost of such high grade plus the usual waste in handling this grade *irrespective of the fact* that the material used may have been salvaged from a lower grade. The same rule applies to all grades which any product may demand. The result as shown by the Shop Lumber account will then reflect the skill and planning of the mill men in cutting and using their material.

Aids to Securing Data of Material Consumption.—There are many circumstances in various industries where securing the data of material consumption is difficult. For the purpose of assisting the reader and for the still more important purpose of impressing the fact that a little ingenuity may nearly always solve these problems of apparently difficult nature, a few odd cases are mentioned.

Very Small Material is handled in special containers or "tote boxes." The tare of each box is known, and the count of the material may be found by weight. Or, if preferred, the material may be counted by use of computing scales.

Standard Sized Material is often put through the shop and kept in stores in special tote boxes which hold an exact quantity. For instance, a half-inch drill may have its own special box holding exactly 100 drills when level full.

Variable Unit Materials may be accompanied by tags which give full details of weight or any other characteristics and which will remain on such material until consumed. An instance of this is found in a rubber tire plant. A roll of frictioned fabric will have a tag attached when it leaves the calendar giving full data as to weight, style, etc. This tag will stay on the roll until used. It will then be used as a requisition, as all data are found thereon. The value of this method may be appreciated when it is remembered that each of those rolls is of different size and weight. The same principle may be used in all cases where units vary in size and weight.

Loose Materials such as sand, fire-clay, coal, limestone, etc. may be handled in various ways in order to arrive at the amount consumed. In all cases, there is a controlling stock record. The inventory at the beginning of a period is known, and all incoming material for the period is also known, but the consumption figure is desired.

Whenever any such material are in bins, the wall of the bin may be marked with a graduated scale, the material leveled and the inventory thereby ascertained. This will enable the consumption to be determined.

Wherever the material is in loose piles, the general storekeeper may scale the pile and compute the cubic yards remaining. This figure when multiplied by the weight per yard of the material will give a fairly accurate inventory, thereby enabling the consumption to be determined.

But in all such cases the consumption may be determined from other sources, and the inventory may constitute simply a check. For instance, limestone is usually measured as used, as is also fire-clay. Coal may be taken from main storage piles by carloads, in which case the car may be run over the track scale before going to boiler house or wherever the coal is to be used. Some believe in counting wheelbarrow loads of sand, coal, etc. The necessities of the case will invariably indicate the proper method to be followed.

Liquid Materials, such as used in oil refineries, chemical plants and the like, are often very difficult to account for. In order to supply proper data for the accounting of such materials manufacturers are spending more and more money for the necessary apparatus. Much of this money is spent for scales incorporated with tanks or kettles at strategic points in the various processes. For instance, in a plant for refining cotton seed or any other kind of oil, the refining kettles are now often mounted on scales. It is obvious that this gives perfect control of weights, and as a result most accurate figures are obtained.

Another method is to figure carefully the capacities of all tanks and kettles whereby a gauge stick may give a reading as to what quantity is in the tank or kettle. This permits the proper determination of consumption and the establishing of yields of the various operations.

Wherever possible accurate metering or weighing should be done in order to safeguard the accuracy of consumption figures.

Garment Materials should always be kept in bundles of whatever size is desired, as for instance in units of 10, 12 or larger. The accounting for the material is thus greatly facilitated, whether the material is in stock or process.

Importance of Accuracy of Original Data.—Very unfortunately, it has been a general practice in the past, when it seemed a little difficult to account for material, to immediately consign this material to the overhead. This is a situation which must not exist if accurate costs are to be found.

The suggestions given in this chapter should make it possible for anyone to work out the disposition of all material which enters into the product through the means of tests where necessary. In this way such items may be eliminated from the various burden accounts where they not only clutter up the accounts needlessly, but at the same time render the costs more or less inaccurate.

As all cost figures are used increasingly for active campaigns of cost cutting, and as executives make greater use of departmental figures, it is obvious that all such figures must more and more truly represent the actual conditions and thereby become a gauge of actual accomplishment. In reaching this condition, the accurate determination and allocation of material consumed is a very important factor.

CHAPTER XV

METHODS OF PRICING MATERIAL REQUISITIONS

The Pricing of Material Requisitions.—After assuring the completeness and accuracy of reports of consumption of material, the next important step is to price properly the materials used. The problem of pricing requisitions involves both the raw materials of all sorts and the manufactured parts, both individual and assembled. There are some points to be considered with respect to raw materials which do not affect manufactured parts, and vice versa.

Raw Material and Supply Material Cost.—The cost of all raw material and of supply material should be understood to mean the complete cost of such material delivered to the plant so far as it can be determined. This will include the invoice cost plus any cost of transportation which possibly can be attached to each specific kind of material.

Particularly in the case of the raw materials which enter into the product the entire cost at the plant should be considered, that is, the invoice cost of the goods, plus the normal and regular cost of transportation to the plant. Where material normally received by freight is received by express on account of running too short or any other necessity, the difference between normal freight cost and the express cost may better bè charged to an expense account reflecting the transportation cost.

Where small supply material which is for general service use, to be used by one department as well as another, is received in small quantities by express or minimum charge freight, the transportation cost of such material may go to an expense account without detriment. It is quite impracticable to do otherwise in most cases, as to attempt to distribute the cost of a trip of a truck among perhaps 25 items in the truck load would be ridiculous. But the reader should remember that this applies only to small items.

Supplies which come in large bulk such as coal and the like should *always* have the transportation charges figured into their cost. This also applies to *all* supplies for specific purposes.

Cost of storing material is very difficult to attach to the materials themselves for lack of any specific basis. Of course, if any specific materials are stored in public warehouses for speculative or other reasons, such storage cost must be figured into the value of the goods. Otherwise, the stored costs are treated as a factory expense.

Transportation charges should always be noted on each invoice, and there combined with the invoice price of the material. This procedure gives the correct unit cost of the material to enter on the stock record sheet.

The Problem of Pricing Requisitions.—The pricing of requisitions involves a number of serious problems which differ in extent in varying industries. In considering these problems, two prime factors require attention:

1. The effect which the method of pricing has on inventory control accounts.
2. The effect on costs.

In connection with the first point, the accuracy of the ledger inventory accounts is of extreme importance. Obviously, material cannot be charged to an inventory account at a unit cost of $1 and credited by pricing of requisition at $1.25 without seriously affecting the accuracy of the ledger balance as representing the true value of the inventory. Therefore, whatever the method used, this point must be continually kept in mind.

As to the second point, that of the effect on costs of the

various methods of pricing requisitions, it is obvious that in regard to product costs particularly, some means must be followed to assure costs which are consistent and comparable. To illustrate, a cotton mill may be receiving each day shipments of cotton on three separate contracts at three different prices, and also some "spot" cotton at a still different price. Obviously, it is impossible and improper to attempt to price requisitioned consumption of cotton in the mill on the basis of either one of the different receipts of cotton. Therefore, it is a matter of using an average—or a standard price—in the pricing of the requisitions as is explained later in this chapter. Where material is more of a supply nature, it can more safely be priced at its cost as actually received.

Therefore it should be evident that the manner of pricing requisitions must safeguard these two points, i. e., accuracy of ledger inventory balances and the effect on costs.

Methods of Pricing Requisitions.—Having established the points necessary to be considered and safeguarded in deciding the method to be used in pricing requisitions for the different types of material, the next step is to consider the methods which can be used. The principal methods which prevail in pricing requisitions are:

1. At actual cost of each lot of material received.
2. At average cost of material on hand at time requisition is filled.
3. At market price of material at the time consumed.
4. At a standard cost.
5. At estimated cost.

Receipts				Requisitions			
Date	Quantity	Price	Value	Date	Quantity	Price	Value
Jan. 1	100	$1.20	$120 00	Jan. 2	50	$1.20	$60.00
" 3	200	1.40	280.00	" 4	40	1.20	48.00
				" 5	10	1.20	12.00
					70	1.40	98.00

1. At Actual Cost of Each Lot of Material.—Whenever possible, material should be priced out on requisitions in the order of receipt of material and at the actual cost thereof. In the instance illustrated in the table on page 179 two lots of material were received; 100 units at $1.20, and 200 units at $1.40 each. These units were partially drawn out on three dates. The first lot issued, 50 units, was priced at $1.20 as well as the second lot of 40. The January 5th issuance was for 80, of which 10 were priced at $1.20, which cleaned up the original 100 units at $1.20 each, and the other 70 were priced out at $1.40 each, as this lot was the next in order received. The January 5th requisition would show two prices, as would be the case with any requisition which spanned the break from one lot with another.

It is clear that this method safeguards absolutely the accuracy of the inventory control account.

As to the effect on the costs, it may be said that, first, in all cases of supply material, that is, all material which does not enter directly into the product, it has no effects which are worth considering. In all cases, however, where the material enters directly into the product, great care must be exercised in determining whether or not to use this method.

An important factor in determining whether to use the method is the proportion of the cost of product which the material bears. For instance, if the material in question is in itself but a small proportion of the cost of the product, the slight variation in the unit cost of the material is lost. In such cases this method should be used. But where the material in question is a large factor in the product cost, and the unit cost is subject to considerable variation, one of the succeeding methods should be used. It is a careful consideration of the extent to which the costs will be affected that will decide where this method should give way to one of the following three methods all of which are designed to remedy this condition.

2. **At Average Cost of Material.**—In the case cited of cotton received on three separate contracts at three different prices together with some "spot" at a still different price, the situation may be handled under methods 2, 3 or 4. For convenience we will use this case to illustrate each method.

If the business is one producing a standard product, where the costs are largely of an operation or process nature, it is advantageous to price the consumption of the cotton on the averaging method. As in the majority of cases of this nature the cost is figured by periods, we will assume a period of one month. To focus this discussion reference should be made to the table below showing how this averaging is accomplished for a month's transaction:

Inventory at beginning of month........	70,000	lb.	at	$0.06	= $ 4,200.00
Received on Contract No. 1	50,000	"	"	0.05	= 2,500.00
" " " No. 2	100,000	"	"	0.055	= 5,500.00
" " " No. 3	300,000	"	"	0.06	= 18,000.00
" " Spot	30,000	"	"	0.065	= 1,950.00
	550,000	"	"	0.0585	= $32,150.00
Consumed during month	460,000	"	"	0.0585	= 26,910.00
Inventory close of month.............	90,000	"	"	0.0585	= $ 5,240.00

It will be seen from this table that the requirement for correct ledger balances of inventory is entirely provided for. It will also be obvious that by this method we get an absolutely average cost, and in a continuous turnover process or operation business on standard product this method is undoubtedly the best one to follow in pricing standard staple materials which enter heavily into the product.

It might be noted that the average unit price shown opposite inventories could be shown to more decimal places and be exactly correct. But as the quantity and total money value is all that is considered in the next period, it is more often the case to show it as the same unit price as was used for pricing out the month's consumption.

This method of pricing is simple but accurate. It may be described as follows:

To the inventory on hand on the first of each period is added all receipts for the period, both in quantity and cost. The total quantity of inventory and receipts, divided into the total cost of inventory and receipts, gives the unit cost. The consumption for the period is extended at this unit cost, and the quantity and cost being deducted from the total receipts leaves the amount and value of inventory on hand at the close of the period. This inventory will then start the same procedure for the next period.

3. **At Market Price When Consumed.**—It is sometimes advisable to use the current market price of raw material in figuring costs, irrespective of what the material actually costs. This may be for a number of reasons:

1. To provide a check on the purchasing department when material is bought on long-term contracts.
2. To place the current costs of production on basis of current raw materials.
3. To place the costs of a business capable of the possible advantages of long term buying on the same basis as that of competitors who are obliged to buy. for current requirements.

In either case, the procedure is the same, and one or more extra or intermediate accounts are required to furnish proper control. The cotton illustration in case 3 will be continued, but additional accounts may be set up for other prominent raw materials as required. The three accounts required to illustrate this procedure are:

1. Raw Cotton account (inventory).
2. Work in Process Material account.
3. Raw Cotton Adjustment account.

Referring to the illustration for averaging the price in case 2, it shows a consumption of 460,000 pounds at $0.0585, amounting to $26,910. This must be credited to the Raw Cotton account in order to clear this amount from the inventory which the company carries at cost. The journal entry is:

Dr. Raw Cotton Adjustment Account..............	$26,910.00	
Cr. Raw Cotton Account..........		$26,910.00

It will be noted that the debit is to the Raw Cotton Adjustment account, and not to the work in Process Material account.

At the same time this entry is made, another entry is made for the same quantity of consumption, but extended at average market price for the period, which we will assume to be $.065 per pound, or 460,000 pounds at $0.65 per pound = $29,900. The journal entry is:

Dr. Work in Process Material Account............	$29,900.00	
Cr. Raw Cotton Adjustment Account.....		$29,900.00

It will be noted that the debit here is to the Work in Process Material account where this amount will actually enter the cost, and the credit is to the Raw Cotton Adjustment account. The ledger accounts now show as follows:

RAW COTTON ACCOUNT

DR.	CR.
Purchases	$26,910.00

WORK IN PROCESS MATERIAL ACCOUNT

DR.	CR.
$29,900 00	

RAW COTTON ADJUSTMENT ACCOUNT

DR.	CR.
$26,910.00	$29,900.00

It is obvious from this illustration that we:

1. Clear the actual cost from the inventory account.
2. Charge work in process with the consumption at current market.
3. Show in the Adjustment account a profit of $2,990 which not only adjusts the difference to profit and loss, but at the same time shows the results of the judgment of the purchasing department in making its long-term contracts.

4. **At Standard Cost.**—When it is necessary or particularly desirable to keep certain material costs uniform, that may be accomplished with safety by providing a control somewhat similar to the illustration in case 3. In this case we should use a standard cost for each material based on past cost coupled with judgment of the future.

The use of this method is particularly indicated in connection with manufactured parts in any industry where it is impossible to wait for actual costs before charging out many of the parts for assembly, although it also may just as well be used with purchased material if desired.

As we are to credit the inventory account for whatever material is issued, we must be sure to debit this inventory account at the same rate per unit, otherwise our inventory control would be inaccurate. At the same time, however, the stock record sheet should show for each item of material exactly what the actual cost is each time the item is run in order to permit a check on the standards.

Variation from standards may be cared for in either of

two ways, both resulting in debiting or crediting an account which may be called "Variation from Standards," which is a factory profit or loss account.

First Method. The Adjustment columns shown on the stock record sheet in Figure 27 may be used for recording the over or under credit in accordance with whether the standard is over or under the actual cost of the material when the cost sheet or invoice for each lot received comes to the stock record for entry. At the close of each month an adding machine accumulation may be made of the over- or under-credits and through a journal entry a correction may be made of the Inventory account, the Variation from Standard account being debited or credited.

For instance, if the total of over-credits was $186 and the total of under-credits was $72, the net over-credit of $114 would be journalized as follows in the case that the group of material was manufactured parts:

Dr. Manufactured Parts Account....................	$114.00	
Cr. Variation from Standards Account.........		$114.00

In other words, the actual cost of the completed parts was $114 less than standard prices at which they were or will be credited out. It is necessary, therefore, to replace this difference in the inventory account for manufactured parts to preserve its accuracy as it has been over-credited.

Second Method. When an actual cost sheet or invoice comes to the stock record sheet, the actual unit cost will be entered thereon, and the "standard" cost will be entered on the cost sheet. Instead of journalizing the actual cost of all cost sheets for the month to the debit of Manufactured Parts account, this debit will be at standard cost. The credit to Work in Process will be at actual cost in order to clear this account accurately. The difference will be a debit or credit to Variation from Standard account according to whether the actual cost was more or less than the standard. Assuming that the total actual costs of completed orders for a month were $14,580, and the same material at standard costs amounts to $14,694, the journal entry would be:

Dr. Manufactured Parts Account..................	$14,694.00	
Cr. Work in Process Account...........		$14,580.00
Variation from Standards Account...		114.00

It will be noted that the result is the same as in the first method, the Variation account getting credit for $114.

5. **At Estimated Cost.**—In a steel or any other foundry, or in many other businesses, it is often the case that deliveries on special orders start considerably before any actual cost is known. Therefore, the material requisitioned to fill the shipping orders must be priced before actual cost is known in order to secure a cost of sales.

In such cases, the original estimated cost may be used as follows: The completed material drawn for shipment will be costed at the estimated cost; but all such requisitions or shipments will be accumulated separately from all others. The total of such requisitions will be journalized separately, charging Sales Cost and crediting Estimated Cost account. For instance, suppose the total amount shipped was $28,000, the journal entry would be:

Dr. Sales Cost Account..........................	$28,000.00	
Cr. Estimated Cost Account.............		$28,000.00

In the inventory statement at the end of the month, the Estimated Cost account would appear immediately following the Work in Process accounts as a deduction in order to give an inventory as accurate as possible. On completion of the orders on which the estimated costs were used, an adjustment is necessary to clean up the records. To illustrate, suppose the estimated cost just used resulted in an actual cost of $29,400, as each case handled this way must be treated separately in order to make proper adjustments. The journal entry to complete this case would be:

Dr. Estimated Cost Account........................	$28,000.00	
Sales Cost Account...........................	1,400.00	
Cr. Work in Process Accounts...........		$29,400.00

It will be noted that this entry cancels the Estimated Cost account as far as this item is concerned, debits the Sales Cost account with the excess over-estimate, and credits the Work in Process accounts with the actual cost.

CHAPTER XVI

HOW TO TAKE INVENTORY

The Necessity of Physical Inventories.—Perpetual inventories carried on through the means of well-regulated stockrooms and controlled by stock records have reached a point of high development. In order to guard against an accumulation of clerical errors, however, it is necessary to check the quantity of the material on hand against the stock records at reasonable intervals, and with even the best conducted system of perpetual inventory a complete physical inventory should be taken at least every five years.

For this reason, and on account of the fact that the work of the cost department is so closely associated with both perpetual and physical inventories, a method of taking inventory which has been very successful is explained in this chapter.

Continuous Checking of Perpetual Inventory.—A checking of the stock records with the physical stock should go on continuously irrespective of when any completed physical inventory is taken. This is done in the following manner:

When and as the various items of material reach a low point where a count is a simple matter, the stock record clerk will list such items on a "test inventory" form as illustrated by Figure 33. Only items belonging to one ledger controlling account will be listed on the same sheet, as this permits of a number of items on one sheet where the adjusting entries will be to the same accounts.

The stock record clerk notes the part number or size and what the material is, together with its location. He does *not* show the stock record balance at this time. The sheet will then go to the storeroom, where the count is made, the sheet

TEST OF INVENTORY

LEDGER CONTROL NO. ______ NAME ______________________ DATE ______________

Part No. or Size	Description	Location			Counts		Physical		Unit Cost	Adjustment	
		Sec.	Shelf	Bin	Store Room	Stock Record	Under	Over		Dr. Mtl. Adj. Cr. Stores	Dr. Stores Cr. Mtl. Adj.

Figure 33.—Test of Inventory. (Size, 8½ x 11.)

being immediately returned with the physical count for each item entered thereon.

The stock record clerk then enters the balance of each item shown by the stock records, computes the quantity that the physical count is over or under the stock record balance, if any, enters the unit cost, and extends the adjustment into the proper adjustment column. If the physical count is less than the stock record, the extension is entered in the left-hand Adjustment column which means that the Stores Control account for this material will be credited, and the Adjustment account debited. In other words, some material has been used without being requisitioned, or was erroneously entered on this record in the first place. If the physical count is more than the stock record, the extension will be entered in the right-hand Adjustment column, which will debit the Stores account and credit the Adjustment account.

In this connection, it is a common occurrence to have many adjustments which almost balance in total. The reason for this is that a requisition for a square head bolt might be filled with a round head bolt and by error the requisition be allowed to go through. This would occasion a discrepancy in each bolt account, but in the count one would offset the other, even though there might be a slight adjustment of value. A case has been known where the net adjustment of many items was but about $200, when the total of each side of the entries amounted to nearly $10,000. This meant that many careless issuances of material had occurred where the requisitions which came through were not changed at the time different material was issued. This condition is also occasioned by erroneous postings of requisitions in the stock record department.

By this continuous checking, where a designating mark is made on the stock records as each item is checked, the entire inventory may be checked up, item for item. Each item should be checked *at least once each year.*

Taking a Complete Physical Inventory.—A very successful and safe method of taking a physical inventory is to use a duplicate tag method.

Under the duplicate tag method, detailed preparations are made long before the date set for starting the inventory, with much the same care that an army general plans his attack. Each employee who will participate in the work is assigned a definite task and is informed as to whom he should consult in case he should need advice. The steps under the new method might be outlined as follows:

1. Issuance of inventory instructions.
2. Counting, weighing, etc., the inventory.
3. Listing the inventory.
4. Pricing the manufacturing inventory.
5. Calculating and extending the inventory.
6. Checking the inventory.
7. Comparing the inventory.

1. Inventory Instructions.—The best plan is to issue the inventory instructions in the form of typewritten sheets or a booklet. They should be distributed long enough before the date of starting the inventory, to permit a thorough study of their contents. Schools of instructions in inventory methods are established in some plants for the benefit of those who will take inventory.

Unfortunately, most instructions are loosely arranged. This fault can be overcome by grouping instructions for each department separately after the general instructions for all departments are set forth. The general instructions usually pertain to the following:

(a) The length of the inventory period.
(b) The personnel of the inventory committee.
(c) The articles to be taken.
(d) Special preparations.

(a) **Inventory Dates.**—The length of the inventory period depends on the size of the plant—perhaps only a day or two, perhaps two weeks or more. In large factories most of the departments cease their activities during this period. In some small plants inventory can be taken without stopping all work, but even in such cases the routine could be expedited if there were a complete cessation of operations.

(b) **Personnel of the Inventory Committee.**—The managers and departments heads are on the inventory committee. The committee is assisted by each superintendent and foreman; by tag-writers who make out inventory tags and list items thereon; and by workers who handle, count, and weigh, etc., the articles to be taken. Sometimes the accounting department supervises the taking of the inventory. In this chapter, the final authority, whether it be the inventory committee or the accounting department, is referred to as the "supervising authority." A chart showing how the plant is organized for taking inventory is sometimes prepared, and always proves of great assistance.

(c) **Articles to be Taken.**—The names, definitions, and locations of the broad classes of articles to be taken, such as raw materials, supplies, machinery and equipment, furniture and fixtures, work in process, finished parts, finished products, etc., are mentioned in the inventory instructions. This broad classification of items is usually the balance sheet classification of assets.

(d) **Special Preparations.**—The heads of departments are instructed to make certain preparations and to furnish the supervising authority with a list of the names and clock numbers of the clerks and laborers needed in order to take inventory in their respective departments. In order to expedite inventorying, various departments are assigned definite tasks as enumerated below.

Inspection Department. The inspection department is instructed to clean and inspect goods in the inspection cribs and work in process. This department also makes a list of defective material capable of correction through repairs.

Salvage Department. The salvage department is directed to prepare a list of all obsolete and scrap material. This material is sent to scrap storehouses if it cannot be corrected. Later the scrap is disposed of by the purchasing department with the aid of the inspection department. If scrap can be corrected, it is retained in the salvage department until inventory is completed. Then it is transported to the proper department for correction with a "corrective work order" attached. The salvage department moves goods sold but unshipped, for which shipping orders have been prepared, to storage places provided.

Production Departments. The production departments are instructed to clean up all spoiled, defective, or scrap goods; to sort and bring together all like job numbers; to put all articles in proper receptacles; and to send scrap to the salvage department. In short, the production departments make a general "house-cleaning." Production departments should minimize requests for materials during the days which immediately precede the beginning of the inventory period, and should bring all work in process so far as possible to the same stage of completion.

Storeroom Department. The storeroom department is ordered to clean up, to sort and stack its material, and to place all articles in proper receptacles, marked so as to be readily identified. Scrap and obsolete material is weeded out and sent to the salvage department. Deliveries from storeroom to factory should cease or slow down several days prior to inventorying.

Purchasing Department. The purchasing department is instructed to draw up a list of unfilled purchase orders and contracts, arranged according to part numbers or names of material, as of the closing date of the inventory period, say December 31. All purchase invoices in dispute are promptly adjusted with vendors and sent to the accounting department before December 31. Invoices passed for payment prior to December 31 are recorded on the books, and goods covered thereby are considered as a part of the inventory even though not yet received. If sellers' invoices have not come in, memorandum invoices are made out by the purchasing department and sent to the accounting department for goods received prior to the beginning date of the inventory period, say December 29. All invoices which have been received from goods still in transit should be segregated and listed separately. These may or may not be taken into consideration, but it is sometimes good practice to do so, as goods shipped f.o.b. vendor's works are, according to law, the *property of the buyer when in transit.*

The purchasing department requests outside concerns which have in their possession certain materials, tools, patterns, etc., belonging to the company which is making the inventory, to submit sworn statements covering such articles. It also requests them to furnish a list of the above assets which they may have shipped back to the company a certain number of days prior to December 31. The purchasing department is urged to minimize the amount of material received during the inventory period. One way to help in this respect is to slow up delivery by ordering goods to be sent by freight which ordinarily are carried by express.

Receiving Department. The receiving department is directed to clear its floors of all goods received up to the time of starting inventory. Receiving records covering such goods are to be completed and quickly forwarded to the accounting department. Goods received after inventory has started are sometimes kept in the receiving room but are not included in the inventory. This is bad practice, as all dates must necessarily show as of the month which is included in the records. This of course applies only to goods actually received before final inventory date.

General Accounting Department. The general accounting department is instructed to obtain a list for the sales department of goods billed but unshipped prior to December 31, so that these goods will not be included in the final inventory. The goods may be inventoried, but the figures are subtracted from the "total" inventory to give the amount of the inventory to be used in preparing statements, etc.

If the general accounting department supervises the taking of inventory, it will have charge of all the tags and inventory sheets. Acting in this capacity, it will charge the tag-writers with the tags and sheets as issued and credit them with returns. The fact that tags are serially numbered helps the general accounting department to keep its records straight. When inventory has been taken, tags are returned to this department. Then they are checked by serial numbers and are sent to the cost accounting department.

Cost Accounting Department. The tags which the cost department receives from the general accounting department are sorted by classes. From these tags inventory sheets are prepared.

The cost accounting department is instructed to charge all manufacturing costs incurred before December 31 to the various classes of orders. It must see that price records are up to date so that goods may be priced correctly. The cost accounting department or the inventory committee is ordered to price, to calculate and extend, to check, and to compare the inventory.

Co-operation of Departments. The inspection, salvage, and production departments—in fact all departments—are instructed to co-operate prior to the inventory period for the purpose of minimizing the obsolete and defective material which cannot be corrected.

2. **Counting and Weighing the Inventory.**—Before inventory starts, instructions are issued and studied. Each employee knows what he is to do. When the signal is given to begin, the workers in the charge of foremen or department heads commence to count, weigh, measure, or size inventory items. Goods should be counted, weighed, etc., *twice* before the tags are filled out.

3. **Listing the Inventory.**—The results of counting, weighing, etc., are recorded in indelible pencil on the tags by clerks known as tag-writers. These tags are procured from the supervising authority. When obtained each contains a serial number only.

The tags for material are made in duplicate with perforated stubs and with wires for attachment to the material. As soon as a lot or section of material is inventoried, one tag is attached by the tag-writer to the lot or section, the other tag is sent to the supervising authority. If a receptacle is empty, a tag marked "empty" is placed therein. Every tag is accounted for. None should be lost, destroyed, nor borrowed. Spoiled tags should be marked "void" and sent to the supervising authority. Sample forms of inventory tags are shown in Figures 34 and 35.

Most of the data on the tags is self-explanatory. Figure 34 is an inventory tag used in taking the inventory of material and supplies. The inventory tag for finished material has the same arrangement.

Figure 35 is an inventory tag for work in process. It requires a slight explanation. Assuming that the standard operations on the work in process which is being inventoried are known, it is sufficient to enter in the designated space only the number and name of the last operation. This shows the condition of the work in process. If the sequence of operations is not known, however, it is necessary to count the number of pieces of work in process completed under each operation and to show in detail the operations completed on each piece.

In the "Condition" or "Last Operation" space, is written information as to whether the goods are new, old, or usable.

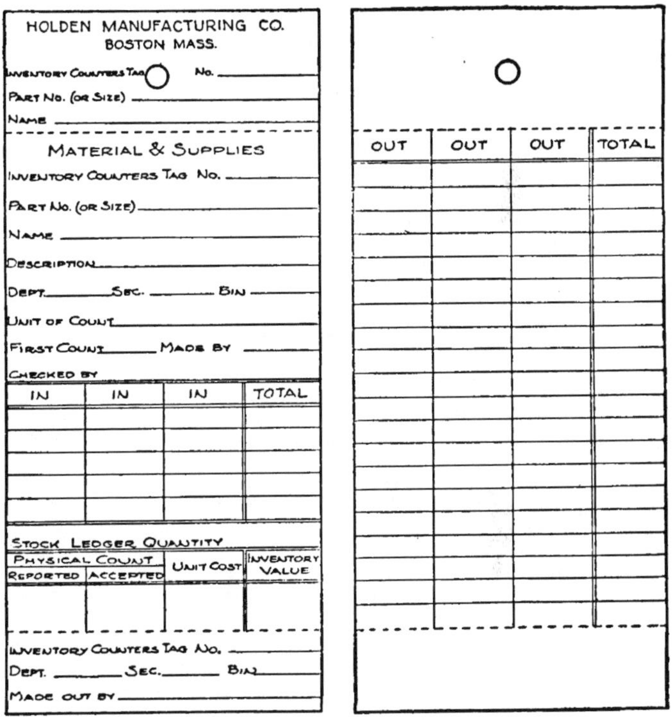

HOLDEN MANUFACTURING CO.
BOSTON MASS.

INVENTORY COUNTERS TAG No. ______
PART No. (OR SIZE) ______
NAME ______

MATERIAL & SUPPLIES

INVENTORY COUNTERS TAG No. ______
PART No. (OR SIZE) ______
NAME ______
DESCRIPTION ______
DEPT. ______ SEC. ______ BIN ______
UNIT OF COUNT ______
FIRST COUNT ______ MADE BY ______
CHECKED BY

IN	IN	IN	TOTAL

STOCK LEDGER QUANTITY

PHYSICAL COUNT		UNIT COST	INVENTORY VALUE
REPORTED	ACCEPTED		

INVENTORY COUNTERS TAG No. ______
DEPT. ______ SEC. ______ BIN ______
MADE OUT BY ______

OUT	OUT	OUT	TOTAL

Figure 34.—Inventory Tag for Material and Supplies (face and reverse). (Size, 3½ x 7.)

It is the practice sometimes to assign one or more engineers to special departments so that materials may be accurately described and last operations properly designated. If engineers are not assigned, tag-writers should possess sufficient information to fill out tags properly. The "Unit of Count" may be the pound, the barrel, piece, etc. Metal tags rather than paper tags are attached to machinery and equipment, to furniture and fixtures, and to assemblies.

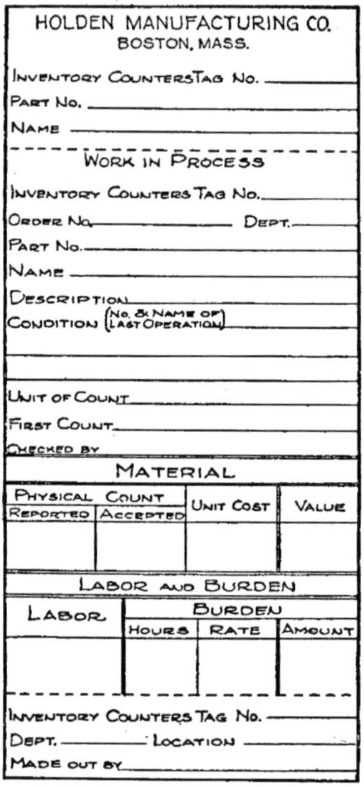
HOLDEN MANUFACTURING CO.
BOSTON, MASS.

Inventory Counters Tag No. ______
Part No. ______
Name ______

Work in Process

Inventory Counters Tag No. ______
Order No. ______ Dept. ______
Part No. ______
Name ______
Description ______
Condition (No. & Name of Last Operation) ______

Unit of Count ______
First Count ______
Checked by ______

Material

Physical Count		Unit Cost	Value
Reported	Accepted		

Labor and Burden

Labor	Burden		
	Hours	Rate	Amount

Inventory Counters Tag No. ______
Dept. ______ Location ______
Made out by ______

Figure 35.—Inventory Tag for Work in Process. (Size, 3½ x 7.)

As soon as inventory is completed in each department, the supervising authority is notified. Representatives of the supervising authority visit the department to see if everything has been inventoried. If so, tag-writers and others who have been working there are released and are assigned, if necessary, to other departments. The next step in inventorying is to pull —or detach—the original tags. No tags are pulled without the order of the supervising authority. After the tags have been pulled in a department, regular operations may be resumed, provided they do not interfere with work in other departments. Tags pulled are sent to the supervising authority and compared with duplicate tags. If the tags do not agree, a recount of the material represented by the tag is ordered, if the discrepancy is large enough to warrant a recount. Someone other than the person who took the original inventory makes the recount.

After the tags have been pulled, they are sorted according to the balance sheet classification of assets. The tags not only show quantities but also unit and total prices. In such cases the data on tags are entered on inventory sheets (Figures 36 and 37) which are in the charge of the supervising authority. After sheets are filled out they are sorted according to numerical sequence, are checked as to completeness, and are then re-sorted according to the balance sheet classification of assets. That is, all raw material items appear in one batch of sheets, work in process in another, and so on. The complete inventory is then recapitulated on summary sheets, consecutively numbered—one sheet showing the totals of each asset.

4. Pricing the Manufacturing Inventory.—The pricing of the manufacturing or work in process inventory must necessarily be effected through the current cost records.

Every order representing the work in process has its time cards and requisitions filed in the work in process files, and if a physical inventory is taken, the notations on the physical inventory as to operations completed should agree with the information given by the cost files as to number of pieces completed under each operation, which also gives the cost of same.

The requisitions in like manner should also account for

the direct material cost and what is on the floors in process, thereby taking care of this feature.

In adding up the time cards in the files and extending these totals on the inventory sheets representing the work in process, the extensions of the burden at the standard rates for each department will furnish the total of the work in process burden.

With these three items of work in process cost ascertained from both the physical count and the current cost files, it is then an easy matter to arrive at the totals and thereby check the controlling accounts in the ledger.

These costs are always carried at what is shown in the work in process files, it being absolutely impossible to alter them to agree with any market conditions, as any change would be altogether impossible to accomplish.

Use of Records in Pricing. Raw material may be priced from stock record sheets, purchasing department records, accounting department records, market quotations, or by the engineering department or the works engineer.

Some persons hold that work in process is difficult to inventory. If material requisitions and time tickets have been properly filed behind orders in the standing order files, or posted to cost sheets, the calculation of work in process values is simply one of arithmetic. In some plants, cost sheets are not filled out until orders are completed, in which event the order files rather than cost sheets must be resorted to in figuring work in process inventories. This is the preferable practice. Under process systems the stage of completion of work in process is ascertained, the total cost of each process is ascertained, and the total cost of all processes is calculated. Work in process cannot be so easily figured under an estimating system.

Finished parts and finished products are priced from individual part cost sheets, assembly cost sheets, estimated records or stock record sheets.

HOLDEN MANUFACTURING CO.
BOSTON, MASS.
PHYSICAL INVENTORY
________ MATERIAL ________

Period Ended ________ Page No. ________

PHYSICAL COUNT							STOCK LEDGER		DIFFERENCE			
		DESCRIPTION							OVER		SHORT	
TAG NO.	QUAN.	Part No.	Name	UNIT PRICE	UNIT	VALUE	QUAN.	AMOUNT	Quan.	Amount	Quan.	Amount

Figure 36.—Inventory Sheet for Material and Supplies. (Size, 14 x 11.)

HOLDEN MANUFACTURING CO.
BOSTON, MASS.
PHYSICAL INVENTORY
WORK IN PROCESS

Dept. ________ Period Ended ________ Page No. ________

TAG NO.	ORDER NO.	PART NO.	NAME	NO. OF PIECES	MATERIAL			LABOR		BURDEN			REMARKS
					Unit Price	Unit	Amount	Last Oper. No.	Amount	Hours	Rate	Amount	

Figure 37.—Inventory Sheet for Work in Process. (Size, 14 x 11.)

All of the above inventories should be priced at manufacturing cost. Selling and administrative overhead should not be capitalized in work in process, finished parts, and finished product inventories.

5-7. Final Steps in Taking Inventory.—The supervising authority has charge of calculating, extending, checking, and comparing the inventory. Much of the detailed work is facilitated by the use of various mechanical devices. All calculations on inventory sheets should be made twice, and the extensions and figuring checked.

Figure 36 is an inventory sheet for the physical inventory of material and supplies. The same form is used for finished material or product. Figure 37 is an inventory sheet for the physical inventory of work in process. Two copies are made for each inventory sheet. The copies remain together until the inventory is priced. They are then separated and given to two separate clerks who extend the values without any connection one with another. The sheets are then brought together and the extensions compared, a method which will immediately expose any differences in extension requiring correction.

After the totals of the sheets which represent the material covered by each controlling account are ascertained, the controlling accounts may be verified and whatever adjustments are necessary can be made.

The inventory sheets are then separated and made up into books, one copy being filed away as a permanent record, and a copy used for current purposes in connection with stock records, etc.

CHAPTER XVII

ADVANTAGES OF STOCK RECORDS

Stock Records an Aid to Entire Business.—The stock record is the keystone, so to speak, of the material cost records. It aids especially the purchasing, storeroom, production, and cost departments. With a knowledge of requirements, orders, balances on hand, past consumption, minimum and maximum quantities, purchasing can be carried on intelligently. With stock records the storekeeper can properly account for materials, parts, etc., under his supervision. Production can be controlled, through a knowledge of requirements, orders, and balances on hand, etc. Material costs can be controlled if stock records are maintained, because such records provide the means of showing quantities and values requisitioned for individual orders, etc. Furthermore, they show balances on hand which can be compared with physical inventories.

The advantages of stock records cannot be fully appreciated until after a knowledge of the technic of stock record accounting has been gained. The advantages set forth in the following pages, therefore, should be studied in conjunction with the main sections of the modern stock record sheet discussed in Chapter XIII.

Purchasing and Production Aided by Listing Requirements.—If the plant has detailed specifications of the product (see Chapter IX) which show the material and parts necessary for its manufacture, the stock record clerk can intelligently fill out the "Requirements" columns. Unfortunately, however, relatively few concerns have exact specifications regarding their product, operations, and machines. Without them neither proper planning nor accurate accounting for costs is possible. Lack of proper specifications is one of the most frequent reasons for the failure of cost methods. With a knowledge of the material requirements for parts and products, however, necessary materials, etc., can be provided in advance of actual needs, and thus production is facilitated.

Records of Consumption Aid Economical Buying.—Stock record sheets show requisitions of each class of stock and also indicate the destination of material, whether to job numbers, contract numbers, departments, etc. Such consumption data are serviceable to the management in estimating future requirements of stock and facilitating economical ordering.

Savings Effected by Proper Ordering.—If purchases are kept within the maximum and minimum limits recorded on stock record sheets, too much capital is not tied up in stock, with the accompanying excessive storage, interest, and insurance charges. Nor do delays in production ensue because of lack of materials. Close and persistent examination of purchase orders, purchases, deliveries, requisitions, and stock balances, together with a careful graphical study of price movements of material, is of inestimable service in preventing these unfortunate and expensive conditions.

The amount of material to be ordered when the balance of stock approaches the minimum is known as the "quantity to order" or "order point." The "quantity to order" is taking the place of the "maximum quantity" in many factories. The figures in the "Year," "Quantity," and "Time Required to Get" sections of the heading of the stock record sheets aid greatly in calculating the minimum, maximum, and quantity to order. Knowledge of the time required to get materials after placing an order also aids the planning department in scheduling the work of the operating departments.

Steady Production Aided by Prompt Ordering and Urging.—Not only must the quantities of material ordered be sufficient, but deliveries from vendors must be kept ahead of consumption needs. It often becomes necessary for the buyer to send an urger or inquiry to the seller. Prompt urging is indeed as important as prompt ordering. It should be done in a spirit which recognizes that tardy deliveries are often due to forces beyond the control of the shipper. The need for urging may arise from the inability of the seller to ship according to schedule; or from the fact that the buyer consumes material quicker than he anticipated because of wasteful use of stores or the filling of rush orders. Nevertheless, if material is not received on time, production will slacken or stop. Lack of sufficient supplies causes manufacturing losses which, although often unnoticed or ignored, are probably greater than any other losses with respect to stores. A slowing-up or stoppage in operations prevents the filling of orders according to contract. That results in cancellation of orders, and that in turn increases unit manufacturing costs, since the overhead has to be apportioned over reduced sales.

Savings by Keeping Deliveries Within Contract Limits.—Stock records facilitate checking receipts of stock against purchase orders, special contracts, etc. Material may be specially contracted for, long before delivery. If prices rise during the delivery period, vendors may be tempted to charge the buyer the new market price before all deliveries have been made on the old contract, trusting to the buyer's forgetting that the old contract has not been completely filled. On the other hand, if the market price has fallen prior to the completion of deliveries on special contracts, the vendor may try to overrun contract requirements, trusting that the buyer will continue to pay the former market price. When a concern is purchasing regularly from a given firm, it is especially possible for such malpractice to occur. The way to prevent it is to scrutinize very carefully special contracts and the deliveries applicable thereto, as shown by the stock records.

Elimination of Wasteful "Help-Yourselves" Methods.—Properly kept storerooms and a system of stock records eliminate the wastes from promiscuous access to stock. If everybody has free access to stock which is not under lock and key, the natural result is that foremen and workers, because of self-interest and departmental interest, accumulate reserves of stock near their work places. That causes an inequitable distribution of stock throughout the plant and hinders efficient production. Such departments will have material in excess of requirements; other departments will not have enough.

Stock records provide the medium for discovering abnormal consumption of stores due to such "help-yourselves" methods. For example, a certain plant was located on the bank of a river. Its workers had for years been throwing spoiled product into the river. As workmen could procure stock at will, unusual consumption of material had never been detected. During a drought the river almost dried up and the large quantities of spoilage were discovered. The discovery so astounded the management that it installed a perpetual inventory immediately.

A stock record reduces spoilage, scrap, and waste losses because it registers unusual consumption, and because it makes for orderliness, always the foe of waste.

Deliveries Facilitated by Appropriation of Stock.—If materials and parts are appropriated for production orders according to their priority, the product can be made and delivered to customers on time, provided no unforeseen delays occur. The production departments, therefore, are vitally interested in appropriations. The purchasing department, unlike the production departments, is not interested in the appropriation of stock, since its chief function is to order the proper material to supply requirements.

Ready Knowledge of Balances on Hand.—As mentioned in Chapter XIII, the running total columns of a modern stock record sheet eliminate the need of a balance on hand column. The balances on hand, however, can be quickly determined by subtracting requisitions from receipts. With a knowledge of the quantity and cost of materials, etc., on hand, the estimating department can intelligently estimate new work called for by the sales department. Purchasing and production, likewise, are materially benefited by information of available balances of parts, materials, supplies, sub-assemblies, etc.

Reduction of Obsolete Stock.—Since the stock record shows the dates on which supplies were received, the age thereof can be determined. If the storekeeper keeps in close touch with the stock movements, he can ascertain whether or not his old stock is obsolete or obsolescent. Such stock should be disposed of in some way, because it is more or less of a dead loss. Accumulations of obsolete stock decrease the stores turnover, which in turn decreases the profits.

Makes Possible Monthly Financial Statements.—When stores records are maintained, financial statements can be compiled frequently—every month if desired—without the necessity of taking a physical inventory in the different storerooms and departments. It is true that the values of the book and physical inventories may not be the same, but the former are more likely to be correct because of the greater chance of error in taking physical inventories. The financial statements prepared monthly upon the basis of book inventories are very accurate. A monthly physical inventory of all the stock is not practicable because of the labor entailed and the time lost in production due to the partial or whole shut-down of the concern.

Fire Loss Adjusted Equitably.—One of the most important advantages of the perpetual inventory is that it facilitates an equitable settlement with insurance adjusters in case of fire loss. Insurance adjusters naturally try to keep settlement amounts as low as is consistent with good business policy. But some adjusters have opinions with respect to stock records that are difficult to understand. A certain adjuster, for example, contends that a stock record is not advantageous in settling fire losses. He admits that insurance adjusters after a fire are under the necessity of receiving an inventory, prepared by an appraisal company for what it may be worth, just as they would receive any other evidence submitted for their consideration; and furthermore, that the inventories prepared by such a company are in excellent form and in very minute detail, prepared very conscientiously, and as near correct as it is possible to make them, since the property owner desires exact truth with respect to his property both for loss and for coinsurance purposes. He urges, however, that as values are subject to fluctuation, an inventory made one year may not be of much value the next year. This adjuster, considering the matter of the value of stock records from the viewpoint of the insurance company, fails to get the manufacturer's viewpoint.

Accountants do not agree with all the views of this adjuster. They contend particularly that in any event a stock record makes possible a more equitable settlement than could otherwise be had, since comparisons between past perpetual inventories and past physical inventories can be made. If the comparisons disclose substantial agreement between these two classes of inventories, the adjuster should be willing to consider the book inventory at the time of the fire loss as indicative of the physical inventory burned up. To be sure, the book inventory carried at cost prices may not represent market prices at the time of the fire loss. Even so, book records are indispensable evidence of losses in respect to quantities and values. In fact, book inventories are usually more correct than physical inventories. This view is not enough appreciated.

Advantages of Stock Record Sheet Illustrated.—Special points in connection with the modern stock record sheet as shown in Chapter XIII, Figure 27, may be mentioned as follows:

1. Running total
2. Requirements and ordered
3. Appropriated
4. Received
5. Issued

1. Running Total Columns.—By many tests made during the actual operation of stock records, it has been proved that the number of times a balance is actually used is very small in comparison with the number of times it was computed. It has also been proved that an enormous amount of extra work is involved in the use of the balance method in answering questions of the purchasing, production, sales, and other departments with reference to the quantities used in given periods.

The reason for this extra work has been the necessity of adding the full detail of the entries for the period desired. By the use of the running total method, figures desired can be quickly obtained through subtraction. For example, the balance on hand can be quickly determined by simply subtracting the total requisitions in the running total column from the total receipts in the running total column. Furthermore, the running total method increases the accuracy of the stock records because it involves mostly addition and little subtraction, more errors being made in subtraction than in addition. Balances of material on hand, determined by the balance method, disclose only a net result. Balances arrived at by the running total method not only disclose that information but also enable questions as to quantity to date for any period to be instantly answered.

Stock record clerks should watch every item of material,

noting the length of time it has been in stock, how quickly it moves, etc. Whether or not stock records are a constant and useful source of cost data, depends largely upon the diligence, watchfulness and accuracy of the stock record clerks.

2. **Requirements and Ordered Columns.**—Because of the close relation between the Required columns and the Ordered columns of stock record, they are here discussed together.

The recapitulation of the requirements of material parts, etc., needed for the product that is to be manufactured is entered in the Requirements columns. This information is obtained from production schedules, shipping orders, and breakdowns of assemblies. The requirements are compared with the quantities ordered, as shown in the Ordered columns, in order to ascertain whether or not requirements are being covered by either production or purchase orders—production orders in the case of manufactured parts, purchase orders if material and parts are bought.

In some cases only the actual or net requirements are entered. In other cases the minimum of material to be carried is recorded and added to the net requirements. This obviates an error which might otherwise arise through mentally adding the minimum to the requirements.

When the minimum is entered in the Requirements columns, the total of the Ordered columns must always equal the total of the Requirements columns. If this practice is not followed, however, the minimum must always be mentally added to the total in the Requirements columns so that the quantity required can be compared with the quantity ordered.

3. **Appropriated Columns.**—The quantity of material which it has been decided to use for machine schedules, assemblies, and shipments, is entered in the Appropriated or Reserve columns. Thus production control and the scheduling of shipments are facilitated. The Appropriated columns are arranged

in such a way that a running total of the appropriations on each order, as well as the grand running total of appropriations on all orders, may be kept.

4. **Received Columns.**—There is little to be said about the Received column, for the data entered in it are self-explanatory. As orders are received in full, the entries in the ordered columns should be checked off. In this way the management can ascertain whether the quantities which have been ordered to cover requirements have been received.

The Amount column must be filled out because the invoice cost and transportation charges of material are often entered separately. The unit price, which includes both the invoice cost and the transportation charges, is then recorded.

5. **Issued Columns.**—It has been found of little value to have the stock record clerk stop to extend the amount in the Issued Amount column, or to make the entry after the extension has been made by a calculating machine operator. In fact, on some stock record sheets the issued amount column has been omitted.

It is sufficient to enter the price of stock issued, as that affords enough information to enable all of the material received at one price to be properly cleared when entries are being made for requisitions.

Relation Between Columns of a Stock Record Sheet.—In general, the relation between the different columns of stock record sheets may be summarized as follows:

1. "Requirements" less "Appropriations" equals the balance of materials or parts, etc., not scheduled.
2. "Requirements" less "Ordered" indicates whether requirements are covered.
3. "Requirements" less "Received" shows how far behind the plant is in getting material and parts needed for

requirements, either from the outside or from manufacture.

4. "Requirements" less "Issued" shows requirements not issued from stock.
5. "Appropriated" must never be greater than "Received."
6. "Appropriated" less "Issued" equals balance of appropriated material not issued.
7. "Ordered" minus "Received" equals amount due on orders, either purchase or production.
8. "Ordered" must exceed "Requirements" by the amount of the minimum.
9. "Received" less "Issued" equals balance on hand.

Advantage of Carrying Money Values on Stock Records.—Money values of all purchased raw materials, purchased supply material, all individual parts, sub or minor assemblies, and full assemblies—where the product is manufactured in standardized and segregated lots—should appear on stock records. There are a number of reasons for this procedure:

1. It is the only way to price out correctly material used. (See Chapter XV.) The safest and easiest method of pricing out material is by actual lots. It gives inventory balances that are correct and enables correct financial statements to be compiled. In cases where material is bought on more than one contract and is consumed in large quantities, it may be priced at average cost.

2. It saves clerical work. The stock record clerk should price each requisition, passing it on to the calculating machine operator for extension, and then it should be forwarded to the cost department. If values were not carried on stock records, it would be necessary to enter the quantity of each requisition on the stock records, to send it to some other clerk for pricing, and then to still another for computing and cost work.

Furthermore, pricing should be done by the stock record clerk, since the stock record is the *only* record showing when each lot of material is exhausted. To prove this, consider the case of a price book kept in the purchasing department containing, for example, the following data:

March	1,	500 pieces,	$2.00 each		....	$1,000.00
"	25,	1,000 "	2.25	"	....	2,250.00
June	15,	2,000 "	2.35	"	....	4,700.00

These were spot purchases made at different prices. The material is used in odd quantities, some of it being consumed as late as July and August. In this case what price should the purchasing department use—$2, $2.25, or $2.35? If the purchasing department cannot price material in such a way as to allow accurate detailed costs to be kept, neither will the controlling accounts for material and supplies be accurate. If, on the other hand, the stock record clerk prices requisitions, the items thereon can be easily identified, thereby insuring accurate pricing.

To have pricing done by some department other than the stock record department is not desirable. Requisitions are not in shape for proper accounting of the material consumed. (See Chapters XIV and XV.) On the other hand, each stock record sheet kept for each class of material shows the name or number of the controlling account for that material. The stock record clerk marks the controlling account number or name on each requisition before it is entered on an accumulation sheet and then filed in the cost department. Thus proper credits can be made to material control accounts.

An ideal perpetual inventory system involves a constant and systematic checking of items in order that the plant will not have to shut down for inventory. A cycle of checking for each control account should be completed at least once a year. When the cycle is completed and the individual stock record sheets show that each item has been verified, the dates on which the balances of the different accounts are to be struck are selected.

The balance of each item must always be priced properly. This means that if the balance is larger than the last lot in, and the previous lot price is different from the last, the balance will be priced at the last lot price to the extent of the lot, and the rest of the balance will be priced at the previous cost.

CHAPTER XVIII

ACCOUNTING FOR LABOR—IN THE PLANT

The Importance of Labor Accounting.—The accuracy and utility of cost records depends very largely on the excellence of the original data secured in the plant. This has already been brought out in connection with the material records.

As compared with material data, however, the accuracy of labor data is of far greater importance. Material data can be checked at any time and in various ways, and no particular human relation is involved. But with labor data it is a different matter. They *must be accurate,* as the efficiency of men—workers, foremen, superintendents and even the executive management—is being expressed in terms of time and money units through the use of the labor data.

Broad Steps in Labor Accounting.—It is of advantage to consider now the broad steps of labor accounting. These may be regarded as follows:

1. Gathering of original data
   (a) Regular cases
   (b) Special cases
2. Checking and extending the time cards
3. Preparing the pay-roll.

The first step is naturally carried out in the plant. The second step is sometimes and probably most often carried out in the plant. The third step is carried out by the pay-roll department, and this is described in the following chapter:

Objectives of Labor Accounting.—Accounting for labor in the plant and in the pay-roll office has four main objectives:

1. To ascertain the amount of wages due each worker so that pay-rolls can be prepared.
2. To ascertain the time spent on each production order by pieces, operations or processes worked on.
3. To ascertain the time spent on the expense or burden standing orders.
4. To provide data through the foregoing procedure whereby proper control of labor costs may be maintained.

Chief Forms Used in Labor Accounting.—It will be useful to enumerate here the chief forms used in order to reach these objectives, together with a brief explanatory comment of their functions. These forms are:

1. *Weekly In-and-Out Card.* A clock card (Figure 38) is assigned to each worker in order that he may record thereon the time when he arrives in the plant and leaves it—in other words the in-and-out time. The function of this card is the same in every plant, although its form may vary slightly.

2. *Time Card.* Time cards (Figures 39 and 41) vary according to the kind of labor information desired and the system of wage payment in use in the plant—regular day-work, piece-work, or premium or bonus. As a matter of fact, the accounting for labor on time cards and other labor records probably depends more upon the system of wage payment than upon any other factor. Certain special cases that arise in accounting for labor will be discussed in this chapter along with the regular procedure of labor accounting.

3. *Late and Absent and Overtime Reports.* If a worker is present during the full working day his in-and-out card and time cards will show this fact. If he is late or absent, or if he works overtime, this fact is entered on a late and absent or an overtime report (Figures 45 or 44), as the case may be.

4. *Pay-Roll Sheet.* The pay-roll sheet (Figure 46, Chapter XIX) is used to assemble the pay of each man from the

time cards representing the detail of work performed, and supplies the basis for the journal entry for the distribution of pay-rolls. (See Chapter XXIV.)

5. *Labor Transfer Record.* The labor transfer record (Figure 48, Chapter XIX) is used to record the time and cost of workers temporarily loaned by one department to another.

6. *O. D. S. O. Transfer Record.* The O. D. S. O. transfer record (Figure 49, Chapter XIX) is used to record the details of work on other department standing orders.

WEEK ENDING ....192.....

No.
NAME

	MORNING IN	NOON OUT	NOON IN	NIGHT OUT	EXTRA IN	EXTRA OUT	

TOTAL TIME..HRS.

RATE..................................

TOTAL WAGES FOR WEEK $ ....

Figure 38.—Weekly In-and-Out Card. (Size, 3¼ x 5½.)

Weekly In-and-Out Clock Cards.—The weekly in-and-out clock cards show the time the worker enters and leaves the plant each day. The difference between the two figures for each day is the time when he is supposed to be in the plant. This figure is checked up with the time reported on the time cards. Inasmuch as the time cards show the time worked as well as the cost of the labor performed by each worker, it can be ascertained whether or not he was idle during any of the time that he was in the plant. Still another use is made of in-and-out cards, namely, to aid the pay-roll department in locating differences in the pay-roll.

The Time Clerk.—An important essential to be considered at this point is that of how the gathering of original time data is accomplished. The filling out of time cards by workers is the worst way, and only in very exceptional cases should be used.

Requiring foremen to fill out time cards is not practicable except in exceptional circumstances, or in very slack times. A foreman has far more valuable duties to perform than clerical work.

The accepted practice in this respect is to have timekeepers in the various departments who, not only will secure the time records, but also will assist the foremen in many other ways. The time clerk will see that the workers stamp in-and-out cards properly. Each week these clerks forward the in-and-out cards, after they have been properly stamped, to the pay-roll department to be filed consecutively by workers' numbers. The in-and-out cards do not show the actual time and cost of work done, nor do they show the workers' idle time. The detailed accounting for labor in the plant does not really begin until the time cards are filled out. This work should be done by the time clerk. If workers are permitted to fill out time cards, a part of their productive time is lost. Furthermore, they may lose the cards or get them so dirty that they are illegible.

Before taking up in detail the preparation of time cards, the various duties of the time clerk, in so far as his duties in connection with timekeeping are concerned, may be outlined as follows:

1. To account for all working hours of employees in their departments.
2. To enter on time cards the time when operations are commenced by workers.
3. To place the card in a rack under the proper working place number.
4. To remove the card from the rack when the job is finished.
5. To enter the quitting time.
6. Usually to calculate on the cards the elapsed time.
7. To turn in for each worker enough cards to represent the entire time he was present. These time cards are checked with the late and absent, and overtime reports for the purpose of noting any deviation from the standard number of working hours.
8. To stamp night and overtime on cards for night work and overtime.
9. To enter the quantity of work accomplished as called for in each case.
10. To enter all idle machine time on idle machine cards as specified. (See Chapter XXXIII.)

Time Cards.—There are two principal kinds of time cards —one for direct or productive work (Figure 39a) and another for indirect work (Figure 41).

The direct-labor card is used to record labor which is chargeable to a production order; the indirect card is used to record labor chargeable to a standing order.

All time cards are similar in a general way, though they differ as to detail. The time cards illustrated here show the greatest amount of detail ever necessary even for the operation of a production control system. Much of this detail may be omitted in most cases.

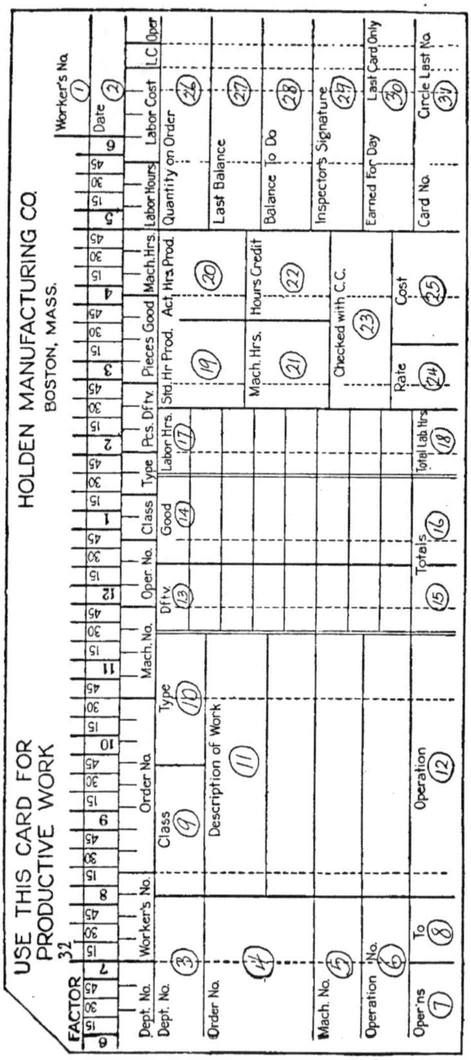

Figure 39a.—Direct Labor Time Card. (Size, 7⅜ x 3¼.)

This form is used for recording direct, that is to say, productive work, whether it be done under the regular day-work, piece-work, or premium or bonus system of wage payment, the forms used under each of these systems differing from the others in color only.

Time Cards for Direct Labor.—The same form of direct-labor card is used for all direct, that is to say, productive work whether it be done under the regular day-work, piece-work, or premium or bonus system of wage payment—the regular day-work card being different from the piece-work, bonus or premium card in color only. A recapitulation card—called the bonus and premium report—is used in conjunction with the direct-labor card under the premium or bonus system.

The day-work system is not as common as formerly, owing to the adoption of piece, premium, bonus, and other special methods of wage payment.

The following is a detailed description of the data on the time cards for direct work (see Figure 39a). The circled figures appearing upon the card have been inserted merely for the purpose of identifying the columns referred to in the following discussion.

1. Worker's Number. The worker's time-clock card number.
2. Date. Stamped with date stamp.
3. Department Number. The number of the department on whose pay-roll the worker belongs.
4. Order Number. This is secured from the production order or the standing order code.
5. Machine Number. The number of the machine which the employee is operating.
6. Operation Number. The identifying number of the operation being performed.
7. Operations. The total number of operations which are to be performed on the material.
8. The next operation to be performed on the piece.
9. Class. The class of goods being made, as shown by the product code.
10. Type. The type of goods being made, as shown by the product code.
11. Description of Work. A description of the goods being made.
12. Operation. The name of the operation being performed by the worker.
13. Defective. The number of pieces spoiled during the operation.
14. Good. The number of good pieces finished during the operation.

15. Totals. The sum of (13).
16. Totals. The sum of (14).
17. Labor Hours. See description of (32) "factor."
18. Total Labor Hours. See description of (32) "factor."
19. Standard Hourly Production. The standard rate per hour for this operation.
20. Actual Hourly Production. The actual rate per hour accomplished.
21. Machine Hours. Total number of machine hours.
22. Hours Credit. Number of good pieces divided by standard hourly rate of production.
23. Checked With Clock Card. A distinguishing check mark or the initials of the dispatch clerk who checks the labor card with the in-and-out clock card is entered in this space.
24. Rate. The rate of pay.
25. Cost. The labor cost which is the rate, piece or day (24), multiplied by the total number of good pieces made (16) if piece-work, or the number of hours (18) if day work.
26. Quantity on Order. The total quantity of the particular product ordered.
27. Last Balance. The balance of the order left after the previous quantities made have been subtracted from the quantity on order (26).
28. Balance To Do. The quantity of the order which is still unfinished which is obtained by subtracting the total good (14) and defective (15) pieces from the last balance (27).
29. Inspector's Signature.
30. Earned For Day. Total earnings for day are extended on last card for day only.
31. Card Number. Each worker's cards are numbered consecutively using 1 for the first card in the morning, 2 for the second card, etc. A circle is placed around the last card number. Cards are numbered consecutively for workers who have more than one card for a day's work, in order to insure the receipt of cards for the entire day.
32. Factor. The use of all time cards except the bonus card involves a somewhat special feature known as the calculation of factors.[1] The factor is the term given to the number of machines a worker operates. It is shown on the horizontal scale across the top of the card.

By reference to the three cards (Figure 39b, c, and d) the method of calculating factors can be understood. Employee No. 526 started work at 7 A. M. on three machines, each of which is represented by one of the cards. At 10 A. M., machine No. 950 stops because of a breakdown. The hours that machine are idle are reported on idle machine cards. The worker continues to operate the other two machines, Nos. 951 and 952. From 7 A. M. to 10 A. M., therefore, worker No. 526 has operated three machines. Hence, his factor for that period is 3, that is, the same as the number of machines he was running. The factor is indicated on three cards by drawing heavy vertical lines at 7 A. M. and 10 A. M. respectively, and writing the figure 3 between the lines. The difference in time as shown by the number of hours between vertical lines is 3. This figure is divided by the factor for that period, which is also 3, and the result is the labor hours—1—to be entered in space (17) (labor hours) on each card. While worker No. 526 continues to operate two machines his factor is 2. He resumes operations on machine No. 950 in the same production order at 3 o'clock and consequently his factor again becomes 3. Heavy vertical lines are drawn at 3 o'clock on all of the cards. On the cards shown in Figure 39c and d, 2 (the factor) is written between the 10 o'clock and 3 o'clock lines. The period represented by the difference in hours between the line is 4, as one hour is taken off for lunch. This is divided by the factor 2 and the result—2—is the number of labor hours to be entered in column (17) on the second line on Figure 39c and d.

Suppose the worker No. 526 quits at 6 o'clock. From 3 to 6 o'clock he has been operating three machines. His factor for that period is 3. The labor hours are 3÷3, or 1, and are entered in column (17) on each of the cards. The next step is to calculate the labor hours on each card which are entered in space (18). These hours are 2, 4, and 4, respectively. The elapsed machine hours as shown by the cards are 6, 10, and

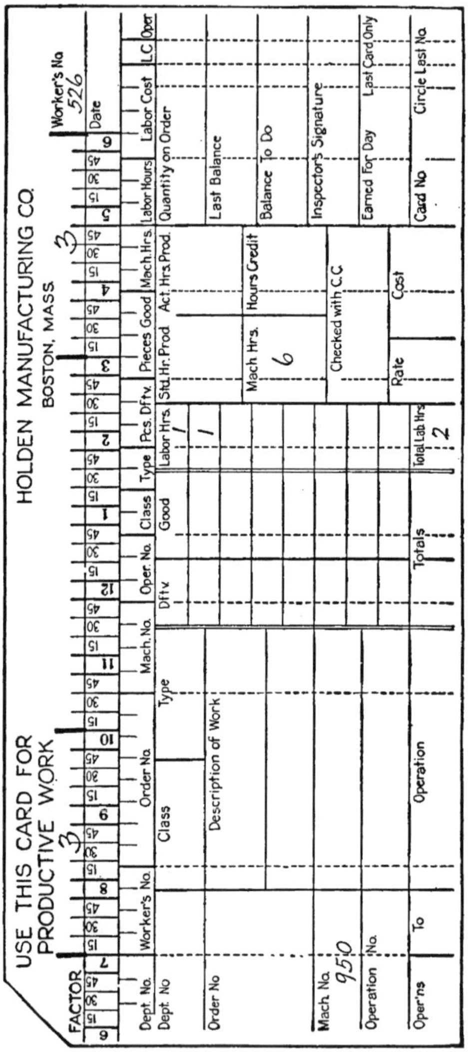

Figure 39b.—Direct Labor Time Card Filled in to Indicate Use of Factors. (Size, 7⅜ x 3¼.)

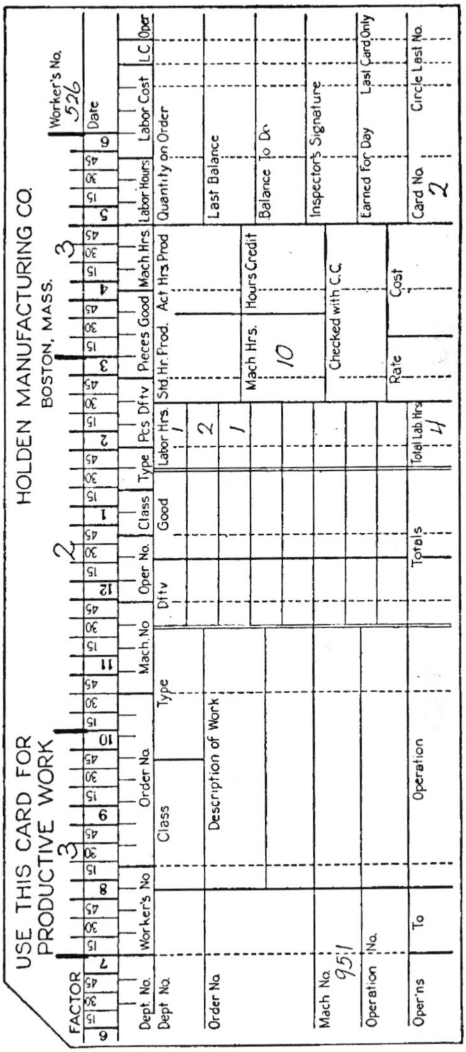

Figure 39c.—Direct Labor Time Card Filled in to Indicate Use of Factors.
(Size, 7⅜ x 3¼.)

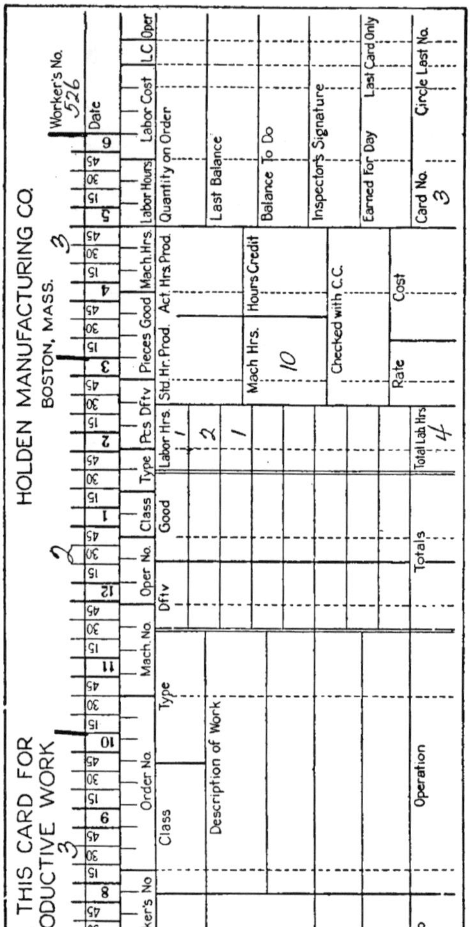

Figure 39d.—Direct Labor Time Card Filled in to Indicate Use of Factors.
(Size, 7⅜ x 3¼.)

10 hours respectively. These figures are entered in space (21) on each card.

When the factor does not divide evenly into the elapsed hours (as 1¼ hours divided by the factor), arbitrarily divide the time into even 15-minute periods.

Bonus or Premium Report Card.—The method of accounting for labor under the bonus or premium method of wage payment involves the use of regular time cards and the bonus or premium report card (Figure 40), which is a recapitulation card of the bonus or premium earned by the worker. These cards are made out in duplicate. The original bonus report or premium card is given to the worker so that he himself can check up the calculations of bonuses and premiums made by the office, and the duplicate is forwarded with the product to the inspector of the product, and later the cards are forwarded to the pay-roll department. It should be clearly kept in mind that the bonus or premium reports do not obviate the need of regular time cards.

On the bonus or premium report are entered the basis of payment made to the worker, the date, time, and pieces made. The bonus is calculated as follows: The number of pieces required per hour is multiplied by the number of hours worked during the period. The result is subtracted from the number of pieces made to find the number of pieces on which a bonus is earned. The bonus rate is multiplied by this number to find the bonus earned. A glance at Figure 40 will make this clear. On December 1 and 2 the employee whose card is shown worked 4 and 6 hours respectively, which means that he had to produce more than 400 pieces (40 x 10) in order to earn a bonus. The record shows that he actually made 450 pieces during that period. As 2 cents is paid for each piece on which a bonus is allowed the worker earned a bonus of $1.

The bonus is then entered on the card and is added either to the regular pay-roll or to a special bonus pay-roll.

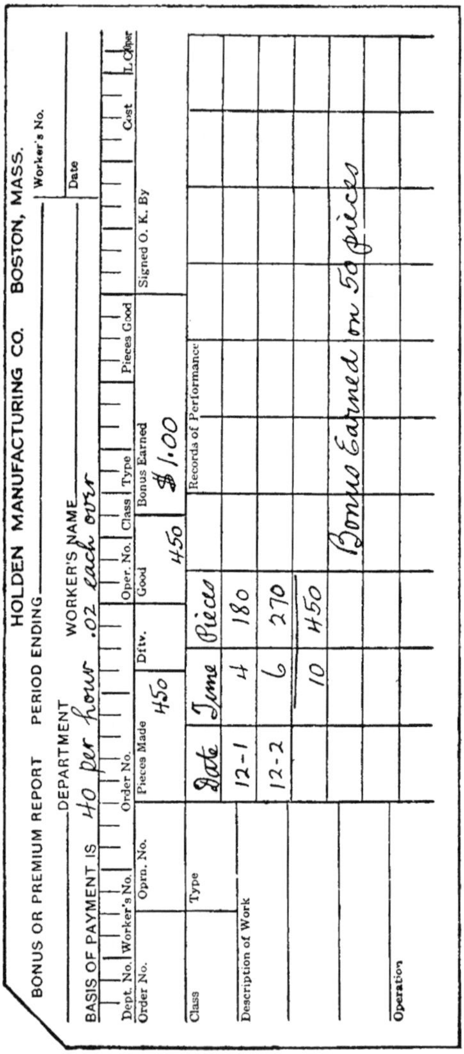

Figure 40.—Bonus or Premium Report Card. (Size, 7⅜ x 3¼.)

Inspection Reports.—The time cards for direct labor discussed in this chapter call for entries of good and bad pieces. As it is frequently impossible to inspect the product in time, however, it is often necessary to record the number of pieces completed, whether good or bad, and to have a separate inspection report follow later.

Time Cards for Indirect Work.—Another important feature of labor accounting occurs in connection with indirect work. It will be remembered that time cards for direct work are chargeable to production orders. Time cards for indirect work (Figure 41) are chargeable to standing orders.

Cards for indirect work are filled out as follows:

1. Worker's Number. The worker's time-clock card number.
2. Date. Stamped with date stamp.
3. Department Number. The worker's home department number.
4. Order Number. The standing code order number outlined on the order which accompanies the work or from the standing order code.
5. Labor Hours. The time spent on the work.
6. Rate. The worker's rate per hour.
7. Labor Cost. The time spent, times the rate per hour.
8. Description of Work Done. The description should be complete, e.g., "Repairing machine 50."
9. Complete. A check mark is placed here if work is complete.
10. Incomplete. Checked here if work is incomplete.
11. Earnings for Day. Extension of total earnings for day to be on last card for day only.
12. Card Number. Worker's cards are numbered consecutively. A circle is placed around the last number.

Time Cards, 3″ x 5″.—The illustrations of time cards in this chapter have been punched cards. Where electric machines are not used, the same information can just as well be entered on smaller cards.

For the purpose of illustrating such cards, Figures 42 and 43 are shown, being designs of direct and indirect time cards in small size. While called "time cards," these forms are better

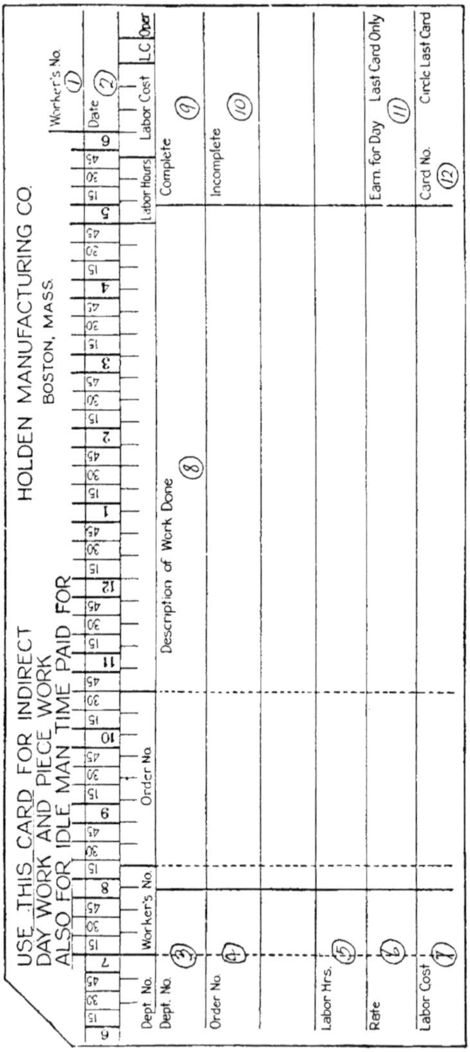

Figure 41.—Indirect Labor Time Card. (Size, 7⅜ x 3¼.)

Account No.		From	To	Workers No.		
Dept.	Work Place	Est. Time		Date		
Descriptive		Complete	Incomplete	Spec. Order No.	Checked	
				Inspected	Card No.	
				TIME ANALYSIS FACTORS		
					Stop	
					Start	
					Elapsed	
INDIRECT TIME CARD	Mach. Hrs.	Burden Rate	Amount Burden	Labor Hrs.	Labor Rate	Amount Labor

Figure 42.—Small Indirect Time Card. (Size 3 x 5.)

Order No.	Quantity on Order	Part or B. P. No.		From	To	Workers No.
This Operation Name				No.	No. of Op'ns.	Date
Dept.	Workplace		Descriptive			
Last Bal.	Shp. Credit	Next Shp. Debit	Dfty.	Good	TIME ANALYSIS FACTORS	
Bal. to Do	Next Shp.				Stop	
Inspected	Checked	Card No.			Start	
					Elapsed	
DIRECT TIME CARD	Mach. Hrs.	Burden Rate	Amount Burden	Labor Hrs.	Labor Rate	Amount Labor

Figure 43.—Small Direct Time Card. (Size, 3 x 5.)

printed on cheap paper in order that they may be easily handled when being accumulated by adding machine.

All time cards may also be designed to permit the use of one of the various job time recording clocks which are available.

Recording Special Cases.—It will be remembered that the steps mentioned in accounting for labor were:

1. Gathering of original data
   (a) Regular cases
   (b) Special cases
2. Checking and extending the time cards
3. Preparing the pay-rolls

Special features are:

1. Recording the time of loaned workers.
2. Accounting for work on other department standing orders.
3. Accounting for labor costs on short operations.

1. Recording Time of Loaned Workers.—The first special case in connection with accounting for labor occurs in the recording of the time of loaned workers. When a worker is on a certain pay-roll and is loaned to another department for temporary service, and when no burden charge is involved, it is of course impracticable to change the worker's number. In such cases, accordingly, the following very serviceable method is used:

The time clerk of the worker's home department makes out two cards for the loaned worker, entering thereon the worker's number, the date and the time the worker reported for duty in the department borrowing him. These cards will be either direct or indirect, in accordance with the nature of work to be done by the man borrowed.

Both cards are then stamped diagonally in the description of work space, "Transfer to Department Number . . ." The time clerk fills in the number of the department to which the man is transferred. One card is placed in the worker's space on his home dispatch board as a memo, and the other card is given to the worker to turn over to the time clerk of the department to which he is loaned.

The time clerk of the department borrowing the man fills in all other information as if the worker were one of his own men. He makes out any additional cards necessary to cover the man's time for the period, stamping all other cards the same time as the first. At the close of the day—or upon return of the worker to his home department—the time clerk sends the cards back by the worker, who reports back to his home time clerk.

These cards are then forwarded to the pay-roll office like all other cards. The memo card held by the home time clerk is destroyed—or used again after erasure of entries. The further special procedure in connection with the transfer is explained later in Chapters XIX and XXIV.

2. **Other Department Standing Order Accounting.**—The second special case in accounting for labor occurs in connection with charges made by one department to any other department in a plant where the burden of the originating department must be incorporated in the charge.

While the filling out of the card is identical with any other entry of indirect labor, the card must be specially stamped in order to insure proper handling in the subsequent operations in connection with the pay-rolls. These cards are accordingly marked with a rubber stamp "O.D.S.O." in large letters. They should be stamped diagonally across the description of work so that they may be quickly and easily detected in the pay-roll department. Other than this, the entries on the cards are the same as in all other cases, the only difference being in any one department when the standing order number will be for some department other than the one performing the work. The special handling of these cards is described in Chapters XIX and XXIV in connection with the pay-roll distribution.

3. **Short Operations.**—The third and last special case in accounting for labor has to do with recording the labor costs of short operations. Many manufacturing operations are of

such short duration that it is impracticable to charge the direct labor involved to production order numbers through time cards. Hence, these operations are known as "short" operations and code numbers are provided for them.

This situation in accounting for labor is exactly the same in principle as in the case of glue, paint, etc., explained in Chapter XIV as representing materials that cannot conveniently be charged directly to orders. In fact, not only the principle is the same but the procedure of handling is almost the same.

An illustration of this may be cited in the hardening of taps. Many sizes are handled together—and each size may be on a separate order. To separate the time on each size and order is impracticable. Therefore all hardening time is charged to a code order or account called "Hardening."

It is necessary, however, to enter the actual cost of hardening each of various sizes of taps on the cost sheets. These costs may be estimated as follows: The cost of hardening each of six or eight sizes is determined by means of tests the results of which are then plotted on a chart. A curve drawn through these points will indicate the approximate cost of hardening intermediate sizes. The standard costs thus derived should be used on all cost sheets and the code order or Hardening account credited with like amounts. The total of standard costs entered on the cost sheets during a given period should approximate the total amounts charged against short operations during the period. If a discrepancy exists, adjustments should be made and the standard cost should be revised.

Although the time of short operations is not kept, a list of all products, their production order numbers, and quantities, should be kept under each operation, so that the orders to which standard short-operation costs are applicable may be known.

Standard costs should be listed or shown graphically in some way. They remain fixed unless changed conditions affect the amount of standard costs, in which case the standards should be revised. It should be clearly kept in mind that short operation accounts are not a cure-all for everything; these accounts should be minimized and used as infrequently as possible.

Checking Labor Cards.—The second principal step in accounting for labor consists of checking the labor cards. The

HOLDEN MANUFACTURING CO.
BOSTON, MASS.

OVERTIME REPORT

DEPARTMENT____________________ DATE__________

WORKERS' NO.	NAME	TIME IN	TIME OUT	TOTAL OVERTIME
		SIGNED		

Figure 44.—Overtime Report. (Size, 5 x 7¾.)

time cards for each day are checked the following morning. Each time clerk must see that the time cards for all workers in his department are checked. In order to do this properly he must be provided with a list of the numbers of the workers in his department and must prepare overtime reports (Figure 44) and late and absent reports (Figure 45). For exceptions to the regular hours of employment the procedure is as follows:

Shortly after the whistle blows in the morning, and after the lunch hour, each time clerk takes the cards left in the "out" rack and keeps them in his time booth. Any worker who is late reports to the time booth for his time card and the time clerk fills out on the late and absent report the worker's number and name, and the rest of the data called for on the report—which is self-explanatory. Absent time is recorded in the same general way from the cards of absent workers and during the day

HOLDEN MANUFACTURING CO.
BOSTON, MASS.

LATE AND ABSENT REPORT

DEPARTMENT ________________________ DATE ____________

WORKERS' NO.	NAME	MORNING		AFTERNOON		TOTAL TIME ABSENT
		IN	OUT	IN	OUT	
	SIGNED					

Figure 45.—Late and Absent Report. (Size, 5 x 7¾.)

for all workers who leave the plant before the regular quitting time.

From the passes issued for overtime the dispatch clerks prepare the overtime reports, which are also virtually self-explanatory.

For all workers who are present for the full day's work, the time on the time cards must total the regular hours—8, 9, or 10, as the case may be. After time cards are checked by time clerks for full labor hours as well as for full machine hours, they are placed in numerical sequence and are then forwarded to the pay-roll office.

Extension of Cards.—The next step in accounting for labor is the extension of time cards. In different plants there will always be found a difference of opinion as to who should have charge of the file of day and piece rates, in order to accomplish the proper rating of the cards. In some cases the files of such rates are in the shops, and in other cases in one of the office departments, usually the pay-roll department. It is probably best to have the rating of the time cards as to rates per hour and piece rates confined to the office, if possible, in order that the information as to day rates, in particular, shall not be a matter of common knowledge. Irrespective of where it is decided that this work shall be done, after the contributing data have been entered on the cards the next natural operation is to have them rated and extended. This is purely a matter of referring to the day rate files in the case of straight day-work and in bonus or premium system based on day-work, and to the piece-work files in cases where the work is performed in this manner. The extensions on the cards should be made clearly and distinctly, and in all cases checked by someone else in order to insure absolute accuracy. After the cards have been rated and extended they are passed on to the pay-roll department, the detail procedure of which is described in the following chapter.

CHAPTER XIX

ACCOUNTING FOR LABOR ON PAY-ROLLS

Purposes of Pay-Roll Sheets.—The pay-rolls constitute the analysis of the total amount of wages paid whereby the departmental controlling accounts receive their entries. The grand total of the amount paid out as pay-roll is of no use as a controlling account as it in no way reveals the nature of work paid *for*. The pay-roll sheets serve the following purposes:

1. To arrive at the total pay of each worker.
2. To analyze the pay-roll for the accomplishment of certain controls.

Condition of Time Cards on Delivery to Pay-Roll Department.—Before the pay-roll sheet is taken up, however, it might be well to insert a word about the condition of the time cards when they reach the pay-roll department. By turning over these cards in orderly and proper shape, the time clerk can help the pay-roll department greatly.

It is very important, for instance, that the time cards be delivered to the pay-roll department with all cards representing the day's work of each man. The cards for each man should also be in their numerical sequence, it being remembered that when a man uses more than one card per day the various cards representing his day's work are serially numbered.

It is natural that the cards should be in order, as the last move made by the time clerk should be to verify the fact that a man's entire time is represented by the time cards—after they have been checked with the late and absent reports and the overtime reports.

The cards should also be in sequence according to the

worker's check number, as this is the condition in which they should be handled in the time booth in the shop.

Arrangement of Pay-Roll Sheets.—A careful study of the pay-roll sheet in Figure 46 should be made. These sheets should be in binders and should be made ready for the entries of a pay period before the entry of the pay-roll is started. This means that the full data at the top of each pay-roll sheet should be filled in, including the department name, the name of the worker, his day rate, his check number, and the pay-roll period.

If the sheets are prepared ahead of time from the list of check numbers last known to be employed in the department, a great deal of time will be saved in the current work of entry.

In some places it has been found of advantage to have the pay-roll sheets loose during the posting period, as the sheets will then lie perfectly flat for entry. If this method is used, however, great care must be taken to see that none of the sheets become separated from the file.

Details Shown on Pay-Roll Sheet.—The first column on the pay-roll sheet is the date column, in which it is necessary to enter only the day of the month, as the period date at the top gives the other information desired.

The column headed "Slip Number" is for the purpose of entering the serial number of the slips for the worker when more than one time card is required to represent his work. In this connection it is to be remembered that the serial number on the last card representing the day's work should be enclosed in a circle. This automatically shows the pay-roll clerk that all the cards for each worker are in hand. The column headed "Charge" is for the entry of the order number covering the work accounted for by the time card. This may be either a standing order number or a production order number. The nature of this order number regulates the entry of the time in the columns which follow.

There are five main blocks of columns across the sheet.

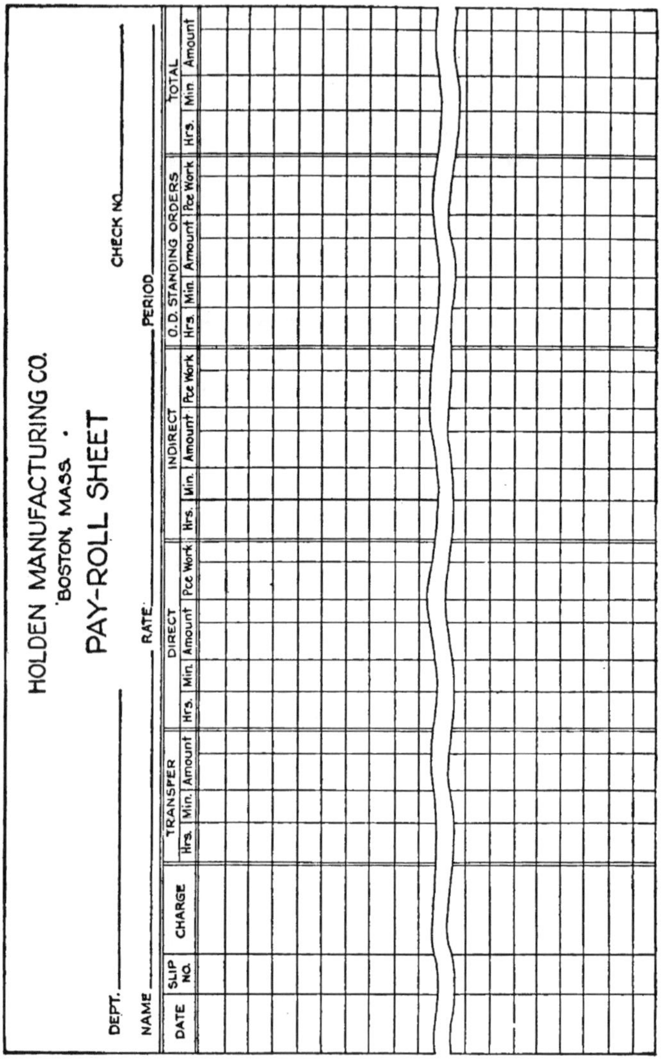

Figure 46.—Pay-Roll Sheet. (Size, 13 x 8½.)

The first four of these are of extreme importance, as they become the basis of the controls for each subsequent movement of labor through the medium of journal entries. Each has a very specific use, and too strict attention cannot be paid to mastering and understanding fully the uses to which they are put. The blocks are herewith described in regular order:

1. **Transfer.**—The time card procedure in connection with labor which is loaned by one department to another has previously been described. When one department loans a man for some hours or days to another department, the time of loaning is usually not sufficient to warrant changing his check number, and therefore the method described in the previous chapter is used to obviate the mix-ups which might otherwise arise.

When the pay-roll clerk of the department recording the pay of a man who has been loaned to another department finds a card stamped "Transferred to Department A," he should enter this card under the transfer heading. This entry has the effect of registering the man's time for pay on his own pay-roll, and at the same time providing the entry in a column ready for use in connection with the labor transfer record as described later in this chapter.

2. **Direct.**—A card whereon the order number shown is that of a productive order of the home department, should be entered in this block. It will be noted that there are two main columns shown in this block, as well as the two succeeding blocks, one headed "Amount," and the other headed "Piece-work."

The object of this distinction is to separate day and piece-work in order that the pay-rolls may automatically show how much of the direct labor is operating under day-work as against any special inducement method other than day-work. It might be noted here that the straight-time earnings under bonus work or any other kind of premium work should be also entered in the piece-work column, this heading being used for any kind of work other than straight day-work.

3. **Indirect.**—The indirect block is arranged exactly as the direct block. Entries to be made therein are confined to work performed by anyone in the department on any standing order number of his department. In other words, no work must be included which is done by the department on the standing order number of any other department or any general department. The entries must be confined wholly to work on the standing orders of the department of which the worker whose pay-roll sheet is being prepared is a member.

4. **O. D. Standing Orders.**—The term "O. D. Standing Orders," that is to say, other department standing orders, is designed to cover the entry of any work performed by the department of which an employee is a member, on the standing order of any other department in the plant, where the department burden should be charged. This also includes work charged to any machine rate expense codes, even though these machines may be in the same department as the worker.

The work entered in the O.D.S.O. columns is of the same nature as that entered in the Direct column, so far as the originating department is concerned, and must be considered in conjunction with the direct in finding the basic figure for the burden rate.

An instance of this might occur in case a grinding department ground some tools for another department. To the grinding department this work is the same as work done for an outsider, and the department receiving the benefit should pay not only the direct-labor cost but also the burden in connection therewith. It is, therefore, exceedingly important to be certain that every entry made in the O.D.S.O. columns is for the work on other department standing orders.

In this connection it may be thought that many times a department might do work which would not carry overhead as against another department. In cases of this sort the entry should be carried out under the transfer scheme rather than through the O.D.S.O. scheme. Further description of the treatment of O.D.S.O. time is found later in this chapter.

5. **Total.**—The entries in the Total column consist simply of the total time and amount, and show the total earnings for each day, as well as the total time for each day. In this connection, it might be brought out that even though the time cards are supposed to have been verified by the dispatch clerk as to the total elapsed time for each day, the clock cards are brought to the pay-roll department at the close of the week for a final check against the time as shown daily on each man's pay-roll sheet, to doubly safeguard the accuracy of the pay records.

Closing the Pay-Rolls.—As each day of each man's time has been entered, the total time and amount has been brought out to the Total column. At the close of the period the entire sheet is footed vertically in all its columns, and cross-footed to agree with the vertical footing of the Total column. This makes an absolute check on the accuracy of the time and money entries and is a valuable feature in connection with the technic of pay-roll accounting.

If bonus or premium systems are in effect, it is then in order to enter at the bottom of the pay-roll sheet the bonus or premium which is due each man, in case there is no special bonus or premium pay-roll sheet provided therefor. Deductions from the pay-roll which may be necessary on account of subscriptions, rent, or many other purposes, should then be entered. After these additions and deductions have been made, the net amount of pay for the man can be computed, and the pay envelope made out accordingly.

Splitting Pay-Rolls at Close of Month.—Many times when the pay-roll period is one week, the end of the month comes in the middle of a week. In such cases it is necessary to enter the cards of the last working day of the month and to rule footing lines after the entries of this day. The entries for the remaining days of the week are then made, and after all the entries are in for the last day of the week, another sub-footing line is ruled in. It is then necessary first to add the sheets down to the first sub-footing, and then the balance of the days of the week down to the second sub-footing—each section separately. The two sub-footings must then be added to arrive at the total for the week. The use of these sub-footed totals will be explained later in this chapter.

Pay-Roll Totals.—The next operation is to arrive at the total of the pay-roll for each department. The procedure consists merely of adding the total time and amount of money for each block, whereby is shown the total for transfer, direct labor, indirect labor, O.D. standing orders, as well as the total pay-roll. Note that the totals are to be in both time and money.

This total must be arrived at for each individual pay period, but in addition to this a monthly total will be made up by recapitulation as follows:

The last sub-total of a split pay-roll at the beginning of the month starts the recapitulation for the month. The full pay-rolls during the course of the month are then taken, and to them is added the first part of the split pay-roll at the end of the month. This gives the exact total of the pay-roll during the current month, which then becomes the basis of the journal entries to effect the controls referred to in other chapters. A pay-roll sheet may be used for this recapitulation as shown in Figure 47.

In this connection it should be stated that the total of the full week's pay-roll is the amount for which the pay-roll check is drawn and which credits cash and charges the pay-roll account. It will be seen by this that the credits which are made to the pay-roll accounts because of transfers to the various

HOLDEN MANUFACTURING CO.
Boston, Mass.
PAY-ROLL SHEET

Dept. A
Name ______ Rate ______
Check No. Recap
Period July 1925

Date	Slip No.	Charge	Transfer			Direct				Indirect				O. D. Standing Orders				Total		
			Hrs.	Min.	Amount	Hrs.	Min.	Amount	Pce. Work	Hrs.	Min.	Amount	Pce. Work	Hrs.	Min.	Amount	Pce. Work	Hrs.	Min.	Amount
			Recapitulation of Pay Roll - July 1925																	
Sub Tot		1-5	10	15	6 15	600	—	480 00		200	30	160 40		50	—	40 00		860	45	686 55
Week		Ending 12	20	—	12 00	700	—	560 00		100	—	80 00		10	—	8 00		830	—	660 00
"		" 19	10	—	6 00	670	30	496 40		50	—	40 00		18	30	14 80		699	—	557 20
"		" 26	30	—	18 00	680	—	544 00		75	—	60 00		12	—	9 60		797	—	631 60
Sub Tot		27 - 31	5	—	3 00	410	45	328 60		10	—	8 00		2	—	1 60		427	45	341 20
			75	15	45 15	3011	15	2409 00		435	30	348 40		92	30	74 00		3614	30	2876 55

Figure 47.—Pay-Roll Sheet Illustrating Split Pay-Roll

control accounts are in advance of the payment of the last pay-roll, which in turn explains the reason for there always being in the balance sheet an accrued pay-roll in the liability section. Only the actual pay-roll of the month being figured is used for control purposes.

Analyzing Pay-Roll Records.—After obtaining the totals for each department of the headings as shown on the pay-roll sheets for the entire month, the journal entry is prepared, crediting the actual pay-roll figures for the month to the pay-roll accounts, and charging the various control accounts involved.

It is important to note that there must be a pay-roll for each producing department where a burden rate is involved. The necessity of this is obvious when it is remembered that the pay-roll gives an automatic analysis whereby the total amount of direct labor in the department is known as well as the total labor charged to the code of expense orders for the month.

All men working in the general expense departments, such as electric power, steam, and all other departments of non-producing or service nature, may be included in a "general" pay-roll.

In compiling the journal entry of labor distribution, all burden accounts for the various departments are grouped together in order of the departments as they appear in the standing order code—all expense accounts in their order, and the Work in Process Labor account for each department in the same order as the burden accounts. Two other accounts will be shown in the debit side of this entry, namely, an account called "Transfer," and one called "O.D.S.O. Clearance."

The method, then, of filling out the journal entry is to take each department's total of the various blocks as described, and enter it against the corresponding heading in the journal entry. Two exceptions to this are in the case of the Transfer account and the O.D.S.O. Clearance account, where it is necessary to recapitulate the debits to these accounts from all departments, combining them into one grand debit for each of these accounts which later is distributed as described in following pages.

Thus the total for each department of the direct block is entered opposite the work in process labor title for this department in the journal entry. The total of the indirect block is entered opposite the items showing debit to the burden account for this department. The total of the transfer for this department is combined with the total transfers of all other departments and entered opposite Transfer account in the journal entry. The O.D.S.O. block is handled in the same way.

The credits of this journal entry are the total of the total block for each department, which entry would be made against the credit item of the Pay-roll account for each department.

Following is an example of a journal entry distributing labor charged to the code of expense orders for the month:

Debit:

Machine Shop Direct Labor
Assembly Direct Labor
Molding Direct Labor
Pattern Shop Direct Labor
Machine Shop Burden (on labor)
Machine Shop Burden (machine hour)
Assembly Burden
Foundry Melt Account
Molding Burden (on labor)
Molding Burden (machine hour)
Molding Sand Cost
Flask Cost
Core-Making Burden (on labor)
Core-Making Burden (machine hour)
Finishing Cost
Annealing Cost
Pattern Shop Burden
Electric Power
Steam Expense
Teaming Expense
General Expense

Transfer Account
O.D.S.O. Clearance Account

Credit:
Accrued Pay-Roll

Result of the Foregoing Distribution.—It may be now easily seen that the journal entry as above described will debit the various control accounts which have been described in other chapters. (See Chapters XXI and XXV for the procedure which governs the crediting out of these costs in connection with the burden statements.)

Work Performed by One Department for Another.—At all times the cost man has been confronted by the knotty problem of how to dispose of time when men are loaned to another department for a longer or shorter period, or when work is performed in a department for another department on which the burden of the originating department should be charged.

It should be constantly borne in mind that the pay-rolls of each operating department must be maintained intact, or there will never be any known basis of the total direct-labor cost or labor hours on which to establish the control of the work in process labor or compute the burden. Nor will there be any accurate control of the indirect labor, unless the pay-rolls accurately represent what has transpired in connection with the men who are listed for each particular department.

There have been many ways of solving these problems, one favorite way, in the case of a loaned man, being to give the man a new check number in the department to which he was loaned. This has resulted, and might at any time result in his being paid double, as the two check numbers would automatically mean that he would have two pay envelopes.

A method is here presented for safeguarding the records without issuing a new check number. While perhaps appearing complicated on first consideration, it is quite simple when thoroughly understood.

Loaned Workers.—The procedure under this method, so far as it relates to the shop end, is described in detail in Chapter XVIII under the heading "Recording Time of Loaned Workers." From that description it will be seen that when a man is loaned from one department to another, his card, stamped with "Transferred to Department Number . . ." is entered on his home pay-roll. All cards of this nature are entered on the regular pay-roll sheet for this man under the block heading "Transfer."

After the pay-roll entries for each day are made and proved up, the cards stamped "Transfer" and also those stamped "O.D.S.O." are thrown out. Those stamped as loaned are then sorted according to the departments to which the workers were loaned. The cards will then be sorted as to direct or indirect time. They are next footed for the direct and indirect hours and amount for each department which received the benefit of the loaned labor. These totals are then entered on the labor transfer record (Figure 48) of the department which received the benefit of the work, in either the Direct or Indirect columns, as the case may be, under the main heading "Transferred to this Department," always also entering under "Department" in the same section the designating number of the department from which the labor was borrowed.

On the Labor Transfer Record of the department making the loan should be entered the total hours and amount *loaned,* under the heading "Transferred By." This entry may either be for *all* labor loaned for the day, irrespective of how many departments were loaned to, or an entry may be made to represent the total loaned to each department if more than one. In such a case, the designating number of the departments loaned to will be shown as called for.

It will be noted that by this method of entry the transfer

LABOR TRANSFER RECORD

DEPT.________

Date	Transferred to This Department by the Departments as Shown Below					Transferred by This Department to the Depts. as Shown Below		Date	Transferred to This Department by the Departments as Shown Below					Transferred by This Department to the Depts. as Shown Below	
		Direct		Indirect						Direct		Indirect			
	Dept.	Hrs.	Amount	Hrs.	Amount	Dept.	Amount		Dept.	Hrs.	Amount	Hrs.	Amount	Dept.	Amount

Figure 48.—Labor Transfer Record. (Size, 8½ x 11.)

sheets become a journal, and that the grand total of all entries under "Transferred To" should always balance the grand total of all entries under "Transferred By." It should be noted also, that the total for the month of entries under "Transferred By" for each department should exactly equal the total for the month of all entries in the transfer block of the pay-roll sheet for the same department.

At the close of the month all columns on all labor transfer record sheets are footed, and a journal entry prepared which completes the transfers and clears the Labor Transfer account which has been charged through the pay-roll distribution. This journal entry is made up as follows:

Debit Side:

1. The Direct Labor account of each department which shows entries under "Direct" on its labor transfer sheet in the block "Transferred To."
2. The Burden account of each department which shows entries under "Indirect" on its labor transfer sheet in the block "Transferred To."
3. The expense account of each department as in the case of Burden account.

Credit Side:

The grand total from transfer sheets of the figures under "Transferred By."

This credit should exactly equal the debit to the Transfer account received from the pay-roll journal entry.

It must be borne in mind that the "hours" transferred must be added to the "hours" as shown by the pay-roll in order to get total direct hours for each department before computing each departmental burden rate.

Other Department Standing Order Labor.—The problem in connection with the other department standing order labor is far more difficult and one which not only involves the labor expended by one department on the standing orders of another department, but in addition the burden on this labor. The handling of this class of charges, however, is accomplished in somewhat the same manner as in the labor transfers.

The procedure is as follows: As in the case of the loaned workers, the cards charging other department standing orders, which are stamped with the rubber stamp in large letters "O.D.S.O.," are thrown out, after the pay-roll has been completed for the day and proved up. These cards are then extended with the proper burden for the department, and a super machine rate, if such is called for. These extensions are made on each card with red pencil in the lower right-hand corner under the heading "Circle Last Number."

The cards are next sorted by the departments as charged, in exactly the same manner as the loaned labor cards were handled.

The cards for each department are then totaled for the total labor charge and also for the total burden charge, as shown by the red figures. The total for each department is entered on the O.D.S.O. transfer record (Figure 49) in the columns headed "From," with the exception that in addition to the labor amount there is entered also the total of the burden charge.

The total of all the departments to be charged by the originating department is found and entered on the O.D.S.O. transfer record of the originating department under the heading "To," showing the labor and the burden separately.

At the close of the month a journal entry is prepared in practically the same manner as in the case of the labor transfers as follows: The total of the "From" columns for each department, including both labor and burden, is the debit to the Burden or Expense account of the department shown at the head of the record. This applies equally to each department and the result is a debit to each burden or expense account involved in the plant.

The credit side of this original entry, however, is radically different from that in connection with the labor transfer. The total of all the labor under the heading "To" on all transfer sheets is found and combined into one figure, which is shown in the journal entry as a credit to the Other Department Standing Order Clearance account. This figure should be absolutely identical with the debit to O.D.S.O. Clearance account in the journal entry distributing the pay-roll for the same month. In this way the O.D.S.O. Clearance account is "cleared."

HOLDEN MANUFACTURING CO.
BOSTON, MASS.
O. D. S. O. TRANSFER RECORD
Dept.__________

Date	From			To			Date	From			To		
	Dept.	Labor	Burden	Dept.	Labor	Burden		Dept.	Labor	Burden	Dept.	Labor	Burden

Figue 49.—O.D.S.O. Transfer Record. (Size, 8½ x 11.)

The balance of the credit side of the journal entry, however, consists of a credit to the Work in Process Burden account of each department which has performed work for other departments, provided that there is a Work in Process Burden account for each department. If there is but one Work in Process Burden account for the entire plant, the credit naturally consists of only the one entry to this account.

This entry completes the transfer of the work done by the various departments for the other departments of the plant. The entry just completed will appear as follows:

Debit Side:

1. The Burden account of each department which shows entries under "From" on its O.D.S.O. transfer sheet.
2. The Expense account of each department as in the case of Burden account.

Credit Side:

1. The O.D.S.O. Clearance account for the grand total of all labor on O.D.S.O. transfer sheets.
2. The Work in Process Burden account of each department, which shows entries under "To" on its O.D.S.O. transfer sheet, or the Work on Process Burden account for the entire plant if there is no account for each department.

Final Filing of Both the Labor Transfer and O.D.S.O. Cards.—Each day, after the entries have been made on the labor transfer record and the O.D.S.O. record, the cards in the transaction are filed under the production or standing order numbers as shown on the cards. It will be noted that these order numbers are all for departments other than the department where the men who performed the work belong, but as the money value has been transferred from the originating department to the departments which received the benefit of the work, it is now possible to file the cards under the standing orders where they belong. As a matter of record, no further thought is to be given to these cards, excepting to foot them into the various burden and expense accounts wherever they are found as the control accounts have been made to conform to the details by the procedures just described.

It may be repeated that the journal entries effecting this transfer reduce the labor costs of the originating departments to the amounts actually used by themselves on their own standing orders, and increase the control accounts of all other departments by the amount of labor and burden involved in the work which was done for them by departments other than their own.

CHAPTER XX

EXPENSE AND BURDEN ACCOUNTS

Importance of Clear Understanding.—As the flow of cost procedure is approaching the stage of compiling the costs, it is important to understand clearly the meaning and use of expense accounts and burden accounts. While these two classes of accounts are very similar in construction and in their degree of use for managerial control purposes, their treatment from a cost accounting standpoint differs largely.

It may be urged, and with truth, that all cost other than the direct charges of material and labor is expense. Many years ago, however, the term "burden" was given to that expense which requires a method of allocation to the cost of product in ways other than by a direct charge (as in the case of labor or material, which are definitely measurable in respect to a given item of product). In other words, the direct cost was obliged to carry a *burden* or load of indirectly chargeable expense.

The term "overhead" in reality should be understood as applying to *all* cost other than that which may be directly allocated to the product. Therefore, overhead covers all such expense as service, office, sales and administrative expense and the various producing department burdens.

Admittedly, there is much disagreement as to the correct terminology to be used in respect to the various classes of accounts used in cost accounting; but at the same time it is desirable so far as possible to bring out clearly the nature of the account.

For this reason we will consider as a general rule that the indirect costs are treated in two main classes of accounts:

1. *Expense accounts,* which are, after compilation, distributed to the other expense accounts and to burden accounts.
2. *Burden accounts,* which are, after compilation, figured into the cost of the product, always being the indirect expense account of a producing department.

1. **Expense Accounts.**—Expense accounts as a class may themselves be subdivided into three classes:

(a) Expense accounts which are distributed both to other expense accounts and to burden accounts.
(b) Expense accounts which are distributed to burden accounts only.
(c) Expense accounts which do not at any time appear in the cost of the product as a manufacturing cost.

Each one of these subdivisions will now be explained:

(a) Expense accounts such as steam expense, electric power expense, teaming expense, and the like, are distributable both to other expense accounts and to burden accounts. For instance, if the electric power plant has steam engines, a steam charge is made from the steam expense. At the same time the steam plant is lighted by electricity and receives a charge for electric power. The teaming expense benefits the general stores expense to the extent of the amount of teaming it supplies to the storeroom.

The burden accounts also receive benefit from these same expense accounts for the steam, electric power, teaming, etc., received.

(b) Expense accounts such as General Superintendent's Office Expense, Cost Department Expense, Pay-Roll Department Expense, General Stores Expense, and the like, are usually distributed only to burden accounts. If the cost procedure was carried to the finest degree, it might be stated that all expense accounts as well as burden accounts should receive charges for supervision, accounting and other service. But this complication is of little value and its carrying out entails much extra work. It can, of course, be done if desired, but it is not nearly so necessary as in the cases of steam, electric power, etc., where the services performed are large and of great value.

(c) Expense accounts which do not appear at all in the manufacturing costs are such accounts as Administrative Expense and all the various Sales Expense accounts. Financial Expense, so called, including interest on loans and such costs as do not appear in manufacturing costs, is an item appearing only on the profit and loss statement.

The Administrative and Selling Costs may be treated in different ways, and a full explanation of the matter will be found in Chapters XXVI and XXVII.

The distribution of all expense accounts is on the basis of the benefits given in each individual case. Further details as to this procedure are explained in the following chapter.

2. **Burden Accounts.**—Burden accounts, let us remember, are those accounts which are the final resting place of all indirect manufacturing costs, and are figured into the cost of product by various methods.

Burden accounts may not always be called burden accounts in actual practice, largely for convenience. In some of these exceptions, there may be even a mixture of what might be regarded as direct and indirect costs. We, therefore, may regard burden accounts as falling into three classes:

(a) Burden accounts which are figured into the cost of the product on the basis of productive man effort, either on the basis of hours or the dollar value of these hours.

(b) Burden accounts which are figured into the cost of the product on the basis of productive machine effort, which is always by hours.

(c) Burden accounts which are figured into the cost of the product on the basis of the measure or weight of the product itself, which accounts are often termed simply "cost" accounts.

Each of these subdivisions may be explained as follows:

(a) Burden accounts which are figured into the cost of the product on the basis of man-effort, consist of cases where nothing in the department indicates the necessity of more careful or more closely defined treatment. For instance, an assembly department in a machine shop or *any* department in any industry where no worker employs equipment of greater value or expense of upkeep than another may operate with a single burden rate, preferably on the basis of the hours of work directly applied to the product.

In the case of the spinning room in a textile mill, the machine equipment is, of course, valuable; but if all workers are using the same class of equipment, machine rates are needless. The building room of a tire plant furnishes each tire builder with an expensive machine to use; but *all* the builders use such a machine and therefore the machine expense is common to all.

This type of burden account is equally valuable where the use of the equipment may be charged to the product by a machine rate. In such cases all machine upkeep is charged to machine burden accounts, and does not appear in the general burden account of the department. In this case not only the burden per hour would be used, but also the machine burden as described later.

(b) Burden accounts which are figured into the product on the basis of productive machine effort are of two kinds: First, where *all* the department burden is figured into the cost of product through the use of machine or cost center rates; second, where only the cost of the machine upkeep, power, depreciation and (if desired) interest is handled through the machine rate, the general department burden being handled through a man-hour rate.

The first case has been and still is popular, and in some

instances may be best. The second case is much more desirable in many cases. This matter will be fully discussed in a later chapter.

(c) Burden accounts which are figured into the cost of the product on the basis of the weight or measurement of the product itself are illustrated by the cost of melt in a foundry. Here there is little ground for designating any of the work in connection with melting iron as direct labor. Therefore, all labor cost, combined with the material used other than the actual iron melted becomes a burden *per pound* of iron melted. In this case, the term "burden" may not be used, this cost being usually known as "Cost to Melt" or "Conversion Cost." This same principle applies to open hearth steel furnaces, the washing of rubber in a rubber plant, kiln drying of lumber and other cases.

Expense and Burden Accounts as Control and Aids.— As has been stated previously, if all that was desired should be to *account* for money, there would be no need of paying so much attention to the details of expense and burden accounts. But if there are violent fluctuations in cost, how can one tell why it happened and how we can stop it without detailed knowledge as to what makes up the total expense or burden and how each item thereof compares month by month?

Furthermore, the correct distribution of each expense account on the basis of benefits given, and the proper allocation of burden accounts have a vital bearing on the accuracy and reliability of the final costs. For these reasons this chapter was designed to impress on the reader the necessity for thoroughly understanding expense and burden accounts before attempting to master the details of their treatment.

CHAPTER XXI

DISTRIBUTION OF EXPENSE ACCOUNTS

Discussion of Expense Accounts.—In the history of cost accounting there has been a great divergence of both opinion and practice regarding the distribution of certain originating expenses, and a good deal of inaccuracy. When two different methods are used for identically the same distribution, one must be right and one must be wrong. The reader's attention is directed to certain underlying arguments which may be applied to the problem of distributing initial expenses.

Probably because the majority of manufacturing institutions, at least up to recently, distributed their indirect cost on the basis of direct-labor cost, a misconception arose as to the distribution of certain expenses of a business other than those of the actual operating department—whose burden cost, of course, should be accurately found.

Some of the expenses referred to will be found in any plant of average size. For instance, a plant may have a general superintendent in whose office will be an assistant general superintendent, two or three stenographers, and half a dozen clerks for various general purpose work. The plant may have also a cost department of, say, 5 to 20 people who are keeping the costs, both direct and indirect, of the entire plant. In addition there will probably be a pay-roll department employing 5 or more persons who compile the pay-rolls for the entire plant.

At the same time there may also be an engineering department, consisting of the chief engineer, two or three clerks and a half dozen draftsmen. In addition there also may be a well-organized inspection department with 15 employees who devote practically all their time to inspecting the product.

In the past, all of this expense has usually been thrown into one general account. That is still the practice in many plants. In occasional cases there might be an account for each division as specified above, but the procedure of distributing the expense to the operating burden accounts would be the same. That procedure in the majority of cases consisted of prorating this general expense to the operating burdens on the basis of the direct-labor cost or the direct-labor hours of each department—a method which can be proved to be entirely inaccurate and unreasonable. It is, of course, easy and simple, but no more so than the correct way.

Probably the only reason that could be urged for this method of distribution is the mental effect of the fact that *after* the expense has reached the operating burdens it is applied in the cost sheets on the direct-labor cost or the direct-labor hour. The reasoning here involved, however, is entirely wrong. The general superintendent's office, the cost department, the pay-roll department, and all other such general departments, are concerned exactly as much with the indirect labor as with the direct. It takes just as much, if not more effort on the part of the general superintendent to regulate the indirect as the direct workers. Likewise, it is just as much work to account for the wages and cost of the indirect workers as for the direct workers. Therefore, the splitting up of this expense among the operating burdens on the basis of direct-labor cost or hours alone is entirely wrong. Department A, for example, may require 80 direct workers with only 20 indirect workers. Department B may be just the reverse, namely, a department in which the direct workers required are only 20 as against 80 indirect. A divergence as wide as that has been known to exist in many plants.

If these general expense accounts were distributed on the basis of the direct labor alone, department A would be charged four times as much for the general expense as would department B, and yet each department had the same number of men, all of whom had to be supervised and watched over by the general superintendent, accounted for by the pay-roll department, the cost kept by the cost department, and so on through whatever divisions are in like relation.

It should be quite evident, therefore, that the proper basis of distribution of those expense accounts should be on the basis of the *total* labor hours or *total* labor cost of each department.

In the case of the engineering department, however, there is an entirely different condition. The distribution of the engineering department expense should be on the basis of the time spent by the department in connection with work for other departments. For instance, if a new machine is being designed for one of the production departments, the time of engineering and drafting, plus its proportion of the clerical and supplies expense of the engineering department, should be charged to the department receiving the benefit. It will be noted that this distribution differs entirely from that of the general departments previously described.

The distribution of the inspection department is still different. In this case the inspectors are following the product. This immediately implies *direct* labor as the basis for distribution. Therefore, the total inspection expense may very properly be distributed on the basis of the direct-labor hours of the departments whose work is inspected.

This brings out very forcibly the fact brought out in other chapters, that too much attention cannot be given to the problem of properly departmentalizing the indirect operations whereby an absolutely and perfectly correct distribution of all these expenses may be made to the various burden accounts.

The problem connected with what might be called "super expense" accounts is entirely different from that involved in the burden accounts which are used directly in figuring the productive costs. (See Chapter XXIII.)

For this reason this chapter is set aside for descriptions of a few of the expense accounts, set forth in sufficient detail to illustrate what must be done, and to give enough clues as to the proper procedure to enable anyone to work out individual problems in his own plant.

Trucking Expense.—The trucking expense of a company is made up of charges for labor, the cost of gasoline, oil, etc., or of horses, the cost of repairs of the truck equipment and of the building which houses them, together with depreciation and other fixed charges which may apply.

It is easier to get the total cost than to distribute it and to establish a basic unit whereby the efficiency with which the trucking is handled may be checked. In many institutions the nature of the trucking is such that a tonnage basis is best. This applies particularly to some plants in large cities where all material is trucked to the plant, and the finished product away from the plant.

In other plants it is better to work on the basis of the trucking hour, that is, the actual number of hours of trucking performed. If this plan is followed, the trucks should be divided into classes, and the trucking hours found for each class. The point to be brought out, however, is that some cost basis should be established, both to show the effectiveness of work performed and also to distribute properly the trucking expense to the departments affected.

Steam Expense.—This particular expense is quite difficult to control on the basis of unit of performance, unless a company goes to the expense of installing flow meters in order to know not only what is produced, but how the steam produced is distributed among the various departments. When steam is a very large cost, however, some steps should be taken to provide a basis for knowing production and distribution, even to the extent of installing flow meters to check the quantities. If the total steam produced is accurately known, the control feature of the steam cost will be effective. Without flow meters, the distribution of steam cost to departments which use the cost must be estimated by the engineering department on the basis of the equipment involved, including heating apparatus.

Electric Power.—Plants which produce their own power naturally measure the total amount of power produced, as it is of far greater importance to know this figure in the matter of generating electricity than in the case of steam. In up-to-date plants the consumption of power by each department is metered. In such cases, the distribution is easy and accurate, and the control of efficiency is assured.

In plants without metered consumption, it is necessary to go through the various departments and count the number of lamps, motors, etc., listing their rated consumption. But at best this is inaccurate, as the length of time each unit will consume power is unknown. A portable recording meter may be used to good advantage by running tests covering a week or more for each department.

Compressed Air.—The increased use of compressed air in connection with the operation of machines affords possibilities of enormous wastes unless some steps are taken to control its production and consumption. Steam leaks can be seen—like water leaks. Air, however, can leak without any check whatever. Very large sums of money may be wasted without anything to indicate that the air is leaking at perhaps every joint in the line.

Many plants have used compressed air with such prodigal abandon that the compressed air expense amounts to large figures before it is realized. For this reason it is urged that those responsible for the costs use every endeavor to check up the consumption and use of this commodity in those plants where it has become of general use.

Here, as in the case of steam, the use of meters is best. The next best plan is for the engineering department to estimate the consumption of each department on the basis of its equipment.

Internal Transportation.—In the studies of cost reduction, it has been found by many plants to be of advantage to concentrate truckers and material handlers in a central gang. In such a case, the obvious basis of distribution is on the direct hours of the production department served, as rarely do the units of material afford a proper basis.

Restaurant.—Many companies maintain a restaurant for the convenience of employees. Even if some charge is made for meals it is rarely that the restaurant runs even. In cases of loss, it is equitable to distribute the loss on the basis of the total employees or hours, both direct and indirect, of all the departments of the plant, as the restaurant is operated for the convenience of all.

Rent.—In those plants operating on a rental basis a number of things have to be taken into consideration in prorating the rent to the various departments. The square-foot basis is not sufficient, as for instance, in a foundry the building may be high and equal to four or five floors of the machine-shop section of the same plant. In fact, no specified rule can be laid down for the distribution of rent, since the proportionate value of the space used by the various departments is a matter of judgment. It is suggested, however, that when a company rents a plant they request from the owners a detailed valuation of the various buildings. This would be of assistance in prorating the rental as between a foundry building, machine shop, or forge shop. The latter would be higher than a machine shop, but possibly not as high as a foundry.

Unfortunately, the cubic foot basis does not entirely solve the problem, as naturally a foundry with a high roof does not cost as much as an equivalent height of building with three stories. On the other hand, it is fairly easy to take these things into consideration and prorate to the various departments the value of the space which they use. Without doubt, aside from buildings, such as foundries, forge shops, etc., it is perfectly allowable to use the square foot arrangement for the normal shop of one floor in height.

Taxes.—In cases where plants are owned by the operators the distribution of taxes is somewhat along the same lines as rent, and is so closely allied that the comments made under Rent may very well apply to this heading, as far as buildings are concerned. Taxes on personal property should be distributed on the basis of the value of the equipment involved in the complement of each operating department.

Depreciation.—In a large measure the principles governing the distribution of depreciation, so far as buildings and plant facilities are concerned, are somewhat similar to the principles involved in distributing rent and taxes. The distribution of depreciation, however, is a far more important matter in that the largest consideration of depreciation is centered in the equipment used by each department, which in many cases may be very expensive.

Yet in a plant which has its appraisal of buildings and particularly of machine equipment, the problem is not difficult, as it then becomes a matter of fixing the depreciation on each unit and assembling therefrom the total depreciation for the department. This depreciation will, of course, be divided between buildings and equipment as the principles involved in each are separate.

Many pieces of equipment will have perhaps a depreciation of 25% because of their special nature, either as to delicacy of construction or because they quickly become obsolete. Other pieces of equipment may be subject to a depreciation of only 5%, as in the case of standard lathes and other machine tools which, with proper care, will be as good—as regards design—twenty years from now as at present.

The depreciation of buildings, therefore, should be on the basis of value of building used by each department, and depreciation on machine tools and equipment on the basis of the actual circumstances as stated above.

In all cases it is best to use what is called the "straight-line" method for recording depreciation—namely, a regular amount per month rather than a diminishing charge.

Fire Insurance.—This item should be distributed on the basis of the valuations made for insurance purposes. This basis is largely parallel to that which is used for depreciation of buildings and equipment. This would apply particularly in instances where the insurance rate is high.

In cases where plants are running under factory mutuals and have a very low rate of insurance, it sometimes does not pay to try to distribute the fire insurance on the basis of equipment, because of the fact that the insurance is a blanket proposition and the total expense for such insurance each year is very small indeed. In many cases of this sort the amount is so small that the fire insurance is included in a general expense account and distributed with other items on the basis of total labor. It should be understood, however, that this is only in cases where the insurance cost is very small.

Liability and Compensation Insurance.—Unlike any other kind of insurance, liability and compensation insurance depends entirely on the amount of pay-roll paid out and also upon the classes of labor, as specified by the insurance policy. In this instance therefore—particularly inasmuch as this very distribution must be made for the auditor of the insurance company—the most simple and accurate method is to classify the pay-rolls of each department each month as specified by the insurance policy and ascertain the actual insurance which will have to be paid for each department.

With this classification, accurate figures of liability and compensation insurance expense can be obtained. It will also save a tremendous amount of work in classifying the pay-rolls at the end of the year, in order to satisfy the requirements for premium payment.

Telephone.—In most large institutions the telephone service involves a great deal of equipment, such as switchboards, extension instruments, special gongs, and other appliances. It has been found best to take all regular monthly charges for switchboard rental, extensions, etc., into one controlling account.

This account is distributed monthly through the journal as follows: The total cost of the telephone expense for switchboard, extensions, trunk lines, etc., is divided by the number of instruments actually connected with the board in the plant in order to establish a flat rate per instrument, including all regular monthly expenses. To determine the amount to be charged to each department the rate should be multiplied by the number of phones used by the department.

Long-distance and toll charges should not be included in this computation but should be charged to the departments for whose benefit the calls were made. Such calls affect principally the sales department and the purchasing department.

Engineering Department.—In addition to what was said at the beginning of this chapter it may be said that many problems arise in properly distributing the expense of a drafting department. For instance, owing to the varied nature of its work, the draftsmen prepare skeletons or drawings for estimates for the sales department, new equipment in the plant, repair parts for the plant, new building layouts, etc.

All that can be said within the space allotted here is that a method of time reporting should be installed in the drafting room along the lines of the method used in a producing department. In other words, job numbers should be assigned to special work done by the draftsmen, and standing order numbers to regular routine work.

Those expenses of the department of a general nature which make up the overhead can be charged to the sales department, to new equipment, and all other points, on the basis of the time reported as shown on the records of work performed by the draftsmen.

Stores Expense Accounts.—In dealing with the various stores expense accounts, it may be found that one stores item may be entirely for the benefit of one particular department, another for the benefit of two departments, and another for the benefit of many departments. This must be taken into consideration when working up a distribution of the expense accounts of the various stores and of the general stores.

For instance, if it is thought best to have a complete store unit for some particular department, this expense naturally should be charged to that department. At the same time this department may also share in the expense of a general storeroom as it is served by the general as well as its own storeroom.

About the only basis for distributing stores charges is on the basis of total number of men in the departments served. This has exceptions in some plants where special storing facilities are provided for very valuable and special goods or for specially hazardous articles. The man basis, however, is as a usual thing, about the only practical one to use.

In some cases it is possible and best to distribute stores expense with purchasing and receiving on a percentage basis on material value.

General Expenses.—It is urged that the title "General Expenses" be avoided and that the general expenses of the plant be split up into segregated expense accounts, such as Purchasing Department, Pay-roll Department, Cost Department, Statistical Department, General Superintendent's Office, Industrial Relations, Dining-Room Expense, House Publication Expense, and any other accounts which will quickly answer the question as to where the money in the general expense has gone.

It has been found best, as a general rule, to distribute all of the expense accounts just enumerated to the various operating burden accounts on the basis of the total number of men, the total labor hours, or the total labor value for each department.

CHAPTER XXII

DEPARTMENTAL BURDEN RATES AND THEIR APPLICATION

Necessity for Intelligent Burden Distribution.—Cost accounting has developed in the last few years to a point where it is quite generally acknowledged that departmental burdens are a necessity, not only for the accurate accounting of cost, but also for the greater necessity of managerial control. The rapid development of the use of budgetary control is an indication of the desire on the part of management not only to establish control of expenditures, but beyond this, to tie in more closely the thought and interest of all the heads of departments so that they may feel their responsibility more keenly and be in a far better position to carry out this responsibility.

The compilation of a burden cost account with no basis for comparison of periods or for application to the cost of the product is obviously wasted effort. There must be a basis on which the periodical costs can be compared, and on which the burden may be applied to the final cost of the product. Before taking up the modern practice in respect to burden rates, a brief survey of the more important steps in the evolution of burden (or overhead as it is often called) distribution will be made.

Evolution of Burden Distribution—Fixed Percentage Method.—What was probably the first method of distributing burden—known as the fixed percentage method—was arbitrary and for that reason inaccurate. Under this plan manufacturing cost was ascertained by simply adding, usually to the prime cost (direct labor and material), a fixed percentage to cover manufacturing burden or overhead, as it was then called. To manufacturing cost was added another fixed percentage to cover selling and administrative burden. The addition to this cost figure of further percentages to represent profit, furnished the figures employed for the arbitrary fixing of selling prices.

Prices so fixed were satisfactory because competition was not so keen as it is today, because profits thus figured were deemed sufficiently accurate, and because income tax laws had not literally forced manufacturers to realize the need of more accurate costs. Today the situation has changed and slipshod methods of cost accounting are not found in progressive plants. But the evolution of accurate burden distribution has been gradual.

Blanket Rate Method.—The next step after the fixed percentage method was the use of blanket rates. This method increased the accuracy of burden incidence. At the beginning of each fiscal period, blanket rates were calculated for the period, based on total direct-labor costs or total direct-labor hours for the *whole plant* during a past period. Material costs, prime costs, and machine hours were also used, occasionally, as burden bases. The blanket burden rates for each factory was calculated by dividing either the total direct-labor costs or total direct-labor hours on all jobs into the total manufacturing burden or overhead. No separation of burden was made by departments, and only in rare cases was any itemized cost of this general overhead maintained. It was a "front office" secret—a closed book to the rank and file of the organization.

This blanket rate was then applied to either the direct-labor cost or direct-labor hours of each individual job according to the burden basis selected, in order to ascertain the burden cost of the job. If in a given case the total manufacturing burden and total direct labor costs were $50,000 and $100,000 respectively, the blanket rate of burden ratio would be 50%. This rate would be applied during the ensuing period to the labor cost of each job. Suppose a job had the following prime cost: Direct material $1,000; direct labor $3,000. Its burden cost would have been $1,500 ($3,000 x .50). The sum of this burden cost ($1,500) and prime cost ($4,000) gave the manufacturing cost of the job ($5,500).

Both fixed percentages and blanket rates were open to serious objection. Neither method considered differences among productive departments with respect to equipment, labor hours, machine hours, labor costs, etc., which caused burden to vary for each department. Both methods ignored the fact that departments were the only natural units for the calculation and application of burden, and nothing whatever was considered in respect to the necessity for costs to be used for control and cost reduction purposes. Fixed percentages and blanket rates have been very largely supplanted by departmental burden rates.

Departmental Burden Rate Method.—The next step in the evolution of burden distribution was the use of departmental burden rates. This method is generally regarded today as the best method of applying burden to product. The steps involved in the calculation and application of departmental burden rates and in the preparation of expense and burden statements may be summarized as follows:

1. Adequate organization of all operations into proper departments or "cost centers" as they are sometimes referred to. (See Chapter III.)
2. The provision of a proper code of standing orders for each department. (See Chapter X.)
3. The provision of proper means to secure accurate allocation of time and material to the standing orders. (See Chapters XIII and XVIII.)
4. The compilation of burden accounts through use of the procedures which are explained in this volume.
5. The selection of the proper bases on which to compute the burden rates.

6. The determining of the normal capacity for each department.
7. The predetermination of the standard departmental burden rates on the basis of normal capacity.
8. The application of burden to the cost of product at standard rates, such detailed charges appearing on the actual product cost sheets.
9. The disposition of the under- or over-absorbed burden in the profit and loss account, this being the difference between the actual burden and amount of burden applied to orders at the standard rates.
10. The revision of the standard departmental burden rates when current conditions so demand.

Steps 1 to 4 inclusive are dealt with in great detail in other chapters. Steps 5 to 10 inclusive will now be explained:

5. The Selection of Proper Burden Bases.—The selection of the proper bases on which to compute the burden rate for each department requires a careful analysis of the nature of the work performed by each department, together with a consideration of the various methods or bases to be used in the distribution of burden.

The general theory underlying the calculation of departmental burden rates is that a proportional relationship exists between the burden of each department and some production basis. The major problem, therefore, is to select the basis best suited to existing conditions. The same basis is not necessarily used for all departments or for all the burden in any one department. The most satisfactory bases for the calculation of departmental burden rates are:

(a) Direct-labor hours
(b) Direct-labor cost
(c) Machine hours
(d) Weight or measurement of product

Other bases, such as prime cost, sold-hour plan, overhead day, and list percentage plan, are either obsolete or of limited use.

The relative value of these four bases will be discussed in Chapter XXIII. The pages here following describe in detail how they are used.

(a) *Direct-Labor Hours Basis.* The direct-labor hours method is somewhat similar to the direct-labor cost method, except for the fact that the hours of labor applied become the basis for the application of the burden, rather than the amount paid for the hours. When this method is used, time must be carefully kept on all operations, no matter what the basis of payment may be, and an absolute total of all direct hours applied on productive orders must be found and used in computing the rate per hour of the burden of the department. The amount of burden to be applied to each order will be the number of direct-labor hours charged to the order, multiplied by the standard rate per hour as predetermined for use in each department, the monthly burden statements showing how the actual rate per hour compares with the standard rate per hour.

(b) *Direct-Labor Cost Basis.* Under the direct-labor cost basis, burden is applied to the product by means of a percentage on the direct-labor cost. This is done as follows: The total cost of labor applied to all productive work is assembled. At the same time the total burden for the department is assembled. The latter figure divided by the former gives the percentage of burden to be applied to each individual order on the basis of the direct-labor cost which is known. As in the case of the direct hour basis, a standard percentage is used for costing purposes, which standard rate is checked each month with the actual as shown by the burden statements.

(c) *Machine-Hour Basis.* The method of using machine hours as the basis for application of burden cost has been developed in many cases into such a complicated procedure, that the effect has been detrimental to the progress of the science of cost-keeping.

The machine-hour method is based on the theory that a portion of manufacturing burden should be applied to the work performed, on the basis of the time which each unit of production requires of the machines which are necessary to produce the goods. As to the justice of this contention there can be no question, and in the majority of manufacturing institutions this truth must be taken into account if the costs found are to be at all correct, and are to be regarded as safe for actual use.

On the other hand, to take all the manufacturing burden of the department into consideration on the basis of distribution through machine hours is not only erroneous, but is productive of an enormous amount of detail which succeeds only in beclouding the cost records. Supervision, timekeeping, transportation of material around the shop, inspection, and many more of the items which make up a regular manufacturing burden, have really no relation whatever to the machine-hour basis. It would seem, therefore, to be going too far from the lines of sensible procedure to try to establish items in the machine cost which really have no purpose therein.

As a usual thing the items which are really involved in a machine rate are:

1. Depreciation on the machine unit.
2. Maintenance of the machine unit.
3. Power to operate the unit.
4. Interest on the machine unit when desired.

Some other items may be included, such as insurance, etc., but these other items are usually so small that they really have no bearing on the eventual result.

It is advocated, therefore, that the machine-hour rates be confined to the items which really have a large bearing on the additional cost to be charged against production for the use of the machine units involved, and that the balance of the burden be handled through the use of the productive-hour rate as a general burden charge for the department. Admittedly this means the use of two rates in many cases; but the greater degree of accuracy and especially the greater degree of managerial control which results fully justifies the use of the two rates. (See Chapter XXXVII for more detailed discussion of machine rates.)

The technique of determining a machine rate is not difficult; it is simply a matter of determining at the start the amounts to be allowed for proper depreciation, maintenance, power and interest if used, and then dividing this by, say, 80% of the total possible hours to establish the predetermined rate. Each month thereafter the actual depreciation, maintenance, power and interest will be known, and this should be divided by the hours which the machines actually run to arrive at a regular monthly figure as to the cost per hour for operating the machine. The actual and standard figures will be compared monthly which will furnish a constant check on the standard rate being used.

(d) *Weight or Measurement of Product Basis.* In Chapter V mention was made of the melting or conversion cost of the metal in a foundry as an example of a class of costs which are in reality a kind of burden. The reason for classing this as a burden cost is that the metal at its rate per pound to melt is figured *directly* into the cost of the product.

Another example of such a cost is the annealing or case hardening of metals. In a malleable plant where the castings are packed into the annealing furnace either in boxes or otherwise, the cost of the labor of packing is the smallest part of the cost; neither can it in any way be attached to any individual items of product. It is necessary, therefore, to compute this cost on the pound basis of castings annealed.

Whenever there are similar circumstances, where the cost

of the product must be figured on the volume produced, and where this cost appears directly in the cost of the product, the weight or measurement basis is indicated for use.

In all such cases, the principle of establishing a standard rate applies with all the bases, and the actual for each cost period will be compared with the standard.

6. The Determination of Normal Capacity.—At the International Conference of the National Association of Cost Accountants in 1921, a representative group of cost men who had discussed the meaning of "normal capacity" agreed on the following definition of what is meant by normal capacity:

"The normal capacity basis is the total possible time (meaning any kind of work, machine or other) *less* a reasonable allowance for break-downs, repairs, inefficiency, reasonable lack of operators and all other regular normal delays outside of lack of orders to run on." [1]

To arrive at the percentage of normal capacity, therefore, the full capacity of a department will first be figured. The foreman of the department is best fitted to set this figure. Let us use for an illustration the sewing machine department of a garment plant. There are 100 machines in all. Fifteen of these machines are "standby" machines held in reserve to accommodate operators from machines that break down. Therefore the maximum capacity is 85 operators, which, at 8 hours per day gives an absolute maximum capacity in hours of 680 hours per day, or for 300 working days in the year a total maximum yearly capacity of 204,000 hours.

The plant is located in a city where it is difficult to get operators, and this has been found to affect the actual capacity to quite an extent. The same scarcity of help means that the training time for the new operators is also a considerable factor. As 15 standby machines are provided, the breakdown and repair factor is practically eliminated.

[1] Year Book of National Association of Cost Accountants, 1921.

Considering past records, the present labor supply and all other factors, it seems impossible to expect better than 75% continuous operation of the maximum capacity, even on the assumption of having plenty of orders. Therefore, 75% of 204,000 hours, or 153,000 hours, will be the normal capacity of this department.

This principle applied to every department will furnish the normal capacities which become one of the factors in arriving at the standard or predetermined rates used in connection with all burden accounts.

If dollar value is to be used as the burden basis, multiply the hours by the average rate per hour for total dollar labor value.

7. The Predetermination of Standard Burden Rates.—Having explained the method of arriving at normal capacity, the next step in the predetermining of standard burden rates is the adjusting of the actual burden to a normal basis.

The ideal situation is to be able to have actual burden costs for exactly normal speeds of operation. Should this ever happen, it would be a perfectly simple thing to divide the burden on the normal basis for a year by the normal hours. The ideal, however, is never found, and it is necessary to examine the burden figures for various months and determine as nearly as possible what the burden would be if exactly normal conditions prevailed.

To illustrate: Let us assume that the supervision of the department remains the same as in the case of the burden figures we are adjusting. As production averages but 60% of normal in the burden cost figures being adjusted, the foreman and cost man decide that normal capacity would increase the inspection cost by 20%; would make no change in the timekeeping cost; would increase the cost of labor in handling material by 30%; of cleaning and sweeping 10%, and so on through all the items including repairs and supplies.

The fixed charges apportioned from the reserves would remain the same, except that liability insurance increases with the labor cost, and the general plant charges would slightly increase with the higher speed of operation.

In this manner, the available burden figures are adjusted to normal capacity; in fact this is also a very fair illustration of budgeting.

When the burden has been thus adjusted to the normal speed of operation, all that remains is to divide the normal burden for the year by the normal capacity in hours if an hourly rate is to be used, or by the total direct labor value if the direct labor cost basis is to be used.

This method of predetermining the standard rate of burden is similar in all cases, whether for general departmental burdens, machine rates or on product costs by weight or measure.

8. **Application of Burdens to Cost of Product.**—The cost sheets for products of all kinds are always arranged for entry of the direct labor, usually both hours and value, and machine hours if any machine rates are used.

To apply the burden cost to the product, the standard per direct-labor hour, the standard percentage of the direct labor, the standard rate per machine hour or the standard cost per weight of material—whatever the method used, is entered on the cost sheet and extended.

9. **Over- and Under-Absorbed Burden.**—It is obvious that when standard rates based on normal capacity are used for departmental burdens, it would be pure coincidence if a department ever ran exactly at normal. If a plant became very busy, so that operators worked overtime, and the maximum capacity was reached, the use of the standard normal burden in cost figuring would charge to the product a quantity of burden larger than the actual. The reverse would occur when-

ever the department operated at less than normal capacity. The credits to burden to balance the debits to product cost at standard rates are regarded as the "absorption" of burden. Therefore, when the plant runs at full speed, the actual burden is "over-absorbed," and when the plant runs at a slower speed than normal, the burden is "under-absorbed."

It may be contended that this feature of cost accounting is not in keeping with *actual* or *accurate* costing. But nevertheless from a practical standpoint it is the only possible way to figure costs. A few reasons for the use of standard rates of burden are:

(a) It is the only way to level erratic burden costs to a usable mean.
(b) It recognizes the fact that *abnormal* running cannot be used as a basis for selling products.
(c) It is the only method which permits intelligent estimating of new work and prompt costing of orders.

(a) *Levelling Erratic Burden Costs.* It is impossible for the actual burden costs to run alike month after month even though the flow of production is constant. This should be very clear when it is remembered that every manufacturing plant chooses dull periods, or at least a temporary slack period, for overhauling equipment. Obviously, therefore, the repair costs are actually *higher* in dull or slack times. This in itself would be a sufficient argument against the actual burden for any one month as the cost or burden to be added to the direct labor basis for the same month?

In any steel industry using open hearth furnaces, major repairs to each furnace involving heavy expense are made at about three month intervals. This consists of replacing all the brick work above the checkers. In addition, at longer intervals, perhaps once a year or once in two years, the checkers which are in the lower part of the furnace must be replaced.

Manifestly, no one month's cost can be used in this case. The same situation exists in greater or less degree with many of the items which make up the burden cost. Obviously, the major repairs to open hearth furnaces cannot be handled otherwise than through a monthly rate which considers its pro rata share of such repairs. Therefore, the standard rate is designed to represent the *over all* conditions; and in the months where no major repairs or other expense occurs, there naturally will be an "over-absorbed" balance. But when the months arrive when the major repairs take place, the over-absorbed balance is quickly dissipated or perhaps transformed to an "under-absorbed" balance.

In some cases a cycle of two, three or even five years must be considered, particularly where major repair items occur only at such intervals. This can, however, be more safely handled by reducing such major repairs to a monthly charge of a special depreciation, creating a reserve for major repairs. When such repairs are actually made, they should be charged to this reserve.

(b) There has been much controversy as to the use of normal capacity as the basis of standard burden rates. Probably the best argument for its use is the fact that an *abnormal* basis is most certainly out of the question, as no business could be obtained if prices should be based on slack running costs, and vice versa prices would be too low when running at high speed.

This point is best understood by an illustration showing various conditions:

Maximum Capacity	10,000 hours
Normal Capacity at 80%	8,000 hours
Burden at Normal Capacity	$6,400

Assume that the plant runs at different speeds of operation with the following results:

% of Normal	Hours	Burden	Actual Rate per Hr.
125	10,000	$7,000.00	$ .70
100	8,000	6,400.00	.80
50	4,000	4,000.00	1.00
25	2,000	2,500.00	1.25
0	......	1,000.00	?

It must be remembered that volume of business is dependent not only on economic or trade conditions but also on the efficiency of the selling organization. What chance of securing business against a competitor who is running at normal or near it has the sales department of this company if the selling prices were figured on the basis of 50% of normal running? The following table shows what would result from using the popular but somewhat doubtful method of adding straight percentage for administrative and selling, and 10% for profit:

COST OF AN ARTICLE

% of Normal	Material Cost	Direct Labor Cost		Actual Burden	Total Mfg. Cost	20% Admin. and Selling	Total Cost	Selling Price at 10% Profit
		Hrs.	Cost					
125	$20.00	40	$32 00	$28 00	$ 80 00	$16 00	$ 96 00	$105 60
100	20.00	40	32 00	32 00	84.00	16.80	100 80	110.88
50	20.00	40	32.00	40.00	92.00	18 40	110 40	121.44
25	20.00	40	32 00	50 00	102 00	20 40	122.40	134 64

Any company at any time may become the victim of inefficient selling. Ordinarily, in normal times, a company would sell this article at $110.88. The selling department slips back, and the plant is forced to operate at 50% of normal. Under these circumstances can the company hope to get $121.44 for the same article? Obviously not; and any such attempt would close the doors of the plant.

Neither can the company hope or expect the customers to pay for idle capacity in dull times. Why should they?

By proving the fact that costs for *abnormal* running *cannot* be used, it should be evident that a standard rate of burden based on normal capacity must necessarily be used in figuring product costs.

(c) *Standard Rates Permit Accurate Estimating.* From the foregoing it will be clear that under no circumstances could the estimating of new work be accomplished on any other than the basis of a standard rate based on normal production. Certainly, the future must be considered as holding possibilities of business on which to operate; and there can be no doubt that the only safe premise on which to base calculations is the normal capacity of the plant.

The costing of current orders could not be accomplished in any reasonable time unless a standard burden rate is used. To wait for actual burdens for each month would not only project the costing of orders far from their time of completion, delaying the preparation of the monthly statements in like proportion, but the final costs when secured would be so erratic that useful comparison would be impossible.

Finally, when product is in process for months the accounting for the actual burden for each month on the exact direct labor or machine effort for each month would entail a volume of work which would be prohibitive. And as already proved, the costs would be entirely worthless when finally completed.

By the use of standard rates of burden based on normal capacity, orders may be costed immediately on completion; correct work in process accounts may be maintained, and the under- and over-absorbed burden balances will provide a means of knowing just how the standards, and the business as a whole are progressing.

10. Revision of Standard Burden Rates.—The actual burdens for each month are known in detail. The productive effort for each month, its relation to normal, and the balances of over- and under-absorbed burdens are also known. Constant watchfulness is necessary to detect when a standard rate is in need of revision. When the accumulated actual burdens have developed conditions which are out of alignment with normal, the standard should be changed, the work in process burden accounts adjusted to the new rate, and the new rate put into use for all estimating and costing purposes.

Burden and Burden Credit Ledger Accounts.—In Chapter VI the use of burden control accounts was explained. It was made clear that for each departmental burden a corresponding control account was maintained in the general ledger.

To these accounts are debited all charges from any source which affect the burdens. No credits, however, should go to those accounts, except for correction or adjustment of debits which may be in error.

Instead, there is a "credit" account corresponding with each burden account. For instance, if there should be a Spinning Room Burden account, there will also be a Spinning Room Burden Credit account. The burden credit accounts receive no debits except for correction or adjustment of errors as in the case of the credits to the burden accounts.

At the end of the year when the books are closed, each of these accounts will be entirely closed by journal entries transferring them to profit and loss. During the year the balances will be used in making up the statements but no active journal entries will be made. The reason for this method of handling burden controls is to permit the use of the monthly and accumulated balances to date in the preparation of burden statements. An example of each account as shown below should make this clear.

In May the total debits to the burden account amounted to $2,600 of which $100 were in error as per the adjustment entry. The detailed burden account will balance with this figure, and will show just how this money was spent.

After adjusting an error in the journal entry crediting the Burden Credit account for May, the net credit to this account

BURDEN ACCOUNT

DEBIT	CREDIT
Total debits for May from all sources..................$2,600 00	Adjustment of an item found to be charged by error in May..$100.00
2,500.00	
Total debits for June....... 3,000.00	
5,500.00	
Total debits for July........ 3,200.00	Adjustments for July......... 85.00
8,615.00	

BURDEN CREDIT ACCOUNT

DEBIT	CREDIT
Adjustment for May when part of another department was included in error.....$2,200.00	Transferred to Work in Process Burden on basis of standard rate direct hours for month of May....... $4,800.00
	2,600.00
	Transferred to Work in Process Burden for June..... 2,900.00
	5,500.00
	Transferred to Work in Process Burden for July..... 3,000.00
	8,500.00

is $2,600. This credit is for the amount of burden at the *standard rate* on the actual direct hours applied to product during the month. For instance, the pay-roll distribution shows 3,250 direct hours. The standard rate being 80 cents per hour, the actual amount of applied burden is therefore 3,250 hours x 80 cents or $2,600. This is credited to the Burden Credit account and debited to Work in Process Burden account, the nature of which is explained under the next heading. This same procedure follows for June and July.

So as a result not only the amount for the month for each account is known, but so also is the accumulated total to date as shown by the small figures. Both of these figures are used for the control of burden statements, as on these statements are shown the burden for the current month, the credits by transfer to Work in Process Burden, and also the total burden and credits to date for the year. It is obvious that this procedure furnished the check or control for the statements.

It will also be noted that the difference between the burden and the Burden Credit account balances for both month and year to date gives the exact amount of over- and under-absorbed burden. This must check with the same balance shown on the detailed burden statements. In May there was an over-absorbed balance of $100, meaning that the credits to the Burden Credit account exceeded the actual burden cost for the month. In June the credit under-absorbed the actual by $100, there being no balance between the accounts to date. In July the credits were $115 less than actual, which produced an under-absorbed balance both for the month and for the year to date.

Work in Process Burden Accounts.—The debit side of the entry crediting the burden credit account always debits a work in process burden account. The work in process burden may be cared for by an account for each department or by one Work in Process Burden account for the entire plant. In perhaps the majority of cases only a single account of this sort is used. This account represents the inventory of burden on orders in process of production. It is the amount of burden which the company is entitled to inventory, the balance of over- and under-absorbed burden being treated each month and at the close of the year as a profit or loss.

Whenever a change in a standard rate of burden is made, it is necessary to find from the work in process records the amount of direct labor expended by the department whose rate is to be changed on the uncompleted orders. A journal entry should be made correcting the work in process burden to the new rate, the other side of the entry being to the Burden Credit account. To illustrate, a rate of 80 cents per hour is to be changed to $1 per hour. The uncompleted orders show 3,000 hours of work by this department uncosted. It is known that the Work in Process Burden account holds a balance of 3,000 x 80 cents, or $2,400. The new rate of $1 would bring this balance to 3,000 x $1, or $3,000. A journal entry is necessary, debiting work in process burden with the difference of $600, crediting the Burden Credit account. If this were not done, and the orders were costed at $1 per hour when the Work in Process Burden account had been built up on the basis of 80 cents per hour, it is obvious that the inventory account of work in process burden would receive a credit for something that did not belong to it. Further, the Burden Credit account would not receive its additional credit, and the profit and loss would be in error by the amount of $600.

The Work in Process Burden account is credited by the amount of burden at standard rates on completed orders. Therefore, at all times this account should represent the correct value of the burden applied to labor which rests in the files of uncompleted orders.

The Treatment of Over- and Under-Absorbed Burdens.—Reference has been made to the definition of Normal Capacity as agreed on at the 1921 conference of the National Association of Cost Accountants at Cleveland. At the same session, a further agreement was reached as follows:

> It was the consensus of opinion that in the regular financial accounting of the company all over- and under-absorbed burden should be carried to profit and loss at the end of the year. This does not mean, however, that in the regular operation of the business it is not perfectly proper to take into consideration over- or under-absorbed burdens of any year or past years in setting standard rates for future operations. This means that it is perfectly in order for records to be kept separate from the general accounting, whereby it will be possible to intelligently take into consideration all facts in connection with the various burdens. But these records will be entirely aside from the financial accounting, it being the consensus of opinion, as stated above, that in the actual records of the company, the over- and under-absorbed

burdens should be written off to profit and loss at the end of each fiscal year.

The primary reason for this is that carrying over these balances involves treating as either an asset or a liability whatever the balances may be. Obviously, an unearned or unabsorbed burden has absolutely no value, therefore cannot be carried as an asset. Any over-absorbed burden is likewise no liability as it is not owed to anyone. Therefore, the under- and over-absorbed balances should be carried to the profit and loss each month on the statements, and actually closed to profit and loss by journal entry at the close of the year.

CHAPTER XXIII

ADVANTAGES AND DISADVANTAGES OF DIFFERENT METHODS OF APPLYING BURDEN

Theories of Applying Burden.—In this discussion, the distribution of such expense accounts as power, steam, etc., to *other* expense accounts and to the actual manufacturing burden accounts should not be confused with the actual application of the burdens to the cost of the articles actually manufactured for sale.

Moreover, this discussion naturally does not deal with costs which are in the nature of process or operation costs, but only with manufacturing burden which can be distributed to units under a job cost system only through the means of some basic vehicle, such as labor hours.

The original theories which underlie *all* methods of application of manufacturing burden to costs are quite clear. Theoretically, the proportion of supervision cost to be assumed by any unit of product varies according to the length of time the operator was supervised. The same theory holds true in regard to the cost of timekeeping. So also do the costs of rental and heat, and the cost of power used in driving the machine enter into the cost of the unit in proportion to the time each of these factors is involved in its production.

The same may be said of the depreciation of all facilities, either building or equipment. Theoretically—and quite actually so in general—the *length of time* worked is the measure of the service necessary to keep the worker supplied with material and relieved of completed material, of keeping the working place clean, of oiling the shafting, and so on through almost all the burden items which are necessary to keep the direct workers busy.

The *applied hour,* therefore, is without question the most theoretically accurate basis for the application of burden to costs. Of course, there are some items of burden, such as idle time or general labor, which cannot be reconciled to this or any other reasonable method of distribution. These items are few, however, and not of sufficient volume to amount to much in any event.

Methods Actually Used.—Actual practice in the application of manufacturing burden has developed more or less along the lines of least resistance. The three principal methods discussed in this chapter, with brief preliminary comments thereon, are as follows:

1. *Direct-Labor Hours Method.* This is without doubt the most accurate, especially when used in combination with a "super-rate" covering machine expense.

2. *Direct-Labor Cost Method.* This is a substitute for the direct-labor hours method. The value of the direct labor is used instead of the measure of time applied. It can probably be shown that in every case where this method is used it was adopted because it is cheaper to operate than the direct-labor hours method. The latter necessitates keeping an accurate account of applied time, which is not the case in a piecework plant. Under the direct-labor cost method, however, the great advantage of knowing elapsed time for schedule and planning purposes is entirely lost.

3. *Machine-Rate Method.* When machines are a prominent factor in production, it naturally follows that it is necessary to take into consideration the time and costs of machine use. But to make the machine hour the basis of all kinds of charges is much overdone and useless, even to the point of being obscure and inaccurate.

Advantages of Direct-Labor Hours Method.—The basis of applying burden according to the direct-labor hours method is *time*—the number of direct-labor hours consumed in producing a certain quantity of one unit, in one operation. As stated above, this is beyond a doubt the most accurate method of applying burden. The attitude of the cost accountant toward accuracy depends to a large extent upon his reasons for distributing burden. If he looks upon the application of burden as a purely accounting necessity, he is not apt to be influenced largely by a desire for accuracy, and will probably use the most convenient method available. If, on the other hand, the cost records are to be used as a means of increasing production, accuracy is obviously one of the most important attributes of any method.

Supposing, for example, a plant runs under a piecework system, it is, of course, *easy* to use the method of applying burden on the basis of *value* of the applied work. But what becomes of the element of *time* as between fast and slow workers?

If costs are really to be cut down and *production* increased, the costs should always show the elapsed time for each and every operation. If this is done, and if the hours applied are kept, the results will convince anyone that the direct-labor hours method is of the greatest advantage, both from an accounting standpoint, and even more from a managerial standpoint.

The following is an illustration of an advantage of the use of the direct-labor hours basis for the application of burden. Two men on like work and using like equipment are working at the *same* base rate under a bonus plan. One man is a hustler and turns out 20% more work than his neighbor, receiving for this a bonus of 20% on his pay. This obviously indicates that the good worker works 20% less time than the other on the *same number of pieces*. Therefore, he uses 20%

less supervision, timekeeping, heat, light, etc., as all or the majority of burden items are directly in proportion to time.

By the direct-labor hours method, the burden is charged to the job in proportion to the time. If the direct-labor cost were used, the cost of the pieces made by the man who made the bonus would be flagrantly penalized by the burden on the *bonus earned,* while the slow man would carry less burden as he earned no bonus.

The great advantage of bonus methods is that *more* product is obtained from the *same* burden; therefore, unless the direct-labor hours method of burden application is used, the whole object of the bonus is defeated so far as the costs are concerned.

Disadvantages of Direct-Labor Hours Method.—The disadvantages of the direct-labor hours plan are small when compared to its advantages. One of the disadvantages frequently mentioned is that the time, as well as the costs, of jobs must be calculated. This double calculation, so it is said, involves extra clerical work. But if workers are paid under a system other than the piece-rate system, the time spent by employees *must* be figured in detail in order to determine wages. Where piecework prevails, extra time for calculation is required, but after the great value of this knowledge is realized, the "disadvantage" disappears.

Another alleged disadvantage is the tendency of department heads and foremen to reduce the time required for the manufacture of work to an unreasonable degree. The contention with respect to this disadvantage is as follows: Inasmuch as the burden is proportioned to time, a saving in time will consequently reduce the overhead charged to orders. Hence, the time element may be overemphasized, with the result that the quality of product deteriorates unless it is carefully inspected, the wear and tear on equipment increases, and the health of the workers may even be impaired. Department heads and foremen may ask for the purchase of time-saving and labor-saving machines without considering fully the increased capital and running costs of the machine which may offset the savings in time and labor. In other words, not enough attention is given in such cases to the operation of the economic principle of selection or substitution. This is all a fallacy, as the speeding up of work is the great goal of today; and under real control is, and will be, the great secret of success.

Advantages of Direct-Labor Cost Method.—Despite all the criticism and disadvantages of the direct-labor cost method, also termed "productive-labor cost method" and "percentage on wages method," it is still the most common method of applying manufacturing burden. Its popularity is due to simplicity and convenience.

A blanket rate for the whole factory, or rates for each department, may be computed. The latter method is the only accurate one. In either case the ratio of total burden (plant or department) to direct-labor cost (plant or department) is ascertained. The ratio is then applied to the direct-labor costs of individual units in order to determine the overhead chargeable to the units.

The direct-labor cost plan has other advantages. When labor charges are about equal in amount for each worker and the amount produced by each worker is about the same, the plan may be fairly satisfactory. Such uniformity occurs if goods are manufactured in large quantities—"mass" production—and are uniform in character. This uniformity is present where process methods of production are used. Hence, each unit of output requires about the same amount of labor time and labor cost in the technical processes. Because of these uniform conditions, either direct-labor cost or direct-labor hours will prove a satisfactory basis for applying overhead.

On the other hand, though uniform conditions may prevail in a single department, they seldom exist throughout an entire factory. The direct-labor cost method, therefore, is of limited use. Rarely is it the best method for a whole plant.

About all that may be really said as to the real advantages of the direct-labor cost method of applying burden is that in plants where piece rates prevail, and when in such instances the elapsed time on jobs is not an absolute necessity to get the direct-labor cost, a small saving in clerical expense is made by its use.

But if the reader will carefully study the arguments for the direct-labor hours method and the need for some recognition of machine rates, it is difficult to conceive of much that may be said as to the advantages of this method.

Disadvantages of Direct-Labor Cost Method.—It has been shown that the greater part of all indirect expenses are really increased or diminished according to the *time* it takes to do the jobs, as well as according to the number of jobs completed. The severest criticism, therefore, of the direct-labor cost method is the fact that it is not based on *time* but on *cost*. Inasmuch as time is the most important factor which affects burden, any burden method based on factors other than time is inherently faulty. But the dominant weakness of the direct-labor cost method is too often overlooked because of its simplicity and convenience.

If the uniform conditions mentioned on page 294 are not present, the direct-labor cost plan is disadvantageous. The following tabulation will serve to illustrate the point: Assume that a considerable difference exists between the rates of pay of two workers, A and B—A gets 80 cents per hour, and B, 40 cents per hour—and that each can complete a given job in 5 hours. Assume further, that the departmental burden rate is 50% based on direct-labor cost, and that each of the jobs consumes material costing $1.

A

Material	$1.00
Labor ($.80 x 5)	4.00
Burden (50% of $4)	2.00
Total manufacturing cost	$7.00

B

Material	$1.00
Labor ($.40 x 5)	2.00
Burden (50% of $2)	1.00
Total manufacturing cost	$4 00

The example discloses that A's product is charged with twice the overhead that is charged to B's product. This is obviously wrong, as A is a better man, more experienced, and therefore requires less supervision. Even though this were not true, what is the justification of charging *twice* the burden against A's job, when exactly the same elapsed time was spent by both, using the same value of burden in both cases?

Advantages of Machine-Rate Method.—The deficiencies of the direct-labor cost plan are strikingly apparent when brought into contrast with machine-rate plans, or a combination of machine-rate and labor-hours plan. Under all methods of distributing overhead, with the exception of certain machine-rate plans, overhead rates are calculated for whole plants or single departments, and not for individual machines or groups of machines. If one stops for a minute to consider the intricacy and complexity of technical processes in a modern plant, he is struck with the idea that homogeneous operations are limited to small areas. Machines and equipment are vastly different and each machine affords a natural rather than an artificial unit for the allocation of burden. Machine rates, therefore, should be used in distributing part of the burden where production is dependent primarily on machines. Machine rates are determined in advance, as in the case of burdens. The total estimated overhead charges for an ensuing fiscal period are distributed over different work places (production centers, which may be work benches, machines, groups of like machines, or assembly spaces) according to different bases. The total charge for each work place is then divided by the estimated number of hours that the work place will operate during the period. Thus, the factors involved in the use of machine rates are predetermined, and subsequently actual conditions are compared with estimates. The plant may not run during all of the estimated period. But burden items proportional to time accrue anyway. Such charges are known as "unabsorbed burden."

The best development of machine rates is very simple, and consists of what may be termed a "super-rate" to cover machine expense. This method allows all the burden of a department, other than four items mentioned below, to be handled through the regular burden account, and be applied to the cost of machined work on the basis of direct-labor hours.

A special super-rate, however, is set up on either individual machine units or groups of approximately like machines, either from actual design of machines or from the standpoint that they are of about the same nature from a cost standpoint. A rate for each machine or group is set up, based on these cost factors:

1. Depreciation
2. Power to operate
3. Maintenance
4. Interest if desired.

The great advantages of this method of having the departmental general burden and a super-rate for machines are: simplicity, accuracy, and flexibility.

Imagine a machine or pair of machines threading pipe in a tube works. Some sizes require three men in the gang and others four. The work can even be done in a pinch with two men.

By this method we get the following:

CASE 1—3 MEN

1 man 5 hrs. at $.75 per hr.	$3.75	
" " " " " .60 " "	3.00	
" " " " " .50 " "	2.50	
Direct labor 15 hrs.		$ 9.25
General burden " " at $.80 per hr.		12.00
Machine rate 5 " " 1.50 " "		7.50
		$28.75

CASE 2—4 MEN

1 man 5 hrs. at $.75 per hr.	$3.75	
" " " " " .60 " "	3.00	
" " " " " .50 " "	2.50	
" " " " " .50 " "	2.50	
Direct labor 20 hrs.		$11.75
General burden " " at $.80 per hr.		16.00
Machine rate 5 " " 1.50 " "		7.50
		$35.25

Note that the machine hours are the same, and that the flexibility and accuracy is shown by the simple addition of another man with his general burden for the number of hours he worked. This flexibility and accuracy is especially apparent in all cases where more than one operator is on a machine. It is just as apparent when an operator is running *more* than one machine.

Disadvantages of Old-Style Machine-Rate Methods.—Except in a very few isolated cases, the great detail heretofore expended in the adjustment of machine rates has been too laborious and unnecessary. When it comes to great units like armor-plate forging, where the units require almost a whole building, then more detail must enter into machine rates. But these cases are in the great minority; and unfortunately it has happened that such conditions have influenced the attempt to apply an enormous amount of detail in shops of all kinds where it only resulted in ridiculous red tape and perhaps failure.

The setting aside of so much floor space for a group of machines or for an individual machine is in 99% of cases absolutely unnecessary. This is usually done with the aim of splitting up many and doubtful expenses and distributing them to each machine unit. Such an attempt at distribution usually causes a cost method to sink of its own weight.

The modest method of the super-rate, however, is one which gives very accurate costs and at the same time is simple and flexible.

CHAPTER XXIV

PREPARATION OF JOURNAL ENTRIES

Principal Journal Entries.—The journalizing of all monthly entries is a very important part of cost accounting. Even those entries which are entirely confined to the general accounting department have a more or less intimate relation to the cost department, as the effecting of proper controls starts with each entry in the general books of account.

The principal monthly journal entries are divided into two main classes: Entries made on the original books and internal or cost entries. These may be classified as follows:

Entries in Original Books:
1. Voucher Register
2. Cash Receipts
3. Cash Disbursements
4. Sales Register
5. Customers Credit Memo Register
6. Purchasing Department Debit and Credit Register

Internal or Cost Entries:

1. Distributing Material Requisitions
   " Material Credit Memos
   " Expense Debit Slips
2. " Scrap Tickets
3. " Labor Pay-Rolls
5. 6. " Fire and Other Property Insurance
7. " Taxes
8. " Depreciation
9. " Liability Insurance
10. " Departmental and General Expense accounts
11. Journalizing Burden to Work in Process Burden

12. Distributing Completed Production Orders
13. " Cost of Sales

As many of these journal entries require some special means of preparation, each entry will be separately described.

Entries in Original Books

1. **Voucher Register.**—The voucher register and its journal entry are described in detail in Chapter VII. There is also described the method of analyzing the columns through the use of code numbers for the various material and pay-roll accounts.

It is allowable to post the entries from the voucher register in one of the two following ways:

(a) After ascertaining the sub-analysis, such as the payroll and material accounts specified in Chapter VII such analyses may be copied into the voucher register, thereby showing a complete analysis on the last page of the monthly record to be distributed. If desirable, the posting to the general ledger can be made direct from these figures.

(b) Instead of copying the detailed analysis on the last page of the month's entries in the voucher register, this detail may be copied in the general journal and posted to the ledger from that point.

The journal entry method is preferable—even though it involves a little more work—because it concentrates in the general journal all the distributions of the various books of original entry.

The journal entry of a voucher register would appear as follows:

Dr.	Rubber Account	$15,600.00
	Fabric Account	20,000.00
	Direct Raw Materials Account....	8,500.00
	General Stores Account......................	4,200.00
	Department A Pay-Roll Account..............	10,500.00
	Department B " " "	8,400.00

General Pay-Roll Account	$3,600.00	
Expense Ledger Arcount........................	854.00	
Freight Cut on Sales Account..................	1,200.00	
Freight to be Deducted Account................	800.00	
Freight to be Added Account...................	350.00	
Miscellaneous General Ledger Accounts........	250.00	
Cr. Vouchers Payable Account............		$74,254.00

2 and 3. Cash Receipts and Disbursements.—The same may be said of the cash receipts and disbursement totals for the month as was said in relation to the voucher register. The journal entry should be made in the general journal and the postings made from there.

There should be very few entries from this book, as the responsibility of distribution should be placed on the voucher register.

4 and 5. Sales and Customers Credits.—The prevalent method of recording sales and credit memos is to assemble a numerical file of copies of invoices and credit memos in a binder. By the use of adding machines total sales under the various sales divisions, together with all items of postage, freight, etc., which enter in, can be easily accumulated.

In all cases, what is known as a "top sheet" is prepared which gives the total sales as represented by the sheets in the binder, together with the total prepaid postage, freight, etc., involved in the billings. In some cases postings are made direct from these top sheets to the general ledger accounts, but it is best, as with other books of original entry, to copy this entry into the general journal and from there to the general ledger.

Invoices to customers and credit memos to customers are of course accounted for in a similar manner, except that the operation is reversed.

6. Purchasing Department Debit and Credit Memos.—Where the plan is in force of using purchasing department debit and credit memos as described in Chapter XI, the treatment is the same as with sales and credits to customers, except that different accounts are involved.

INTERNAL OR COST ENTRIES

1 and 2. Material Requisitions and Credits.—It must be remembered that the basic distribution to the various control accounts of all material drawn from stockrooms on requisition must be made before these requisitions are filed under the accounts to which they are charged. Therefore it is important that the procedure here outlined be carried out.

After the material requisition slips have been received from the storerooms with all data properly filled in, and have been entered on the stock records so as to show the price and the number or name of the ledger account which holds the value of the material issued, the cost department proceeds as follows:

(a) All requisitions are sorted daily according to the controlling inventory accounts which hold the value of the material used.

(b) After sorting, the requisitions are footed and the total amount to be credited to each material inventory account is found.

(c) These totals are then entered on an accumulation sheet which is simply a columnar-ruled analysis paper with the name of an inventory account at the head of each column.

(d) Each requisition is then stamped with a rubber stamp "Credit Footing."

(e) The requisitions are then sorted again into piles which represent the control accounts to which they are charged, namely, the various expense accounts, burden accounts, and Work in Process Material accounts.

(f) After sorting, they are footed in order to ascertain the total debit to each of these controlling accounts and entered on another accumulation sheet whereon is a column headed with each expense, burden, or work in process account.

(g) After these footings have been made each requisition will then be stamped with a rubber stamp "Debit Footing."

These two accumulation sheets representing the credit and debit entries should at all times be exactly balanced and should be kept continually under this proof.

With these steps completed, the requisitions are filed under their proper order numbers to permit constant closing of production orders and to be ready for the closing of the expense and burden statements at the end of the month.

The preparation of the journal entry then becomes a matter simply of taking the column totals from the credit and debit accumulation sheets. This transfers from the material accounts to the expense, burden, and work in process accounts the materials drawn out on requisition and leaves a true balance of the value of material on hand in each material inventory account.

Such a journal entry would appear as follows:

Dr. Department A Work in Process Material.. ..	$ 3,254.00	
" B " " " "	12,861.00	
" A Burden Account........... ...	1,846.00	
" B " "	947.00	
Electric Power Account......................	128.00	
Steam " "	725.00	
Other Expense Accounts (specify)...........	500.00	
Cr. General Stores Account....		$ 5,862.00
Raw Material Accounts (specify)....		14,399.00

The treatment of material credit memos is exactly the reverse of that used for requisitions.

3. **Expense Debit Slips.**—The use of the Expense Ledger account and the expense debit slip has been discussed already in Chapter VII. It is necessary, however, to compile the figures carefully and to journalize the expense charges properly, if proper controls are to be maintained.

The expense debit slips are made out daily according to the

charges to the expense ledger. Before filing the slips under their order numbers—which it must be remembered are only the expense or burden standing orders—an accumulation must be made as in the case of the material requisitions. The difference is that in this case there is only a single credit—to the Expense Ledger account. In order to prove up daily, the accounting department should furnish the cost department with the totals for the day which are covered by the expense debit slips turned over to the cost department. The procedure is as follows:

(a) Upon receipt of the expense debit slips, the cost department sorts them according to the controlling expense and burden accounts, and finds the total chargeable to each of these accounts.

(b) These totals will be entered on an accumulation sheet similar to that used for requisitions where each control account has its accumulation column. One column of this sheet may be used as the credit column, in which will be entered the daily total as given by the accounting department, representing the total charge made daily to the Expense Ledger account. This sheet must be kept in balance daily as in the case of the material requisition distribution.

(c) After this footing is completed, the debit slips will be stamped with a rubber stamp "Debit Footing" and the slips filed under the order numbers to which they are charged.

At the close of the month it is, therefore, a simple matter to prepare the journal entry debiting the various expense and burden accounts and crediting the Expense Ledger account.

It will be noted that the credit to the Expense Ledger account should exactly clear this account of all charges made to it during the month. That consummates in an orderly and accurate manner the direct charging of expense items which in the past has been a source of numberless errors in the handling of cost records.

The journal entry would appear as follows:

Dr.	Department A Burden Account..................	$ 28.00	
	" B " "	122.00	
	Electric Power "	3,576.00	
	Steam " "	28.00	
	Other Expense Accounts (specify)..............	100.00	
	Cr. Expense Ledger Account..............		$3,854.00

4. Scrap Tickets.—All scrap tickets before being filed with order numbers are entered on an accumulation sheet with two main divisions, one side for debit and the other for credits. Plain columnar paper is well suited for this accumulation, as the accounts affected vary from month to month. It is usually best to enter each ticket, transferring to the accumulation sheet the journal entry which is on each scrap ticket.

If the three scrap tickets illustrated in Chapter XIII were recapitulated, and there were no other tickets, the combined journal entry would be:

Dr.	Returnable Scrap Account..........................	$ 25.00	
	Bad Returnable Castings Loss Account............	26.00	
	Spoiled Work Account...........................	51.00	
	Scrap Account	2.00	
	Material to be Salvaged Account..................	61.00	
	Cr. Work in Process Material Account........		$ 75.00
	Machine Shop Direct Account............		42.00
	Machine Shop Work in Process Burden Account		36.00
	Spoiled Work Account..................		2.00

5. Labor Pay-Rolls.—From the voucher register, distribution of moneys paid out for labor is made to a pay-roll account for each department. These accounts constitute what is known as the original pay-roll and are subject to analysis through the medium of the pay-rolls in order to establish the controls needed for the operation of monthly profit and loss accounts.

The analysis of the pay-roll is discussed in Chapter XIX.

Here, therefore, it is necessary only to point out that after the analysis of the pay-roll of each department for each month is completed, a journal entry must be prepared, crediting the Pay-Roll account with the total pay-roll for the exact month and debiting the control accounts which are affected by the distribution as found by the pay-roll analysis and as explained in Chapter XIX. It is best not to make an individual journal entry for each department, but instead to make one large journal entry for all the labor distribution, crediting all the pay-roll accounts and debiting the control accounts which cover the Work in Process Labor, the various expense accounts, the various burden accounts, the "Other Department Standing Order Clearance" account, and the "Transfer" account. The data for these entries is easily obtained if distribution of the pay-rolls is carried out.

It should again be brought out that there is nearly always a credit balance in the pay-roll accounts on the first of each month, as the distribution of the pay-rolls precedes the payment of at least some days of the weekly pay-roll. This is classed as "accrued pay-roll" with the liabilities on the balance sheet.

An entry for distribution of pay-rolls would appear as follows:

Dr. Department A Direct Labor Account	$8,400.00	
" B " "	3,000.00	
" A Burden Account	7,200.00	
" B " "	2,500.00	
Electric Power Account	1,700.00	
Steam " "	1,500.00	
Other Expense Accounts (specify)	1,300.00	
Labor Transfer Account	800.00	
O. D. S. O. Clearance Account	700.00	
Cr. Department A Pay-Roll Account		$12,400.00
" B " " .		10,500.00
General Pay-Roll "		4,200.00

6 and 7. Fire and Other Property Insurance—Taxes.— Fire insurance and taxes are so nearly in the same class that they will be considered together.

In both cases, the actual payments may be made at different intervals. In each case they are charged to their separate accounts when paid. But in preparing the monthly journal entry which should remain standard for a year, the value of the departments must be known and the proportion for each department computed as described in Chapter XXI.

When the monthly charge for each is computed, this will be set up into journal entries which will be used each month for the year covered by each expense.

Each entry will be similar in form, and along the line as follows:

Dr.	Department A Burden Account	$500.00	
	Department B Burden Account	400.00	
	Electric Power Account	250.00	
	Steam " "	180.00	
	Other Expense Accounts (specify)	650.00	
	Cr. Prepaid Insurance		$1,980.00

8. Depreciation.—In the matter of depreciation there are found two elements: depreciation on buildings and depreciation on equipment.

In respect to the depreciation on buildings, the total amount should be settled and this total prorated to the various departments in a similar manner as insurance and taxes. The journal entry would also be similar unless it is combined with the equipment depreciation entry.

In the case of depreciation on equipment, an entirely different problem is involved, for here the values of all equipment must be known in detail. Further, each piece of equipment is subject to a different rate of depreciation, based on its nature as respects durability and the likelihood of its becoming obsolete.

Each piece of equipment should be on record in a plant ledger, and all details concerning each should be shown. From this record, which groups the equipment by departments, the total equipment depreciation may be summarized.

The monthly entry for depreciation may be set up either separately or combined with the entry for depreciation on buildings. As this entry is similar to those for insurance, taxes, etc., no example is necessary. The same entry will remain standard until changes in equipment or location of departments are made.

9. **Liability Insurance.**—Liability insurance should not be prorated to departments by percentage. Every company pays for liability insurance by classified rates according to different kinds of work, and the insurance companies require an accurate statement of these classes at the close of the year.

A columnar sheet should be used, and each pay-roll should be immediately classified. The distribution of pay-roll entry gives the figures of exactly what is being charged each department. The classification of labor in each department is known, and therefore it is simply a matter of entering the amount of labor for each insurance classification for each department. Knowing the rate for each classification, the amount of liability insurance for each department is easily and accurately computed, and a journal entry prepared charging each burden and expense account and crediting Accrued Liability Insurance account.

10. **Departmental and General Expense Accounts.**—As Chapter XXI described in great detail the method of distributing the various expense accounts, it needs but to be mentioned here that a journal entry for each expense account is actually made each month clearing out each account completely. In this the expense accounts differ from the burden accounts which are actually closed out by journal entry but once a year.

Journal entries for expense accounts differ largely, according to their nature. The principle, however, is the same in each; i.e., to charge whatever account has been benefited on the basis of the service given, the credit to each account always balancing the account.

An illustrative journal entry may be shown, taking the electric power account as the example:

Dr.	Department A Burden Account .... (80,000 kilowatt-hours at .04)	$3,200.00	
	Department B Burden Account .... (60,000 kilowatt-hours at .04)	2,400.00	
	Cr. Electric Power Account		$5,600.00

11. Burden to Work in Process Accounts.—In the payroll distribution, Department A direct labor was charged with labor of $8,400, and Department B with $3,000. Assuming, for example, the standard burden rate per hour of Department A as 80 cents, and that of Department B as $1, the journal entry transferring the standard burden to the Work in Process Burden accounts would be:

Dr.	Department A Work in Process Burden	$6,720.00	
	" B " " " "	3,000.00	
	Cr. Department A Burden Credit Account		$6,720.00
	" B " " "		3,000.00

Chapter XXII describes the principles of this transfer very fully. In the case of machine rates exactly the same principles apply, the basis being the number of machine hours applied to productive effort. These hours are kept in a subsidiary record which accounts for the time of all machines.

12. Completed Production Orders.—The preceding journal entries have brought the accounts controlling operations into three main accounts, as follows:

(a) Work in Process Labor, usually called "Direct Labor"
(b) Work in Process Material
(c) Work in Process Burden

If at all possible it is unquestionably best to have one of each of the above work in process accounts for each operating department, although in many cases this involves too much detail, and in other cases is impossible. In this connection it may be stated that the names of the work in process accounts given above are subject to considerable broadening when it becomes necessary to have special kinds of work in process accounts in order to control clearly and concisely the operations of the plant.

As production orders are completed, the accounts belonging to the three above-mentioned main classifications receive credit for the cost of the orders which are completed, and the various other accounts are debited as hereafter described.

The adoption of the best method of handling the detail work will aid greatly in accumulating the figures upon which journal entries are based. For instance, if a sales book is used in which each sale is entered, columns may be provided to represent the cost of the sale, together with the work in process accounts which would receive credit for the cost. This, however, occurs in very few cases as it is usually better to work by a different method.

Probably in the majority of cases, work which is completed in the shop is charged daily to a Finished Stock account, and in such cases it is necessary to do one of two things.

(a) To maintain an accumulation sheet for all completed orders, which sheet will show the work in process accounts to be credited and the various finished stock accounts to be debited, as well as the sales cost accounts to be charged if the debit of cost is to be made direct to cost of sales.

(b) To file a duplicate of each cost sheet and at the end of the month recapitulate, by the use of electric or manual adding machines, the credits and debits involved.

As stated before, it is usually best to pass all completed orders through a finished stock account as this greatly simplifies all work in connection therewith. It is, therefore, recommended that an accumulation sheet of completed orders be maintained for each operating department. Then as the cost sheets are completed each day, either for individual or assembled parts, they should be footed for credits to the proper work in process accounts of the department and also for debits to whatever finished stock account is to be charged with the material. As this accumulation sheet will be carried on for the month and must be kept in balance, the making of the journal entry crediting the control accounts and debiting the cost accounts is simply a matter of copying the totals as shown by the sheet. It should be remembered, however, that the accumulation sheet must be kept in balance.

It often happens that a department does a great deal of work which never goes into a stockroom. In such cases the work should be charged out immediately upon completion. This can be handled on an accumulation sheet for completed orders, provided there be added to the debit side of the accumulation sheet columns representing the cost of sales accounts which will hold the cost of the goods which have been charged out.

Great care must be taken in this respect, however, as confusion is very easy. Goods which are supposed to be charged out direct find their way through a storeroom and become mixed in with that material which must be extended with its proper cost for credit to the finished stock account when shipped.

An illustration of a journal entry which "clears" completed production orders is as follows. In this example it is assumed that *part* of the product did not pass through Finished Stock.

Dr.	Finished Stock	$22,100.00	
	Special Product A Sales Cost Account	1,800.00	
	" " B " " "	400.00	
	Cr. Dept. A Work in Process Labor....		$6,500.00
	" B " " " "		2,300.00
	" A " " " " Mat'l.		3,800.00
	" B " " " " "		4,200.00
	" A " " " " B'rd'n		5,200.00
	" B " " " " "		2,300.00

13. **Cost of Sales.**—In probably the great majority of manufacturing institutions material is manufactured and passed through the stage of finished stock. The debits to the finished stock accounts come through the journal entries just described, together with a few debits direct to the Sales Cost accounts.

In respect to the Sales Cost accounts, it is necessary to consider the *Sales* accounts. As will be seen in Chapter XXVII on Sales and Distribution Expense, a prominent factor in the control of the various sales branches is the knowledge as to *gross profit* on sales. As this is an important point, it obviously follows that the *Sales* accounts to which are credited all sales of product *must* be arranged in sufficient detail to give the necessary data. For instance, supposing that a company has five branches, and that the product sold consists of four clearly defined classes, there would be twenty sales accounts as follows:

Branch A –	Product	Class	1	account
" A	"	"	2	"
" A	"	"	3	"
" A	"	"	4	"
Branch B	"	"	1	account
" B	"	"	2	"
" B	"	"	3	"
" B	"	"	4	"

And so on for the other three branches.

For each sales account there is always a sales cost account to which is charged the manufacturing cost of the goods sold. This enables an absolute statement as to the gross profit earned by each branch on each product class.

An intermediate step to charging sales cost is necessary in many companies. Whenever branch warehouses are a part of the distribution plan, the unfinished stock at the factory is transferred from the factory to a distant warehouse. This brings in a new element, i.e., the freight from the factory warehouse to the branch warehouse. This freight is carried as an inventory, and as shipments are made from branch warehouses, this freight at a standard amount per product, plus the freight from the warehouse to customer is charged either to customer or to freight out on sales as the terms may dictate.

In any event, the finished stock in branch warehouses is therefore carried at exactly the same value as in the factory warehouse, the added cost being handled as just described.

To arrive at the journal entries necessary to credit the factory or branch warehouse finished stock accounts and to charge the various cost of sales accounts, great care must be taken. If *all* shipments come out of finished stock, the process is very easy. If some shipments of goods are made which do not come through finished stock, the protection of the procedure must start at the time of issuance, not only of the shipping order, but also of the production orders which may cover the shipping order.

Each shipping order must state whether shipment is to be made from stock or directly from production orders. When shipment is to be made directly from production orders the number or numbers of these production orders must be shown. For the same reason, the production orders must show "charge sales cost" instead of "finished stock." If these precautions are taken, no trouble will be encountered.

A duplicate copy of each shipping order goes to the cost department. Copies of all notices of shipments also go to the cost department. The stock record keeper prices the outgoing shipments at cost (see Chapter XIII), and the cost clerks price the items which are shipped directly from production orders.

An accumulation sheet will be maintained for the recapitulation of cost of goods shipped. This sheet will have as many debit columns as there are sales cost accounts, and as many credit columns as there are finished stock accounts (including branch warehouses), and as many work in process accounts which are credited with completed product charged directly to the cost of sales. Obviously the debits must at all times balance the credits.

The journal entry is prepared by simply using the totals of the columns, and may be illustrated as follows:

Dr.	Branch A Product 1 Sales Cost Account......	$2,800.00	
	" A " 2 " " "	3,300.00	
	" A " 3 " " "	2,200.00	
	" A " 4 " " "	3,100.00	
	" B " 1 " " "	2,400.00	
	" B " 2 " " "	850.00	
	" B " 3 " " "	600.00	
	" B " 4 " " "	950.00	
	And so on with other branches................	12,500.00	
Cr.	Branch A Warehouse Account		$9,400.00
	" B " " .		3,300.00
	" C " "		2,400.00
	" D "		4,400.00
	" E "		1,730.00
	Finished Stock Account		3,500.00
	Dept. A. Work in Process Labor Acct.		900.00
	" B " " " " "		500.00
	Dept. A " " " Mat'l. "		1,100.00
	" B " " " " "		250.00
	" A " " " B'rd'n. "		720.00
	" B " " " " "		500.00

In this entry, some material was shipped from headquarters finished stock and some directly from completed production orders.

On material from warehouse stocks the freight from factory at standard rates must be computed and journalized to Freight Out on Sales for each branch if it is not chargeable to customers. This journal entry will credit the Warehouse Freight account, thereby keeping the inventory of freight in correct ratio to the warehouse stock. An illustration of such an entry follows, where one Freight Out on Sales account is maintained for each branch. If one such account is possible for each product class, the greater detail may or may not be kept, as may be desired.

Dr.	Branch A Freight Out on Sales Account............	$300.00	
	" B " " " " "	650.00	
	" C " " " " "	520.00	
	" D " " " " "	900.00	
	" E " " " " "	750.00	
Cr.	Branch A Warehouse Freight Acct.........		$300.00
	" B " " " ...		650.00
	" C " " "		520.00
	" D "		900.00
	" E "		750.00

The proportion of this freight to cost of product sold is of course greater for distant warehouses.

In General Regarding Journal Entries.—It cannot be impressed too strongly that the accuracy of cost records depends entirely on the proper transfer of figures as the work progresses from one stage to another. With the careful journalizing of all steps, based on the data which come from accurately working shop conditions, it is entirely feasible to maintain through the control accounts a monthly profit and loss statement and balance sheet which are even more accurate than those based on an annual inventory. The whole procedure is based on the recording of all cost items, such as labor, material, etc., as they are incurred rather than waiting to see what is left at the end of the year after the money has been paid out—as was the case under the old methods of compiling annual profit and loss statements.

No industrial institution can live today without a close check on all of its operations, and it should be evident to anyone who will carefully study the progressive steps outlined in this chapter that, with the care which should be given to every operation in an industrial plant, figures can be produced which will be of incalculable benefit to the management. Warning is given, however, that the proper journalizing of the principal steps must be carried out strictly, in order to establish proof of all figures used in the compilation and statement of costs.

The slightest relaxation in accuracy will probably result in erroneous figures which cannot but prove disastrous.

On the other hand, continuous figures showing every month exactly how work is progressing may *save* the company from disaster. If it should enter on a dangerous road it will not have to wait till a year passes before discovering the fact. It is just this point which constitutes the great value of cost accounting. If to this is coupled the value of the uses of costs to be made by department heads, it may quickly be realized that the cost figures, when properly controlled and safeguarded, become a sure and constant guide for every responsible head in the organization.

CHAPTER XXV

EXPENSE AND BURDEN STATEMENTS

General Nature of Expense and Burden Statements.[1]— The attractiveness of expense and burden statements for management and department heads depends largely upon their proper compilation and presentation. A poorly presented, badly arranged statement of indirect cost, even if perfectly accurate, will receive scant attention. A well-arranged, easily understood statement of indirect cost, with comparisons of the costs on a unit basis month by month will not only command attention, but *will be used.*

After all the items chargeable to each expense and burden account are properly taken care of under each of these accounts, the next step is to assemble all the figures under their proper order numbers, or their designation, in order to arrive at the total cost of each account, and thereby reach the point of assembling the expense and burden statements.

In order to derive real benefits from such figures, the matter of compiling the figures in usable shape becomes one of the greatest importance. Many industrial institutions, though they assemble thousands of figures, neglect to do more than file the figures in obscure places, making no real managerial use of them. The greatest attention should be paid, therefore, to the collating of such figures into neat, attractive, and comprehensive statements which not only are correct and properly reflect the conditions as they exist, but are so presented that it is a pleasure for anyone to study them. By so doing one becomes very deeply interested in accomplishing reforms based on the figures shown.

[1] Illustrations of Expense and Burden Statements and their relation to other financial statements will be found in Chapter XXVIII.

The great importance of establishing the basis of costs, and also the great need for and benefits to be accrued from the proper departmentalization of the plant, have been taken up in detail in other chapters.

The present chapter deals with the matter of expense and burden statements, a matter which if not properly handled will entirely nullify all efforts to produce useful results from assembling indirect costs. In other words, the culmination of all that has been outlined is reached in the effectiveness with which the elusive indirect costs can be set down in the expense and burden statements.

Distinction between Expense and Burden Accounts.—As has been explained elsewhere, indirect costs are treated in two main classes:

1. Expenses, which are, after collection, distributed to other expense accounts or to burden accounts.
2. Burdens, which are the final collection of all indirect costs of each operating department, and which appear in the actual cost sheets of goods produced.

The Great Value of Detail.—It is in the presentation of the various expense and burden accounts that the great value of detail is realized. By this is meant good, wholesome, analytical detail which is designed to answer automatically all questions before they are asked.

A short time ago a case was noted in which five expense order numbers were used. In one department, four of these numbers which specified certain operations showed a total altogether of about $1,200, whereas the fifth order number, entitled "Miscellaneous," had over $12,000 against it. A statement of this sort is valueless.

Within reason, the standing order code should be sufficiently detailed as to analysis of cost to make the statements tell a complete story. If fifty orders are necessary to do this

—have fifty. A statement of lump sums is a wasted statement and had better not be compiled.

Fallacy of High Cost of Detail.—Many managers, and lesser lights as well, rebel at a well-analyzed standing order code, saying that the work is so great and the cost of keeping the records is so high that it is impracticable. This is a most unfortunate mistake. It must be that such judgment is expressed in ignorance of true circumstances, and through an entire lack of real study of the subject. A little reasoning will clear up this point.

A standing order code is prepared, and a comprehensive and well-detailed dissection of all expenses and burdens is made. This is quite a task, but it needs to be done only once. The code is then printed in book form and becomes permanent. Putting the code number for the work performed on the time card covering the work involves simply the very slight time necessary to refer to the code book, to make sure of the right order number. This in itself is soon a matter of memory. When filing the cards in cost files it is practically as easy to file to fifty order numbers as ten.

Footing the time cards for entry on statements takes a little more work—but only that of clearing the adding machine fifty times instead of ten and putting down the totals. This comes, moreover, but once a month. The truth is, the fear of having too much detail is entirely without ground, and a careful investigation would soon prove that a detailed analysis of indirect cost is a valuable asset.

Proving of All Statements.—Before going on with the technic of making up statements, it is important to emphasize strongly the absolute necessity of proving all steps performed. This is done through the aid of controlling accounts.

It will be remembered that a controlling account must be set up in the ledger for each expense and burden account.

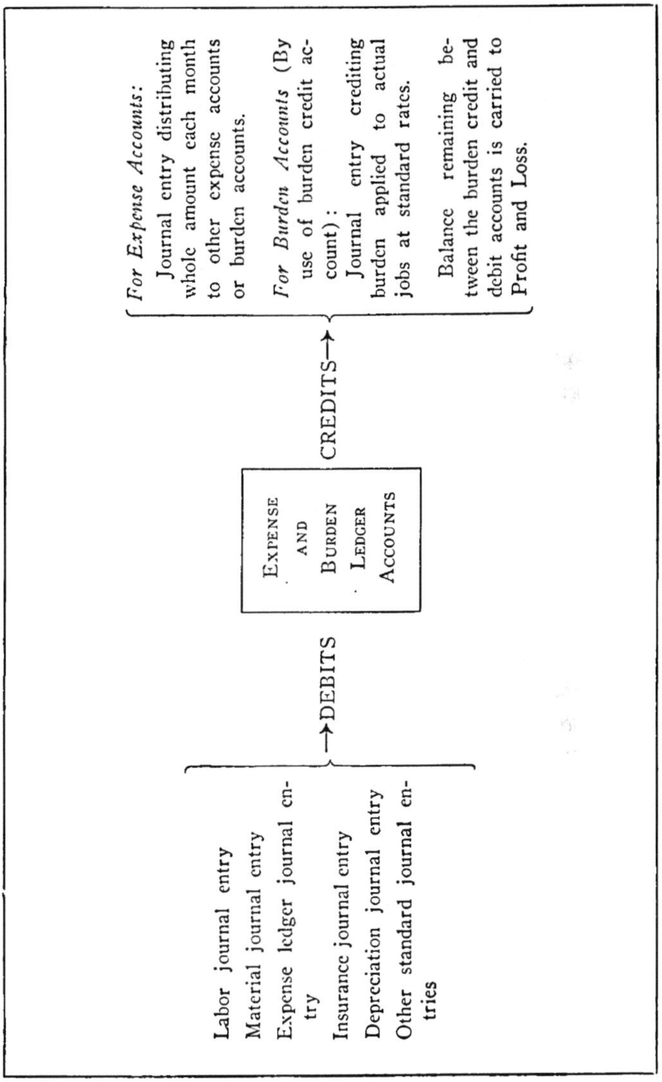

Figure 50.—Chart Showing Flow of Costs in and out of Expense and Burden Accounts

Debits to these accounts are distributed through the journal from the following originating sources:

1. Labor, from a recapitulation of time cards.
2. Material, from a recapitulation of requisitions.
3. Expense, direct from voucher register, a recapitulation of expense debit slips.
4. Miscellaneous apportioned charges from standard monthly entries and other expense distribution.

As all plant expense accounts are credited out in full each month, the control account of each plant expense is used merely as a collecting and proving account so far as the ledger is concerned, and does not appear on the trial balance.

A semigraphic illustration of the flow of entries into and out of the expense and burden ledger accounts is shown in Figure 50.

The burden control accounts are never credited during the year except for correction, the credits for burden applied in costs being credited to a paralled "Burden Credit" account. (See Chapter XXII.) This is done in order to allow the burden accounts—both debit and credit—to accumulate, thereby giving a control for statement purposes which otherwise would be impossible.

Structure of Statements.—In general, all expense and burden statements include three main features:

1. A section showing the entire cost for the month and period to date in sufficient detail to make clear the disposition of every dollar.
2. A section showing the distribution of this total monthly cost to date.
   (a) In the case of expense accounts the complete distribution of each account to other expense accounts and to burden accounts.
   (b) In the case of burdens, the amount for each burden account which has been transferred to Work in

Process Burden at the standard rate, the balance left being the over- or under-absorbed burden.

3. A section showing in comparative form the total unit cost of each expense account for the month and to date, and for each burden account the actual burden rate for the month and to date.

Preparing Skeleton Statements.—At odd times during a month, the skeleton statements may be prepared for use after

HOLDEN MANUFACTURING CO.
BOSTON, MASS.
EXPENSE AND BURDEN ACCOUNT
COLLATING SHEET

Month of____________ Name of Account____________

Order No.	Own Labor	O.D.S.O. Charges	Req.	Expense Debit Slips	Total	Total Last Month	Total To Date

Figure 51. Expense and Burden Account Collating Sheet. (Size, 8½ x 11.)

the month closes. These skeleton statements are as follows: (1) the form of statements as they are to be presented (shown on pages 370 and 371; (2) the working sheets for assembling the figures to be entered on the regular statements (shown in Figure 51).

These sheets should be prepared, so far as possible, before the end of the month in order to speed up the work when the month closes. This will include headings, account numbers (and names on the regular statements), and

1. On the regular statements, the figures for the previous month.
2. On the working sheets, the *total* to and including the previous month.

Preparing Data.—After all time cards, requisitions, and expense debit slips are properly filed, the first step in preparing the statements is to sort all data under each order number.

1. Time cards should be sorted into:
   - (a) Cards which account for "own labor," i.e., work done by men belonging to the department being accounted for, and where no burden of another department is involved.
   - (b) Cards which account for work done by other departments and where the burden of the other department is charged.

2. Requisitions and expense debit slips should be sorted so that they may be added separately.

Footing and Entering Data.—With all details ready, the next step is the accumulation and entry of the various order number totals on the collating sheets. The procedure is the same whether the work is done by manual labor or on electric machines.

1. The time cards of "Own Labor," representing the work done by any department on its own standing orders, is footed for each order and entered under this heading on the collating sheet.
2. The time cards stamped "O.D.S.O.," representing work done for one department by other departments, and which are extended not only with the labor cost of the work performed but also with the amount of burden thereon, will be footed to show the total for each order of both the labor and burden cost. (See Chapter XIX.) These totals will be entered in the column headed "O.D.S.O. Charges."
3. The totals of all requisitions for each order are accumulated and entered on the collating sheet under "Requisitions."
4. The totals of all expense debit slips for each order are accumulated and entered under "Expense Debit Slips."

The foregoing complete all entries which come through the mediums mentioned.

Entry of Journal Entry Data.—All apportioned expenses come through the medium of journal entries. While the main posting of the journal entries is, of course, to the control accounts in the ledger, a short-cut is here possible by also posting the same entries direct to the collating sheets. This saves a special journal debit form which otherwise would be necessary.

In making the entries of the journal entry data in connection with the apportioned expenses, the only columns on the collating sheet to be used will be the last three columns, namely, total, total for last month, and total to date.

The names of the various expenses will be written on the sheet starting with the order number column and writing over the next column. This may appear rather unbusinesslike, but as the greatest use of the form is for the information as called for by the headings, and as the various statements for the expense accounts vary so much in size, it is about the only economical way to use the form.

Completion of Collating Sheets.—When all data have been entered, all entries opposite each order number are cross-footed and the totals entered under the heading "Total." This gives the total cost of each standing order for the month. The next step is to add the total for the month for each order to the "Total for the Last Month," thereby arriving at the "Total to Date" for each order. When cross-footing is complete, the vertical footings are entered on the collating sheet.

The various section totals are cross-footed, and as they must agree with the total of the cross-footed items, it will be noted that the sheet is self-checking so far as the work upon it is concerned.

The expense accounts closed out monthly will of course have no total to date.

Proving the Working Sheets with Controls.—It is noted that both the total cost for the month and the total cost to date for each account have been found.

The total cost to date must agree with the balance of the ledger control account for each burden account, and each monthly expense account will of course also agree with the ledger control for the month.

If all work has been done correctly, each expense and burden account will come out exactly right. But unfortunately errors happen, and it is the use to which the controls may be put in finding these errors that justifies the apparently extra work of establishing controls.

The checking out by sections is as follows

1. The total "Own Labor" for each account must equal this total found in the summary of the pay-rolls, adjusted by the transfers of loaned labor.
2. The total of the O.D.S.O. charges must equal the total of the debits to the control account, according to the journal entry of same described in Chapter XIX.
3. The total of requisitions for each account must equal the total debit for the same account on the accumulation sheets for the requisition journal entry.
4. The total of expense debits for each account must in like manner equal the corresponding total debit on the accumulation sheets for the expense debit slips journal entry.
5. The postings under "Apportioned Expenses" may be checked directly against the journal.

If the foregoing rules are kept in mind, the errors can be quickly located and straightened out.

Completing the Statements.—With the collating sheet proved up and correct, the making up of the actual statements is an easy task.

The first move is to copy the current month and total to

date into the proper columns on the statement. After this has been done, two things remain:

1. On expense statements, to work out the distribution.
2. On burden statements, to ascertain the total basic units applied to production orders, which are either:
    (a) Direct-labor hours
    (b) Direct-labor cost
    (c) Machine hours

In this connection, the collecting of the basic data for distribution of expense accounts and the hours or other data for burden accounts should be carefully regulated.

In the case of expense accounts, reports must be received from the various expense departments as to the data required in connection with the distribution and the figuring of comparative cost tables for each department. This includes:

Department From	Data
Electric Power	Total kilowatt-hours produced and number of kilowatt-hours consumed by each department.
Steam Power	Total pounds steam produced and the consumption of each department.
Compressed Air	Total feet free air compressed and consumption of each department.
Trucking	Total team hours by classes and hours of service given each department (or tonnage if that unit is used).
Restaurant	Meals served. (The balance is distributed on the same basis as in the case of the General Superintendent's office.)
Internal Transportation	The pay-rolls give the hours of direct labor served.

These figures should be submitted in good form and the reports filed by the cost department. A loose-leaf book should be maintained to record this data properly in permanent shape.

The journal entries for distribution of pay-roll deal simply with money. It is therefore necessary for the hour data to be cared for independently, and here again a recapitulation of all the hour data should be secured from the pay-rolls and recorded in an orderly manner in a loose leaf book. Great care must be maintained to correct the direct-labor hours shown by the pay-rolls with the amount of transferred hours shown by the labor transfer records.

The machine hours will also need careful recording from the special accounting of machine time as explained in Chapter XXXIII. A record for each machine or machine group having a machine rate must be maintained.

Sequence of Compilation of Expense and Burden Statements.—Naturally, as explained in other sections, not all expense and burden accounts can be closed at once. Expense accounts, such as Steam, Electric Power, Trucking, etc., must close out first, their distributing journal entries being made, and posting made to other expense controls before they are closed.

Then the second set of expense accounts are closed out, and so on until the entire indirect cost is concentrated in the final set of accounts known as burden accounts. This final set of accounts is that whose cost, represented by a standard, appears in the actual cost sheets of the goods produced.

Comparison of Indirect Costs—1. Expense Accounts.—There remains to be discussed the comparisons of the indirect costs which are designed to give a direct and true line on the results of the work.

It has been brought out before that in every possible case each expense account should be so designed as to give some line—for comparative purposes—on the efficiency of each segregated group. If no check of this sort is maintained, the great advantage of keeping the indirect costs is lost, as a volume of figures without any resulting unit comparison is of no use from a managerial standpoint. The nature of the expense accounts depends largely on the plant which is installing the cost methods, but careful thought will bring about a grouping of expense accounts which will accomplish the desired end.

Nearly every plant, for instance, has a Trucking or Teaming Expense account, and from the nature of the business it can be decided whether or not a section unit can be kept in one of two ways: hours of actual trucking, or tonnage trucked. Then, if the cost of trucking is kept, there can be a very usable and valuable unit cost ascertained on one or the other unit.

A great many plants generate at least a portion of their own power. Even where the power is purchased, more or less equipment is always required to transform and distribute it. Thus a knowledge of unit cost is desirable. The cost per kilowatt hour can be accurately determined, if a meter is installed to show the total number of killowatt hours generated or purchased and transformed.

If a plant wishes to go to the expense, almost the same procedure can be followed in the case of steam by the use of flow meters. Unit costs can thereby be arrived at which will give a decided check on the production of steam.

The majority of expense accounts belonging to the second set—those which are to be distributed entirely to the burden accounts—are preferably compared on the basis of the total hours spent by the departments which the account serves. The second choice of a basis of comparison is the total pay-roll in dollars. This may be illustrated in the case of a Pay-Roll Department Expense account where the cost of operating the department is almost in direct ratio to the number of hours of work or value of the hours which the clerical department has to account for. This would apply equally to the cost department, the general superintendent's office, etc.

By all means, care should be taken to avoid an error which is largely prevalent today, namely, of regarding the cost of such departments as being distributable and comparable on the basis of the direct-labor hours or cost of the operating departments. This is entirely wrong, the reason being that a payroll department or a cost department or the general superintendent's office is just as deeply involved with the handling of the indirect labor as it is with direct labor. Therefore, the cost of these departments should be distributed to the operating departments preferably on the basis of the *total* labor hours both direct and indirect, and comparisons made on this basis.

2. **Departmental Burdens.**—The basis for comparison to be used for the operating burdens will depend entirely on the method chosen as being the best or most available for cost purposes. By this is meant that the burdens will be applied and used in the costs on the basis of either direct-labor hours, direct-labor cost, or machine hours. Regardless of what method is chosen, there should be for each expense and burden account some comparative table (on the basis of what has been previously explained) in order that a true measure may be obtained of the efficiency of each division of the indirect cost. These comparisons will be set up along the lines of the table on page 372. This table shows a comparison for some months back of the burden account and also of the Trucking Expense account illustrated on page 372.

It will be noted that this table shows:

1. The expense for each month and the total to date.
2. The number of basic units for each month with the total to date.
3. The cost per unit for the month and the average per unit to date.

Through the medium of these comparative tables, constant watch can be kept as to the accomplishment of each department. The unit cost for each month can be immediately compared with the unit costs of previous months. The average unit cost to date gives still further information.

In the burden accounts particularly, the total units of direct-labor hours for each month show how near to normal the department is running. The burden for the month may be compared with other months of equal speed of running, and the average actual burden rate to date shows immediately how each department is operating as compared to the standard rate of burden which is used in figuring the cost of product.

All burden statements are of the same form, as illustrated in Chapter XXVIII. Attention may be called to the fact that the three sections referred to on page 330 are, in this statement:

1st Section—Down to and including "Total Burden."
2nd Section—The credit by transfer to Work in Process Burden.
3rd Section—The comparative tables for this Burden account, shown on page 372.

Expense statements are of similar form, as illustrated in Chapter XXVIII. The three sections as referred to on page 330 are, on this statement, the total cost, the tabulated distribution, and the comparative table shown on page 372.

Where large comparative burden sheets are used as illustrated in Figure 53, Chapter XXXI, the typewritten statements may in many cases be omitted, as for instance in the copies for foremen or other department heads. The comparative form gives much more information.

Proper Presentation Indispensable.—The fact should be emphasized again that it is wholly useless to spend the money to collect a mass of figures and fail to display them in presentable and useful form. The ultimate presentation of any figures whatever in connection with an industrial institution is the final and actual test as to the real value of all the endeavor which has been made.

A great many people think that it is unnecessary to spend money for neatly typewritten statements. They are much inclined to use pencil memoranda and rough sheets of figures which should never be dignified by the name of statements. The truth is, too much attention can hardly be paid to the neatness and clearness of the presentation of any figures which may be assembled for managerial or other purposes.

CHAPTER XXVI

ADMINISTRATIVE EXPENSE

What Administrative Expense Includes.—The manufacturing cost of product never includes the general administrative or selling expense. These expenses, sometimes called commercial expenses, are of an entirely different nature from the costs incident to manufacturing and have no relation to them.

The administrative expense has to do wholly with the general administration of the company's affairs, with the work of accounting for all its general transactions, and such general functions which in no manner affect any specific division of the company. Should any employees, including the president of the company, perform work for both the administrative and manufacturing divisions, a prorating of the salaries of such employees should be made in the distribution of salaries as explained later in this chapter.

Administrative expense in most cases includes all cost which is not distinctly a cost of manufacturing, selling or of *money*. What is included depends upon the way the offices of a company are organized. For instance, the billing is often a sales department function, although it is better to have it a general function under the controller. The departments or functions whose costs are usually included in the administrative expense are:

1. Executive Offices
2. Treasurer's Office
3. Credits and Collections
4. General Accounting
5. Billing (sometimes in Sales Expense)
6. General Stenographic Department

7. General Office (not including Manufacturing or Sales Office)
8. Statistical Department
9. General Filing Department

The general office includes only that which is actually for general service, and includes such items as the cost of messenger boys, general clerks, door attendants, telephone operator if desired, janitor service and the like. This is of course with the idea that the office manager is in charge as well of the other specified divisions, which are, as a matter of fact, divisions of the general office.

The Compiling of Administrative Expense.—Reference to Figure 18, in Chapter X, will give the basis on which the various divisions of the administrative expense are compiled. It is not enough to have simply an administrative expense account.

Admittedly, the cost accountant sometimes has his troubles in getting the management to allow a detailed expense code analysis of all this expense, but progressive executives now have the "close at home" expense followed as closely as the expenses of manufacturing.

By the use of a code of orders as illustrated, the cost by details of each division of the administrative expense is gathered. Except in a few cases, it is largely a salary cost, with supplies of small nature being concentrated in the general office division. Stationery, particularly of a special and expensive kind, bought in large quantities should be charged to stores and requisitioned by packages.

Classification of Salaries.—Practically all the charges to the various divisions of the administrative expense for salaries come from the salary pay-roll, which is altogether too frequently kept as a sacred and secret document. It may be remarked here in passing, that the secrecy usually surrounding this pay-roll is unfortunate, as it is apt to suggest that someone has something or is doing something which he is ashamed of. If, however, the pay-roll has to be kept as a secret document, it is necessary to have a distribution worked out by the one who is in charge of it, whereby the salaries chargeable to each division may be known. The distribution may be as follows:

Distribution of Salaries

Employee	141	142	143	144	145	146	Etc.

By this method each employee on the office pay-roll will be allocated to the division in which he or she works. The total for each division will appear on the statement of administrative expense opposite "Salaries." This means that each division head should keep the employee in charge of the salary-roll fully informed as to any changes of employees, and vice versa the salary-roll clerk should check up frequently to be sure that the distribution of employees as between divisions is correct.

Allocation of Other Charges.—Charges for many of the items of the administrative expense come directly through the Expense Ledger account by use of the expense debit slip as explained in Chapter VII. Exactly the same procedure applies as if the charges were for some plant expense or burden account. Many charges to these code numbers come from the plant. For instance, all repairs and maintenance are usually cared for by the plant employees. In such cases exactly the same procedure is followed as in the case of any one of the Manufacturing Expense accounts. The office departments will also requisition many things from the general stores, and other stores departments, but the treatment of such charges is exactly the same as for any other expense account.

The Statement of Administrative Expense.—The preparation of the statement of administrative expense is exactly similar to any plant expense account statement, the same collating sheet being used.

An additional journal entry is made to distribute the salary-roll to the administrative and also the selling expense divisions. This entry will debit each division as shown on the Administrative Expense statement, and also each division of the Sales Department. A control account may be maintained for each division of the administrative expense, although often but one control account is used, as the control of each division of the administrative expense has no such importance as the control of the plant expense accounts.

A condensed administrative expense statement is shown below. The arrangement shows an average by months, a feature that means a good deal in this statement, as the expense is more definitely and permanently fixed than in the plant statements.

Control of Administrative Expense.—It is unfortunately not possible to use the administrative expense details for control purposes as fully as with the plant expense accounts. It is a fact with many companies that a slackening down of business actually increases the cost, or at least the work, in many divisions of this expense. This is accounted for by the fact that in "hand-to-mouth" times customers order in small lots—perhaps four or five orders for what in good times would come through on one order. This means more orders, bills, accounting entries, credit visés, and more correspondence.

But this condition need not prohibit the measurement of much of the expense on the basis of what is produced. For instance, the billing cost per invoice may be found and watched, for the number of invoices is known. The same basis gives a fair control of the work on the customers' ledgers. The stenographic department in many businesses is controlled by the number of lines of transmission and dictation.

Administrative Expense
Month of July, 1924

	Jan. 1 to July 31 1924	Month of July 1924	Month of June 1924	Average per Month
General Administrative:				
10101 Salaries	$ 8,750.00	$1,250.00	$1,250.00	$1,250.00
4 Travel and Entertainment	665.	60.	99.00	95.00
6 Sundries	70.	10.	9.00	10.00
7 Telephone and Telegraph	315.00	40.00	52.00	45.00
14 Legal	700.00	100.00	100.00	100 00
	$10,500 00	$1,460.00	$1,510.00	$1,500.00
Treasury Office:				
10201 Salaries	4,914	702.	702.00	702.00
4 Travel and Entertainment	70.	12.	9.00	10.00
5 Office Supplies	42.	11.	0.00	6.00
6 Sundries	35.00	5.00	3.00	5.00
7 Telephone and Telegraph	49.00	10.00	11.00	7.00
	$ 5,110.00	$ 740 00	$ 725.00	$ 730.00
Credits and Collections:				
10301 Salaries	5,264.00	832	825.00	752.00
4 Travel and Entertainment	280.00	50	25.00	40.00
5 Office Supplies	84.00	3	9.00	12.00
6 Sundries	42.00	7.00	4.00	6.00
7 Telephone and Telegraph	140.00	28.00	17.00	20.00
	$ 5,810.00	$ 920 00	$ 880.00	$ 830.00
General Accounting:				
10401 Salaries	7,245.00	1,110.00	1,023.00	1,035.00
5 Office Supplies	70.00	7.00	11.00	10.00
6 Sundries	35.00	3.00	6.00	5.00
	$ 7,350 00	$1,120.00	$1,040.00	$1,050.00
Billing:				
10501 Salaries	2,065.00	330	300 00	295.00
5 Office Supplies	35 00	0.00	7.00	5.00
6 Sundries	70 00	0.00	13.00	10.00
	$ 2,170.00	$ 330 00	$ 320 00	$ 310.00
Stenographic:				
10601 Salaries	5,153	870.	779.00	736.14
5 Office Supplies	49.00	0.00	8 00	7.00
6 Sundries	28.00	0.00	3.00	4.00
	$ 5,230 00	$ 870 00	$ 790.00	$ 747.14
Forward	$36,170.00	$5,440.00	$5,265 00	$5,167.14

ADMINISTRATIVE EXPENSE
MONTH OF JULY, 1924

	JAN. 1 TO JULY 31 1924	MONTH OF JULY 1924	MONTH OF JUNE 1924	AVERAGE PER MONTH
Forward	$36,170.00	$5,440.00	$5,265.00	$5,167.14
GENERAL OFFICE:				
10701 Salaries	$ 1,537.00	$ 213.00	$ 220.00	$ 219.57
5 Office Supplies	630.00	64.00	59.00	90.00
6 Sundries	28.00	3.00	5.00	4.00
8 Postage	630.00	100.00	110.00	90.00
10 Repairs	175.00	28.00	14.00	25.00
11 Grounds Expense	280.00	52.00	25.00	40.00
12 Dues, Subs., Gratuities	210.00	50.00	6.00	30.00
	$ 3,490.00	$ 510.00	$ 439.00	$ 498.57
STATISTICAL:				
10801 Salaries	1,495.00	245.00	230.00	213.57
5 Office Supplies	70.00	0.00	15.00	10.00
6 Sundries	35.00	5.00	3.00	5.00
13 Tabulating Rentals	1,050.00	150.00	150.00	150.00
	$ 2,650.00	$ 400.00	$ 398.00	$ 378.57
FILING:				
10901 Salaries	841.00	190.00	170.00	120.14
5 Office Supplies	35.00	0.00	5.00	5.00
6 Sundries	14.00	0.00	3.00	2.00
	$ 890.00	$ 190.00	$ 178 00	$ 127.14
GRAND TOTAL	$43,200.00	$6,540.00	$6,280.00	$6,171.42

The main control as regards the administrative expense, is the judgment of the executive as to the relation of this cost to the volume of business as a whole, and much study is required to form this judgment.

CHAPTER XXVII

SALES AND DISTRIBUTION EXPENSE

Closer Scrutiny of Sales Costs.—Great pressure has for years been put on the manufacturing department of industrial plants to reduce costs. While this pressure was being exerted, the sales department went blissfully along spending the money saved in the manufacturing. Competition has now become so great that the same pressure must be applied to the sales and distributing end of the business as has been so rigorously applied to the manufacturing end. The cost department in the past has had nothing to do with administrative and sales cost. These expenses have, as a too general rule, been bunched into some grand total and allowed to go unchallenged. The cost department in the future will find a greater field in these general or commercial expenses, as in many instances the manufacturing departments have been squeezed to the limit for savings. This is particularly true in many businesses where the selling and distribution cost is larger than the manufacturing cost.

Branch Expenses.—As so many companies now have branches, either simply selling offices or selling and warehousing offices as well, this chapter will deal with a simple case along branch lines. If a company has no branches, it becomes simply a case of treating the entire sales department as one branch is treated.

The code of standing orders (see Chapter X) is the basis for charging all expense in the selling department. The methods of charging are exactly similar to those for the administrative expense except as noted under the next heading. The main point is to be sure that the sales department is organized with clearly defined lines of demarcation between its several branches in order that sales and expenses may be properly allocated.

Charging the Sales Expense.—When a company maintains branches, it is usually necessary to provide each branch with a fund with which to operate. Sometimes even the branch salaries are paid out of this fund, although in most cases salary checks are sent out from the main office from the source previously mentioned in the chapter on administrative expense.

At regular intervals the branch office sends in an expense report of monies paid out. After audit this report may be handled in one of two ways, according to how it is planned.

1. It may be handled as a journal voucher and entries made directly to expense accounts by means of debit slips.
2. It may go through the voucher register as any invoice and be handled in regular form through the expense ledger.

Probably the second method is best, as this permits of the maintenance of a regular standard fund at the branch, often called an imprest fund.

In either event, the expenses finally come to the cost files as in the case of the administrative expense and the various branch statements are made out as well as the general sales expense. The procedure is exactly the same as with the administrative expense and needs no further comment.

Branch Sales and Cost Statement.—Below is shown a statement such as would be made out for each branch. The sales items come from the general ledger, and the sales cost items from the sales cost journal entries. All the other entries come through the regular procedure as explained.

This statement gives the branch manager a complete story of his operations. The general sales manager and the chief executive also get the same statement.

It may be noted that the branch here reported on is not in good condition. In the first place, it fell behind in its gross profit. Its percentage was 23.3 while the standard was 25.8. Its selling expense was high as is shown by the comparative sales expense statement below.

It is obvious that a study of such a statement, compared with other branch statements cannot fail to suggest ways of saving money. Ways may be found for helping the branch, which should always be the first consideration. If the condition stays chronic, the branch may have to be closed. In any event, the detailed facts must eventually bring action.

BRANCH A EXPENSE
July, 1924

	SALES	COST OF SALES	GROSS PROFIT	% COST Standard	% COST Actual
Product 1	$ 3,640.00	$ 2,800.00	$ 840.00	30	30
" 2	4,026.00	3,300.00	726.00	25	22
" 3	2,948.00	2,200.00	748.00	30	34
4	3,442.00	3,100.00	342.00	20	11
Total	$14,056.00	$11,400.00	$2,656.00	25.8	23.3
LESS FREIGHT OUT ON SALES			927.00		8.1
NET TRADING PROFIT			$1,729.00		15.2
SELLING EXPENSE					
Salaries—Manager and Salesmen			$ 500.00		4.3
Salaries—Office			250.00		2.2
Traveling and Entertainment			450.00		3.9
Sundries			52.00		.5
Telephone and Telegraph			68.00		.6
Office Supplies			44.00		.4
Postage			45.00		.4
Branch Advertising			360.00		3.2
Warehouse Wages			225.00		2.0
Warehouse Expense			98.00		.8
Total Branch A Expense			$2,092.00		18.3
NET LOSS BRANCH A			$ 357.00		(3.1)

NOTE: Remember that the general selling expense is to come in the profit and loss statement.

Comparative Sales Expense Statement.—It often is bad policy to compare actual dollar and cent figures in statements issued to department heads. A comparison of results by percentages, however, permits no divergence from the facts brought out by comparison.

Herewith is shown a comparative sales expense statement for sending out to branches on which nothing but percentages appear.

COMPARATIVE SALES EXPENSE
July 1924
For Issuance to Branches

	Branches				Total
	A	B	C	D	
Product 1	30	29	28	32	31
" 2	22	25	23	24	24
" 3	34	28	30	29	31
" 4	11	22	20	19	18
Total	23.3	25.2	25.1	26.9	25.8
Freight Out	8.1	6.4	7.1	7.2	7.0
Net Trading Profit	15.2	18.8	18.0	19.7	18.8
SELLING EXPENSE					
Salaries—Sales	4.3	3.2	4.5	3.8	4.80
Salaries—Office	2.2	1.8	2.5	2.5	2.20
Traveling and Entertainment	3.9	2.9	4.0	3.1	2.96
Sundries	.5	.4	.6	.4	.36
Telephone and Telegraph	.6	.5	.5	.5	.44
Office Supplies	.4	.8	.7	.6	.36
Postage	.4	.3	.5	.4	.44
Branch Advertising	3.2	2.1	3.2	2.0	1.92
Warehouse Wages	2.0	1.8	2.5	1.6	1.64
Warehouse Expenses	.8	.7	1.1	.6	.34
Total Branch Expense	18.3	14.5	20.1	15.5	15.46
Net Profit or Loss	3.1*	4.3	2.1*	4.2	3.34

* Loss.

The first section gives the comparison of percentage of profit by products, and for the freight out. Note the divergence between branches in the net trading profits. The next section compares the details of the selling expenses. Here an examination, item by item, shows another wide divergence between percentages on like items of expense.

This statement permits each branch manager to see how each of his items compares with similar items for the other branches, and with the average.

The labor of making up the statement is small, as it consists of simply copying the figures of percentages from each branch statement, and the total from the general sales statement.

GENERAL SALES STATEMENT
July 1924

	Sales	Cost of Sales	Gross Profit	% Cost Standard	% Cost Actual
Product 1	$17,040.00	$13,000.00	$ 4,040.00	30	31
" 2	18,600.00	15,000.00	3,600.00	25	24
" 3	13,100.00	10,000.00	3,100.00	30	31
4	14,160.00	12,000.00	2,160.00	20	18
	$62,900.00	$50,000.00	$12,900.00	26.1	25.8
Total Freight Out on Sales			3,500.00		7.0
NET TRADING PROFIT			$ 9,400.00		18.8
FIELD SELLING EXPENSE					
Salaries—Managers and Salesmen			$ 2,400.00		4.80
Salaries—Office			1,100.00		2.20
Traveling and Entertainment			1,480.00		2.96
Sundries			180.00		.36
Telephone and Telegraph			220.00		.44
Office Supplies			180.00		.36
Postage			220.00		.44
Branch Advertising			960.00		1.92
Warehouse Wages			820.00		1.64
Warehouse Expense			170.00		.34
TOTAL BRANCH EXPENSES			$ 7,730.00		15.46
PROFIT ABOVE BRANCH EXPENSES			$ 1,670.00		3.34
GENERAL SELLING EXPENSE					
Salaries			$ 820.00		1.64
Traveling and Entertainment			380.00		.76
Sundries			40.00		.08
Telephone and Telegraph			120.00		.24
Postage			90.00		.18
General Advertising			1,200.00		2.40
Distribution Division Salaries			450.00		.90
Distribution Division Expense			80.00		.16
TOTAL GENERAL SELLING EXPENSE			$ 3,180.00		6.36
NET LOSS BEFORE ADMINISTRATIVE			$ 1,510.00		3.02

General Sales Statement.—This general sales statement shown above is a composite of the branch statements with the addition of the general selling expense at the bottom of the statement. This statement requires no special comment as its value and use is obvious.

Further Costs of Selling.—In the control of selling expense, much greater detail may be worked out by means of subsidiary statements.

Sales are nearly always allocated to salesmen, and a statement of sales by salesmen may be made up and compared with the cost of the salary and expense of each salesman. In fact this should always be done.

In various lines of business some companies have worked out records whereby the cost per call of salesmen is found. Where this can be done at all it is a particularly valuable practice, and by the use of standards a very positive control may be exercised over the salesmen. For instance, the calls per customer, with the cost per call, compared with the yield in business from the customer, will show whether the business from this particular customer pays or not.

Freight Out on Sales.—Many accountants have claimed that the cost of delivering goods to customers, that is, freight out on sales, should be treated as a selling *expense*. Others claim that at least a portion of such charges should be so treated. For instance, the following condition is cited. A salesman works under the usual terms, whereby his customers must pay freight for the delivery of goods. He can sell a first order to a new customer providing he allows freight on the goods to the customer's plant. He gets authority to grant this allowance. In this case it is claimed that the freight cost of this delivery should be charged to selling expense in order to penalize the sales department, as the allowance was made in order to land the new customer, and therefore this becomes a sales policy expense.

Granting the fact that this is a sales policy expense, it is wrong to charge it to selling expense, as by so doing it creates a *cost which is prorated over all other business.* Obviously, the allowance for freight was a plain reduction in price, and the branch allowing the reduction should take its penalty in its freight out on sales account where it has to answer for any increase as shown in its statement. In the desire to penalize a selling branch there is no need to resort to incorrect accounting to accomplish the penalty. One might as well start the penalizing of selling expense with injudicious uses of trade discounts.

Cash Discount Taken by Customers.—Many companies include in selling expense the cash discount taken by customers at the time they settle for invoices. This is an erroneous practice.

When terms are offered of, say 2% 10 days, this becomes an inducement to customers to pay promptly in order to provide a quick turnover of the capital of the company. It is a *financial* inducement, and therefore the cash discounts allowed become a charge to profit and loss as is the case with interest paid for any other money.

The inclusion of cash discounts in selling expense would also automatically hold out an inducement to the sales department to *discourage* customers from discounting their bills, as by so doing the selling expense would be decreased by the amount of discount which could be prevented.

General Selling Expense.—The prevailing custom of prorating the general selling expense, that is, the headquarters expense which is entirely apart from any branches, to the various branch selling cost accounts deserves comment at this time. However, the illustrations given do not show such prorating.

From the standpoint of the actual use of statements of expense with the organization, and equally from the standpoint of accounting principles, nothing is to be gained and much is to be lost by prorating the general selling expenses to the branches. There are many reasons for this, and the principal ones are as follows:

1. There is no tenable basis for such prorating. About the only basis other than purely arbitrary is the basis of sales volume for each branch. Careful investigation will usually develop the fact that the greatest expenditure of effort by headquarters is on weak points—branches whose sales are lagging and which need help. Therefore, the prorating by sales volume often if not usually causes charges which are just the *reverse* of what they should be. In other words, the strong branches requiring little support and producing good sales volume are *penalized* for the weak ones that are getting strong support. This is a very unfair and inaccurate proceeding.
2. The prorating of a large percentage of the general selling expense to the strong branches as a penalty for large sales will cause resentment on the part of the branch management that will draw all constructive thought away from the purely branch costs for which they *are* responsible. This would entirely defeat the object of accurate cost statements; i.e., to stimulate cost reduction.
3. Nothing is to be gained in any way by prorating the general sales cost to branch costs, since the branch costs are for control purposes only, and are rarely used in any price setting, the total selling cost being the price fixing medium.
4. Except in a few cases, the great bulk of selling expense is directly chargeable to branches if the selling department is property organized.

It is therefore, far more equitable and useful to concentrate the general selling expense in one account and make no distribution thereof to branch selling expense. The combined statement of sales cost gives the total selling and distribution cost, and the branches cannot be held responsible except for what they have under their control.

CHAPTER XXVIII

FINANCIAL STATEMENTS

Value of Financial Statements.—The ultimate object of any manufacturing institution is to make money. The measure of every operation is its value in assisting to attain the ultimate object.

The older custom of retaining all cost figures, direct and indirect, in the executive offices imposed a responsibility which rarely, if ever, was fully carried out. Statements of the burden and expense accounts mean comparatively little to one who is not directly concerned with the work whose cost is reflected compared to what they mean to those who are directly responsible for the departments.

It is quite obvious, therefore, that the executive use of financial statements is divided into two parts:

1. The balance sheet and statement of profit and loss are essentially for the use of the executives.
2. The burden and expense accounts are essentially for the use of the responsible department heads who should not only be furnished such statements, but constantly urged to study and use them to the greatest possible extent.

In the past, executives of manufacturing plants paid a preponderance of attention to those details which have largely to do with the actual manufacture of the product. This led many managers to give subordinates too much leeway in the purchase of the machinery and equipment directly used in the producing of goods, and as a result too little consideration was given to the contributing features which have an essential bearing on the effective operation of the equipment.

It was then found out that the actual mechanical operations of production were largely hampered if they were not properly served by the contributing operations of storing and supplying of material to be used in the manufacture. This caused more attention to be paid to all matters of storage and facilities for delivering the various raw materials and supplies to the scene of action. As time has gone on, it has come to be realized that still other matters required additional attention, in fact, that there must be a tightening up of all procedures which have to do with the management of not only materials, but men.

All this has brought about a perfecting of methods of control through the medium of records, the necessity of which is apparent to anyone who desires to manage a business on the basis of actual knowledge, not guesswork. This perfecting of records has not only extended to matters connected with the handling of materials in the plant, the scheduling of production, and the like, but has become most important in the accounting of costs—particularly as high wages have made it necessary to be absolutely sure as to how far anyone can go with safety and still manufacture goods at a profit. Therefore, the importance of financial statements from a managerial standpoint can readily be seen.

Nature of Statements.—Statements for managerial purposes must be complete. This does not mean that they should be voluminous—a manager should not be obliged to wade through a large volume of figures to find out what he wishes to know. But it does mean that the statements which are presented to the manager shall be in such condition that he will be able to find the answer to almost every question without having to ask for special figures.

In other places in this volume, emphasis has been laid on the necessity of monthly statements. The methods set forth have been designed to enable anyone to work up an accurate balance sheet and statement of profit and loss, verified by the control accounts in the ledger. These statements should be so arranged and tied together that it is unnecessary for the manager to study all statements to get the knowledge needed to enable him to perform intelligently his duties as manager. The statements should be assembled in approximately the following order.

1. **Balance Sheet.**—The balance sheet will show the assets and liabilities in exactly the same form as they are usually shown once per year. The figures for this statement are obtained from the trial balance of the various control accounts. The balance sheet shows also the profit for the month and for the year to date, which profit verifies the Profit and Loss account.

In connection with each balance sheet there should be shown subsidiary statements or schedules giving information in regard to various items which appear on the balance sheet, for example:

1. Schedule of notes receivable.
2. Schedules of general ledger accounts receivable, meaning other than customers' accounts receivable.
3. Schedule of raw material inventory balances, there being only one figure put in the statement representing the total.
4. Schedule of work in process account balances. Schedules (3) and (4) may be combined into one statement.
Schedule of finished goods inventory balances.
Schedule of plant investment accounts.
Schedule of prepaid accounts.
Schedule of notes payable.
9. Schedule of general ledger accounts payable, meaning accounts other than those of creditors.
10. Schedule of accrued items.
11. Schedule of reserve accounts if not deducted from corresponding assets.
12. Detail of surplus account.

The above schedules are given merely for illustrative purposes. In small businesses the items themselves may all appear in the balance sheet, but in larger institutions it is better, when making up a balance sheet, to cover the detail with only one item, in order to present a balance sheet in one-sheet form.

It is always desirable to present a balance sheet on a single sheet of paper, if possible, and to have the explanatory schedules in their proper order on other sheets. When this method is followed, it is always best to follow each item on the balance sheet with a reference figure or letter, designating the subsidiary schedule, and to head each schedule with its reference figure.

It is usually best to assemble two kinds of balance sheets, one of them designed for presentation to banks, and a comparative form which is of great value to the manager. The form for bank use is illustrated on page 361, and the comparative form for managerial use on pages 362 to 364. This form of balance sheet is approximately that recommended by the Federal Reserve Board.

It will be noted in the second statement on page 364 that two columns of increase and decrease are shown, one being the increase or decrease over the end of the previous year, and the other over the previous month. These comparisons are decidedly advantageous, as they bring out constantly the increase or decrease in all such vital items as inventories which, from a managerial standpoint, are exceedingly important.

The financial end of the business is most decidedly interested in the fluctuation of inventories, which results often in very stringent action to curb the amount of money tied up in them. That in turn results in pressure to liquidate raw material inventories and to take special measures to decrease the amount of work in process in the plant and turn it into money.

2. **Profit and Loss Statement.**—The profit and loss statement is shown in condensed form on page 368. Here again,

the device of subsidiary statements is used, in order to reduce the size of the profit and loss statement. In smaller enterprises it is possible to put all detail in the profit and loss statement itself, but it is usually found best to confine the main profit and loss statement to the headings as shown in this illustration, relying on the subsidiary schedules to give greater detail if desired. In connection with the illustration shown, the following schedules may be required for further analysis of items shown in the profit and loss statement:

Schedule of Sales Results. Nearly every industrial institution finds it advantageous to have more than one sales account. For instance, an agricultural implement manufacturer may find it of advantage to have a Tractor Sales account, a Tractor Repairs Sales account, a Cultivator Sales account, a Cultivator Repairs Sales account, and so on, with proper analyses of the sales. In connection with each Sales account there should always be two other accounts—Freight Out on Sales and Cost of Sales. Therefore, a subsidiary statement of sales would have for each Sales account a statement of the gross sales, and a statement of the freight paid on delivery of such sales deducted from the gross sales, which leaves the net value of each sales division. There would be shown also the cost of sales, which means the figured cost of the articles shipped, covering material, labor, and factory overhead at *standard* rates. This would then leave the net result of each particular sales division, permitting the figuring of the percentage of profit in each case.

The net results of all the individual sales accounts would equal, in total, the accumulated figure shown in the profit and loss statement for each item of sales, freight out on sales, sales cost, and gross profit.

Schedule of Plant Balances. In any institution where the number of operating departments is quite large, and where it is not an advantage to carry into the plant balance section of the profit and loss statement the balance of over- or under-absorbed burden of each department, it is an advantage to have a subsidiary statement called "Plant Balances" on which these over- or under-absorbed balances are shown after each department has been given credit for the actual burden applied to costs.

The net result as shown by this statement is either a deduction from or an addition to the gross profit shown under the sales headings. That gives in the profit and loss statement, after this deduction or addition has been made, the net manufacturing profit on the goods sold.

Schedule of Administrative Expense, and Schedule of Selling Expense. As these two headings require the same comment on account of being largely of the same nature, they are here grouped together.

Even though these expense accounts are compiled in the cost department, their treatment in the profit and loss statement is necessarily different from other expense accounts. That is, the total of each expense is shown in the profit and loss statement, and the detail is shown on subsidiary statements. This permits of a condensed profit and loss statement, but with full detail quickly available through reference to the itemized statement for each expense.

Financial Section of Profit and Loss Statement.—In the financial section of the profit and loss statement appear the following headings:

1. Discount Taken.
2. Interest Received
3. Dividends Received
4. Discount Given
5. Interest Paid on Notes
6. Interest Paid on Bonded or Other Indebtedness

It may be well to discuss briefly some points in connection with these accounts, particularly in connection with the fact that they should always be shown separately in the profit and loss statement, and not included either as a debit or credit to any expense account which is included in the cost of goods.

1. *Discount Taken.* In many manufacturing plants the discount taken on purchases has been deducted from the invoice price of the material and the material entered on the stock records at the discounted value. This is believed to be bad practice.

The discount referred to, it should be remembered, is merely the cash discount taken on account of paying bills promptly. It is not to be confused with trade discounts which are involved in actually adjusting the price at which the material is bought in the first place. The cash discount is purely a financial transaction. The reduction of the cost of the product is made possible merely because the company is in such a prosperous condition that they have cash enough to discount their bills. The cash discount, accordingly, should be a direct credit to the Profit and Loss account in the financial section as an added profit to the company on account of being able to pay bills promptly.

2. *Interest Received.* Interest received is also a straight profit derived from good financial management, and may be received as a result either of open accounts or of large bank balances, loans, or investments. Interest should not be credited to anything other than the straight Profit and Loss account. It usually acts as an offset to transactions which affect the Profit and Loss account in the opposite way as explained later.

3. *Dividends Received.* Many times a manufacturing plant is successful to the point where it is possible to invest money in the stock of another company from which dividends are received. Such dividends most certainly constitute a straight profit and loss item, being a financial profit which accrues from the fortunate situation of being able to make the investments.

4. *Discount Given.* The cash discount allowed customers who pay their bills on a cash or short-term basis is unfortunately often included in the selling expense section. It is argued by many that the cash discount is a deduction from the price at which the goods were sold and therefore should be debited as an expense, entering into the final cost of the goods through the medium of the selling expense.

While it is, of course, important to safeguard the affairs of any company by crowding into the cost all possible items, the true theory here is that the selling expense should *not* be burdened with this cost. In fact, a selling department which is jealous of its costs most certainly has reason to object to this item being put in as a part of the expense incurred in selling goods. Whether the account is paid in a week or 10 days or net 30 days, is indeed a matter of no interest to the selling department. In fact, in such a case a selling department would be quite justified, with customers of good credit, in recommending them to pay in 30 days, so that the selling cost should not be burdened with the cash discounts which might be taken.

Discount given should certainly be a debit to the Profit and Loss account in the financial section. The discount is merely an inducement offered by the financial department of the business to obtain quick money returns on sales made, and thereby be enabled to make a much faster turnover of the company's working capital.

5. *Interest Paid.* The disposition of interest in the general accounts has been much debated. While a company will have entries in both the Interest Received and the Interest Paid accounts, the entries usually appear in volume in only one of the two accounts. If a company is prosperous, the preponderant entries will be in the Interest Received account; on the other hand, if the company is not well fixed financially, and is therefore obliged to borrow from banks to a considerable extent,

the natural result will be a preponderance of entries in the Interest Paid account.

Interest received is rarely credited either to any administrative expense account or to any other account except as a straight profit and loss item. That being the case, why should interest paid be included in the administrative expense?

Interest paid is largely brought about by the fact that a company has not sufficient capital to take care of its financial obligations properly. On the other hand, the usual reason for borrowing money is that a company does not care to increase its capital stock, as it is figured that money can be borrowed at 6%, and that a manufacturing profit of, say 15% or 20%, can be produced, leaving a net additional profit of from 9% to 14% to go into dividends for the existing stockholders, instead of dividing this additional profit with the additional stockholders who would participate if the capital were increased to obviate the necessity of borrowing the money. It would seem quite proper, accordingly, to class interest on borrowed money as a *reduction of dividends,* this being the actual result as outlined above.

The suggestion has been made that placing the interest paid in the administrative expense will permit the recovery of the interest as part of the cost before the selling price is set. This is a very fine plan in theory and perhaps in some cases works all right, but not in the case of two plants manufacturing identically the same product, by identically the same process, and with approximately the same grade of organization.

One of these plants has no need of borrowing money, whereas the other is undercapitalized and is obliged to borrow a good deal. Their manufacturing costs up to the administrative expenses may be regarded—for the sake of a highly competitive illustration—as the same. The result, therefore, is that the company with plenty of capital has an administrative expense lower by the amount of the interest which the other company is obliged to pay and which is added to its administrative expenses.

Each company it is assumed, sets its selling price on the basis of a percentage added to their total cost, which immediately places the selling price of the company which is short of capital at a figure somewhat higher than the other company. Only one result occurs, namely, that the company with the higher price loses the business, and the fine theory in regard to the recovery of the interest vanishes in the cold fact of lack of orders.

A company with large bank loans may attempt to put its interest into its costs and may temporarily succeed. A time arises, however, when the banker suggests that the lines of credit are too large and that an issue of preferred stock should be put on the market. This is done. The result is that the very same interest which was paid on the bank loans is now paid as dividends on preferred stock and the administrative expense is immediately relieved of the charge which it has been standing for the interest on the borrowed capital. Is this illustration alone not sufficient to convince one of the fact that interest on bank loans is really in the line of a deduction from dividends?

The main point, however, is that it is a real and serious fallacy to believe that the inclusion of interest on loans in the administrative expense is a means of recovering this interest as against competitors who sell goods without such a charge in their costs. To include the interest in the cost is in reality dangerous in the extreme as affecting the volume of business. While it may not be noticed in any particular cases, the company is actually put into sharp competition with companies who are not subject to such a volume of interest on borrowed capital. Therefore, it seems beyond question that interest paid on bank loans should be a direct profit and loss item and should not be included in any way in the cost of the goods.

3. Burden Statements.—Next following the profit and loss statement, with its subsidiary statements, should follow the burden statements in the order of the departments as specified in the standing order code. (See Chapter X.) An illustration of a burden statement is shown on page 370. The number of these statements will depend entirely on the number of departments which require a statement of their burden.

Each statement will be numbered or lettered at the top with its designating number or letter, which is its identifying reference in the plant balances statement, the net result of which is shown in the profit and loss statement under the heading "Plant Balances." These identifying letters are also used in the distributions made in the expense accounts which follow.

Each burden statement is made up of the three main sections, namely: burden labor, maintenance and supplies, and apportioned expenses. In the burden statement shown on page 370 the large group of burden known as "Maintenance and Supplies" is shown under two headings: "Maintenance" and "Sundry Expense Material." Under the apportioned expenses, each item is followed by a reference to the expense statement whence it comes, to enable quick reference. The over- and under-absorbed balances of each burden account will have the reference letter showing the statement to which this balance was carried in the Profit and Loss.

4. Expense Accounts.—Immediately following the burden accounts will be the various expense accounts arranged in the same sequence in which they appear in the standing order code —as illustrated on page 371.

In these accounts, there are two main sections, the first being the charges made directly to the account, and the second being the apportioned charges.

Here again, the index letters will be used to show the origin of certain charges which are made to the accounts and the accounts which are charged by the distribution of the expense accounts.

Plan of Statements.—The ideal plan for statements is to have them in such order and so keyed together that the manager may go just so far as he cares to, and may have a complete story at any stage. For instance, the balance sheet with its subsidiary schedules gives the profit for the month and to date, together with all other usual balance sheet information. If this is sufficient information for the executive he may stop.

If further study is desired, the statements which follow in order may be examined step by step, giving him answers to questions as to where the various figures come from. Naturally the answer as to *why* the figures are as they are recorded is another matter. To answer this question and to *control* the figures at their source the manager may make fullest use of costs by providing each department head with his statements and stimulating their use.

The order of statements in an average business is as follows:

A—*Balance Sheet:*

A1 – Schedule of Notes Receivable
A2 – " " General Ledger Accounts Receivable
A3 – " " Raw Material Accounts
A3 – " " Work in Process Accounts
A3 – " " Finished Goods Accounts
A4 – " " Plant Investment Accounts
A5 – " " Prepaid Accounts
A6 – " " Notes Payable
A7 – " " General Ledger Accounts Payable
A8 – " " Accrued Miscellaneous
A9 – " " Reserve Accounts—unless deducted
A10 – Analysis of Surplus Account

B—*Profit and Loss Statement:*

B1 – Schedule of Sales Accounts
B2 – " " Plant Balances
B3 – Administrative Expense

B4 – Selling Expense

B4a – Branch A Selling Expense

B4b – " B " "

B4c – " C " "

C—*Burden Statements:*

C1 – Dept. A Burden Account

C2 – " B " "

C3 – " C " "

C4 – " D " "

C5 – " E " "

C6 – And up – Other Burden Accounts

D—*Expense Statements:*

D1 – General Plant Expense

D1a – General

D1b – Accounting

D1c – Purchasing

D1d – Stores

D1e – Shipping

D2 – Engineering Department

D3 – Electric Power

D4 – Steam Power

D5 – Compressed Air

D6 – Teaming

D7 – Maintenance

D8 – Personnel

It will be noted that the order of statements is exactly the reverse of the order in which they are normally prepared. In other words, the final statement of results is the balance sheet. Therefore, this appears first. The expense accounts which are distributed to the burden and to other expense accounts are the last ones shown. Obviously, the manager wants the final result first, the major details next, and the minor details last.

In the following pages are given examples of all statements and schedules, showing their form and how they are keyed together. But one of each of the burden and expense accounts is shown, as each class of statements is similar for each department. Selling cost statements are shown in Chapter XXVII, administrative cost statement in Chapter XXVI.

A

Balance Sheet—July 31, 1924

Assets

CASH:			
Cash on Hand—Currency and Coin		$ 3,000.00	
Cash in Banks		148,560.00	$151,560.00
NOTES AND ACCOUNTS RECEIVABLE:			
Notes of Customers	(A1)	$ 30,580.00	
Accounts Receivable—Customers		346,000.00	
Accounts Receivable—General Ledger	(A2)	10,450.00	
		$387,030.00	
Less: Provision for Bad Debts		15,045.00	371,985.00
INVENTORIES:			
Raw Material on Hand	(A3)	$252,600.00	
Goods in Process	(A3)	185,900.00	
Finished Goods	(A3)	154,650.00	593,150.00
OTHER QUICK ASSETS:			
Raw Material Paid for Undelivered	(A3)		62,000.00
TOTAL QUICK ASSETS:			$1,178,695.00
SECURITIES:			
Liberty Bonds			40,000.00
FIXED ASSETS:			
Real Estate and Buildings	(A4)	$263,000.00	
Machinery and Equipment	(A4)	195,800.00	
		$458,800.00	
Less: Reserves for Depreciation	(A4)	83,900.00	374,900.00
DEFERRED CHARGES:			
Prepaid Expenses	(A5)		8,520.00
OTHER ASSETS:			
Stock of a vendor company			25,000.00
Good Will			50,000.00
TOTAL ASSETS:			$1,677,115.00

Liabilities

BILLS, NOTES AND ACCOUNTS PAYABLE:			
Notes Payable	(A6)	$100,000.00	
Accounts Payable—Vendors		150,180.00	
Accounts Payable—General Ledger	(A7)	15,680.00	
Accrued Pay-Roll		7,690.00	
Accrued Miscellaneous	(A8)	850.00	$274,400.00
OTHER CURRENT LIABILITIES:			
Due future date on stock subscriptions			2,100.00
TOTAL CURRENT LIABILITIES:			276,500.00
FIXED LIABILITIES:			
Mortgage on Plant due 1925		$ 75,000.00	
Bonded debt due 1935		350,000.00	425,000.00
CAPITAL LIABILITIES:			
Preferred Stock		$250,000.00	
Common Stock		250,000.00	
Surplus	(A10)	475,615.00	975,615.00
TOTAL LIABILITIES			$1,677,115.00

A

COMPARATIVE BALANCE SHEET

July 31, 1924

Assets

	Dec. 31 1923	July 31 1924	June 30 1924	Inc. or Dec. over Last Month	Inc. or Dec. over End Year
Cash:					
Cash on Hand	$ 3,000.00	$ 3,000.00	$ 3,000.00	$ 0.00	$ 0.00
Cash in Banks	62,300.00	148,560.00	134,900.00	13,660.00	86,260.00
	$ 65,300.00	$ 151,560.00	$ 137,900.00	$13,660.00	$ 86,260.00
Notes and Accounts Receivable:					
Notes of Customers (A1)	$ 15,400.00	$ 30,580.00	$ 23,900.00	$ 6,680.00	$ 15,180.00
Accounts Receivable—Customers	286,760.00	346,000.00	322,740.00	23,260.00	59,240.00
Accounts Receivable—General Ledger (A2)	7,640.00	10,450.00	9,320.00	1,130.00	2,810.00
	$ 309,800.00	$ 387,030.00	$ 355,960.00	$31,070.00	$ 77,230.00
Less: Provision for Bad Debts	16.00	15,045.00	12,980.00	2,065.00	7,585.00
	$ 302,340.00	$ 371,985.00	$ 342,980.00	$29,005.00	$ 69,645.00
Inventories:					
Raw Material on Hand (A3)	$ 348,945.00	$ 252,600.00	$ 329,225.00	*$76,625.00**	*$ 96,345.00*
Goods in Process (A3)	123,850.00	185,900.00	162,350.00	23,550.00	62,050.00
Finished Goods (A3)	170,480.00	154,650.00	167,900.00	*13,250.00*	*15,830.00*
	$ 643,275.00	$ 593,150.00	$ 659,475.00	*$66,325.00*	*$ 50,125.00*

OTHER QUICK ASSETS:					
Raw Material Paid for Undelivered . . (A3)	$ 0.00	$ 62,000.00	$ 38,000.00	$24,000.00	$ 62,000.00
TOTAL QUICK ASSETS	$1,010,915.00	$1,178,695.00	$1,178,355.00	$ 340.00	$167,780.00
SECURITIES:					
Liberty Bonds	$ 40,000.00	$ 40,000.00	$ 40,000.00	$ 0.00	$ 0.00
FIXED ASSETS:					
Real Estate and Buildings . . . . (A4)	$ 241,000.00	$ 263,000.00	$ 261,500.00	$ 1,500.00	$ 22,000.00
Machinery and Equipment . . . . (A4)	188,900.00	195,800.00	193,400.00	2,400.00	6,900 00
	$ 429,900.00	$ 458,800.00	$ 454,900.00	$ 3,900.00	$ 28,900.00
Less: Reserves for Depreciation . . . . . (A4)	74,050.00	83,900.00	82,400.00	1,500.00	9,850.00
	$ 355,850.00	$ 374,900.00	$ 372,500.00	$ 2,400.00	$ 19,050.00
DEFERRED CHARGES:					
Prepaid Expenses . . . . (A5)	$ 2,550.00	$ 8,520.00	$ 7,580.00	$ 940.00	$ 5,970.00
OTHER ASSETS:					
Stock of a Vendor Company	$25,000.00	$ 25,000.00	$ 25,000.00	$ 0.00	$ 0.00
Good Will	50,000.00	50,000.00	50,000.00	0.00	0.00
	75,000.00	75,000.00	75,000.00	0.00	0.00
TOTAL ASSETS	$1,484,315.00	$1,677,115.00	$1,673,435.00	$ 3,680.00	$192,800.00

* Italics indicate decrease.

Continuation—**A**

COMPARATIVE BALANCE SHEET

July 31, 1924

Liabilities

	Dec. 31 1923	July 31 1924	June 30 1924	Inc. or Dec. over Last Month	Inc. or Dec. over End Year
BILLS, NOTES AND ACCOUNTS PAYABLE:					
Notes Payable.................. (A6)	$ 75,000.00	$ 100,000.00	$ 100,000.00	$ 0.00	$ 25,000 00
Accounts Payable—Vendors..........	73,980.00	150,180.00	139,460.00	10,720.00	76,200 00
Accounts Payable—General Ledger (A7)	8,200.00	15,680.00	13,600.00	2,080.00	7,480.00
Accrued Pay-Rolls..................	5,400.00	7,690.00	6,250.00	1,440.00	2,290.00
Accrued Miscellaneous............ (A8)	1,120.00	850.00	370.00	480.00	*270.00*
	$ 163,700.00	$ 274,400.00	$ 259,680.00	$14,720.00	$110,700 00
OTHER CURRENT LIABILITIES:					
Due on Stock Subscriptions..........	$ 2,100.00	$ 2,100.00	$ 2,100.00	$ 0 00	$ 0.00
TOTAL CURRENT LIABILITIES...........	$ 165,800.00	$ 276,500.00	$ 261,780.00	$14,720 00	$110,700 00
FIXED LIABILITIES:					
Mortgage on Plant..................	$ 75,000.00	$ 75,000.00	$ 75,000.00	$ 0.00	$ 0.00
Bonded Debt......................	350,000.00	350,000.00	350,000.00	0. 00	0.00
	$ 425,000.00	$ 425,000.00	$ 425,000.00	$ 0 00	$ 0.00
CAPITAL LIABILITIES:					
Preferred Stock....................	$ 250,000.00	$ 250,000.00	$ 250,000.00	$ 0.00	$ 0.00
Common Stock.....................	250,000.00	250,000.00	250,000.00	0.00	0.00
Surplus...................... (A10)	393,515.00	475,615.00	486,655.00	*11,040.00*	82,100 00
	$ 893,515.00	$ 975,615.00	$ 986,655.00	*$11,040.00*	$ 82,100.00
TOTAL LIABILITIES..................	$1.484,315.00	$1.677,115,00	$1.673,435.00	*$ 3,680.00*	$192,800.00

* Italics indicate decrease.

SUPPORTING SCHEDULES FOR BALANCE SHEET

Schedule of Notes Receivable — A-1

John Doe Company	$15,580.00	
James Doe Company	5,000 00	
Construction Co., Inc	10,000.00	$30,580.00 (A)

Schedule of General Ledger Accounts Receivable — A-2

Due from Employees on Stock	$ 7,000.00	
James Mahoney—Loan	500.00	
Freight to be Deducted	1,940.00	
Freight to be Added	1,010.00	$10,450.00 (A)

Statement of Inventories — A-3

Raw Materials—On Hand:		
Rubber	$98,500.00	
Fabric	52,700.00	
Direct Materials	42,000.00	
Stores	59,400.00	$252,600.00 (A)
Raw Materials—Paid for Undelivered:		
Rubber—en route	$40,000.00	
Fabric—in Public Warehouse	22,000.00	$ 62,000 00 (A)
Goods in Process:		
Work in Process Material	$99,800 00	
Direct Labor	33,500 00	
Work in Process Burden	52,600.00	$185,900.00 (A)
Finished Goods:		
Main Warehouse	$96,400.00	
Branch A Warehouse	23,600 00	
Branch B Warehouse	15,900 00	
Branch C Warehouse	18,750.00	$154,650.00 (A)

Real Estate, Building and Equipment — A-4

Real Estate and Buildings:			
Land Plant 1	$ 24,000.00		
Land Plant 2	32,000.00	$ 56,000.00	
Buildings Plant 1	$ 93,500.00		
Buildings Plant 2	113,500.00	207,000 00	
Total		$263,000.00	
Less Reserve for Depreciation		29,400 00	$233,600.00
Machinery and Equipment:			
Machines Plant 1	$ 62,600 00		
Machines Plant 2	73,700.00	$136,300.00	
Fixtures Plant 1	$ 21,400.00		
Fixtures Plant 2	19,000 00	40,400.00	
General Equipment		9,700.00	
Office Furniture and Fixtures		9,400.00	
Total		$195,800 00	
Less Reserve for Depreciation		54,500.00	141,300.00
Net as shown on Balance Sheet			$374,900.00 (A)

Deferred Charges — A-5

Prepaid Fire Insurance	$ 3,650.00	
Prepaid Taxes	2,420.00	
Prepaid Group Life Insurance	2,450.00	$ 8,520.00 (A)

Notes Payable — A-6

City Bank	$50,000.00	
Country Bank	25,000.00	
Western Bank	25,000.00	$100,000.00 (A)

General Ledger Accounts Payable — A-7

James Doe—Salary Withdrawn	$ 8,600.00	
John Jones—Bonus Credit	4,500.00	
Thomas Mann—Bonus Credit	2,000.00	
Disputed Claim—P. R. R.	580.00	$ 15,680.00 (A)

Accrued Miscellaneous — A-8

Accrued Compensation Insurance	$ 650.00	
Accrued Boiler Insurance	200.00	$ 850.00 (A)

Reserve Accounts — A-9

Reserve Accounts are in this statement deducted in Schedule A-4.

Surplus Account — A-10

Surplus Balance January 1, 1924		$393,515.00
Deductions Since January 1, 1924:		
Jan. 15 Preferred Dividends, 4%	$10,000.00	
Jan. 15 Common Dividends, 10%	25,000.00	
March 15 Federal Taxes for 1923	16,900.00	
April 7 Adjustment of Patent Case	17,400.00	
July 15 Preferred Dividend, 4%	10,000.00	
July 15 Common Dividend, 10%	25,000.00	
July 15 Extra Common Dividend, 8%	20,000.00	124,300.00
		$269,215.00
Additions Since January 1, 1924:		
January Profit	$31,650.00	
February "	24,900.00	
March "	28,400.00	
April	12,600.00	
May "	41,290.00	
June	33,600.00	
July "	33,960.00	206,400.00 (B)
Balance July 31, 1924		$475,615.00 (A)

GENERAL PROFIT AND LOSS
Month of July, 1924

B

	TOTAL TO DATE	JULY, 1924	JUNE, 1924	INCREASE	DECREASE
Total Sales (B1)	$1,126,410.00	$168,000.00	$162,500.00	$5,500.00	
Freight Out on Sales (B1)	57,400.00	8,750.00	7,940.00	810.00	
Net Sales (B1)	$1,069,010.00	$159,250.00	$154,560.00	$4,690.00	
Total Sales Cost (B1)	763,940.00	110,770.00	108,340.00	2,430.00	
Gross Profit at Stds. (B1)	$ 305,070.00	$ 48,480.00	$ 46,220.00	$2,260.00	
Percent on Cost	40.0	43.8	42.6		
Plant Balances (B2)	$ 14,580.00	$ 2,120.00	$ 3,010.00		$890.00
NET MANUFACTURING PROFIT	$ 319,650.00	$ 50,600.00	$ 49,230.00	$1,370.00	
Percent Profit on Net Cost	42.7	46.6	46.7		
ADMINISTRATIVE AND SELLING;					
Administrative Expenses (B3)	$ 43,200.00	$ 6,540.00	$ 6,280.00	$ 260.00	
Selling Expenses (B4)	54,450.00	8,460.00	6,820.00	1,640.00	
	$ 97,650.00	$ 15,000.00	$ 13,100.00	$1,900.00	
PROFIT ABOVE MFG. ADMIN. AND SELLING	$ 222,000.00	$ 35,600.00	$ 36,130.00		$530.00
FINANCIAL:					
Income:					
Discount Taken	$ 9,450.00	$ 1,650.00	$ 1,140.00	$ 510.00	
Interest Received	3,750.00	940.00	230.00	710.00	
Dividends Received	400.00	200.00	0.00	200.00	
	$ 13,600.00	$ 2,790.00	$ 1,370.00	$1,420.00	
Deductions:					
Discount Given	$ 5,680.00	$ 980.00	$ 760.00	$ 220.00	
Interest Paid	23,520.00	3,450.00	3,140.00	310.00	
	$ 29,200.00	$ 4,430.00	$ 3,900.00	$ 530.00	
NET PROFIT	$ 206,400.00	$ 33,960.00	$ 33,600.00	$ 360.00	

Analysis of Sales B1

	Total to Date	July, 1924	June, 1924	Increase
Group A Sales......	$765,950.00	$119,600.00	$112,650.00	$6,950.00
Freight Out on Sales	40,480.00	6,050.00	5,180.00	870.00
Net Sales.........	$725,470.00	$113,550.00	$107,470.00	$6,080.00
Group A Sales Cost.	535,980.00	78,680.00	74,940.00	3,740.00
Gross Profit........	$189,490.00	$ 34,870.00	$ 32,530.00	$2,340.00
Percentages on Cost	35.3	44 0	43.4	
Group B Sales......	$360,460.00	$ 48,400.00	$ 49,850.00	*$1,450.00**
Freight Out on Sales	16,920.00	2,700.00	2,760.00	*60.00*
Net Sales..........	$343,540.00	$ 45,700.00	$ 47,090.00	*$1,390.00*
Group B Sales Cost.	227,960.00	32,090.00	33,400.00	*1,310.00*
Gross Profit.......	$115,580.00	$ 13,610.00	$ 13,690.00	*$ 80.00*
Percentages on Cost	50.7	42.4	41.0	

* Italics indicate decrease.

Plant Balances B2

	Total to Date	July, 1924	June, 1924
Dept. A........................(C1)	$ 5,290.00	$ 860 00	$ 620.00
Dept. B........................(C2)	4,230.00	790.00	560.00
Dept. C........................(C3)	*1,680.00**	*360.00**	210.00
Dept. D........................(C4)	6,740.00	830.00	1,620 00
Total............................	$14,580.00	$2,120.00	$3,010.00

* Italics indicate decrease.

Administrative Expense B3

This expense statement would be similar to the one shown on page 337, but of course with figures to fit this business.

Selling Expense B4

This expense statement, with its subsidiary statements for branches, would be similar to those shown on pages 341 to 343, but of course with figures to fit this business.

DEPARTMENT A (31) BURDEN ACCOUNT—July, 1924 C1

	JAN. 1 TO JULY 31, '24	MONTH OF JULY, '24	MONTH OF JUNE, '24
DIRECT HOURS	51,450	7,516	7,200
LABOR:			
3101 Supervision	$ 2,130.00	$ 308.00	$ 312.00
2 Clerical	875.00	125.00	125.00
3 Inspectors	840.00	120.00	120.00
4 Cleaning and Sweeping	210.00	28.00	34.00
5 Handling Materials	814.00	125.00	110.00
6 Expense on Account of Shop Error	165.00	38.00	12.00
7 Idle Time	70.00	11.00	18.00
8 General Labor	91.00	8.00	19.00
	$ 5,195.00	$ 763.00	$ 750.00
MAINTENANCE:			
3121 Machinery	$ 1,625.00	$ 258.00	$ 240.00
22 Tools	1,520.00	290.00	229.00
23 Dies, Jigs and Templates	210.00	32.00	28.00
24 Buildings and Grounds	470.00	41.00	34.00
25 Fixtures	132.00	18.00	16.00
26 Pipe and Power Lines	115.00	21.00	9.00
27 Electrical Apparatus	180.00	9.00	18.00
28 Other Equipment	88.00	11.00	16.00
	$ 4,340.00	$ 680.00	$ 590.00
SUNDRY EXPENSE MATERIAL:			
3141 Small Tools	$ 772.00	$ 65.00	$ 152.00
42 Lights	126.00	16.00	19.00
43 Oils and Waste	154.00	24.00	21.00
44 Emery Wheels	183.00	16.00	53.00
46 Miscellaneous	215.00	22.00	35.00
	$ 1,450.00	$ 143.00	$ 280.00
TOTAL PURELY DEPARTMENTAL	$10,985.00	$1,586.00	$1,620.00
APPORTIONED EXPENSES:			
Prop. of Gen. Depts. (D1)	$ 2,522.00	$ 325.00	$ 357.00
" " Elec. Power (D3)	3,115.00	440.00	452.00
" " Steam Power (D4)	840.00	120.00	120.00
" " Compressed Air (D5)	196.00	28.00	28.00
" " Teaming (D6)	525.00	62.00	82.00
" " Personnel (D7)	350.00	48.00	50.00
Depreciation (J.E.)	735.00	105.00	105.00
Taxes (J.E.)	224.00	32.00	32.00
Liability Insurance (J.E.)	915.00	148.00	130.00
Telephone and Telegraph (J.E.)	28.00	4.00	4.00
	$ 9,450.00	$1,312.00	$1,360.00
Total Burden	$20,435.00	$2,898.00	$2,980.00
Carried to Work in Process Burden at 50 cents per Hour	25,725.00	3,758.00	3,600.00
Balance (B2)	$ 5,290.00	$ 860.00	$ 620.00

Teaming Expense (24)—July 1924 **D6**

	Jan. 1 to July 31,'24	Month of July, '24	Month of June, '24
Labor:			
2401 Supervision	$ 1,400.00	$ 200.00	$ 200.00
2 Clerical	525.00	75.00	75.00
8 Labor	4,400.00	560.00	490.00
	$ 6,325.00	$ 835.00	$ 765.00
Maintenance:			
2421 Trucks	$ 1,750.00	$ 274.00	$ 368.00
4 Buildings	280 00	28.00	16.00
5 Fixtures	240.00	19.00	32 00
7 Electrical Apparatus	280.00	38.00	17.00
	$ 2,550.00	$ 359.00	$ 433.00
Expense Material and Service:			
2442 Lights	$ 126.00	$ 11.00	$ 15.00
3 Oils and Waste	560.00	76.00	58.00
5 Fuel—Gasoline	1,750.00	250.00	175.00
6 Miscellaneous—Materials	80.00	9.00	12.00
6 Outside Teaming	1,951.00	195.00	190.00
	$ 4,467.00	$ 541.00	$ 450.00
Apportioned Charges:			
Prop. of Electrical Power (D2)	$ 1,699.00	$ 175.00	$ 182.00
Depreciation (J.E.)	630.00	90.00	90.00
Taxes (J.E.)	84.00	12.00	12.00
Liability Insurance (J.E.)	875.00	125.00	116.00
Car Insurance (J.E.)	462.00	66.00	66.00
	$ 3,750.00	$ 468.00	$ 466.00
Total Teaming Expense	$17,092.00	$2,203.00	$2,114.00

Distribution for Month of July

Total Teaming Hours 1,200. Cost per Hour $1.836

Dept. 13	220	hours	(Dld)	$ 403.92
" 14	350	"	(Dle)	642.50
" 22	80	"	(D4)	146.88
" 31	286	"	(C1)	525.00
" 32	90	"	(C2)	165.24
" 33	70	"	(C3)	128.52
" 34	30	"	(C4)	55.08
" 35	74	"	(C5)	135.86
	1,200			$2,203.00

Note: Sub-analysis may be made for cost of sizes and types of trucks.

COMPARATIVE TABLES
Dept. A (31)
Cost per Hour of Burden

Continuation—**C1**

Month	Direct Hours		Burden		Cost Per Hour	
	For Mo.	Total	For Mo.	Total	For Mo.	Average
1924						
January	$6,934	$ 6,934	$3,560.00	$ 3,560.00	$51.34	$51.34
February	7,500	14,434	2,750.00	6,310.00	36.67	43.72
March	7, 60	22,034	2,680.00	8,990.00	35.26	40.80
April	7,400	29,434	2,807.00	11,797.00	37.93	40.08
May	7,300	36,734	2, 60.00	14,557.00	37.81	39.63
June	7,200	43,934	2,980.00	17,537.00	41.39	39.91
July	7,516	51,450	2,898.00	20,435.00	38.56	39.72
August						
September						
October						
November						
December						

TEAMING COSTS PER HOUR

Continuation—**D6**

Month	Direct Hours		Burden		Cost Per Hour	
	For Mo.	Total	For Mo.	Total	For Mo.	Average
1924						
January	$1,600	$1,600	$2,400.00	$ 2,400.00	$1.50	$1.50
February	1,300	2,900	2,600.00	5,000.00	2.00	1.72
March	1,500	4,400	2,625.00	7,625.00	1.75	1.73
April	1,400	5,800	2,940.00	10,565.00	2.10	1.82
May	1,300	7,100	2.210.00	12,775.00	1.70	1.80
June	1,100	8,200	2,114.00	14,889.00	1.92	1.82
July	1,200	9,400	2,203.00	17,092.00	1.84	1.82
August						
September						
October						
November						
December						

Interpretation of Statements.—One of the most welcome and valuable documents to a manager is a letter accompanying a completed set of statements, calling attention to points—good and bad alike—which should be noted by the manager. No one is in a better position to interpret the figures than the cost accountant; at least so far as the cost figures are concerned. This letter may be a joint letter by the cost and general accountants.

Very few managers will take the time to study the details of statements and many are not so inclined. For such managers, the letter of interpretation is invaluable. It will create in the minds of such managers a far greater sense of appreciation of what is received for the money that is spent for gathering and compilation of costs. And better still, such interpretation will nearly always stimulate a healthy use of cost figures, with the result that the profits of the company will be increased.

CHAPTER XXIX

BUDGETARY CONTROL

Factors of Budgets.—In simple language, budgetary con trol means a plan whereby a goal is set for future operations, and where the actual accomplishment is compared with the budget to find where and for what reason the differences occurred. In other words, based on a combination of past and current knowledge, a standard of accomplishment is set up for the future, to act as a guide and particularly a stimulant to the organization.

In the preparation of budgets, as they are usually known, there are two very important factors:

1. The quotas
2. The budgets of expense or cost

These two factors work so closely together that the term "budget" is used for both, as for instance the budget of sales for given periods. For the purposes of this discussion, however, these two factors will be explained as being separate.

The Quotas.—A complete budget for a manufacturing institution usually starts with the sales quota. This does not mean that budget plans cannot be used in any other way than for the complete business, as it is perfectly possible to budget portions of the business to advantage. But in any event, every budget must start with a quota or goal of accomplishment.

If the sales department only is budgeted, the first item is the quota of expected sales. Following this will come the budget of expense considered necessary to accomplish the sales quota.

If the manufacturing department or any division thereof is to be budgeted, the first and controlling item is the quota or accomplishment of production expected in the period or periods budgeted. Then follows the budget of cost considered necessary if this goal is to be reached.

The Budgets of Expense or Cost.—The money outlay required for carrying out the quotas makes up the budget of expense or cost. That is, if a quota is set for a certain speed of production in a manufacturing plant, an estimate is made of the cost involved in operating at this speed, based on past performances. This is by far the most difficult part of the budget plan, as so many items are involved.

Computing the budgets of cost requires a complete knowledge of past performances at varying volumes both of sales and production, a knowledge of present conditions particularly as to comparative wage and salary rates, and a careful judgment as to the probability of wage conditions for the period in the future covered by the budget.

The Scope of Budgets.—The order of precedence in budgets depends on the nature of the business. If a business *makes to sell,* i.e., is a highly specialized business manufacturing articles such as stoves, for example, the manufacturing quota is likely to be the first consideration. If a business is of the reverse type, i.e., *sells to make,* such as many machine shops, foundries, etc., where the plant depends on what is sold for its manufacturing schedule, the sales quota is naturally the controlling factor.

Assuming for our discussion, that a business is of the "selling to make" type, the scope and procedure of the budget would be as follows:

1. **Budget Department.**—The responsibility for the budget should be definitely fixed by creating a budget department.

2. **Sales Quotas.**—An estimate of the future sales is made by months for such a period in the future as is thought

practicable. In some businesses this period may be a year. In others six or even three months are all that can be considered with any degree of accuracy.

Basis:

(a) Past experience with each customer or, in some cases, territory, in dollar volume.
(b) Past experience with each customer or territory in units of product where possible.
(c) Knowledge as to present customer and territorial conditions.
(d) Judgment as to future customer and territorial conditions.
(e) Specific trade conditions.
(f) General economic conditions.

Set By:

(a) Salesmen who will state what they believe they can sell each old customer, or at least the principal ones, with an estimate of new business.
(b) Branch managers who examine the estimates of salesmen and parallel with their own estimates.
(c) Headquarters who examine both the salesman and branch managers' figures and finally set the quotas.

3. **Sales Expense Budgets.**—From past records, and after consultation with all concerned, standard budgets of branch and general selling expense are set up. This involves very careful study and vision.

Basis:

(a) Records of past performances for each branch and for the general sales office.
(b) Decisions as to advertising policy. A percentage of expected sales is a good basis with a company which is well started.
(c) Study of quotas as to whether or not any additional or less sales personnel is anticipated.

(d) Knowledge as to anticipated salary changes in the budget period.

Set By:

(a) Cost department, which estimates the expense.
(b) The branch manager, who studies the cost department estimate and suggests changes.
(c) Headquarters, which finally passes on the estimates.

4. Manufacturing Quotas—Goods to Make.—The sales quotas become the basis of the manufacturing quotas. In some cases the sales quotas become the actual manufacturing quotas as in the case of all perishable goods manufacturing.

In most cases, however, the manufacturing quota must be arrived at after careful consideration of the policy of the company as to what stocks of finished goods are to be kept on hand over and above the sales requirements.

The setting up of a manufacturing quota in businesses manufacturing but a few standard articles is comparatively easy; but where a business manufactures many different articles —thousands of them, perhaps—it is not only more difficult to set up such a quota but many times it can only be set on a percentage of operating capacity without attempt to itemize the product to be made.

As this discussion of budgets is confined to one chapter, the finer details of budgeting cannot be covered. The description, therefore, will be confined to companies manufacturing standard products such as automobiles, tires, flour, textiles, steel and other such products.

Basis:

(a) The sales quotas.
(b) Adjustment of sales quotas by finished stock on hand with consideration of the policy of the company regarding what is to be carried for the future period.
(c) A consideration of the season or time of year. (See Section 7.)

(d) A consideration of labor supply where this may be influenced by time of year.

Set By:

(a) The planning department, if such exists, the cost department, or whatever department has the responsibility of ordering and scheduling work, assuming that the stock records are either a part or are closely associated with this function.
This is accomplished by the following steps:
I Analysis of the sales quota into manufacturing units.
II Subtraction or addition of stock on hand or undelivered orders on hand respectively.
III Addition of stock to be kept on hand above the sales quota, which gives the parts to make.
IV Extension of raw materials required for the schedule.

(b) The works manager, or whoever is the officer charged with the responsibility of approving manufacturing programs.

5. **Manufacturing Quotas—Operations.**—The detail of recapitulating all the labor and machine operations required to perform a certain fixed manufacturing schedule is great. It can be done when all operations are definitely specified, as described in Chapter IX. But even then it is extremely doubtful if the effort would pay.

In most companies, the quota of sales required by the budget as explained in Section 2, corrected by stock on hand as explained in Section 4, is a definitely known percentage of the plant capacity. If the plant is at all well balanced, this will automatically indicate the capacity of each department required to carry out the quota. In any event, this method of using a percentage is probablv as accurate as is necessary.

Basis:

(a) The percentage that the manufacturing quota is of plant capacity.

(b) The actual operation requirements if such should be figured out on the basis of the specifications of manufacturing operations.

Set By:

(a) The planning department, if such exists, the cost department, or whatever department has the responsibility of scheduling work.

(b) The works manager, or whoever is the officer charged with the responsibility of approving manufacturing programs.

6. **Manufacturing Budgets.**—The normal or, if desired, actual capacity of manufacturing operations, having been arrived at, the preparation of the manufacturing budget by departments is a comparatively easy operation.

(a) The average direct labor cost at the normal speed of each department is known. Therefore, the percentage of capacity called for by the manufacturing quota will give the direct labor cost requirement for the budget by departments.

(b) Past records will have permitted the preparation of standard burdens for different percentages of capacity operations. (See Figure 52, page 383.) These burdens include *all* plant indirect expense and can be used as such in making up the main budget. This eliminates any consideration of the various plant general or service expense accounts, as these are represented by prorating in the burden accounts. This would also eliminate any other budgeting of supply materials, as this cost is also represented in the burdens, either direct or through the prorated expense accounts. If it is desired to go to the great work necessary, the burden and expense accounts may, of course, be broken down to the labor, material and other charges which make them up. This is, however, unnecessary for the purpose of budgeting.

Basis:

(a) For direct labor, the percentage of normal operation called for by the manufacturing quota.

(b) For burdens, the standard burdens for the percentage of normal operation called for by the manufacturing quota.

Set By:

(a) The cost department.

(b) The works manager, or whoever has the responsibility of approving programs.

7. Raw Materials Budget.—The purchasing department will receive the details of the raw materials required to carry out the approved programs. The cost of the materials required may be extended by the stock record department, and if so the purchasing department will visé and correct the prices where conditions are changed.

As the schedule of requirements is by months, it still remains for the purchasing department to prepare the schedule of exactly when this material will come in, as in many cases the materials may not come in at the time when its use is scheduled. By this is meant that for economy of purchase, some items of material will come in at once in sufficient quantity for an entire program, while other items will come in as required for use.

The resulting schedule of the purchasing department will give the cost to be covered in the procurement of the raw materials.

Basis:

(a) Requirements of raw materials for manufacturing program, extended at the cost of the last lot.

(b) Current prices and trade conditions as a check on past prices.

(c) Consideration of economical quantities for purchase.

Set By:

(a) The purchasing agent, after correcting prices and arranging deliveries.
(b) The works manager, or whoever is responsible for approving programs.

8. **Plant Additions Budget.**—In case the program is larger than the existing plant capacity, the cost of additional buildings and equipment is required to make possible budgeting the money to be provided for such extensions.

Basis:

(a) Buildings or equipment required.

Set By:

(a) The engineering or plant operating departments.
(b) The works manager, or whoever has the responsibility of approving programs.

9. **Administrative Expense Budget.**—The administration expense budget is largely of the same nature and is to be treated in about the same manner as the plant burdens. This is a very easy expense to budget, as it changes less for different volumes of operation than any other expense.

Basis:

(a) Past records of expense.
(b) The volume of operation.

Set By:

(a) The cost department.
(b) The general manager, or whoever is responsible for final approval of budget programs.

10. **Financial Budget.**—After all other quotas and budgets have been worked out, a very important operation is the computing of the financial budget.

In computing the financial requirements, the following major considerations are involved:

(a) How accurate are the sales quotas, as in considering the available income the financial department must be fairly sure of the turnover?
(b) What percentage of sales will be discounted, and what percentage will take the full time allowed or even more?
(c) What available bank lines exist?
(d) What terms govern purchases of raw materials; that is, what are the due dates for these purchases?

In order to compute properly the budget of financial requirements, a very careful survey must be made of the exact time that money will flow in and the exact time when obligations are to be met. The money requirements do not correspond with the months when the actual physical transactions take place.

It is very necessary that the exact requirements of money be known, as on this depend the plans of the treasurer for his bank loans.

Basis:

(a) Budgets of all departments.
(b) Expected movements of income and outgo.
(c) Past history of money movements.

Set By:

(a) The budget department.
(b) The treasurer.
(c) The general manager, or whoever is responsible for final approval of budgets.

The Adjusting of Burdens to Different Speeds of Operation.—A very important part of budgeting is the adjustment or setting of a standard budget of burden for various speeds of operation.

It is suggested that standard burdens be set for each 10% of normal production capacity; that is from 0 to 10, 10 to 20, 20 to 30, 30 to 40, 40 to 50, 50 to 60, 60 to 70, 70 to 80, 80 to 90, 90 to 100% of normal production capacity.

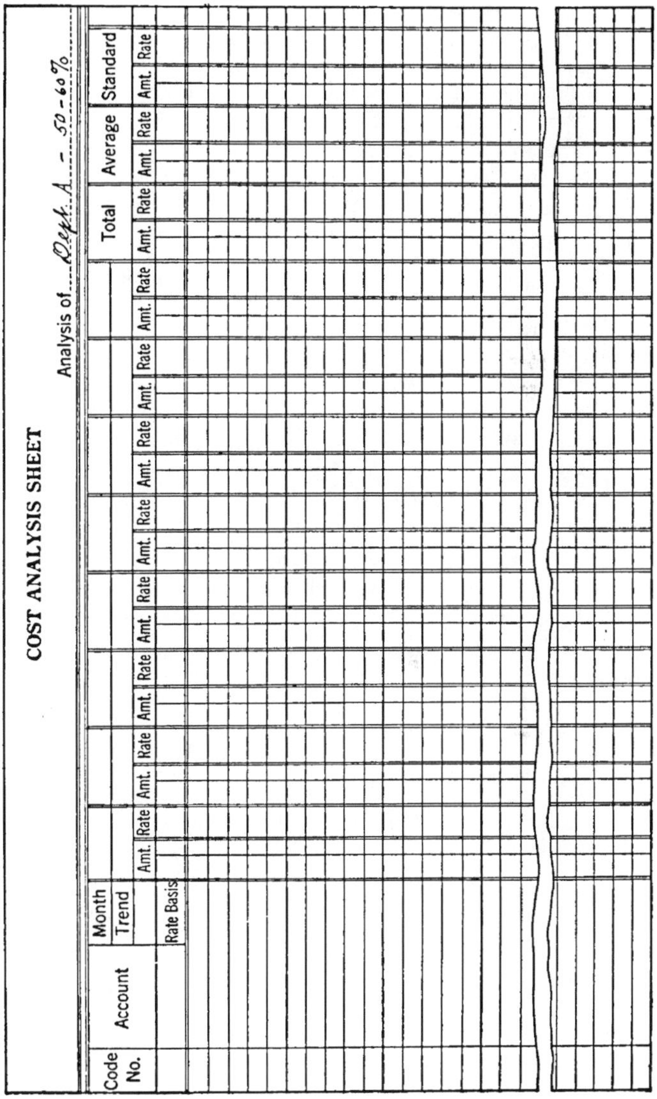

Figure 52.—Cost Analysis Sheet. (Size, 23 x 18.)

Figure 52 is designed to assist in this work and is used as follows:

1. The normal production capacity for each producing department is fixed. This also fixes the normal capacity of the plant.
2. Analysis sheets will be started for each expense and burden account, each sheet being titled with one range of operation; that is, say, 50 to 60%.
3. Going back over as many past years as is practicable, the percentage of total capacity used for each month should be computed.
4. In the case of expense accounts, the expense for each month which falls in each range (10 to 20, 20 to 30, etc.) should be entered on its proper analysis sheet, giving at the head of the column the exact productive effort for the month in hours for the entire plant. Enter on the analysis sheet each item of expense and its unit cost. Also enter at the head of each column whether trend of production was upward or downward.
5. In case of burdens, the same procedure holds, with the exception that the range of capacity controlling is of the department rather than the entire plant.
6. When all months have been copied to their proper sheets, cross foot and find the average for each item for all months posted.
7. Each item should then be carefully examined for anything at all out of the ordinary, and notes made as to where the items seem out of line, and what they should be.
8. After assuring that the items with any adjustments are correct, enter in the last column the standard for each item to be used for this range or operating capacity. This will then give the standard budget to be used for each range of capacity use.

In General Regarding Budgets.—The subject of budgets is very extensive and requires great study and vision. It is obvious that such a subject cannot be covered in one chapter. To discuss all phases of budgets would require an entire volume. Some kinds of business lend themselves to budgetary control much better than others, and it is obvious that it is impossible to treat all phases of this subject in one chapter. The authors do not apologize for the limited way in which the subject of budgets has been covered in this chapter, but do express their regret that the space at their disposal could not permit much more as to the procedure.[1]

The object of this brief sketch of budgeting is simply to impress the fact that cost accounting plays a most prominent part throughout the whole procedure. In fact, it is naturally the back-bone of the budget structure. It seems but fair to state that no company can hope to operate a budget plan which has not been working under a good cost plan for some time previous to instituting the budget plan. It is almost useless to expect foremen or anyone else to estimate capacities of departments and requirements of labor and material unless they have records back of them. In fact, no human mind can safely be depended on for such data.

[1] On account of the importance of budgeting to industry today, the reader is referred to J. O. McKinsey's "Budgetary Control," Ronald Press Company, New York.

CHAPTER XXX

USE OF COST REPORTS BY EXECUTIVES

Cost Reports a Practical Guide.—It has been repeatedly brought out in this volume that the greatest value of cost figures lies in their use throughout the entire organization for cost reduction. The responsibility for such use rests wholly on the chief executive of the business.

Few executives are sufficiently conversant with the detailed methods of cost accounting to understand fully how to interpret the figures. This one point has caused much trouble in business, as in many such cases the cost and general accountants have failed to present their figures and statements to the management in such form that they were used, or even understood.

With proper interpretation of all figures, no cost accountant should have the slightest difficulty in being supported by the management in getting the figures used. On the other hand, no executive, superintendent, foreman, sales manager or any other department head will ever use obscure or too detailed statements. Neither will anyone use statements which in themselves are so arranged that further effort is necessary to arrive at conclusions.

A Quick Survey of Statements by the Executive.—Consider the position of a manager receiving a set of statements for the month.

It is natural, first of all, to look at the profits in the balance sheet to see how much money was made during the month. It is assumed that this profit was either larger or smaller than anticipated—on the basis that a manager is usually either surprised or disappointed. At the same time the manager has been quite concerned over the amount which it has been necessary to borrow from banks, and therefore wishes to find out why the bank account is so small.

He therefore first glances at the raw material and manufactured stock inventory in the balance sheet and discovers that it has gone up very materially during the month. He then turns back to the statement which shows the detail of inventories and discovers that the steel stock took a decided jump of, say, over $60,000.

He immediately rings for the purchasing agent and receives the explanation that a lot of old stock orders had been received and paid for during the month. He also learns that in the meantime certain orders for spot delivery had been placed to keep the plant going, and that this material was in reality surplus stock which was largely unnecessary.

It then becomes a purely executive matter not only to decide what to do about this particular material, but to survey the conditions of other outstanding orders, in order to curb the amount of material coming in if the financial conditions of the concern so demand.

He then gives attention to the fact that the profit is smaller than was anticipated. Turning to the profit and loss statement (page 368) for an explanation, he sees that the shipments have been normal and that apparently the percentage of profits at standard rates of burden is satisfactory. But in looking at the plant balance he finds a heavy penalty in under-absorbed overhead which leads him to turn to the subsidiary statement of plant balances for an explanation. Here he finds that in four or five of the most important departments there is a very large amount of under-absorbed burden which accounts, to a considerable extent, for the penalty in the profit and loss account.

He therefore turns back to the burden accounts of these particular departments and he finds that the actual expenses of the departments were on a normal basis, but that the productive hours of work accomplished during the month were very low—in fact much lower than the preceding month. He now has located the cause of the losses, but this, of course, is as far as the financial statements can go.

He therefore calls for the general superintendent to explain the conditions, who in turn calls for the manager of the industrial relations department to account for the heavy decrease in productive hours. It is learned that in one department the foreman has not treated the men very well and as a result he has had a very heavy turnover.

He also learns that in another department the help has been largely made up of a certain nationality who have become very independent and have during the month availed themselves of many holidays on account of events of special interest to their people.

In other departments he finds other features of labor conditions which may or may not account for the heavy shortage in the productive hours applied in the plant.

He is in a position, therefore, to expect action on the part of the industrial relations department and of the general superintendent, perhaps by changing the foreman in the department where the men cannot get along, and by taking steps to sprinkle in different nationalities in the department where there was a large concentration of one element, in order to stabilize conditions there.

In turning back to the expense accounts, the manager also notes that the Electric Power account has increased to a very considerable degree during the last month.

He then remembers that the power company has been able to secure a large increase in rates. He realizes that the result in his expense account is such an increase as to make it apparent that the company may well consider the installation of their own auxiliary power plant to take the peak loads, instead of being obliged to pay a large service charge for power which sometimes is not used.

Attitude of Executives in Using Cost Figures.—The attitude of the chief executive toward cost figures of all sorts is sure to be reflected throughout the organization. If he uses them as a means of hounding and harassing his subordinate heads of departments, then this method will be used by the subordinates. If he doubts any figures, almost everyone down the line will doubt all figures.

On the contrary, when an executive, after assuring himself that every possible effort is made to have all figures accurate, takes the position that the facts as shown by the various statements and reports are correct, the effect on the organization is magical. No time is wasted in discussing whether something is so or not, but instead, all this effort is put into finding out *why* it is so.

The first duty of the chief executive toward cost reports is to be assured of their proper construction and accuracy. When thus assured, the next duty is to convince every responsible head of the organization that the figures *are* dependable. The third, and most important duty, is to promote the idea of *using* the figures as the principal guide for all operations.

Methods of Using Figures.—The methods of using cost reports depend entirely on the extent to which the development of figure controls have been carried. While the use of budgets has not been developed to a very general degree, there can be no doubt but that the budget method offers a fertile field.

By using budgets, each department of the business is on record for what and how it proposes to operate. When the actual accomplishments are placed against the expected, it is obvious that the differences, item by item, form the basis for careful research.

But the budget method at best is far from a cure-all; there is always danger of setting and perpetuating too slow a pace. To reach the best results it requires much study and research beyond simply the setting of an estimate.

A very valuable use of costs is the comparison of both direct and indirect costs, particularly the indirect costs, at like speeds of operation at different times. This plan, which is taken up in detail in Chapter XXXI, is very valuable for the executive in his campaign for the stabilization of costs.

The executive who educates his department heads to look for and use his costs, finds in such use the greatest advantages. Comparisons through budgets on any other method are merely details. The principal goal of the executive is to be sure that costs are considered; that they are the uppermost thought in the mind of every responsible head; that it becomes an obsession with everyone in the organization to stop and think before spending money in time, material or any other expense. When this is accomplished, the profits will materially increase.

Organizing for Cost Reduction.—The executive is responsible for the organization of efforts to reduce and keep down costs. The extent to which such efforts can be organized depends entirely on the nature and size of the business.

If the executive succeeds in getting a strong spirit of "save cost" throughout the organization, he will find himself where calls for assistance from department heads will be very insistent. If a business is large enough, a "cost research" department is a most valuable adjunct. This department would be placed at the disposal of each department head for investigation of cost items which are high, and which the department head desires to be studied. The cost research department would also initiate studies on its own account, but always carrying out all investigations and studies *in conjunction with* the head of the department whose expense it is.

Some companies have organized "cost committees" for such work, and have been highly successful. But even though such a committee exists, some one person or department should be responsible for carrying on the detailed research required to reduce costs. Such a person or department will enlist the effort and thought of everyone who can help and thereby produce results.

The executive should promote, either directly or through the cost research department, active steps whereby the workers, so far as possible, are interested in cost reduction. In many industries, where unusual and exorbitant demands for wages are made, it is obvious that eventually the workers must be educated to the fact that a balance must exist, and that there is a positive limit to the wages which can be paid. This feature, however, can only be carried to a conclusion when the executive is sure that wastes in the burden and expense accounts are entirely eliminated.

Determining Selling Prices.—The advantages of costs as aids in establishing selling prices has been over-emphasized. It holds true where a concern works on a cost plus contract, when it has a monopoly, and when its product is highly specialized—as in the case of a number of jobbing industries—and therefore considerably different from products of other concerns.

But even industries manufacturing standard competitive lines of products must have definite bases for determining where the selling prices of products indicate the articles on which selling pressure should be the greatest, and what articles should be treated as a matter of good policy sales. Some selling prices are established by "charging what the traffic will bear"; but usually prices are set by competition.

Selling prices frequently influence costs. Thus, in packing concerns and chemical plants, costs of major, joint and by-products are distributed, in many cases, over these products according to respective sales (market) prices of these products.

Instead of saying that one function of cost accounting is to enable a concern to establish intelligent selling prices, it is better to say that cost accounting aids in establishing the *lower limit,* below which there is no profit on sales, called the "point of profit" or "stop-loss point." Too frequently, in determining selling prices, volume is disregarded by managers who do not consider that there are certain fixed expenses which do not fluctuate much, whether volume is great or small. Consequently, the higher the volume of sales is above the fixed expenses, the greater the chances are for making money.

The basic theory that might be advanced, then, is that the manufacturer should try to obtain at least such a volume of business as will pay the fixed expenses of operating his plant, and also the variable expenses which rise in proportion to the volume of production. Expressed in other words, each concern has what is known as its "point of profit," namely, the sales volume needed to operate without loss and from which profits begin to accrue as the sales volume increases.

It has been conceded by some that a manufacturer should make the major part of his profits on the "effort of manufacture." The more effort one particular product requires over another, the more profit that particular article should bring. The whole theory of manufacture is to purchase material and then apply labor together with its burden in such a manner as to bring about a profit. This theory means effort. The manufacturer who adopts this theory does not consider so much the buying and selling of the raw material as he does the effort (labor and burden) put on the materials.

Where particular attention is paid to using the "effort of manufacture" as the controlling basis for setting selling prices, a jobbing percentage is added to the material cost, and a larger percentage is added to labor and burden cost.

The Addition of Administrative and Selling Cost in Price Building.—Great care must be exercised by executives in the manner of adding administration and selling cost to the manufacturing cost in building up selling prices, or in fixing "over-all" costs (meaning costs which include every known item).

The effort of selling varies greatly in respect to various products. Even in the same general line of goods one item may be very popular and have sales of large volume. The only condition to consider is *price*. That is, the only basis of getting orders is to give a price in line with competitors. In such lines, orders come in almost automatically with no particular selling effort.

It is with the other items, therefore, that the selling effort comes, and as in the distribution of burden in the plant, it is quite clear that a greater selling cost should be added to such items.

A very impressive example of the problem of selling cost distribution is found wherever a manufacturer accepts orders for "private brand" goods, as is customary in connection with orders for goods from mail-order houses, chain stores, large jobbers, etc. In such cases there is no advertising cost whatever; no branch office expense; no warehousing; no traveling or salesman expense. A large deal is arranged by headquarters, and usually for large quantities over a long period. It is obvious that in such cases, the selling price will be built up with little consideration for selling expense, although the administrative expense still applies almost in its entirety.

In other words, great care must be taken in building up selling prices to consider all the circumstances, and no specific rule can be laid down.

Possibilities of Careful Study of Statements.—Limitations of space in this volume prohibit the further analysis of the countless managerial uses which may be made of statements of all sorts. It would require a volume nearly as large as this discussion of cost methods in general, to cover satisfactorily all the uses of a thorough reading of a proper set of statements.

Above all things, a manager should remember that a comprehensive set of statements can be used by him for a most positive regulation of all conditions. Every manager must remember that it is up to him to perfect himself absolutely in the knowledge of how statements are prepared and how to read them, and that if he should so prepare himself, he is in a position to read the efficiency of every responsible official and department in his institution.

CHAPTER XXXI

USE OF COST REPORTS BY DEPARTMENT HEADS

Arguments for Publicity of Costs.—A statement has repeatedly been made that 80% of the blame in the case of non-production lies with the management, meaning that only 20% of the fault can be in any way attributed to the workers.

This failure on the part of the management extends into many branches of the industrial institution, covering not only failure to provide the means of actually producing the goods, including all manner of devices and equipment for facilitating the movement of goods, but also failure to furnish the foremen and assistants with the proper backing in the matter of records showing what they are accomplishing.

Probably in the great majority of manufacturing institutions today, figures by the thousand are compiled and safely salted away in files where no one makes sufficient use of them to warrant their compilation. In fact, it is quite a prevalent habit for plants to consider that cost figures which have been compiled are purely of a confidential nature, and therefore must not be known by anyone who is interested. This is one of the most fatal mistakes that can be made. Its consequence is that no steps whatever are taken to give superintendents and foremen a real knowledge of what is going on, which will prompt them to better the existing conditions.

Importance of Cost Figures to Department Heads.—The objection is often urged that all such figures are confidential; that if they are released for more or less general knowledge, the figures will leak to someone outside of the plant, and as a result some competitor may learn something about the business which otherwise he would not know. As a matter of fact, the figures in respect to the various expenses incurred by the several departments of the business are peculiar to that business alone. Even if they were known by someone else, the chances are very much against their being of any particular use. Even within one industry the internal workings of individual concerns are so different that figures pertaining to any one department are absolutely valueless to an outsider.

The conclusion seems clear that withholding from operating superintendents and foremen, from sales managers and other department heads the figures which would mean so much to them if available in comprehensive and usable form, is plain failure on the part of the management. It is most strongly urged, accordingly, that all possible use be made of cost figures, even to the point of preparing special statements on special forms for the various department heads in order that they may know exactly what they are accomplishing.

Burden Statements for Foremen and Department Heads.—The head of each operating department should be provided each month with a copy of the statement of his burden for the past month. Figure 53 illustrates a form for such a statement. Although this statement is called a "Burden" statement, it is used for all expense accounts as well as burden accounts.

It will be noted that this form provides for the figures for six months, together with the average of the previous six months. It is not sufficient to supply a man with the figures for a single month. The great value of figures lies in making possible the comparison of present and past. This form enables the recipient to get the true measure of how each item which makes up the burden is running as compared with past experience, both as to money and as to the ratio of each item to the basis used for the application of burden.

The form is quite simple and practically explains itself, so that only a slight description is necessary. The first two columns provide for the standing order numbers and the name of the account, or the work covered by each order. This is followed by the column in which is entered the average of the previous six months.

With the exception of their month headings, the next six blocks are absolutely identical, the amount of money for each standing order for each month, and the unit cost of each item being entered in each block. The third column in each block shows the average unit cost from the beginning of the six months' period for each item.

In entering figures on the form, all unit costs which are higher than the figure for the same item for the previous month are entered in red. In other words, if an item showed $300 last month and $320 this month, the $320 would be entered in red. If it should have happened that the direct labor basis had also increased and the unit cost of this item for the month had decreased, the unit cost would be entered in black. If, however, the unit cost had increased, as well as the amount of money, it would be entered in red.

By means of this scheme attention is directed graphically to all figures which are increasing, which make it far easier to detect the matters in the report which need attention.

The amount of money can easily increase and yet the result be satisfactory. This, however, will be plainly indicated by the unit cost. It is perfectly natural for a business which is increasing to have larger sums of money spent for each item, but so long as the ratio of this expenditure and the direct or productive work which it is serving stays the same or diminishes, the department is running in a way which is to be commended.

Use of the Burden Statements.—If a careful study is made of the comparative burden report just described, it may easily be seen what far-reaching benefits will accrue from its use. The one thing never to lose sight of is that any expense or burden account is made up of small items. Proper regulation

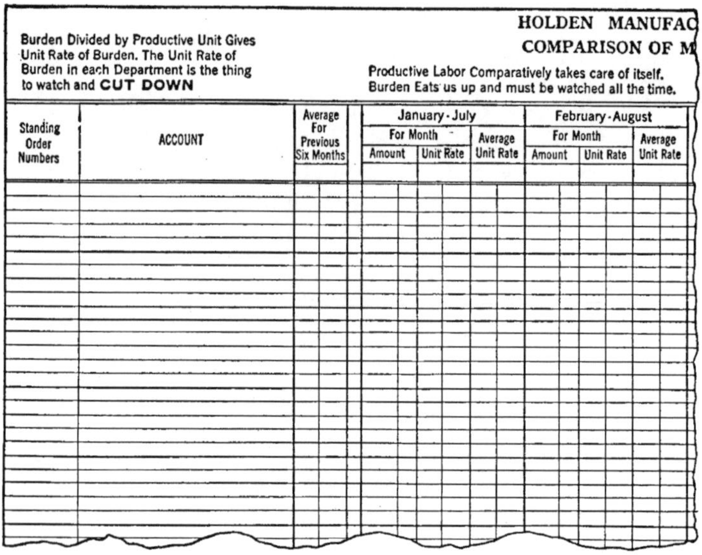

HOLDEN MANUFAC
COMPARISON OF M

Burden Divided by Productive Unit Gives Unit Rate of Burden. The Unit Rate of Burden in each Department is the thing to watch and **CUT DOWN**

Productive Labor Comparatively takes care of itself. Burden Eats us up and must be watched all the time.

Standing Order Numbers	ACCOUNT	Average For Previous Six Months		January-July			February-August		
				For Month		Average	For Month		Average
				Amount	Unit Rate	Unit Rate	Amount	Unit Rate	Unit Rate

Figure 53. Comparative Monthly

of these small items, constant watching of everything that contributes to each of them, and constant vigilance in keeping down the expenditures for every one will decrease the burden cost of the business to an extent which will indeed be surprising.

To give merely one illustration, in the majority of industrial plants, the mechanical work is under the jurisdiction of a master mechanic. The various repair men are detailed from one department to another as their services are needed. These men being under the jurisdiction of the master mechanic are, unfortunately, regarded by the foremen of the various operating departments as being of no particular interest to them. This feeling can be entirely eliminated if the foremen are provided with the statement of their monthly expenses as shown in Figure 53, where they can see the amount of money with which

TURING COMPANY
ONTHLY BURDENS

Increased Unit Rate show in red.
Decreased Unit Rate show in black.

Department..............................
Burden Figured Per..............................
For Six Months Ending..............................

March - September			April - October			May - November			June - December		
For Month		Average	For Month		Average	For Month		Average	For Month		Average
Amount	Unit Rate	Unit Rate	Amount	Unit Rate	Unit Rate	Amount	Unit Rate	Unit Rate	Amount	Unit Rate	Unit Rate

Burden Statement. (Size, 23 x 17¼.)

they are charged for maintenance of equipment in their department.

An instance of this was noted in a large plant where a foreman, on receiving his first statement of his burden expense for the previous month, was instantly struck with the size of the charges to his department for the repairs of certain equipment. He came to the cost office and protested that the repair men spent most of their time sitting around and talking and that the actual repair work only took a few hours.

The net result, however, was that this foreman realized in a way that he never did before that, while the men connected with the master mechanic's staff were detailed to his department, they were in reality his own men, since he had to pay the bills for the time they were there. It is needless to say that thereafter he paid just as much attention to any outside men who were in his department as he did to the men directly on his pay-roll, knowing that he had to pay the bills in his burden account for all the time so spent.

Use of Burden Statements Becomes a Game.—The remark has been made in many plants, after the foremen have been given regular comparative statements of their monthly burdens, that the operation of their departments was like playing a game. By this they meant that they looked forward to receiving these statements with almost as much interest and anticipation as in watching the score-board at a baseball or football game. Many foremen have expressed the opinion that it was even more interesting than any game of amusement could possibly be.

This is but natural, as the game of everyday life is the most important. Nearly all foremen are ready and anxious to use cost figures when furnished them in the proper manner and in the proper spirit. This means that cost figures should no longer be looked on—as once was the case—as a means to "expose" conditions. Shop foremen of the present day are more and more of a highly intelligent type. Many college men are to be found among foremen; and when educated men of this type are sprinkled through an organization they leaven the whole. It is natural that such men not only want but demand records to guide them in their work.

Use of Cost Research Department.—If the chief executive has instituted a cost research department, the foremen will find this a means whereby they can reduce costs to a remarkable degree.

In one instance, under the guidance of a cost research department, and at the request of a foreman, a number of men collaborated in the designing of a variable speed drive for emery wheels, the purpose of which was to keep the speed of the circumference of the emery wheel approximately the same as the wheel wore down. After the installation of the machines it was a constant pleasure to see the decrease in the expense for emery wheels. Far greater efficiency could be obtained from the wheels through keeping them up to speed, and they could be worn to a much smaller diameter by increasing the speed as they wore down. The net result was a decrease in the emery wheel expense of over 80%, an item which amounted to over $30,000 to this department in a year's time.

Every item making up the burden is subject to treatment of the same nature. A careful study of the circumstances in connection with each one will easily develop some method of reducing cost, and as a result of the various schemes worked out, the monthly statement does in reality become a score-board to record the result of the industrial game which is being played.

Problems of all sorts confront a foreman; some are mechanical, some are of personnel nature, some due to shop management, and many due to lack of proper backing from the management. The cost accountant is in an intermediate position whereby he can be of greatest value. His interpretation of costs means much to the department heads and to the executive. The cost research department will be guided by his figures and will rely largely on the cost accountant for guidance of where to look for opportunities to reduce costs.

The foremen will look to the cost research department for investigating materials as to their cost and suitability; for the study of handling materials and where mechanical devices can save man power; for the study of machining operations; for the study of quantities to manufacture, and countless other features.

Use of Costs with Workers.—A great field of the future is the education of workers to more responsibility for costs. Foremen, who are in constant touch with the workers, are in the best position to get them to see slowly but surely that wasted time and effort depress profits which in turn depress wages.

Committees of workers may be organized to take up costs which are seemingly high. Very satisfactory results are found by this procedure, as it gives the workers a first-hand knowledge of the importance to the entire business and to their own interests of careful attention to costs. Such knowledge spreads, and in time an entirely different spirit springs up among the workers.

This committee plan has had remarkable success in safety work, and its application to cost reduction plans can be just as successful.

Use of Costs by Sales Managers.—The form shown in Figure 53 may be used with selling costs just as successfully as with plant departmental costs. In Chapter XXVII are shown statements of selling costs in detail, and also a statement of comparative costs by percentages to be sent out to the branches.

When the detailed cost of selling is entered month by month, each branch manager sees exactly the variances each month, and can study the causes. The unit cost in this case may be figured on the basis either of the total sales of the branch or of cost of goods sold. No matter which basis is used, a comparison is possible month by month of each item and its ratio to what was sold.

A master set of these sheets is in the office of the general sales manager, and he not only can see how each branch is performing as a whole, but the comparison of unit cost for each item for each branch will show exactly how each branch is performing as compared to others. While the action to be taken is of course different, the principle of everlastingly keeping up a cost reduction spirit is exactly the same in sales work as in manufacturing.

Watching Direct-Labor Costs.—Keeping track of the direct cost is different from keeping track of the indirect cost.

To determine how the direct cost is best watched depends very largely on whether or not the manufacturing plant is running under a method of production control.

When a method of production control is followed, and the various direct operations are carefully scheduled at standard rates, the natural way of controlling the direct operations is to keep in constant touch with performance as shown by the control methods. Each operation on each piece, whatever the line of industry, should be subject to some approved standard of speed—a certain number of pieces per hour or per day, as may be best.

Where no planning method is in operation, various methods of watching the direct labor cost may be followed. The method to be used varies very much with the nature of the business. Where the product manufactured gives many pieces produced per day or per hour for each operation, there exist certain methods of watching the direct labor cost. Where the product is such that many operators may work more than one day—perhaps many days—before completing one piece in one operation, the methods must be entirely different.

Taking these two broad classes, and assuming that the time required in both cases is known either through set standards or through estimates, the following methods may be used:

1. *Where product is more than one completed piece per day,* three methods are suggested:

(a) By entering on each daily time card the standard quantity that should have been produced in the time taken, so that the foreman may see by looking through the cards, who is up to standard and who is not.

(b) By having the cost department run off a weekly statement for each worker showing the standard quantity which should have been produced compared with the actual production.

(c) By having a production record card as shown in Figure 54 on which all direct labor cards will be entered before going to the cost department or even to the payrolls. This method constitutes a production control as well as a check on standards.

Other schemes may be used to follow the direct labor, but probably the third plan is, on the whole, the most useful and productive. Besides giving a record from which everyone, the foremen in particular, may know just how work is progressing

PRODUCTION RECORD

Date of Order ________
Due for Completion ________
Date to Start ________
Date Completed ________

Name of Part ________

Part No. ________
Order No. ________

Oper.				Stan.	Oper.				Stan.	Oper.				Stan.	Oper.				Stan.
Date	Check No.	Hrs.	Actual Quan.	Stan. Quan.	Date	Check No.	Hrs.	Actual Quan.	Stan. Quan.	Date	Check No.	Hrs.	Actual Quan.	Stan. Quan.	Date	Check No.	Hrs.	Actual Quan.	Stan. Quan.
Oper.				Stan.	Oper.				Stan.	Oper.				Stan.	Oper.				Stan.
Date	Check No.	Hrs.	Actual Quan.	Stan. Quan.	Date	Check No.	Hrs.	Actual Quan.	Stan. Quan.	Date	Check No.	Hrs.	Actual Quan.	Stan. Quan.	Date	Check No.	Hrs.	Actual Quan.	Stan. Quan.

Figure 54.—Production Record. (Size, 8½ x 11.)

as compared to standards, it works as a very effective purifier of cost records, since a wrong order number of operation on a time card is immediately detected.

As a production control, this method is very effective. The record card shows the date the work should start, and the due date for completion. The clerk handling the production records watches these dates, and if the subsequent operations show no entries after the work starts he can be instrumental in keeping the piece moving by calling attention to the fact that the work has stopped.

2. *Where product is less than one completed piece per day,* greater difficulty is encountered in following the direct labor.

Taking an extreme example, consider a large casting on a boring mill where the work to be performed may take four days or more. To make this case worse, it may be assumed that it is a special job where it will be done but once. If it is done in estimated time or less, a profit is made; if it takes more time, a loss is sustained which can never be recovered.

In such cases the estimate is, or should be, on a square inch basis of cutting. If so, the number of square inches cut for each day can quickly be figured and reported. In this way a daily production can be shown as against the standard which should also be known on a square inch basis.

Aside from the square inch basis, an estimate may be made each night by the foreman of the percentage of completion of such jobs. As these estimates are based entirely on the physical state of the job itself, this percentage of the total estimated time for the operator will give the standard time to enter opposite the actual on the production record.

In any event, the direct labor should be controlled *at the time it is used.*

Watching Direct-Material Cost.—The direct-material cost will show on the cost sheet of the completed goods, and attention should be paid to maintaining the standard material cost. Among the most frequent reasons for diverging from the standard cost are:

1. Inability to secure the standard material.
2. Increase in cost of the standard material.
3. Large spoilages of material.
4. Waste on account of using wrong size of material.

It often occurs in making some product that too expensive material of a given size is used. This may be the fault of the operating department, which has chosen the wrong material, or it may be the fault of general business conditions, which make it impossible to obtain the right kind of material. In either event, the foreman should know exactly what has happened, so that in the future he can choose more wisely, if the fault is his own, or can see that the purchasing department supplies him with the proper kind of material.

As for all the other faults—spoilage, etc.—it is entirely the duty of the foreman to eliminate to the greatest possible extent such causes as tend to increase the cost of the product in his department. It should be evident, however, that no foreman can properly or intelligently act in the best manner unless he is thoroughly posted in respect to what goes on. For this reason it is urged that superintendents and foremen be given constant access to the cost records so they may be fully posted in respect to all that happens. (See Chapter XXXII.)

Using Comparative Cost Sheets.—In any business doing a large amount of rapid work, the detailed cost of each run should be entered on a comparative cost sheet, as illustrated in Figure 10. This comparison will show, side by side, the unit time and cost for each operation and for each period where this particular unit has been in use. Fluctuations in direct cost are the net result of different workers who may run the same machine or perform the same operation. A very careful study should be made of the resulting cost as shown on the comparative sheet. Many times this comparison will bring out possibilities of eliminating the more serious fluctuations—and perhaps reducing time and cost—through careful examination and revision of operating methods.

In many plants more than one departmental foreman may be concerned in the operations shown on the comparative cost sheet. In such cases the superintendent should see that each foreman has the privilege of seeing the results in the operations of his department.

The Spirit of Cost Saving.—Above all things, the departmental heads should strive to develop in their personnel a spirit of cost saving.

The selling department, where such efforts have been little known, is a most fertile field. The use of the comparative monthly costs, the setting of quotas, and the budgeting of sales expense invariably stimulate the interest of each one in the department.

The notion that many in all departments of the business will not be interested in saving costs is untrue. Nearly every human being is susceptible to influence in the direction of making every minute and every penny count. In the last analysis, this is the aim of cost accounting.

CHAPTER XXXII

DEFECTIVE WORK LOSSES

The Ever-Present Result of Carelessness.—One serious drain upon profits is defective work. The losses which result therefrom are largely due to carelessness, although not always owing to carelessness for which someone can be held directly responsible.

Theoretically, if all materials were absolutely perfect, if they were handled in exactly the way they should be, and if all work in connection with them was done in exactly the manner it should be done, the results would be perfect. In actual experience, however, the transformation of any combination of raw materials into a finished product is never so perfect but that some defects are to be found.

Castings, for example, will have blowholes and other defects, and even though not detected at the foundry, these defects seriously affect the working of the metal in the machines during the machining operations. Sand dug from the ground may seem to be in as perfect condition as is thought possible, and yet when used in the mould in the foundry, it develops that the best conditions of venting are not present, and the castings blow as a result of gas pressure. As the condition of the material worked upon has a large bearing on the result of the operation, losses sustained from such imperfections of material are naturally not chargeable to the operator performing that particular operation, because the condition of the material worked on is entirely beyond his control.

On the other hand, in probably the majority of cases, defective work is largely due to carelessness of some kind on the part of the operator. Particularly is this so when wrong cuts are made, and when the completed work does not agree with the blue-print or specifications.

And yet again, far too often verbal directions are given by foremen. In the majority of cases when this is done, it is unfair to hold the worker responsible for mistakes in the machining. In such cases the responsibility for the defective work rests entirely with the management.

Inspection.—Cost records have brought out the industrial importance of maintaining in any manufacturing plant an adequate system of inspection. One of the first results of such a system is the detection of laxity in supplying workers with proper directions, blue-prints, or with proper tools to work with. Inspection is also important in that it leads to the study of the means of correcting errors which are being made. Moreover, inspection enables the management to anticipate the possibility of defective work through the experience gained in going over what has been done and in learning from what quarters errors may be expected and the reasons therefor.

It is not enough to wait until material has been completed and is ready for shipment, but inspection must start almost at the initial operation in order that all succeeding operations may be safeguarded. Intermittent checks during the various processes will prevent the work from going wrong in the first place, with the result that the final inspection becomes more a matter of routine than of finding anything defective.

Methods of Guarding Against Defective Work.—Wherever possible—and it is possible with regard to the majority of manufactured products—gauges and other instruments should be provided for trying out the work, not only as an aid to the inspection department, but also for the use of the operators. It is not safe to assume that an operator at some high-speed point of production will rely on measurement, unless the measurement is made by a fixed instrument and no judgment or brainwork is involved.

In this connection too much stress cannot be laid on the operating results which should follow the exhibits of cost figures, particularly in fortifying all workers and inspectors with proper instruments for minimizing erroneous sizes, and thus preventing defective work.

Various Kinds of Defective Work Losses.—Defective work losses may be grouped, in the main, as follows:

1. Cost of labor and overhead required to salvage defective work.
2. Loss of the unused part of salvaged material.
3. Labor and burden entirely lost when material has to be scrapped.
4. Loss of the difference between original and scrap value of material.
5. Loss of profit due to extra time taken on machines in salvaging material when other new material should have been produced for sale.
6. Loss of profit on material which has to be scrapped.

The last two items, it is true, are never computed in the cost records; nevertheless the loss occurs, as other material could have been made and sold at a profit, if the machines had not been engaged with salvaged material.

Intelligent Salvaging.—In many industries, more labor is put into salvaging material than is warranted by the loss which would be incurred if the material were scrapped in the first place. Particularly is this the fact in the metal industries of all kinds since the developing of the expensive art of electric and oxy-acetylene welding. This comment applies, it is true, more to the salvaging of new material, than to the welding of older material which when accidentally broken frequently affords possibilities of large saving.

But in the production of new material, particularly in operations which are highly specialized, great care must be taken to determine closely the dividing line between a profitable salvaging operation and one whose cost would amount to more than if the piece were entirely scrapped. This problem is a difficult one to solve in the steel-casting industry, where it has become possible to fill in defective spots by means of up-to-date welding apparatus. As welding, however, is so expensive, even though the work turned out is of a wonderful nature, it becomes a question as to how much of it can be profitably done.

Another feature in connection with this or any other salvaging operation is the fact that the possibility of saving the material eases up to a considerable extent the conscience of those responsible for the operations in the first place, with the result that increased carelessness is apt to occur. This tendency can be checked by penalizing either the department or the original operators who produce the defective work with the cost of salvaging the work. It is admitted, however, that inasmuch as costs cannot be determined without difficulty, perhaps this method cannot be carried out in many places.

In every industry there is this ever-present problem of waste. The rubber tire industry is a continuous problem of waste prevention. A "second" tire actually costs more than a "first," and yet of course to sell it as a "second" is more profitable than to sell it as scrap. All woodworking industries are subject to heavy losses through defective work. Chemical industries are subject to heavy losses where carelessness in heat controls and other features may spoil in a moment a lot of valuable material. Much of this material may be salvaged, but some cannot.

In any event, a great deal of study should be given to the question of salvaging, in order that decisions regarding it may be based on economy rather than on simply the idea of saving a particular piece of material, regardless of costs.

Charges for Defective Losses.—As intimated in the previous section, it is always a good plan to charge the department responsible for defective work, either with the cost of salvaging the work or with the losses incurred if the material is scrapped.

If in a rubber plant, for example, the milled compound furnished to the calenders or the tube department is defective, it seems just and fair that the milling department should stand the cost of the losses incurred by the department using the defective material. The management of the department producing this material should most certainly have a continual reminder of the results of the defective work turned out by such department. And in a cost system where all such details are accounted for, every department should stand not only its own cost for defective work, but also that portion of the cost of any other departments occasioned by errors which it has made.

As the excellence of cost-keeping increases, more and more attention is paid to matters of this nature in order that the real efficiency of each operating department may be known.

Analysis of Causes of Defective Work.—One of the most important steps in connection with the handling of defective work losses is that of analyzing and correcting the causes of the defective work. A sample of such analysis is shown in Figure 55—a foundry scrap report used in a grey iron foundry. It will be noted that this report gives a true history of each day's pouring, both as to the number of castings poured and as to the causes of defective work.

This form is shown simply to illustrate the use of analytical statements of defective work. Some form of this nature can be applied in connection with almost every manufacturing operation. In textile industries, for instance, it is easy to prepare a form upon which reasons for defective work may be entered, and to have an analysis sheet showing all defects. A similar analysis as to defective work can be made in industries concerned with the manufacture of wood, rubber, metals—

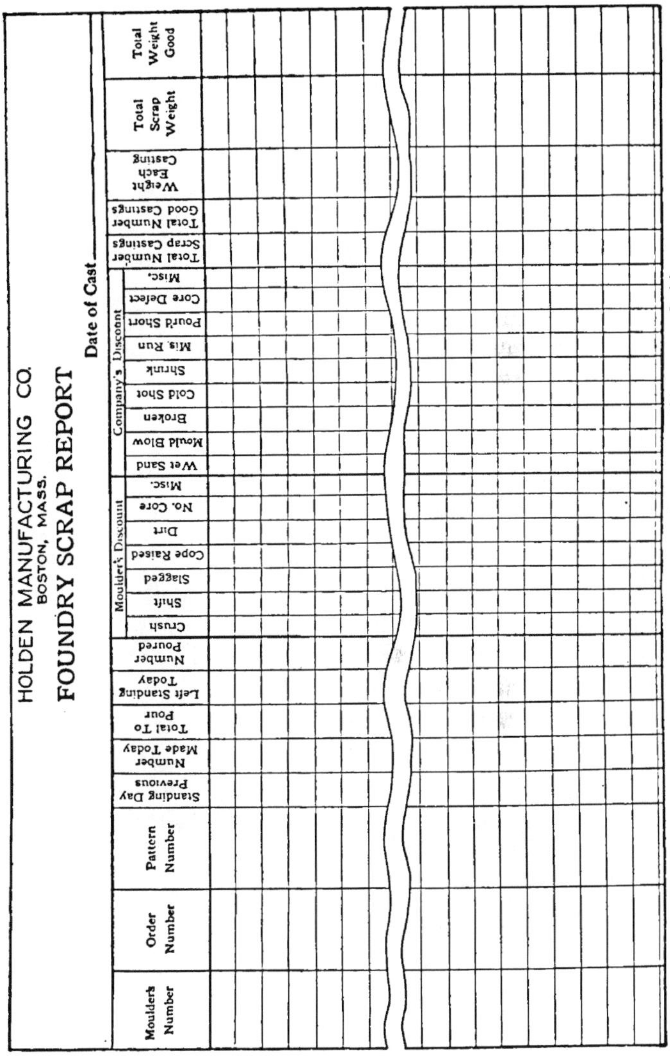

HOLDEN MANUFACTURING CO.
BOSTON, MASS.
FOUNDRY SCRAP REPORT

Date of Cast______

Moulders Number	Order Number	Pattern Number	Standing Day Previous	Number Made Today	Total To Pour	Left Standing Today	Number Poured	Moulder's Discount							Company's Discount									Total Number Scrap Castings	Total Number Good Castings	Weight Each Casting	Total Scrap Weight	Total Weight Good
								Crush	Shift	Slagged	Cope Raised	Dirt	No. Core	Misc.	Wet Sand	Mould Blow	Broken	Cold Shot	Shrunk	Mis. Run	Pour'd Short	Core Defect	Misc.					

Figure 55.—Foundry Scrap Report. (Size, 11 x 8½.)

indeed in almost any industry. It is of little use, however, to have analytical statements unless particular and careful use is made of them.

Statements of this nature show very clearly what might be called "epidemics" in a plant. Very often it happens that a certain class of defects will sweep through a plant and require very stringent action before its course can be stopped. If defects are standardized into a code and analyzed, the means of preventing these epidemics will be discovered. Such analysis of defects often reveals causes that would not have been suspected. For instance, compressed air may be used for various purposes. A lessening of the pressure often causes trouble which would never be successfully coped with unless shown repeatedly on the analysis of defective work.

The usual accounting record of the *cost* of this defective material comes too long after the trouble occurs to be of more than psychological benefit.

Use of Defective Loss Information in Cost Sheets.— With any method of costs in which a classified statement of defects is furnished with each run, it is advantageous to incorporate a statement of these defects in the cost sheet. The statement of defects will not always have an exact value attached to each item, but it will help to explain variation between runs of like material. In almost any industry, the cost of like material produced at different times varies to a considerable extent, and when the material is made on a piecework basis, it is quite difficult to explain this variance unless some automatic means is provided for doing so.

If it were possible, the value of defective work might be taken from a production order cost and transferred to the burden accounts to which it belongs. As an actual fact, however, it often happens that the entire cost of an order is charged up, and divided by the number of good pieces produced. In all such cases it is of the utmost advantage to have the statement of defective pieces and the causes therefor appended to or made a part of the cost sheet.

Defective Loss as Burden vs. Direct Cost.—There has been much argument as to whether or not the cost of defective work should be allowed to remain under a productive order number in a job order cost system, or whether the value of the defective work should be credited to this order and charged in the burden.

If the job under consideration is such that there is little likelihood of its ever being done again, the position that the cost of defective work should be allowed to remain against this particular job is well taken, the argument being that some record should be made of the fact that the work is risky and dangerous and should not be accepted again without due consideration. Work of this nature frequently arises in jobbing factories, machine-shops, foundries, etc.

On the other hand, in a manufacturing plant where the run of work is continuous and where the matter of defective losses may be regulated with care, it is probably best to assemble all defective work in the departmental burden accounts of those responsible for the work, in order to spread the overhead throughout the business.

To back up the argument as to special orders, the foundry may again be taken as an example. An order is received for 2,000 castings which are very difficult to manufacture. The casting is heavily cored, is difficult to mould, and has thin sections adjoining heavy sections. The estimator appreciates the fact that it is a risky casting and the job is taken on the basis of an allowance for, say, 25% or 50% loss. The price, it should be remembered, is given after such a loss has been figured in the estimate. When the run is completed, however, it is found that the loss has amounted to nearly 75%, because of the heavy shrinkage and the heavy discount for cracks caused by the junction of the light and heavy sections.

In cases of this sort each individual run must be considered on its own merits, and most certainly the heavy loss from defective work in the instance cited should not be charged into any burden account to be considered in the figuring of the costs of castings where a normal loss of 5% or 6% would prevail. Beyond question, in any industrial plant which is making a product on a special-order basis of this nature, no matter whether it is a foundry, woodworking plant, or any plant, the defective work in such cases should be allowed to remain as a cost against the particular order, and not spread in any general overhead.

On the other hand, in plants where regular work of repeat nature is the rule and a close study can be made of all defective losses, and where such defective losses are more often the result of causes which have nothing whatever to do with the nature of the material, it would seem more fair and equitable to concentrate such losses as are incurred in the burden accounts of the departments which caused the loss.

This applies particularly, as stated above, in those industries where such losses are occasioned more by changes in personnel, by carelessness, and by the various other causes which are linked up with plant conditions, than with any special features in connection with the work which is being produced.

Accounting for Defective Work.—Chapter XIII described the procedure for using the scrap ticket, the ticket which disposed of defective work to the salvage department when the possibility of salvaging existed, or to scrap account where material was entirely scrapped.

The procedure has been and still is used in many plants to start along immediately new parts to replace those which have become defective, bringing them up to the point where the original pieces were scrapped. This is accomplished through special orders for such parts to be manufactured for such replacement purposes.

This practice, however, is bad in the extreme *except* where the goods being manufactured are very special and no over-run is desired. In most instances the extra cost of setting up machines and equipment to bring up a few parts to replace those spoiled is prohibitive. It is often more profitable to allow in the first place for spoilage and have a slight excess of finished material than to disturb machines with small replacement runs. As a usual thing an allowance for spoilage should be made in quantities ordered. It is usually the case, indeed, that customers either are required or expect to take an over- or underrun of, say, 5% on the quantity ordered. This is especially true with castings.

It is with just such problems that the cost department is wrestling continuously, and where money can be saved through careful study and research.

CHAPTER XXXIII

REGULATION OF IDLE EQUIPMENT DELAYS

Delays of Equipment.—The large investment in the machinery and equipment of an industrial plant necessitates getting the utmost use out of this equipment. Proper planning of production and regulation of plant activities so as to secure this result constitute one of the greatest problems in industrial management. It has been recently stated that the average efficiency of equipment in plants has been about 50 per cent. This seems a ridiculously small percentage, but careful investigation reveals a multitude of causes which result in equipment standing idle and thereby losing the profits which otherwise would be made. It has also been stated that 80% of the causes of idleness of equipment are the fault of the management. When the causes of idle equipment are analyzed, this also may be seen to be entirely possible.

Accountants and engineers have devised almost every conceivable kind of scheme to bring about a greater use of all the facilities of industrial plants. Many of these schemes, however, have failed to reach the root of the trouble *at the time the trouble is occurring.*

They have generally relied upon weekly and monthly reports of the use of equipment—reducing the value of delays to a money basis—and upon elaborate statements prepared therefrom of the money lost in idle equipment. The money loss has then been carried into the burden accounts, thereby loading these accounts with the results of inefficient management, to the point sometimes of producing costs which would partially prohibit the securing of new work on account of high prices.

Practically every plan of reducing idle equipment to a money basis resolves itself into a post mortem proposition which does very little good.

Treating Causes of Delays at the Source.—The principal objective to be secured in connection with delays in the use of equipment is to stop the delays. This seems a simple statement, but it means a great deal. If action is taken at the time delays occur, most of the causes of delay can be readily corrected.

This discussion concerns particularly what is known as "standard equipment," that class of equipment which would be busy all the time, provided the plant management kept the operating departments fully supplied with proper materials, operators, tools, etc. The so-called single-purpose machines are in a class by themselves. With those the problem is one of the sales departments keeping the plant supplied with the particular kind of orders required to keep the special equipment going full speed. It is true that there is another class of single-purpose machines whose operation even for only an hour or two per day makes them well worth the money they cost, because of their high speed and the great savings they effect. Such machines, however, as they are of a highly special nature and relatively very few, are hardly to be considered in the problem of idle time. This is equally true of extra or so-called "stand by" machines.

The chief question is how to deal with the causes of delays at the source. If a machine breaks down, the management should not have to wait till the end of the week to learn that the machine broke down and was idle for two days. The breakdown should be a matter of record 15 minutes after it happens, in order that all the facilities of the organization may be exerted to get the repairs made at the earliest possible moment, thereby reducing the idle time which would result if the repairs were allowed to drag.

Accounting for Idle Time.—As explained in Chapter XVIII, the time clerks have the duty of recording not only the time spent by men on particular jobs, but also the time of idle equipment, using a special card somewhat resembling a time card. Such a card, applying particularly to machine-shops, is shown in Figure 56. The card is of a different color from the time cards, preferably pink or red, in order that when displayed on the time board it will indicate graphically the number of pieces of idle equipment.

The entries are simple, consisting of only the department and machine number and the time idle. The rest of the information is recorded by simply inserting a cross showing the cause of idleness and also whether or not the piece of equipment is a regular, a single-purpose machine or a stand by machine.

On the time board a clip is provided for each working place, that is for each individual piece of machine equipment. At all times, at the clip representing each machine, there will be either a direct worker's card, indicating that the equipment is working, or a pink card, indicating that this piece of equipment is idle.

Action Required to Correct Causes of Delays.—The action required in connection with delays in the use of equipment may be considered under two heads:

1. Anticipative action to prevent the occurrence of delays.
2. Action to be taken while the delays exist.

Preventing delays is by far the more important task. On the thoroughness of such prevention depends the correction of most of the losses from idle equipment. It is an important function to watch and regulate all movements, and thus catch these dangerous and costly delays to equipment at their source. That method is far superior to any possible method of post mortem accounting for value of lost time, which various ma-

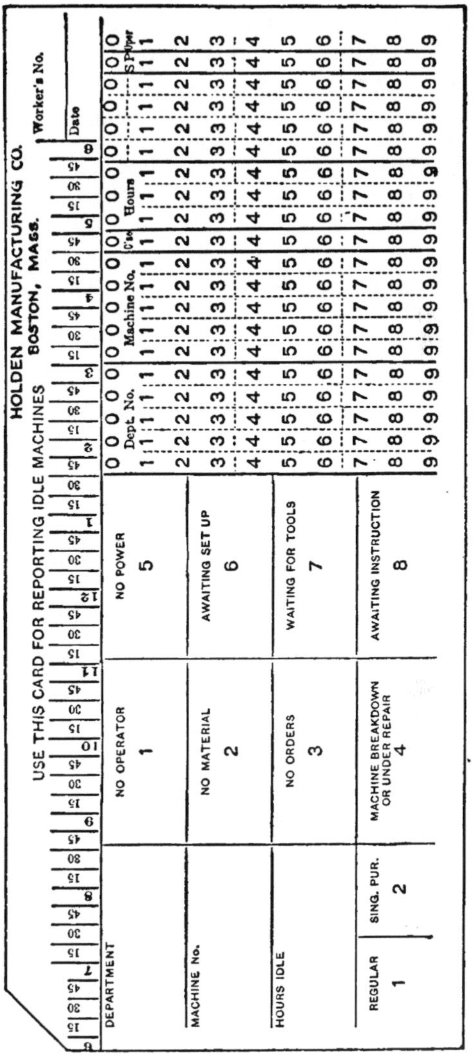

Figure 56.—Idle Machine Card. (Size, 7⅜ x 3¼.)

chine rate and departmental cost systems try so hard to provide. The old saying, "Locking the stable door after the horse is stolen," fits this situation closely. It is of little value to know how much the loss has been in comparison with the steps taken to prevent the loss before it occurred.

Causes of Idle Machines and Equipment.—The principal causes of idle machines and equipment, as indicated on the card shown in Figure 56, are:

1. No operator.
2. No material.
3. No orders.
4. Machine breakdown or under repairs.
5. No power.
6. Awaiting set-up.
7. Waiting for tools.
8. Awaiting instructions.

1. No Operator.—The responsibility for keeping up the supply of operators is primarily within the duties of the employment department. That department has the task of securing and distributing the working forces so that all pieces of equipment shall be kept going full speed, so far as the man power is concerned. It is essential, however, for the employment to keep in very close touch with the operating foremen for two reasons: (1) to be sure that the operating foremen are using the employees in a way to keep them at work and not cause them to quit or stay away from the job; and (2) to overcome the natural conditions of labor shortage which applies to some departments in greater measure than to others.

The time department also has an important function in this connection. It was specified in Chapter XVIII that a late and absent report should be made up each morning. A copy of this report should be sent to the time office, thus enabling that department immediately to ascertain what equipment is idle from the cause of no operator.

A check should be made at once of the schedules on the equipment which may appear to be idle from the cause of no operator, and no time should be lost in getting into communication with the employment department to learn what relief can be obtained there. If no men can be provided through this particular channel, the schedules throughout the shop or in this department and also other departments should be consulted to find some point where operators can be secured to man the idle equipment. In normal times, and even in abnormal times, a great deal can be accomplished in this way, preventing the loss of production which otherwise would result.

2. **No Material.**—Lack of material operates in many ways to delay the equipment, chiefly by—

1. Failure within the department to have the material for a job at the machine at the time the operator is ready to start.
2. Failure of the storeroom to fill a requisition in time to permit delivery to the machine when the material is needed.
3. Failure of the purchasing department to get necessary material to the stockroom to permit delivery at the time the job is ready to be started.

It is of extreme importance that material required for the performance of any operation shall be ready at the machine when the previous job is completed. Failure in this point results in many delays, all of which could be eliminated by the planning department.

Failure within the department to have the material on the spot when a job is to be started is purely a breakdown in carrying out the internal transportation procedure which is under the full responsibility of the planning department. The time clerks have entire jurisdiction over all movements of the material. As they know that a machine will need material for a job at a certain time, it is clearly their duty to see that such material is delivered to the machine in time. Delay from this cause, accordingly, is a delay which should never occur.

Failure of the storeroom to fill a requisition for the raw material or the parts required for an assembly order is in a similar way directly the fault of the planning department through the time clerk. The movement of the raw material from the storeroom is also under the entire jurisdiction of the planning department. This delay also should never occur if the organized procedure is strictly carried out.

Failure of the purchasing department to get material into the plant in time for use is a different matter from the two preceding cases. Nevertheless, except for abnormal conditions, even this delay may be traced back to the stock record division. If the data in connection with all the raw material have been adequately taken into consideration, if sufficient time has been allowed for the process of issuing the purchase orders, for making the shipment, and for the transit of the material, there should be no delays in connection with the receipt of purchased material.

The matter requires close co-operation between the purchasing department and the planning department, but in the last analysis the main responsibility lies with the planning department.

Of course, failure to receive raw material in time does not always result in idle equipment, as a change in schedule may be made which keeps the equipment running full. On the other hand, in specialized plants the results are often disastrous, particularly, for example, in automobile plants, where whole rows of regular machines are set aside purely for performing certain operations on particular pieces of material.

Another illustration may be found in any high-speed manufacturing industry—the manufacture of rubber tires, for emample—where a slip in keeping enough cotton fabric ahead will cripple the entire flow of product and possibly shut down the entire plant. It must always be borne in mind that the function of the purchasing department is to purchase. It is the responsibility of the planning department, however, to see that material is purchased in sufficient time and in sufficient quantity. If this duty is carried out to the letter, the delays due to non-receipt of raw material can be avoided.

3. **No Orders.**—Lack of orders may be owing to either of two reasons:

1. Failure of the plant order department to issue production orders in time to provide the work for the machines.
2. Failure of the sales department to supply the factory with sales orders which are necessary to keep certain kinds of equipment busy.

The first one should be entirely eliminated. It is a matter either of neglect or of overloading on the part of the department issuing the production orders. The production schedules show clearly the work ahead and any failure to issue production orders considerably in advance of the time the work is required for the machines is a neglect which is practically inexcusable.

Yet that very thing happens in many cases, with results that are disastrous to perhaps more than one piece of equipment. The absolute removal of this cause for delay should be a matter of most strenuous action by some responsible executive.

Failure of the sales department to supply the factory with orders is a cause of delay which is subject to considerable debate. It should be said, however, that a planning department which is properly on the job can anticipate shortage of work, and thereby cause action to be taken by the sales department. Otherwise the sales department may know nothing of the fact that certain lines of work are running low.

A good illustration may be seen in a jobbing foundry where special jarring machines may have been installed to take care of work of various sizes. It may be that this particular foundry will do work ranging from small castings in snap flasks to castings weighing two or three tons, which can be made on the large jarring machine equipment which has been installed. The same thing is true of jobbing machine-shops or of any other kind of shop where there is liability of a shortage in various kinds of work.

The planning department, as the only department which has the information as to the exact tonnage ahead, has undeniably the duty of notifying the sales department of the shortage of orders for particular classes of work. If this function is properly performed, in the great majority of cases the sales department can easily secure the orders to keep all classes of equipment going at full speed.

The second reason for delay from lack of sales orders applies most particularly to special or single-purpose machines. It should be given most particular attention by the sales department. Very often the sales department is responsible for installing such machines, agreeing to keep them busy if the investment is made.

4. **Machine Breakdown or Under Repairs.**—The breakdown of machines, which occasions a large percentage of the lost time in the use of equipment, can be reduced to a minimum by proper management. A very effective means is the installation of anticipative inspection, applying the principle of a "Stitch in time saves nine." The fact is, with probably the majority of breakdowns, that if proper inspection of the machinery had been carried out, the weakness which finally resulted in the breakdown could have been eliminated before becoming a serious factor. Speedy attention should be given to each case of breakdown, to get the machine going at the earliest possible moment. This is a function of the planning department, which should follow up the repair department actively and see that all possible speed is used in getting the machine back into production.

Many of the breakdowns occur through breaks of belting, a cause of delay which in nearly every case is absolutely inexcusable. Any mechanic can tell by the looks of a belt whether it is nearing the point of breakdown. A long delay may be easily avoided by having a new belt cut and put into place during the time the plant is not operating.

Inspection of motors should be made daily, particularly in plants where individual motor drives are used, and also when the group plan of drive is used, where the breakdown of a motor is a very serious consequence. It seems almost unnecessary to prescribe this action, but in many plants this inspection is not made and the resulting losses from idle equipment are very heavy. Care in cleaning motors saves many dollars in repairs.

Line shafting should be subject to constant inspection both as to its line-up and as to the matter of constant oiling and care. The pulleys on the line shaft are constantly loosening and need unremitting attention.

The more intricate the machine, the greater the necessity of constant inspection. This applies particularly to such machines as may be found in foundries, grinding departments, and other departments where there is a great deal of dust and a liability to burn out bearings and tie up the machines in other ways.

A matter especially to be considered with regard to inspection is that very often, when a break occurs, the damage done is greatly in excess of what it would have been if the weak point itself had been repaired before the serious break took place. A broken belt has been known to fly through the air and land in the gears of another machine, causing another breakdown and a loss from broken equipment many times the value of the belt which caused the trouble. To this must be added the loss in production occasioned by the breakdown of both machines.

Constant surveillance by foremen prevents many breakdowns. Foremen can require material to be properly piled and small tools to be properly taken care of while lying on the various machine tools, and thus run no risk of causing expensive accidents. Foremen, assistant foreman, and inspectors can earn their salaries many times over by co-operating with machine inspectors in watching all conditions which have to do with causing breakdowns and tying up equipment.

When a machine does break down, the production control department should follow up the repair department to have repairs made and get the machine back into service as quickly as possible. In the case of a breakdown this work has to be done during working hours. All other repairs, however, the planning department should have performed during the regular hours of shut-down rather than during the regular working hours so as to keep the equipment in operation.

5. **No Power.**—Delays due to "no power" are usually caused by breakdowns in the power house in cases where power is generated within the plant. Lack of power may cause a stoppage of work in case of a breakdown or burning out of the motor driving either an individual machine or a group of machines. This cause of idle equipment can be obviated in the majority of cases by the anticipative inspection of electric motors.

In case of delays from this cause when the power is generated by the company itself, the power department must be followed up, so that the supply of power may be reinstated at the earliest possible moment. In the case of failure of power brought in from the outside, it is always necessary to ascertain at once from the distributing station the cause of the failure. It may be that the distributing station knows nothing about the failure of power until notified by the consumer.

6. **Awaiting Set-Up.**—Delays from failure to have machines set up in time for jobs may arise from either:

1. Failure of the operating department to have a sufficient number of set-up men.
2. Failure of the planning department to schedule work so that the set-up of machines is well distributed, in order to avoid peak loads on the staff of set-up men which ordinarily is sufficient to handle the necessary work.

The first cause must be eliminated by the operating department itself, which should maintain a sufficient corps of set-up men. As to the second cause, the planning department must so plan the work that undue bunching of set-ups is avoided.

A well-organized planning department is fortified with the records of set-up time required for each and every job which is to be put into work. If a control board is used, this set-up time appears graphically, and therefore is easily noted. This department is also fully aware of the number of set-up men available in each department. It is entirely the fault of the planning department if a number of jobs which require the services of the set-up men are deliberately scheduled to start at the same time. Neglect of planning, indeed, is usually the largest factor in connection with the delays which occur on this account. Strenuous executive intervention is sometimes needed to overcome this cause.

7. **Waiting for Tools.**—Delay is caused very often by men having to wait for tools, usually because of the failure of the planning department properly to plan and carry out the preliminaries in connection with each job to be performed.

It is a duty of the planning department to safeguard against delays by seeing that all tools including jigs, etc., are ready ahead of the time for starting each job, and that they are delivered duly to the machine.

In the majority of manufacturing institutions the runs of work are sufficient to justify proper tooling. Even in a jobbing-shop where jigs may not be used, it was long ago demonstrated that the regular cutting tools should be ground in the toolroom and kept in readiness. In the production of many pieces of product it is absolutely necessary to have complete and intricate jigs.

The responsibility for supplying jigs rests between the operating department concerned and the planning department. The former must report any breakage or spoilage in tools being used on a job, in order that the latter may have the break repaired before the job is again scheduled.

Special tools damaged in the operating departments should not be returned to the toolroom until they are repaired. In foundries, patterns which are damaged during the progress of a job are often returned to the pattern vault without being put into proper shape for the next job. Patterns are often damaged while in storage. Hence, it is essential for the planning department to check up the tools, etc., sufficiently ahead of the requirements in order to be sure that everything is ready to start the work on jobs.

8. Awaiting Instructions.—In some instances it is necessary to give the operator definite instructions in connection with the work to be performed. The instructions may consist of explaining blue-prints or making clear other details. It is definitely the duty of the operating foremen to be on hand to give the proper instructions at the time the material is delivered to the machine ready for the start of work. The time clerk, moreover, representing the planning department, who is aware of the fact that instructions have to be issued, should make it his particular duty to give the foremen advance notice that this job is about to be started, thereby assuring attention to instructions and elimination of any delay.

Idle Machine Report.—To aid in the careful watching and analysis of delays, an idle machine report is illustrated in Figure 57. This form, it will be noted, gives a statement of the number of hours each individual piece of equipment is idle;

HOLDEN MANUFACTURING CO.
BOSTON, MASS.
IDLE MACHINE REPORT

__________ Dept. Period Ending __________ 19__

Machine Numbers	Stand Hours	Running Hours			Idle Hours									Percentages	
		Regular Stand Hrs	Overtime Hours	Total Hrs. Run	No Operator	No Material	No Orders	Repair	No Power	Await Set Up	Await Tools	Await Inst.	Total Idle Hrs.	% Stand	% Run

Figure 57.—Idle Machine Report. (Size, 11 x 8½.)

the number of hours it should have run, based on the standard hours of the shop; the number of overtime hours run; and the per cent of the total idle time to the standard hours and also to the total hours actually run, a valuable record from the managerial standpoint. This report reflects every week the running conditions of the equipment and shows up both successes and failures of the effort to eliminate idle time of equipment. Perhaps, as a matter of record, the same report should be shown for a complete month.

The point needs to be reiterated that the *elimination* of the causes of idle time is of far greater value than merely holding post mortems. As has been intimated before, the reducing of idle machine time to money cost occurs too late to be of use. This analysis of time without money value follows up by report form the daily and hourly follow-up as the machines are idle.

As machine rates are figured on *normal capacity,* there is no idle machine loss in money until the machine runs less time than normal. Then it is that this analysis is best appreciated in order to know why the machine was idle beyond its reasonable allowance.

CHAPTER XXXIV

JOINT AND BY-PRODUCT COSTS

The Problem of Joint and By-Product Costs.—In the great majority of cases most raw material and labor can be charged directly to the products which are manufactured. In some cases, however, labor is applied to a raw material or a number of raw materials, and more than one product results. This brings about a very perplexing problem in costing, as it is very difficult to properly allocate the total cost to the various resultant products.

In the last analysis there is a very considerable difference between joint products and by-products. What may be a by-product today may be a joint product tomorrow and the main product the next day. The scientific development of uses for materials constantly changes the relation of one to another.

In many industries, such as in the chemical industry, there is encountered a progressive flow of products. For instance, a material may be nitrated. The resultant product will be distilled and a certain marketable product secured. The residue may be precipitated and another marketable product secured. This presents a most complicated problem.

Glue stock may be boiled and a first quality glue drawn off. A repetition of the same process will produce a slightly inferior grade of glue. Repeated again and again still more inferior grades are produced. And yet the original material is used over and over, and the production cost, so far as labor and expenses are concerned is approximately the same for each grade.

We therefore have the feature of what might be called "progressive" products to deal with, and our problem accordingly becomes more and more complex.

Definition of By-Products.—Disregarding any changing conditions, and recognizing only clearly defined facts, a by-product is defined as " an *accessory* product resulting from some specific process." The situation is that some *specific* product is wanted and that in the securing of this product one or more products of varying and doubtful value are secured, none of which would in themselves be desired or practical if alone.

In a woodworking factory the main product may be a line of boxes of fine grade. In cutting the lumber, strips or short pieces are left. If the strips are run through automatic machines into mouldings, and the short pieces made into ink stands, the relationship of these products would be

Main Product – Boxes
By-Products – Mouldings
Ink Stands

In this case, however, no labor or burden expended on the cutting of the lumber for boxes would apply to the by-products—simply the lumber cost would be prorated. The reason for this is obvious, for the labor of cutting the stock for the boxes has no relation whatever to the by-products which by themselves must sustain their own cutting cost.

By-products, therefore, may be regarded as *products recovered from discarded material from a main process or from the production of some major product, and where material value only is to be considered at the time the by-product is severed from its main product.*

Definition of Joint Products.—Wherever a process using one or more materials leads to the production of more than one product, each one of which is a marketable product, and where neither product could be produced without the other, such resultant products are known as joint products.

Many joint products may have originally been by-products; that is, they may have had little or no market, and therefore were simply discards from a main product. A very prominent example of this may be cited in the illuminating gas industry. While naturally the gas is the principal product, the gas plant which is up to date finds coke, ammonia, benzol, toluol and other products to be large factors and approaching the rank of joint products rather than by-products. In the chemical industry will be found an abundance of illustrations of joint products, where an originating process will result in a number of products by successive sub-processes.

In all such cases, the resultant products could never be secured were it not for the original process. Obviously, therefore, not only the material cost of the original process but also the labor and burden cost are rightly chargeable in proper proportion against the succeeding joint products.

Joint products, therefore, may be regarded as *products from an original process where the complete material, labor and burden cost of the original process is chargeable to the various joint products in proper proportion.*

Costing By-Products.—Figure 58 illustrates the method of costing by-products. It will be observed that only the material cost of $70 is carried down to the succeeding products, the bulk, $130, going to the main product.

In this illustration it is indicated that each by-product, B and C, is actually sold by the regular selling forces. By-product B sustains further cost of manufacture, but by-product C is simply sold with no further addition of manufacturing cost. There may be other by-products which should be credited, and without the addition of selling expense and profit.

An illustration in mind is that of slag in an open hearth steel plant. Years ago this slag was carried out to the dump and thrown away with the old molding and core sand. Handling it was an expense, as is the case with all other refuse. Road building has opened a use for this slag, and in many

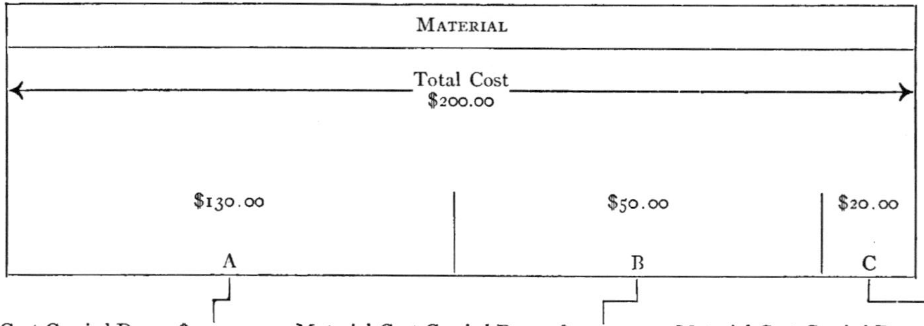

Material Cost Carried Down	$130 00
Other Material Cost	52.00
Labor Cost	75 00
Burden Cost	95 00
	$352 00
Adm. and Selling	35.20
	$387.20
Profit	38.72
Selling Price	$425.92

Material Cost Carried Down	$ 50.00
Other Materials	20.00
Other Labor	10.00
Other Burden	10.00
	$ 90.00
Adm. and Selling	9.00
	$ 99.00
Profit	9.90
Selling Price	$108.90

Material Cost Carried Down	$20.00
Adm. and Selling	2.00
	$22.00
Profit	2.20
Selling Price	$24.20

Figure 58.—Illustration of By-Product Costing

cases an actual income is derived from its sale. Mountainous piles of blast furnace slag, a problem in the past, have become a salable product.

In all cases of by-products, a great deal of analytical thought must be used. In the case of slag, a blast furnace in a large city may derive an income, while one in an out of the way place may derive no income. Thus it is clear that each case must be decided on its own merits.

It will be noted that Figure 58 shows each by-product built up to a selling price with full administrative and selling cost added, and also the standard profit of, say, 10%. The reason for the inclusion of these expenses and the profit may be stated as follows:

To promote the sale of by-products, to sell them and to account for them costs money and may even cost proportionately more than in the case of the main product. The reason for including *profit* is to make sure that the main product carries *full cost* in order that the company may be assured of profits. This will be made clear in the following paragraphs.

Computing Credits to Main Product for By-Products.— Figure 59 shows the actual method of arriving at the figures in Figure 58. Figure 59 shows the eventual disposition of all costs of the process, but in actual practice the figuring begins with the by-products and works back to the main product.

In figuring such costs, it is necessary to start with

1. The amount received for each by-product.
2. The original full material cost of the process.

In the case of by-product B the profit at 10% on cost is first deducted, and then the administrative and selling expenses at 10% on cost. The cost records show a manufacturing cost of $40 to prepare the by-product for market which, being deducted from the previous balance, leaves $50 as the credit to the main product original material cost.

By-Product B

Selling Price		$108.90
Less Profit at 10% on Cost		9.90
		$ 99.00
Less Adm. and Selling at 10% on Cost		9.00
		$ 90.00
Less Cost to Mfr.:		
Materials	$20.00	
Labor	10.00	
Burden	10.00	40.00
Balance—being credit to main product Material Cost		$ 50.00

By-Product C

Selling Price	$24.20
Less Profit at 10% on Cost	2.20
	$22.00
Less Adm. and Selling at 10% on Cost	2.00
Balance—being credit to main product Material Cost	$20.00

Main Product A

Original Material Cost		$200.00
Less:		
Credit from C	$20.00	
" B	50.00	70.00
Net Material Cost		$130.00
Other Material Cost		52.00
Labor Cost		75.00
Burden Cost		95.00
		$352.00
Adm. and Selling		35.20
		$387.20
Profit		38.72
Selling Price		$425.92

Figure 59.—Computation of Credits to Main Product for By-Products, Taking Profit on By-Products into Consideration

By-Product B

Selling Price		$108.90
Less Adm. and Selling at 10% on Cost		9.90
		$ 99.00
Less Cost of Mfr.:		
Materials	$20.00	
Labor	10.00	
Burden	10.00	40.00
Balance—being credit to main product Material Cost		$ 59.00

By-Product C

Selling Price	$24.20
Less Adm. and Selling at 10% on Cost	2.20
Balance—being credit to main product Material Cost	$22.00

Main Product A

Original Material Cost		$200.00
Less:		
Credit from C	$22.00	
" " B	59.00	81.00
Net Original Material Cost		$119.00
Other Material Cost		52.00
Labor Cost		75.00
Burden Cost		95.00
		$341.00
Adm. and Selling		$34.10
Profit		37.51
Selling Price		$412.61

Figure 60.—Computation of Credits to Main Product for By-Products, Omitting Profit on By-Products

By-product C has no additional manufacturing cost; therefore after deducting the profit and expense the credit to the original material cost is $20.

The total credits to the original material cost are $70, leaving $130 as the residual original material cost of the main product. The additional material, labor and burden costs are then combined as usual with the original cost as are also the administrative and selling expense and the percentage for profit, and the result is the selling price which should be received for the main product.

Figure 60 shows the same nature of figuring except that no profit is taken into consideration on the by-products. It is clearly seen that the resultant selling price of the main product is $13.31 less than when profit is taken on the by-product.

The arguments for taking profits into consideration on by-products are that most by-products are subject to further manufacturing after splitting off from the main product; that they require selling effort sometimes greater than main product, that they require as much office, accounting and administration effort as the main product, if not more, and that such effort should produce a profit. When this profit is deducted from the selling prices of the by-products, it naturally reduces the net credit to the main product, thereby showing a higher final cost which the main product must bear, and on which its selling price should be fixed.

Another argument for considering profits on by-products is that every business with by-products is constantly striving to find good uses and markets for the by-products. It often happens, therefore, that almost useless by-products slowly become more valuable, may soon become joint products and later, main products. If, therefore, no profits were taken into consideration on by-products and their value increased, the credit to the main product would become abnormally large and seriously affect the main product cost.

Costing Joint Products.—The costing of joint products is largely similar to the procedure for by-products with one very important exception. This exception is that the total cost of material, labor and burden is prorated to each product rather than just the material cost at the point where the products split apart.

In a dairy plant, whole milk is placed in separators. The centrifugal action of the machine separates the cream from the skim milk. The cream is either sold as such or is used in the manufacture of ice cream and other products. The skim milk may be processed to form the product of skim milk powder. This is a physical process easily understood but exactly parallel to many chemical processes where a material or a number of materials are treated, with more than one product as a result. In the case of the milk, the cost of separating the milk plus the cost of the milk must be prorated to the two joint products. Each of the joint products is then subject to further cost in its own particular process before the marketable products are secured.

Figure 61 illustrates for joint products the break-down of costs. It will be noted that the original cost which is prorated includes labor, burden and material, and not just the material alone as with by-products.

Here again the problem of prorating is confronted, and is somewhat different than in the case of by-products, where the value received for the by-products was worked back from the selling price in order to ascertain the credits to the main product material.

In the case of joint products the ratios to be used in prorating the original cost must be obtained from various sources and in various ways, depending entirely upon the circumstances in each particular case. Another factor which enters into the situation is the purpose of ascertaining the costs—whether for inventory pricing only or to determine selling prices.

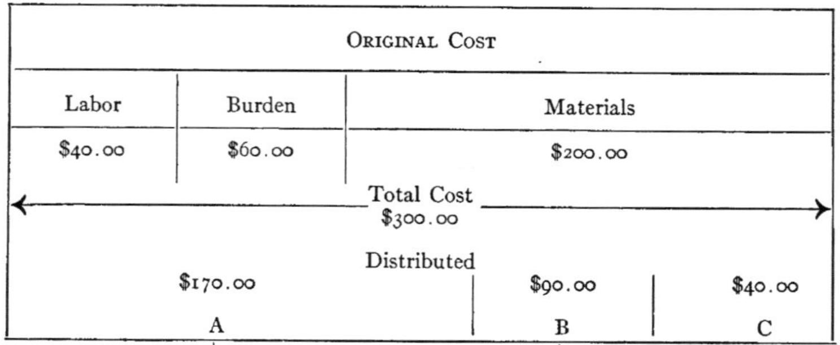

Prop. Carried Down	$170.00
Other Materials	62.00
" Labor	25.00
" Burden	25.00
	$282.00
Adm. and Selling	28.20
	$310.20
Profit	31.02
Selling Price	$341.22

Prop. Carried Down	$ 90.00
Other Materials	10.00
" Labor	20.00
" Burden	40.00
	$160.00
Adm. and Selling	16.00
	$176.00
Profit	17.60
Selling Price	$193.60

Prop. Carried Down	$40.00
Other Labor	15.00
Other Burden	25.00
	$80.00
Adm. and Selling	8.00
	$88.00
Profit	8.80
Selling Price	$96.80

Figure 61.—Illustration of Joint Product Costing

Prorating Original Costs to Joint Product Costs.—The prorating of original costs to joint products will vary in the following situations:

1. Where definite proration may be made on analytical value.
2. Where final weight of yield of each product is a proper basis.
3. Where market values of completed products may be used as a basis.
4. Where a standard proration may be used based on average trade demands or specific internal conditions.

1. *Prorating on Analytical Value.* In the chemical industry many processes produce an "intermediate," so-called, from which certain joint products may be secured. By chemical analysis, the quantity of each of these products to be recovered from the original process is definitely known. This is of course subject to proper yields being secured by the plant, and where any succeeding process fails in its yield it does not affect the original proration at all. Where such chemical basis exists, the prorating may be figured on the basis of the ratio of value of chemicals entering into each product.

2. *Prorating on Weight Basis.* In some cases the joint products may be reduced to a weight basis, and the original process or material cost may be prorated in proportion to the weight apportionment of each product.

3. *Prorating on Market Values of Joint Products.* This method is probably used more than any other at present, largely on account of pressure brought to bear by necessities of securing inventory costs. Thus it may be that tax rulings and accounting expediencies have had too great an influence, and the consideration of the development of processes within an individual company has been neglected.

The method of prorating on the basis of market values is to prorate the cost to the joint products in ratio to their market value. If four products had an original cost of $450.00, this cost would be prorated on a market basis as follows:

	Lbs.	Mkt. Value Per lb.	Amount	Per Cent	Prop. of Cost	Cost Per lb.
Product A..........	300	$ 80	$240 00	40	$180.00	$.60
B..........	400	.60	240.00	40	180.00	.45
C..........	200	.40	80.00	13.33	59.98	.30
D..........	100	.40	40.00	6.67	30.02	.30
	1,000		$600.00	100.00	$450.00	

As stated before, however, the market basis, while probably best for many cases, has its faults. These may be discussed under the following heading.

4. *Prorating by Standard Ratio.* As opposed to any of the other methods, it is believed that this method of prorating the original cost holds more possibilities than any other. It is based on a careful survey of *all* conditions surrounding the joint products, particularly comparing the developments of the processes of the individual company with the industry as a whole.

No two companies are ever exactly equal in the efficiency of processes. One company will develop valuable secret processes which competitors are far from reaching. Another company will concentrate on other products. Therefore, let us consider a case.

Supposing that product A as shown in the illustration on this page, to which was allocated a cost of sixty cents per pound by the market basis method, showed a final cost as follows:

300 lbs. at prorated share of original cost at $.60	$180.00
Further labor cost to complete	25.00
Burden cost	40.00
	$245.00

Administrative and Selling at 10%	24.50
	$269.50
Amount received at market of $.80 per lb.	240.00
Loss on 300 lbs. of product A	$29.50

At the same time, the company has developed some remarkable uses for products C and D where these products could be treated and sold at a large profit even if they had a market price of $1.00 per pound in the case of product C, and $.90 per pound in the case of product D. In the meantime, the costs of product A have influenced the company to cease or slacken efforts to sell product A on account of the apparent loss. Therefore, the whole process suffers, as the production is decreased on account of product A, and there is not enough material to supply products C and D. And as the processes in connection with products C and D are secret, the company does not dare to buy these products in the market.

This case, therefore, is one where the market basis of cost distribution is detrimental, and where a standard ratio based on the conditions of the company itself is called for. Fixing its own market values (which is the basis of figuring its own ratio to be used as a standard) the distribution of the original cost would result as follows:

	Lbs.	Std. Value Per lb.	Amount	Per Cent	Prop. of Cost	Cost Per Lb.
Product A.	300	$.80	$240.00	31.2	$140.40	$.468
B.	400	.60	240.00	31.2	140.40	.351
C.	200	1.00	200.00	26.	117.00	.585
D.	100	.90	90.00	11.6	52.20	.522
	1,000		$770.00	100.0	$450.00	

Products C and D absorb more cost, and products A and B less by this changed ratio. Product A final cost as shown on page 444 would now appear as follows:

300 lbs. at prorated share of original cost at $.468	$140.40
Further labor cost to complete	25.00
Burden cost	40.00
	$205.40
Administrative and Selling at 10%	20.54
	$225.94
Amount received at market of $.80 per lb.	$240.00
Cost	225.94
Profit on 300 lbs. of product A	$14.06

Conclusion.—Accounting for joint products and accounting for by-products differ in but the one feature of the allocation of the original costs to the various products. All the rest of the accounting for the cost is regular procedure.

The discussion in this chapter has dealt with principles instead of taking up many illustrations of specific cases. It is only too easy to attempt illustrations to carry over an illustration from one industry to another where it does not apply, with disastrous results.

The reader must remember that the illustrations of breakdowns of cost as shown in this chapter are for one step only. In the chemical industry one or more of the joint products may be in itself an original cost for further break-down into other products. Coal tar, for instance, is a joint product with coke and other products in a gas or coke plant. But the family of products from coal tar is enormous, including dyes, medicines, high explosives and other products almost without limit.

The great secret underlying the accounting for joint and by-products, as has already been stated, lies in the careful and painstaking study of each individual situation.

CHAPTER XXXV

INTEREST AS A COST

Interest from a Practical Viewpoint.—The question of whether or not interest as a whole, or interest actually paid out versus interest not actually paid out should be treated as a cost is one which cannot be discussed without careful analysis.

It seems without doubt that a very positive error is continually being made in failing to leave aside legal, banking and all other such arguments, and in failing to carefully dissect the problem into its factors, whereby it may be determined clearly just what effect each factor has on business.

The plea, for example, that an inefficient sales department cannot get high enough prices unless interest is included in cost is in itself ridiculous and has no place in the argument. But if the sales department is selling a product manufactured on a high priced machine at a low cost as against a similar product manufactured by a competitor by hand, a selling price which does not include a consideration for interest in the expensive equipment would be wrong and a piece of very bad business.

This chapter, therefore devotes itself to an analysis of the various kinds of interest, the effect they have on business, and their treatment in the records as indicated by the necessities in each case.

This analysis is worked out, fundamentally, from the standpoint of businesses within a particular industry. A packing house competes only with other packing houses, and all have the same general characteristics, but it is not necessary to consider packing houses versus cotton spinning plants.

Kinds of Interest.—Let us consider the various kinds of interest involved. The principal kinds commonly encountered are as follows:

Interest Actually Paid Out:

1. Interest paid on bank loans
2. Interest paid on notes to creditors
3. Interest paid on open accounts owed
4. Interest on bonded indebtedness

Interest Not Actually Paid Out:

5. Interest on buildings and real estate
6. Interest on machinery
7. Interest on fixtures
8. Interest on raw materials in stock
9. Interest on materials, labor and burden in process
10. Interest on finished goods
11. Interest on cash on hand
12. Interest on accounts receivable
13. Interest on other miscellaneous assets

Interest Actually Paid Out

Items 1 to 4 inclusive cover interest actually paid out on liabilities. In this discussion the complete asset side of the balance sheet will be considered. Therefore the interest paid out will be immediately disposed of as a debit to profit and loss. It is manifestly impossible to do otherwise when consideration is given to the question of charging into cost the interest on the various items of investment shown on the assets section of the balance sheet.

Interest Not Actually Paid Out

5. Interest on Buildings and Real Estate.—A very tangible argument exists for charging interest on buildings and real estate to costs.

Within a given industry are concerns which own their own plants and also those which do not. Assuming that each is obliged to defray repair costs, the one owning its plant will be found to include in cost—

Depreciation on buildings
Taxes on buildings and real estate

The one not owning its plant will charge to cost its complete rent, which includes the two items above plus the interest to the owner of the property, in other words—

Depreciation
Taxes on buildings and real estate
Interest on the value of investment

It is evident that the company owning its plant will constantly have a smaller cost by the amount of the interest received by the owner of the property for which the other company pays rent; and to that extent would lose money in prices which are set on cost.

It would seem beyond doubt that this interest should be included in cost. The procedure which may be followed to get this interest into the cost would be as follows, expressed in figures as far as possible.

Value of buildings and real estate		$200,000.00
Rental based on 10% per year (customary percentage)........		$ 20,000.00
Depreciation, say at 2½%	$5,000.00	
Taxes, say at 25 mills	5,000.00	10,000.00
Balance—return at 5%		$ 10,000.00

To follow the procedure for depreciation and taxes as already described in this volume, the $10,000 necessary to bring up the charge to the average full rental could be an added standard monthly journal entry charging each department its proportion of the interest amount on exactly the same basis as the depreciation and taxes are charged. The entry would be:

Dr. Various Departments	$10,000.00	
Cr. Interest Charged to Cost		$10,000.00

The account "Interest Charged to Cost" would be carried throughout the year as a profit and loss account and at the end of the year will be closed out to profit and loss.

6. Interest on Machinery.—The failure to include interest on machinery in the cost of production may often result in very misleading cost figures.

A business that is progressive is constantly installing new, rapid and up-to-date machinery. A printer installs high speed machinery; a founder installs jarring machines; a chemical plant installs the most up-to-date centrifugal machines and vacuum dryers; a machine shop designs special rigs and machines and installs automatics. Such equipment costs large sums of money, and it replaces in recorded capital value a much larger intangible capital value of hand labor.

Obviously there immediately arises the danger of figuring costs which would fail to consider the offset of interest to the saving of labor, unless interest on the high investment is brought into the cost. It must be conceded, therefore, that the safest course is to bring interest on machinery into the manufacturing cost.

The records of the company show the machinery investment for each department, which has already been considered as the basis for depreciation charges. This same investment value—original investment, not considering any deductions for depreciation—becomes the amount of capital value on which to charge interest.

With respect to the rate to be charged, it may be said that 6% is a quite usual rate, but any rate of interest desired may be used.

If this plan is followed, 6% of the full value will be distributed by journal entry in exactly the same manner and on exactly the same value basis as in the case of depreciation on machinery. The entry for interest will exactly parallel the depreciation entry except as to amounts, which of course will differ. If machine rates are used, each machine or group machine rate account will be charged, as will each department if machine rates are not used. This entry would be:

Dr.	Machine Rate Accounts	$2,000.00	
	Departmental Burden Accounts	1,000.00	
	Cr. Interest Charged to Cost		$3,000.00

7. **Interest on Fixtures.**—Assuming that beside production machines, all labor saving devices, and all kinds of material handling devices are included in "machinery," the item of fixtures becomes reduced to inert items wherein one company has no advantage over another. It would seem, therefore, that interest on such items has no grounds for consideration.

8. **Interest on Raw Materials.**—Normal raw material stocks have no special effect on the costs of the business. In this respect every plant within a specific industry is on the same plane. Therefore, there is no advantage to be gained in charging interest on normal stocks to cost.

If on the contrary, a company which has the credit or the cash buys certain raw materials far ahead of normal requirements, pays for them and holds them in warehouse on the argument of "beating the market," it is obvious that the excess material over normal requirements should be penalized with a charge for interest in order to reflect properly the result of the judgment used in making the purchases. Otherwise, the real truth would never be known.

In such cases, the excess material should be entered on a special stock record sheet, a transfer of a month's supply being made from the excess stock to the regular stock as the normal supply period (say 30 or 60 days ahead of manufacturing requirements) is reached. At the time this transfer is made, an interest charge should be added to the original invoice cost for the elapsed time at, say 6%. This charge should be debited to the raw material account and credited to "Interest Charged to Cost." An example follows:

A rubber tire factory requires for normal production per month 500 tons of crude rubber. A normal inward flow on contracts could be maintained, but the following is what actually takes place. The officials believe that the price of rubber is going up. They accordingly buy heavily of spot and other rubber to the extent of ten months' excess requirements, and take it all in. They make no future contracts since the prices for future contracts are higher than what they paid. They had on hand two months' (normal) supply when the large quantity was bought—

Normal Inventory on hand:	
1,000 tons at 22 cents per lb.	$440,000.00
Excess Purchases covering 10 months:	
5,000 tons at 22 cents per lb.	$2,200,000.00

This 5,000 tons is taken in and a special stock record sheet is set up. At the end of one month, a months' normal use of 500 tons is transferred to the regular supply stock record sheet. It will be charged with one month's interest on 500 tons at 22 cents per pound, or $1,100, a journal entry debiting "Rubber" account, and crediting Interest Charged to Cost being made. The 500 tons when entered on the regular rubber stock sheet will be at the pound price of $.2211 instead of at $.22 per pound, the original invoice cost.

The next and each succeeding month will require the same entry except that the interest is for one additional month each time. In other words, the cost per pound for each transfer will run as follows:

1st	month	at	$.2211
2nd	month	"	.2222
3rd	month	"	.2233
4th	month	"	.2244
5th	month	"	.2255
6th	month	"	.2266
7th	month	"	.2277
8th	month	"	.2288
9th	month	"	.2299
10th	month	"	.2310

The total interest at 6% on the entire transaction would be $60,500 for the ten months.

By this method the cost of use of the money for the excess

purchase is placed against the material where it belongs, and the management has an actual record of how the judgment used in the purchase turned out as compared to what rubber could have been bought for during this period. Should the company charge the rubber to cost of production at market each month, and make use of an "Adjustment" account as described in Chapter XXV, a most complete record of purchasing efficiency is obtained.

To summarize, there seems to be no justification for attempting to charge any interest on normal stocks of raw materials, as all companies within an industry are on a like plane. On the contrary, however, there seems a very serious reason for charging interest on excess purchases.

This reasoning should not be applied to small items where monthly requirements are so small that the purchase of a year's supply is only a convenience.

9. Interest on Materials, Labor and Burden in Process.—A very good argument has been brought forward that work which is in process for a long period of time should bear a penalty of interest in order that the final cost should reflect the cost of the excessive use of money. Theoretically no one can disagree with this argument. In actual practice, however, there are two very good reasons for not considering this interest, namely:

1. It is almost impossible to accomplish.
2. In the last analysis there seems no particular practical need for it.

In respect to the first point, it may be that *some* products lend themselves to a fairly easy method of figuring interest on the investment of material, labor and burden for the time the goods are in process. Hams in a packing plant are in process for a fairly well fixed period, and it would be fairly simple to compute an interest charge. Certain products which require a period of aging may also be easily charged with interest, and without doubt should be. But on this particular point, is such process of aging to be regarded as an actual *manufacturing* process? It would seem not. At the same time, while the sawing and piling of the lumber may close the actual manufacturing cycle, there is the year or two required for proper air drying, which absolutely demands the interest charge if its correct final cost is to be accurate. This charge, however, while to *final* cost is *not* a manufacturing cost as manufacturing cost is ordinarily regarded. It is a *carrying* cost; and such a carrying cost applies in many cases.

A heavy machine shop manufacturing large apparatus affords excellent examples of the impracticability of charging interest to cost from the standpoint of penalizing long term orders as against short-term orders. A large pump, for instance, may be in process for months or even a year. A few parts go into process at the start, and a few additional parts every day or two for a long period. To properly penalize this pump with interest on the material, labor and burden involved would require an exhaustive tabulation of the dates each part went into process, and the dates of the expenditure for labor with its burden. How else could an accurate interest charge be figured? It is obvious that such tabulation would be impracticable.

Let us now consider the second point, namely that in the last analysis there is no real need for considering interest on work in process.

Aside from negligent shop management, the large pump just referred to would be in process for a long time no matter *who* manufactured it. That is, every heavy machine shop has orders which are a long time in process. But if every shop in the industry is in just the same position in respect to such work, wherein is the need to safeguard competitive bidding by including interest?

In all packing plants, hams take approximately the same time for production; therefore, at least as between different plants in the industry, there is no need for interest to be considered. If, however, it is desired to penalize hams which are a long time in process as against fresh meats which are disposed of quickly, we have a different proposition. Admittedly there is some justification for charging interest to a product which takes 60 or 90 days to complete, particularly when practically all other products go through and are shipped quickly, and where the products in question are of unit nature and subject to speculation or rapid variation in price. In such cases, the allocation of interest is simple. As the value and time are known, it is easy to figure the interest and charge it to the *product,* and there to credit Interest Charged to Cost.

In general, however, it is almost impossible to see any benefit from charging interest on work in process, as in the same industry, all plants are on the same plane. A fly-wheel casting that takes two weeks to cool in one foundry will take two weeks to cool in any other foundry. Therefore each has the same condition, and interest is unnecessary in so far as this condition is concerned.

10. Interest on Finished Goods.—Here again it is necessary to carefully differentiate as to just what is meant. Lumber, sawed and piled, is green and unsalable until dry. This drying stage is neither a manufacturing process nor is it related to finished stock. It is an aging or drying process, and most certainly interest should be charged for the elapsed time of aging on the value of the product as it left the mill.

When dry and ready for sale, this product becomes *finished stock.* This same reasoning applies to any material which requires an aging, drying or curing period.

In well ordered businesses, the normal finished stock carried is that which the nature of the business requires. If the company is properly managed, the finished stock is kept to a point of normality by the manufacturing schedules.

As stocks of finished goods are practically a *constant* in

every individual business within one industry, there is nothing to be gained by charging interest on this stock, as all units within one industry are on the same plane.

11. Interest on Cash on Hand; 12. Interest on Accounts Receivable; 13. Interest on Assets Not Specified.—Within the same industry, these items are constant in the main, as the terms of sale and other conditions are similar. Therefore, from the standpoint of competition within the same industry there seems no necessity for considering interest.

A good example of such similarity may be found in businesses which follow the custom of "future dating" of invoices. When a product is seasonable, it is often customary to have customers accept goods which are billed with due date perhaps four months distant. This apparent inflation of accounts receivable is in fact to permit a more balanced plant operation, and it so results. As this is the usual custom of any industry which is seasonable, the entire industry is on the same basis, and no consideration need be given to charging interest to cost of production.

Recapitulation.—Interest charged to cost is recommended in the following cases:

1. On Buildings and Real Estate, in order to equalize the property occupancy cost with competitors who pay rent.
2. On Machinery, as nearly every plant has special or high priced machinery for labor saving purposes, and it is necessary to include interest to arrive at the real cost.
3. On Raw Materials which are bought beyond requirements and which should be penalized with carrying charges in order to know their exact cost when included with current stock.
4. On Product going through an aging, curing or drying period. This is a carrying charge rather than an item of manufacturing cost.

Interest charged to cost is not recommended in the following cases:

1. On Fixtures, as there rarely are any fixtures which affect costs.
2. On Work in Process, as all companies within one industry are under like circumstances. Also, it is almost entirely impracticable except in a few cases of individual products such as hams in a packing plant.
3. On Cash on Hand, Accounts Receivable or any other assets other than as already referred to, as such items are constant within the same industry, and therefore require no special interest consideration.

Conclusion.—Interest as a whole is impossible of discussion. Interest in explicit cases and on various phases of the business may be dealt with clearly and with profit.

Perhaps a good rule to follow is: Where interest is obviously an important consideration in an individual situation *use it;* where interest has no apparent value for the safeguarding of the accuracy of costs for competitive purposes, *disregard it.*

CHAPTER XXXVI

ILLUSTRATIVE LEDGER ACCOUNTS AND JOURNAL ENTRIES

Scope of the Chapter.—To specify general ledger control accounts and journal entries to fit every case is, of course, impossible. On the other hand, the fundamental principles underlying the establishment of control accounts and the making of journal entries each month are practically the same in all lines of industry.

This chapter presents a set of general ledger accounts for an average foundry, followed by the usual journal entries which would be involved in handling the cost records. No space is taken up with illustrating the journal entries from the general books of entry, as this matter should be entirely familiar to everyone reading this volume.

The schedule of ledger accounts shown herein, and also the schedule of journal entries which follow the ledger accounts, are taken from the "Standard Foundry Cost System," published by the American Foundrymen's Association.

General Ledger Accounts for Average Foundry.—The schedule of general ledger accounts in the following pages is such as would be required to reflect the details of an average foundry. Subaccounts or additional accounts should be added to represent classes of transactions special to any particular foundry. The schedule and definitions are merely illustrative of the principles involved.

The accounts appear under the following groups which are in the sequence required for presentation on the balance sheet and profit and loss statement, which sequence is important in order to facilitate the work of preparing the statements.

1. Current assets
2. Inventory assets
3. Fixed assets
4. Deferred assets
5. Intangible assets
6. Current liabilities
7. Fixed liabilities
8. Reserves
9. Capital liabilities
10. Surplus and profit and loss accounts
11. Financial profit and loss accounts
12. Operating expense accounts
13. Sundry general ledger accounts

The following detailed accounts are suggested for the general ledger. These may be amplified as much as desired, or as the business demands

1—*Current Assets:*
- 1—Cash in bank (an account for each bank)
- 2—Petty cash
- 3—Notes receivable
- 4—Accounts receivable
- 5—Bonds and other investments

2—*Inventory Assets:*
- 1—Melting stock metals
- 2—General stores (or as many as desired)
- 3—Finished castings
- 4—Work in process

3—*Fixed Assets:*
- 1—Machinery and equipment
- 2—Real estate and buildings

4—*Deferred Assets:*
- 1—Unexpired insurance
- 2—Unexpired taxes
- 3—Prepaid interest

5—*Intangible Assets:*
- 1—Patents
- 2—Good-will

6—*Current Liabilities:*
- 1—Notes payable
- 2—Accounts payable
- 3—Accrued pay-roll

4—Accrued taxes
5—Accrued commission
6—Accrued interest

7—*Fixed Liabilities:*
1—Bonds payable
2—Mortgages payable

8—*Reserves:*
1—Reserve for depreciation on machinery and equipment
2—Reserve for depreciation on buildings
3—Reserve for bad debts

9—*Capital Liabilities:*
1—Capital stock—preferred
2—Capital stock—common

10—*Surplus and Profit and Loss Accounts:*
1—Surplus
2—Income and excess profits account
3—Dividends—preferred stock
4—Dividends—common stock
5—Profit and loss
6—Adjustment account
7—Castings sales
8—Cost of castings sales
9—Miscellaneous sales
10—Cost of miscellaneous sales
11—Freight out on sales
12—Administrative expense
13—Selling expense

11—*Financial Profit and Loss Accounts:*
1—Interest received
2—Discount taken
3—Interest paid
4—Discount given
5—Interest or dividends on investments

12—*Operating Expense Accounts:*
1—Cost of melt
2—Cost of melt credits
3—Molding burden—direct labor
4—Molding burden—direct labor credits
5—Molding burden—machine hour
6—Molding burden—machine hour credits
7—Molding sand cost
8—Molding sand cost credits
9—Flask cost
10—Flask cost credits
11—Coremaking burden—direct labor

12—Coremaking burden—direct labor credits
13—Coremaking burden—machine hour
14—Coremaking burden—machine hour credits
15—Finishing cost
16—Finishing cost credits
17—Annealing cost
18—Annealing cost credits
19—Power, heat, and light expense
20—Pattern-shop expense
21—General expense
22—Expense ledger

13—*Sundry General Ledger Accounts*

1—CURRENT ASSETS

(1-1)—*Cash in Bank:*

Debits—

(1) Open the account with the amount of cash in bank;
(2) Total amount of cash deposited during the month.

Credits—

(1) Total amount of checks issued during the month.

Balance—

Represents the value of cash in bank at end of month. Should be reconciled with the bank's statement to determine outstanding checks and uncredited deposits.

(1-2)—*Petty Cash:*

Debits—

(1) With the value of checks drawn to create or to increase the amount of cash on hand to cover petty expenses for a short period.

Credits—

(1) With any decrease in the amount on hand.

Balance—

Represents the amount set aside for petty cash disbursements.

(1-3)—*Notes Receivable:*

Debits—

(1) Open the account with the face value of promissory notes;
(2) Notes and acceptances received;
(3) Notes renewed.

Credits—

(1) Payments on notes receivable and acceptances;
(2) All notes and acceptances sold or otherwise disposed of;
(3) All notes renewed.

Balance—

Represents the value of all notes receivable and acceptances on hand.

(1-4)—*Accounts Receivable:*

Debits—

(1) Open the account with the total of individual customers' accounts in the accounts receivable ledger;

(2) The total charges to customers as represented by postings on sales register.

Credits—

(1) Total payments received from customers, whether cash, notes or acceptances;

(2) Allowances to customers, including cash discount; in other words, the gross settlements with customers.

Balance—

Represent the net amount due from customers.

(1-5)—*Bonds and Other Investments:*

Debits—

(1) Open the acount with the market value of stocks and bonds on hand;

(2) Market value of other investments;

(3) Cash value of life insurance policies, etc;

(4) Cost of all stocks, bonds and other investments purchased.

Credits—

(1) Cost of stocks, bonds and other investments sold at value carried (any sales of securities at other than the value carried will necessitate entry of the profit or loss to an account representing profit and loss on sales of investment securities).

Balance—

Represents the cost value of stocks, bonds, and other investments owned by the company.

2—INVENTORY ASSETS

(2-1)—*Melting Stock—Metals:*

Debits—

(1) Open the account with the cost value of all melting stock or metals on hand;

(2) All purchases of melting stock metals;

(3) Transportation charges on incoming melting stock metals (distributable according to corresponding invoices);

(4) Charges for unloading in the case of a long-term supply;

(5) Returns to stores of melting stock from melting department.

Credits—

(1) All withdrawals of melting stock metals as represented by monthly summary of metals used;

(2) All melting stock returned to vendors.

Balance—

Represents the value of melting stock metals on hand; should agree with the aggregate of the individual stock ledger sheets or cards.

Note:—The following subdivisions may be maintained:

1. Pig iron
2. Purchased scrap
3. Foundry scrap
4. Ferromanganese
5. Ferrosilicon
6. Other melting stock as required

(2-2)—*General Stores:*

Debits—

(1) Open the account with the value of all general stores material (i.e., other than melting stock metals) on hand;

(2) Purchases of additional material;

(3) Transportation charges on incoming general stores material (distributable according to corresponding invoices);

(4) Returns to stock of general stores material.

Credits—

(1) Withdrawals of general stores material from stock as represented by monthly summary of materials used;

(2) Material returned to vendors.

Balance—

Represents the book value of general stores material on hand; should agree with the aggregate of the individual stock ledger sheets or cards.

(2-3)—*Finished Castings:*

Debits—

(1) Open the account with the physical value of all finished castings on hand;

(2) Deliveries of finished castings as represented by the summary of closed production orders—at cost;

(3) Returns of good material from customers.

Credits—

(1) Material shipped during the period.

Balance—

Represents the cost value of finished goods on hand.

(2-4)—*Work in Process:*

Debits—

(1) Open the account with the cost of goods in process;

(2) With the total amount of molding productive labor and core-making productive labor as represented by the summary of time cards on pay-rolls;

(3) With cost of melt for the month at predetermined rate;

(4) With proper portion of following expense accounts at predetermined rates:

a. Molding burden—direct labor,
b. Molding burden—machine hour,
c. Molding sand cost,
d. Flask cost,
e. Coremaking burden—direct labor,
f. Coremaking burden—machine hour,
g. Finishing cost,
h. Annealing cost;

(5) With cost of castings returned by customers (if finished castings account is not carried).

Credits—

(1) Cost of castings shipped, if finished castings account is not carried, otherwise with cost of finished castings delivered to finished castings stores;

(2) Scrap value of bad castings and sprues returned to melting metals stock;

(3) Losses due to defective work or other errors in service distributable to the departmental expense involved.

Balance—

Represents the cost of finished castings on hand and in process (if finished castings account is not carried), otherwise of castings in process.

3—FIXED ASSETS

(3-1)—*Machinery and Equipment:*
(3-2)—*Real Estate and Buildings:*

Debits—

(1) Open the accounts with the first cost or replacement value of all permanent plant investment represented by the respective accounts;

(2) All expenditures for permanent additions.

Credits—

(1) Value of fixed assets sold or otherwise disposed of.

Balance—

Represents the book value of fixed assets against which as offsetting accounts are the respective reserves for depreciation.

4—DEFERRED ASSETS

(4-1)—*Prepaid Insurance:*

Debits—

(1) Open the account with the amount of unexpired insurance premiums;

(2) Subsequent insurance premiums.

Credits—

(1) Periodical charge equivalent to pro rata insurance cost for period;

(2) All refunds and cancellations.

Balance—

Represents unexpired insurance premiums.

(4-2)—*Prepaid Taxes (If prepaid. See* 6-4):

Debits—

(1) Open the account with total of unexpired taxes paid in advance;

(2) Subsequent taxes paid in advance.

Credits—

(1) Amount equivalent to one-twelfth the annual tax to effect liquidation of monthly charge to taxes in the various expense groups.

Balance—

Represents taxes paid in advance.

(4-3)—*Prepaid Interest* (*See* 6-6):

Debits—

(1) Open with balance of prepaid interest;

(2) All subsequent prepaid interest.

Credits—

(1) With monthly proportions of interest accrued as to the items entered in this account as prepaid.

Balance—

Inventory of unused prepaid interest.

5—INTANGIBLE ASSETS

(5-1)—*Patents:*

Debits—

(1) Open the account with the estimated value of patents owned;

(2) Cost of acquiring subsequent patents including all incidental expenses.

Credits—

(1) Pro rata amount equivalent to one-twelfth the annual charge for the extinguishment of patents. (If so treated.)

Balance—

Represents the book value of patents owned.

(5-2)—*Good-Will:*

Debits—

With value of good-will.

Credits—

With any depreciation of good-will.

Balance—

Net value of good-will as carried.

6—CURRENT LIABILITIES

(6-1)—*Notes Payable:*

Debits—

(1) Payments reducing the notes payable.

Credits—

(1) Open the account with the value of all outstanding notes payable;

(2) All subsequent notes issued.

Balance—

Represents the amount owed by the company on notes payable.

(6-2)—*Accounts Payable:*

Debits—

(1) Payments of accounts payable;

(2) With all contra charges to vendors' accounts;

(3) Value of material returned to vendors for credit;

(4) With amount of notes given vendors;

(5) With all trade or cash discounts allowed by vendors and earned.

Credits—

(1) Open the account with the total of vendors' or purchase creditors' accounts;

(2) Total credits to accounts payable on the purchase journal.

Balance—

Represents the net amount owed to creditors on open account.

(6-3)—*Accrued Pay-Roll:*

Debits—

(1) Amount of wage and salary payments made during the period as represented by cash book entries;

(2) With amounts paid as bonus.

Credits—

(1) Amount of wages, salaries and bonus earned.

Balance—

Represents pay-roll amounts accrued but unpaid.

(6-4)—*Accrued Taxes* (*If accrued. See* 4-2):

Debits—

(1) Actual payment of taxes.

Credits—

(1) Monthly amount charged to operating expense.

Balance—

Represents accrued amounts of taxes accumulated but not yet due.

(6-5)—*Accrued Commissions:*

Debits—

(1) Commissions actually paid agents or sales representatives.

Credits—

(1) All accrued commissions on sales billed (or orders taken) during the period, charging selling expenses.

Balance—

Represents commissions accrued but not paid.

(6-6)—*Accrued Interest* (*See* 4-3):

Debits—

(1) With interest paid as to items entered herein as accrued.

Credits—

(1) Open the account with the amount of accrued interest unpaid;

(2) With amounts accrued monthly on items if interest is accruing.

Balance—

Represents accrued interest on items payable accumulated but not yet paid.

7—FIXED LIABILITIES

(7-1)—*Bonds Payable:*

Debits—

(1) Payments reducing bonds payable.

Credits—

(1) Open with balance of all outstanding bonds;

(2) With all subsequent issues.

Balance—

Represents outstanding bonded indebtedness.

(7-2)—*Mortgages Payable:*

Debits—

(1) Payments reducing the principal of mortgages payable.

Credits—

(1) Open the account with the amount due on mortgages.

(2) Mortgages subsequently issued.

Balance—

Represents the total amount owing on mortgages payable.

8—RESERVES

(8-1)—*Reserve for Depreciation on Machinery and Equipment*

(8-2)—*Reserve for Depreciation on Buildings:*

Debits—

(1) With that portion of the cost which has been depreciated or anything replaced or sold.

Credits—

(1) Open the account with the amount of reserve allowed for depreciation;

(2) Depreciation charge to departmental or general expenses equivalent to a pro rata amount of the annual depreciation charge.

Balance—

Represents the allowance for depreciation of permanent plant investments and maintained as offsetting accounts to the respective fixed asset accounts.

Note:—If the present net book value (first cost less depreciation amount) cannot be determined for any particular article replaced, the first cost should be credited to the fixed asset account and charged to the corresponding reserve for depreciation. If, however, the article replaced is sold or otherwise disposed of at a scrap value, the first cost should be credited to the fixed asset account and first cost less scrap or exchange value should be charged to the corresponding reserve for depreciation. The scrap value should, of course, be charged to the purchaser.

(8-3)—*Reserve for Bad Debts:*

Debits—

(1) With value of accounts receivable considered uncollectible, crediting the individual customers' accounts so written off.

Credits—

(1) Open the account with an amount considered sufficient to cover all losses on accounts considered uncollectible;

(2) Amount based on a percentage of sales billed to provide for losses on amounts charged during the period.

Balance—

Represents allowance reserved for losses on accounts receivable.

9—CAPITAL LIABILITIES

(9-1)—*Capital Stock—Preferred Issued*

(9-2)—*Capital Stock—Common Issued:*

Debits—

(1) With par value of stock returned to or acquired by company.

Credits—

(1) With the par value of stock outstanding.

Balance—

Represents the par value of issued capital stock outstanding, preferred and common, respectively.

10—SURPLUS AND PROFIT AND LOSS ACCOUNTS

(10-1)—*Surplus:*

Debits—

(1) With the amount of dividends at annual closing;

(2) With amount transferred from profit and loss (if loss) at annual closing period.

Credits—

(1) Open the account with the amount of undivided profits;

(2) With profits made during the current year transferred from profit and loss at annual closing.

Balance—

Represents undivided profits, if a credit;

Represents deficit, if a debit.

Note:—Make *no* entries to surplus account except at annual closing time.

(10-2)—*Income and Excess Profits Tax Account:*

Debits—

With amount of income and excess profits tax paid.

Credits—

With any necessary adjustments.

Balance—

Represents amount of income and excess profits taxes paid.

(10-3)—*Dividends—Preferred Stock:*

Debits—

(1) With the amount of dividends paid.

Credits—

(1) With debit to surplus at close of year.

Balance—

Represents dividends paid.

(10-4)—*Dividends—Common Stock:*

Debits—

(1) With the amount of dividends paid.

Credits—

(1) With debit to surplus at close of year.

Balance—

Represents dividends paid.

(10-5)—*Profit and Loss*

At Annual Closing Time:

Debits—

(1) With debit balance of cost of castings sales;
(2) With debit balance of cost of miscellaneous sales;
(3) With debit balance of freight out on sales;
(4) With debit balance of administrative expenses;
(5) With debit balance of selling expenses;
(6) With debit balance of interest paid;
(7) With debit balance of discount given;
(8) With net amount of plant balances (Operating expense accounts Nos. 12-1 to 12-18 inclusive) if such amounts are debit balances;
(9) With debit balance of adjustment account.

At Annual Closing Times:

Credits—

(1) With credit balances of castings sales billed;
(2) With credit balance of miscellaneous sales;
(3) With credit balance of interest received;

(4) With credit balance of discount taken;
(5) With credit balance of interest on investments;
(6) With net amount of plant balances (Operating expense accounts 12-1 to 12-18 inclusive) if such amounts are credit balances;
(7) With credit balance of adjustment account.

Balance—

Represents net profit or loss resulting from transactions of the period accumulated.

(10-6)—*Adjustment Account:*

Debits—

(1) With any determinable decrease in any particular account not traceable to some other account;
(2) With necessary adjustments of any nature.

Credits—

(1) At closing periods with any determinable increase in any particular account not traceable to some other account;
(2) With necessary adjustments of any nature.

Balance—

Represents adjustments necessarily made.

(10-7)—*Castings Sales:*

Debits—

(1) With the billed amount of castings returned by customers;
(2) With allowances to customers as represented by credit memoranda if a sale reduction;
(3) With credit balance, transferring to profit and loss at annual closing time.

Credits—

(1) Total castings sales billed during the month as represented by the sales register, charging accounts receivable.

Balance—

Represents net sales billed.

(10-8)—*Cost of Casting Sales:*

Debits—

(1) Cost value of all material shipped as represented by the summary of daily reports of shipments.

Credits—

(1) Cost of material returned by customers during the period;
(2) With the debit balance at the end of closing periods charging profit and loss.

Balance—

Represents net factory cost of shipments.

(10-9)—*Miscellaneous Sales:*

Debits—

(1) With value at sale price of any returned sales.

Credits—

(1) With sale value of any nature other than castings sales.

Balance—

Value of miscellaneous sales.

(10-10)—*Cost of Miscellaneous Sales:*

Debits—

(1) With cost of above sales.

Credits—

(1) With cost of any returned sales.

Balance—

Net cost of miscellaneous sales.

(10-11)—*Freight Out On Sales:*

Debits—

(1) With all payments of transportation of any nature for delivery of goods to customers.

Credits—

(1) With necessary adjustments.

Balance—

Net cost of delivering sales to customers.

(10-12)—*Administrative Expenses:*

Debits—

(1) With all charges for administrative expenses.

Credits—

(1) With debit balance at closing periods charging profit and loss.

Balance—

Represented aggregate of administrative expenses.

(10-13)—*Selling Expenses:*

Debits—

(1) With the aggregate of charges to all expense accounts classified as selling expenses.

Credits—

(1) With debit balance at closing periods charging profit and loss.

Balance—

Represented aggregate of selling expenses.

11—FINANCIAL PROFIT AND LOSS ACCOUNTS

(11-1)—*Interest Received:*

Debits—

(1) With necessary adjustments.

Credits—

(1) With all interest received for balances or overdue accounts.

Balance—

Net interest received.

(11-2)—*Discount Taken:*

Debits—

(1) With credit balance, transferring to profit and loss.

Credits—

(1) With all cash discounts earned; does not include trade discounts.

Balance—

Represents cash discounts earned.

(11-3)—*Interest Paid:*

Debits—

(1) At closing periods with the amount of interest accrued for the month on items payable, crediting accrued interest or prepaid interest.

Credits—

(1) With debit balance, transferring to profit and loss.

Balance—

Represents amount of interest actually incurred.

Note:—If interest is prepaid, the payment should be charged to prepaid interest (Acct. 4-3). The amount should be liquidated in monthly amounts to apportion the charge equitably over the periods involved. (See Account 6-6.)

(11-4)—*Discount Given:*

Debits—

(1) Cash discounts allowed customers—does not include trade discounts.

Credits—

(1) With debit balance, transferring to profit and loss.

Balance—

Represents cash discounts allowed.

(11-5)—*Interest or Dividends on Investments:*

Debits—

(1) With necessary adjustments.

Credits—

(1) With interest or dividends received on investments. This should be treated as separate from regular commercial interest.

Balance—

Net results of regular income from outside investments.

12—OPERATING EXPENSES

Explanatory Note:

Accounts 12-1 to 12-18 inclusive cover the actual operating accounts; i.e., those that appear in the actual cost sheet, either by pound, percentage, or hour.

If reference is made to the skeleton statements, it will be noted that "Total to Date" is used, both in the body of the statement and in the comparative monthly statement. It is quite evident, therefore, that if there were but one account for each burden and cost statement, which was credited with the transfer at predetermined rates to work in process, there would be no easy way of securing the "To date" figures.

In order to make this easy, two ledger accounts are maintained for each expense or burden account. One, bearing simply the name of the account, is for *debits only*, except where a credit is necessary to *adjust or correct the debits.* The other, bearing the account name followed by "Credits," is for *credits only* of the transfers to work in process, except when a debit may be necessary to *adjust or correct the credits.*

The result is an accumulating figure for each kind of account. This provides, from the general ledger trial balance, the figures to use in the statements of "Total to Date"—the monthly figures coming from the footings for the month's transactions, which *must* balance with the entries for the month in the ledger account controlling each expense account.

It is quickly seen, therefore, that the difference between the "debit" and "credit" account for each expense account is the over- or under-absorbed expense, and will and *must* agree with the monthly statements.

Accounts 12-19 to 12-22 inclusive need but a single account as they are to be *entirely closed out* each month. They are simply collective accounts serving as mediums to split down these expenses to the actual operating accounts.

* * * * * *

(12-1)—*Cost of Melt:*

Debits—

(1) Melting stock metals used (requisitions);

(2) Labor (time cards);

(3) Miscellaneous materials (requisitions);

(4) Charges direct from purchase register (expense ledger charge slips);

(5) Apportioned charges.

Credits—

(1) Adjustments of debits only.

(12-2)—*Cost of Melt—Credits:*

Debits—

(1) Adjustments of credits only.

Credits—

(1) Value of metal poured at the standard predetermined rate.

(12-3)—*Molding Burden—Direct Labor:*

Debits—

(1) Labor (time cards);

(2) Materials (requisitions);

(3) Charges direct from purchase journal (expense ledger charge slips);
(4) Apportioned charges.
Credits—
(1) Adjustments of debits only.

(12-4)—*Molding Burden—Direct Labor—Credits:*
Debits—
(1) Adjustment of credits only.
Credits—
(1) Amount equal to molding direct labor times the standard rate.

(12-5)—*Molding Burden—Machine Hour:*
Debits—
(1) Labor (time cards);
(2) Materials (requisitions);
(3) Charges direct from purchase journal (expense ledger charge slips);
(4) Apportioned charges.
Credits—
(1) Adjustment of debits only.

(12-6)—*Molding Burden—Machine Hour—Credits:*
Debits—
(1) Adjustments of credits only.
Credits—
(1) Amount equal to actual machine hours used times the standard rate per hour.

(12-7)—*Molding Sand Cost (If used):*
Debits—
(1) Labor (time tickets);
(2) Materials (requisitions);
(3) Charges direct from purchase journal (expense ledger charge slips);
Credits—
(1) Adjustments of debits only.

(12-8)—*Molding Sand Cost—Credits (If used);*
Debits—
(1) Adjustments of credits only.
Credits—
(1) Amount equal to total metal poured times the standard rate per pound.

(12-9)—*Flask Cost (If used):*
Debits—
(1) Labor (time tickets);
(2) Materials (requisitions);
(3) Charges direct from purchase journal (expense ledger charge slips);

(4) With total monthly charges in pattern-shop expense accounts Nos. 704 and 705 (by transfer).

Credits—

(1) Adjustments of debits only.

(12-10)—*Flask Cost—Credits (If used):*

Debits—

(1) Adjustments of credits only.

Credits—

(1) Amount equal to total good castings times the standard rate per pound.

(12-11)—*Coremaking Burden—Direct Labor:*

Debits—

(1) Labor (time tickets);

(2) Material (requisitions);

(3) Charges direct from purchase journal (expense ledger charge slips);

(4) Apportioned charges.

Credits—

(1) Adjustments of debits only.

(12-12)—*Coremaking Burden—Direct Labor—Credits:*

Debits—

(1) Adjustments of credits only.

Credits—

(1) Amount equal to coremaking direct labor times the standard rate.

(12-13)—*Coremaking Burden—Machine Hour:*

Debits—

(1) Labor (time tickets);

(2) Material (requisitions);

(3) Charges direct from purchase journal (expense ledger charge slips);

(4) Apportioned charges.

Credits—

(1) Adjustments of debits only.

(12-14)—*Coremaking Burden—Machine Hour—Credits:*

Debits—

(1) Adjustments of credits only.

Credits—

(1) Amount equal to actual machine hours used times the standard rate per hour.

(12-15)—*Finishing Cost:*

Debits—

(1) Labor (direct and indirect unless in large plants) (time tickets);

(2) Material (requisitions);

(3) Charges from purchase journal (expense ledger charge slips);
(4) Apportioned charges.
Credits—
(1) Adjustments of debits only.

(12-16)—*Finishing Cost—Credits:*
Debits—
(1) Adjustments of credits only.
Credits—
(1) Amount equal to molding and core direct labor times the standard rate.

(12-17)—*Annealing Cost:*
Debits—
(1) Labor (time tickets);
(2) Material (requisitions);
(3) Charges direct from purchase journal (expense ledger charge slips);
(4) Apportioned charges.
Credits—
(1) Adjustments of debits only.

(12-18)—*Annealing Cost—Credits:*
Debits—
(1) Adjustments of credits only.
Credits—
(1) Amount equal to total good castings times the standard rate.

(12-19)—*Power, Light and Heat Expense:*
Debits—
(1) Labor (time cards);
(2) Material (requisitions);
(3) Charges direct from purchase journal (expense ledger charge slips);
(4) Apportioned charges.
Credits—
(1) With total net balance at the close of each month distributed to the various operating accounts as explained elsewhere.
Balance—
There should be no balance.

(12-20)—*Pattern-Shop Expense:*
Debits—
(1) Labor (time tickets);
(2) Materials (requisitions);
(3) Charges direct from purchase journal (expense ledger charge slips);
(4) Apportioned charges.
Credits—
(1) With amount which charges the molding burden—direct labor;

(2) With amount which charges the coremaking burden—direct labor;

(3) With amounts which charge the flask cost;

(4) With amount of residue as directed.

Balance—

There should be no balance.

Note:—If the pattern-shop is operated as a producing department, and not solely as a co-operating department, the accounting should be changed to correspond to the condition, and provision should be made for:

1—Pattern production orders;

2—Pattern productive labor;

3—Pattern-shop expense account;

4—Pattern work in process material. The cost compilation must be changed accordingly.

(12-21)—*General Expense:*

Debits—

(1) Labor (time tickets);

(2) Material (requisitions);

(3) Charges direct from purchase journal (expense ledger debit slips);

(4) Apportioned charges.

Credits—

(1) With total net balance at end of each month distributed on the prescribed basis to each operating account.

Balance—

There should be no balance.

(12-22)—*Expense Ledger Account:*

Debits—

(1) At end of each month, with the total of charges made direct to operating accounts, which charges are represented by expense ledger charge slips.

Credits—

(1) With the total of expense ledger charge slips charging the various operating accounts.

Balance—

If any balance exists, it is in error, and the charge slips in the files for month should be checked back to the purchase journal.

13—SUNDRY GENERAL LEDGER ACCOUNTS

In this section of the ledger are located all sundry accounts with firms and individuals, irrespective of whether their balance is debit or credit. There are always a number of accounts of so general a nature that they only properly belong in this section.

When making up a statement, the accounts classify themselves according to their balances into two classes:

General ledger accounts receivable;

General ledger accounts payable.

They will be so entered in the statements immediately under the accounts receivable, and accounts payable respectively.

Journal Entries.—The following sequence of journalizing should be followed in order to distribute the various details into the cost of production and reflect the condition properly on the general ledger:

1. Pay-roll.
2. Materials and supplies.
3. Liability insurance.
4. Depreciation.
5. Taxes.
6. Fire insurance.
7. Power, heat, and light.
8. Pattern-shop expenses.
9. General expenses.
10. Departmental expenses.
11. Reversing foundry scrap.
12. Finished castings.
13. Shipments.

The following pages illustrate the details of the journal entries required:

1. PAY-ROLL:

Debit—

Work in process (direct labor)
Cost of belt (conversion labor)
Molding burden—direct labor
Molding burden—machine hour
Molding sand cost
Flask cost
Coremaking burden—direct labor
Coremaking burden—machine hour
Finishing cost
Annealing cost
Pattern-shop expenses

Power, heat, and light expenses
General expenses
Credit—
Accrued pay-roll

Purpose—
To distribute labor charges for the current month to the accounts receiving benefits.

Source—
Direct labor charges are taken from the molding and coremaking pay-roll sheets and should equal the total of all direct labor daily time tickets under production order numbers or class numbers for the same period.

Indirect labor charges to cost and burden accounts are obtained from the compilation of indirect-labor daily time tickets, filed under the various expense account numbers. . . . The values thus accumulated by summarizing the labor tickets must agree with the total of the pay-roll for the same period.

2. MATERIALS AND SUPPLIES:

Debit—
Cost of melt (Melting and conversion materials)
Molding burden—direct labor
Molding burden—machine hour
Molding sand cost
Flask cost
Coremaking burden—direct labor
Coremaking burden—machine hour
Finishing cost
Annealing cost
Pattern-shop expenses
Power, heat, and light expenses
General expenses
Credit—
Melting Stock—metals:
1. Pig iron
2. Purchased scrap
3. Foundry scrap
4. Ferromanganese
5. Ferrosilicon
General stores
Any other controlling material accounts
Expense ledger

Purpose—
To distribute material requisitions and expense ledger charges for the current month.

Source—

These charges are derived from a monthly summary of cupola or furnace reports, material requisitions, and expense ledger charge slips, representing materials consumed or purchases made during the current month distributed to the cost and burden accounts.

3. LIABILITY INSURANCE:

Debit—

Cost of melt
Molding burden—direct labor
Molding burden—machine hour
Coremaking burden—direct labor
Coremaking burden—machine hour
Finishing cost
Annealing cost
Pattern-shop expenses
Power, heat, and light expenses
General expenses

Credit—

Unexpired insurance

Purpose—

To distribute pro rata amount of liability insurance premiums to the current month.

Source—

This distribution is based on an estimated monthly amount sufficient to absorb the yearly total of liability insurance premiums. The prorating is based on the actual rate of the wages paid in each of the above accounts.

4. DEPRECIATION:

Debit—

Cost of melt
Molding burden—direct labor
Molding burden—machine hour
Coremaking burden—direct labor
Coremaking burden—machine hour
Finishing cost
Annealing cost
Pattern-shop expenses
Power, heat, and light expenses
General expenses

Credit—

Reserve for plant depreciation (As many Reserve Accounts as desired)

Purpose—
To distribute the pro rata amount of annual depreciation charge to the current month.
Source—
One-twelfth of the annual depreciation charge distributed to the various departments, based on the investment in each department.

5. TAXES:

Debit—
Cost of melt
Molding burden
Coremaking burden
Finishing cost
Annealing cost
Pattern-shop expenses
Power, heat, and light expenses
General expenses
(In small plants this may all go to General Expense.)
Credit—
Accrued taxes
Purpose—
To distribute the pro rata amount of estimated accrued taxes to the current month.
Source—
One-twelfth of the estimated amount of yearly taxes distributed to the various departments based on the taxable property in each department.

6. FIRE INSURANCE:

Debit—
General expense
Credit—
Unexpired insurance
Purpose—
To distribute the pro rata amount of fire insurance premiums to the current month.
Source—
One-twelfth of the annual amount of fire insurance premiums.

7. POWER, HEAT, AND LIGHT:

Debit—
Cost of melt
Molding burden—direct labor
Molding burden—machine hour
Coremaking burden—direct labor

Coremaking burden—machine hour
Finishing cost
Annealing cost
Pattern-shop expenses
General expenses

Credit—

Power, heat, and light expenses

Purpose—

To distribute power, heat and light expense of the current month.

Source—

The total of expenses summarized under power, heat, and light expenses. . . .

8. PATTERN-SHOP EXPENSES:

Debit—

Molding burden
Coremaking burden

Credit—

Pattern-shop expenses

Purpose—

To distribute pattern-shop expenses of the current month.

Source—

The total of expenses summarized under pattern-shop expenses. . . .

9. GENERAL EXPENSES:

Debit—

Cost of melt
Molding burden
Coremaking burden
Finishing cost
Annealing cost

Credit—

General expenses

Purpose—

To distribute the general expenses of the current month.

Source—

The total of expenses summarized under general expenses. . . . The basis of distribution is the total monthly labor cost in each of the above departments.

10. DEPARTMENTAL EXPENSES:

Debit—

Work in process

Credit—

Cost of melt (credit account)
Molding burden—direct labor (credit account)
Molding burden—machine hour (credit account)
Molding and sand cost (credit account)
Flask cost (credit account)
Coremaking burden—direct labor (credit account)
Coremaking burden—machine hour (credit account)
Finishing cost (credit account)
Annealing cost (credit account)

Purpose—

To transfer departmental burden and costs at their standard rate for the current month to work in process.

Note:—Each account will have a net debit or credit balance which should be shown each month on the profit and loss statement. Actual closing of these departmental burden and cost accounts will not be made until the end of the year, when they will be closed into profit and loss. Throughout the year the debit and credit postings to these departmental burden and cost accounts will be accumulative totals for trial balance and checking purposes.

11. FOUNDRY SCRAP:

Debit—

Foundry scrap—

Credit—

Work in process

Purpose—

To reverse the scrap value of bad castings and sprues accumulated during the current month.

Source—

The total scrap value of bad castings and sprues as represented by monthly summary of inspectors' rejection reports, showing weights of bad castings and sprues by classes or order numbers.

12. FINISHED CASTINGS:

Debit—

Finished castings (if account is used)

Credit—

Work in process

Purpose—

To transfer from work in process to finished castings account value of finished product delivered to finished castings stores.

Source—

Summary of delivery tickets or scale reports representing the delivery of finished castings to stock.

13. SHIPMENTS:

Debit—

Cost of castings sales

Credit—

Work in process, or

Finished castings (if that account is used)

Purpose—

To cover the cost of castings shipped during current month.

Source—

Summary cost value applied on memoranda of shipments made during the current month.

CHAPTER XXXVII

SPECIAL ADAPTATIONS OF COSTING PROCEDURE

Necessity for Special Adaptations of Methods.—As the science of cost accounting has progressed, it has been found that the circumstances surrounding many types of industries have demanded special adaptations of cost methods to adequately take care of the conditions which existed. Many special conditions of minor importance, conditions that are liable to be found in almost any plant, have been dealt with at various points in this volume.

Many industries, however, require the application of at least two special adaptations of costing methods which are too involved to be here treated in great detail, but which should be briefly described in order that the reader may understand their use and, to a limited extent, the nature of their structure. Either one of these methods would require an entire volume to discuss to a workable extent.

STANDARD COSTS

What is Meant by Standard Costs.—Standard costs are costs of product expressed in terms of what the product *should* cost under normal and reasonable conditions. For many years it has been accepted practice to use standard rates of burden as has been explained at length in this volume. The term "Standard Costs," however, indicates the extension of the standardization of costs to include all of the elements of cost; not only burden, but direct labor and material as well.

The day by day, week by week, or month by month variances in actual costs are important from the standpoint of controlling the expenditure of money, but are confusing in respect to inventory and selling price controls. In fact, many variances are unavoidable and are perfectly normal to a business. But these variances should not be allowed to cause useless waste of time in discussion, and the use of standard costs not only levels the minor variances, but brings out clearly the major variances in a manner which permits of managerial attention.

As with all other plans of cost accounting, the controlling ledger accounts furnish a control which assures confidence in the results shown.

How Standard Costs are Used.—Particularly in those industries where there is a great preponderance of standard lines, where the greater part of the production consists of what is commonly known as "repeat" work, it is of great advantage to place all production costs on a standard basis and deal with the variances from this standard. Based on existing or tested knowledge of actual time and material which *should* be consumed in producing the goods, standard costs are set by operations. Each department of the plant is credited with its production at the standard cost and is debited with its labor, material and all other expense consumed, including its share of all general expenses. The difference becomes a measure of how efficiently the department has operated.

The records are adjusted in such a manner that the variances from standard will be analyzed to indicate the important reasons for the variations, presented in concrete form for managerial use.

The standard costs are not changed unless there is some relatively permanent change in the method of manufacture, in the standard time allowance or in the basic labor rates. The fact that changes in general conditions or in operating efficiency from month to month may occur, is no reason for changing the basic standard costs which should always be used as the basis for setting selling prices.

Example of Standard Costs.—In the manufacturing of an automobile, which is a highly standardized product, it is possible to predetermine costs with great accuracy. The material required for the various parts and assemblies can be definitely specified and all manufacturing operations are standardized as to character, sequence and time required.

The standard material costs are obtained by extending the material specifications, after making allowance for normal and unavoidable waste, at the standard material prices, which, when possible, will be based upon actual material contracts.

The standard cost plan is based upon what is known as the "principle of exceptions." This principle applied to cost accounting means that we are primarily interested in the exceptions or variations from the standard. It is these exceptions which generally represent the inefficiences of plant management and in which the superintendent is most vitally interested.

The operation of the standard cost plan in the automobile factory which has been taken as an example resolves itself therefore primarily into determining what the variations are from the standard costs. If the plant is operated mainly on a piece-work basis, the problem is very much simplified; for piece work and standard being the same, no special cost accounting work is required in connection with these piece-work operations, except to establish the fact that the piece-work pay-roll is based upon correct production data and is priced at the correct piece rates.

In most factories it occasionally happens that work which should ordinarily be performed on a piece-work basis is done as day-work. This is due to a variety of causes, as, for instance, short runs to make up small shortages in stock, or when a new operator is guaranteed his day-work rate and is paid this in place of the piece-work rate when his piece-work earnings fall below what he would have earned on a day-work basis. In such cases it is necessary to figure the standard value of the production and carry the excess of the actual labor cost over this standard value to a loss and gain account. If such excess labor becomes a real consideration, the standard wage rates should be set to cover a reasonable allowance for day-work.

Reoperation work is another exception, and when the operator is paid for this work the cost thereof represents a loss to the company and is charged to the burden account.

In the case of producing operations normally performed on a day-work basis, the standard costs for such operations are figured on the basis of standard time allowances extended at standard labor rates per hour. In order to compare the actual costs of such operations with the standard it is necessary to figure the standard value of this production, carrying any difference between the pay-roll and this standard value of the production to the loss and gain account.

There are of course two main factors entering into variations from standard day-work producing labor costs—namely, time and rates; and it is desirable that variations in such costs be analyzed under these two heads for the information of the operating executives. This can be very easily done as will be evident from the following illustration:

Assume that the standard rate for a certain class of operatives has been taken as being 50 cents per hour, that the actual rate has been increased to 55 cents an hour, and that the actual hours expended in the cost period have been 3,000 as compared with standard time allowances for the work produced of 2,800 hours. Comparisons of actual and standard will then be as follows:

	Hours	Rate	Amount
Actual	3,000	$.55	$1,650.00
Standard	2,800	.50	1,400.00
Increases	200	$.05	$ 250.00

This excess cost of $250 can therefore be analyzed as between rate and time variances as follows:

Increase in Rates—	
3,000 hours at $.05	$150.00
Increase in Hours—	
200 hours at standard rate of $.50	100.00
Total Increase	$250.00

An important item of exceptions or variations from the standard costs is that of spoiled work. Certain operations are properly performed on a part and the operators given credit for the work done. But at last the part reaches a point where for some cause or other it is rejected. Except for the trifling scrap value of the material in the part it is worthless. In such cases it is necessary to figure the standard cost of the part up to the point of its rejection, deduct the value of the scrap and charge the balance to the burden account of the department spoiling the work.

Variances in material costs are divided into two classes, those due to variations from the standard price used in the figuring of the standard costs and those due to variances from the standard specifications. Variances in price are obtained by extending the incoming invoices at the standard prices and comparing the figures so obtained with the actual amounts billed. Variances in quantity are obtained in various ways. In some businesses it is possible to figure the actual material consumption and the amount of excess consumption by keeping careful track of the scrap produced and figuring the standard material value of the parts produced.

Burden variances are determined by figuring the standard burden cost of the production and comparing this with the actual burden costs. The method of determination depends upon the basis of burden distribution adopted. For the purposes of illustration we will assume that the standard burden is figured as a percentage of the standard labor costs which percentage we will say was 90 for the press department. In a given month assume that the standard labor cost of the production was $1,000 and the actual burden cost $950. A comparison of the actual and standard burden costs will be as follows:

Actual Burden	$950.00
Standard Burden—	
90% of standard labor of $1,000	900.00
Increase in Burden	$ 50.00

Now this variance in burden cost of $50 may be due to a variety of causes. It may be due to actual increases in expense or to the fact that the production is less than standard so that the fixed charge expenses require to be distributed over a smaller volume. It is therefore important that an analysis of burden variations should be made as between these two major causes of variations. Taking the example just used, let us assume that the standard burden rate of 90% of standard labor is determined as follows:

Standard Producing Labor in standard cost period		$1,200.00
Standard Burden—		
Variable Charges	$580.00	
(48.33% of standard labor)		
Fixed Charges	500.00	
(41.67% of standard labor)		
Total (representing 90% of Standard Producing Labor)		1,080.00

Further, that the actual burden expenses in the month were as follows:

Variable Charges	$460.00	
Fixed Charges	490.00	$950.00

The following statement is a comparison of the actual and standard burden in the cost period taken as an example:

	Standard Burden Value of Production		Actual Burden	*Increase or Decrease
	% of Std. Labor	Amount		
Variable Charges	48.33	$483.33	$460.00	$23.33
Fixed Charges	41.67	416.67	490.00	73.33*
		$900.00	$950.00	$50.00*

Now the variable charges are assumed to vary directly with the production (or the standard producing labor costs) so that the $23.33 represents an actual saving due to economy. In the case of the fixed charges, though the statement shows an increased cost of $73.33, as a matter of fact the actual expense of $490 is less than the standard of $500, showing a saving in actual expense of $10. The balance of $83.33 is therefore due to idle time and an analysis of the net increase of $50 will be as follows:

Savings in Expense:		
Variable Charges	$23.33	
Fixed Charges	10.00	$33.33
Loss due to Idle Time...........		83.33
Net Loss		$50.00

The correctness of the figure of $83.33 can easily be proved as follows:

The standard fixed charge cost represents 41.67% of the standard producing labor and the loss in production in terms of standard labor costs is $200 (1,200 less 1,000). 41.67% of $200 is $83.33 which is obviously the additional amount of burden which would have been absorbed in the period if the production had been standard.

Advantages of Standard Costs.—The rapid development of standard cost principles is an unquestionable indication of the worth of the method. The advantages from its use are many, a fact demonstrated already by the generally accepted use of standard burden costs.

The use of standard costs reduce clerical work to a minimum. This is an advantage of great value.

The use of standard costs gives a constant comparison of actual results with a fixed standard which should be aecomplished. In contrast to questionable actual costs the advantage gained is obvious.

The setting of selling prices, especially where estimates are involved, is greatly simplified by using standard costs. The valuation of inventories is much more accurate, thereby safeguarding the balance sheet. The control of variations from standard gives the management and the operators of the plant a most intelligent basis on which to act.

In Conclusion Regarding Standard Costs.—Standard costs will probably be carried to a greater extent in the future than any other one development of cost procedure. In reality, standard costs are a part of budgeting; and the development of budget control will necessarily furnish a great impetus to standard costs. Or, vice-versa, the development of standard costs will greatly aid and accelerate budget control.

It is regretted that more space could not be devoted to the subject of standard costs in this volume. But as it is a special adaptation of costing procedure rather than a part of the fundamental principles underlying cost accounting, and as the subject is so extensive, it is possible but to describe briefly the meaning of standard costs and recommend its consideration in actual practice.

Machine Rates

What is Meant by Machine Rates.—Machine rates are rates per hour for each separate production unit which usually include all costs other than direct labor, and in many cases direct labor as well. For instance, a rate of $3.50 per hour for a boring mill in a machine shop might cover *all* cost, including direct labor on machine, all departmental and general expenses and all fixed charges.

The purpose of using a complete machine rate is to establish a lump sum cost rate to be carried by each machine or other production centre, whereby, knowing the hours of work performed, the cost is immediately known.

Where Machine Rates are Thought Necessary.—Machine rates are often thought necessary in heavy work machine shops, where large machinery is manufactured, and where a very large proportion of the cost consists of machinery operations. In addition, machine rates are often considered necessary in jobbing machine shops where much machine work is done on an hourly basis.

In the jobbing shops, there would seem to be a greater need than elsewhere for machine rates on account of the nature of the business, particularly as the means of computing selling prices. Where heavy work machine shops are producing heavy products, especially of a special nature with little prospect of duplication, and where the contracts for machinery are obtained as a result of estimates, there is good reason for using complete machine rates.

One example may be cited in a business manufacturing heavy machines. A set of drawings is submitted to the estimating department, and an estimate is prepared as to the hours of work required for the various machine tools, such as planers, millers, lathes, boring mills, etc. It is then an easy matter to extend these hours at the machine rates set for each class. It is also obvious that a comparison of the hours actually consumed will serve to check the estimate and indicate how well the job resulted by operations.

How Machine Rates are Figured.—Machine rates are arrived at after a careful and very detailed analysis and distribution of all costs. The first consideration is the amount of space required for the machine and its materials in process. Other important bases on which cost is charged to it are its value, its power requirements and the normal hours it is supposed to operate per year.

Without attempting to detail all movements, it may be stated that the following main items of cost are usually charged to each machine as shown.

Power	On the power requirement
Depreciation	On value
Taxes	On value
Insurance	On value
Heat	On floor space
Building maintenance	On floor space
Maintenance of the machine itself	Estimate of annual cost
Departmental burden	Usually on an hourly basis
Crane service	On some basis to reflect service necessary (this varies in different cases)
Direct labor	On normal operating hours

After working out all distributions, the rate per hour for machine is found.

Disadvantages of Machine Rates.—The task of working out machine rates is so great that it can be done only at comparatively long intervals. The scheme of machine rates is most emphatically a cost distributing plan, and as such it relegates into the background the great advantages of controlling costs at their source and thereby maintaining a continuous cost reducing campaign.

Those who use machine rates point out the fact that when machine No. 105 is rated at $2.50 per hour, and machine No. 110 is rated at $3.50 per hour, and a foreman does work on machine No. 110 which could be done on Machine No. 105, the foreman has wasted the company's money. While it is true that the foreman should always use what is obviously (without machine rates) the least expensive machine to operate, the costs which make up these hourly rates are incurred *by others* and in sundry other ways. Therefore, the real control of costs is *not* at the machine where the rates are applied, but at many other points, such as the power house, the indirect labor of the department and all the other divisions of burden and expense as discussed in this volume.

If those who think it necessary to use complete machine rates would also keep up the same activity with all the various cost analyses which provide a continuous check on the costs at their source, then the use of machine rates would not be of any great disadvantage. But when a company sets up machine rates and fails to follow through with the current analyses each month of all the expense and burden accounts, the net result is that the use of machine rates becomes simply a means of distributing costs with doubtful accuracy, with no consistent and continuous means of effective pressure to cut down costs other than the direct applied machine time with its direct labor.

When more than one operator is required for work on some machines where usually a single operator is required, the inclusion of the direct labor in the machine rate causes trouble. Where this is liable to occur, the plan of rates should eliminate the direct labor from the machine rate.

Advantages of Machine Rates.—As stated before, machine rates are really a necessity where machine time is sold as such, as is the case with jobbing machine shops. It is also a convenience in heavy machine shops where large pieces or machines are built.

In some plants the labor and burden portion of the work in process is carried entirely in machine hours. This is accomplished by charging to Work in Process the machine hours performed at their proper rates, crediting the machine hours on completed work at their proper rates. The residue is the inventory. As far as accounting is concerned, this is not at all out of order, and if properly handled is a fair reflection of the actual condition.

If estimates are carefully made rather than guessed at, it is indeed an advantage to check the hours of machine work estimated by the actual hours performed. But as to this feature, there is no necessity of having complete machine rates to accomplish this result, as it can be just as well done with hours alone without money value.

In Conclusion Regarding Machine Rates.—As it is often found that the use of machine rates does not carry with it a close control of the many and important factors which make up the costs, it would seem that it would be better to confine the machine rates to those costs which are strictly machine cost—*i.e.,* Depreciation, Power, Maintenance of the Machine, and Interest on the machine investment.

Superintendence and all the other factors which enter into the departmental burden may more accurately be added by ratio to the time of the indirect labor involved, because if the direct labor varies by changes in number of men necessary on a machine, the burden will automatically vary.

In many cases there may be some expenses other than those mentioned, which may be included in the restricted machine rate. For instance, crane service expense may be collected and pro rated to machines on a more equitable basis than through the medium of direct labor hours. This is especially true where a very heavy machine taking large work, is in the same shop with light machines. The large machines should stand the lion's share of the crane expense.

Machine rates are very necessary in cost accounting. The point is, however, that the attempt to allocate *all* costs through machine rates is not only quite inaccurate, but is also often found to be a bar to better and more profitable methods of controlling and reducing costs.

Developments of Special Adaptations.—Like every other branch of activity, there will and must be a continuous development of special adaptations of cost accounting. The old-fashioned general journal of the accountant has long since been relegated to the background and specially ruled books substituted, such as the voucher register, cash receipts book, cash disbursements book and many others. In fact, much accounting is now done without any books at all, as in the case of records of sales, where the duplicates of invoices serve in place of laborious entry in a sales journal.

So it is and will be in cost accounting. The principles of cost accounting as set forth in this volume are of course necessary of consideration in all transactions; but the volume of entries and the need for inventing short cuts, together with a deep consideration for practicability, demands the application of all possible special adaptations. It is in just such forward movements there will be found the greatest successes in cost accounting.

QUESTIONS AND PROBLEMS

Chapter I—What Cost Accounting Is

Questions

1. What is cost accounting?
2. State the three major objects or purposes of cost accounting.
3. Trace broadly the early beginnings of cost accounting, pointing out the parts played by both general accountants and engineers.
4. Why did the engineer pay so little attention to the overhead in the early days of cost accounting?
5. Make clear just why and in what way the cost man co-operates with the manager, engineer and general accountant.
6. What do you regard as the most important reason why departmental heads should get cost figures?
7. Are "costs" to be regarded as meaning solely the costs of completed products? Give reasons for your answer.
8. What basic condition is necessary if a department head is to be in a position where he can control costs?
9. What are among the more important pyschological effects which result from supplying cost figures to department heads?
10. Name the conventional advantages claimed for product costs.
11. What determines price in a jobbing plant?
12. What determines the prices of staple products made in large quantities?
13. Should non-profitable lines of goods be entirely abandoned or their production and sale curtailed? Why?
14. What general kind of costs is more valuable than product costs?
15. Build up the case for the imperative necessity of cost accounting.
16. Explain in your own words the significance of the charts in this chapter.
17. What is the chief impression made upon you by a reading of this chapter?

Chapter II—Relation of Cost Accounting to Management

Questions

1. Which is more important for a cost man to have, constructive vision or technical knowledge?
2. Why is there often friction between the plant and office?
3. What is necessary to prevent or minimize this friction?
4. Why is the cost department in such a strategic position to promote co-operation throughout the business enterprise?
5. Should a cost accountant gossip? Why?
6. List the characteristics you think a cost man should have?
7. Should a cost man be like a judge, a detective, or a helper? Why?
8. Point out the place a cost man should occupy in budgeting.
9. Why must the cost man be very guarded in everything he says?

Chapter III—Departmentalization

Questions

1. State the essential factors to be considered in departmentalizing a concern.
2. Discuss each briefly.
3. Is it ever necessary to unite two departments under one head? Why?
4. What is meant by a subsidiary or minor department or production center? Give an example.
5. (a) Classify departments from the broad viewpoint of cost accounting.
   (b) Explain each class and give an example.
6. Why are some departments of a hybrid character? Give examples.
7. Why is it necessary to consider departmentalization in building a cost structure?
8. (a) What is meant by direct charging?
   (b) Make clear its significance.

Problem

A plant consisting of the following factors is segregated from a railroad and from any power supply. They have impounded water below the level of the plant which necessitates pumping all their water supply to an overhead tank. All materials in and out have to be trucked. They generate their own steam, which is used in large quantities for production, for heating, for driving turbine engines, for generation of electric power, as well as for pumping water, of which a great deal is used.

One man is responsible for the manufacture and supply of water, steam, and electricity, with assistants directly in charge of each division.

The trucking is under the traffic manager, who also is in charge of all railroad matters.

A very fine stores system is in force under a supervisor of materials.

The product is varied, and the work performed is as follows:

Coke is produced; ore smelted in blast furnaces; rails rolled; wire drawn and various wire products such as nails, fencing, etc., turned out.

The plant is running under well-organized cost and production control, the stores coming under the production control. They have a well-organized industrial relations department that supplies all help, and a good purchasing department.

An engineering department supplies all drawings and designs.

Indicate how you would departmentalize, with consideration for control of costs and production.

Chapter IV—Cost Components

Questions

1. State the broad bases for the classification of costs.
2. Classify costs according to each of these bases.
3. Define and give an example of each major component or element of cost.
4. (a) What is the chief advantage of direct charging?
   (b) What are direct costs and indirect costs?
5. Without reference to the text draw a chart showing the chief components that enter into the total cost of product.
6. What are the uses of complete product costs?

Problem

Classify the following cost items to:

(a) Manufacturing or Selling Costs

(b) Direct or Indirect Costs

1. Foremen
2. Rubber used in making tires
3. Oil used as fuel for boilers
4. Magazine advertising
5. Labor making product
6. Salary of clerk in sales department
7. Oils for lubricating machinery
8. Repairing roof of plant
9. Cost of shipping goods from plant
10. Depreciation on plant
11. Cloth used in making clothing
12. Salesman traveling expense
13. Repairs to machines
14. Blotters sent to trade
15. Cost of electric power
16. Branch office expense
17. Labor inspecting product
18. Labor repairing defective goods
19. Labor keeping time
20. Commissions for selling

Chapter V—Establishing the Bases of Cost

Questions

1. Define a cost basis and give an example.
2. What are some of the reasons for accurate cost bases?
3. What is probably the most prevalent cause of failure of cost methods to operate successfully?
4. Is a single cost basis sufficient for an entire plant? Why?
5. (a) What cost bases may be used in a plant restaurant?
   (b) Which is better? Why?
6. (a) List the cost bases necessary in building up an accurate cost of a cigarette box.
   (b) Why do these cost bases differ?
7. Do the same for the other industries discussed in this chapter.

Problem A

What cost unit would you use for final units in the following manufacturing plants?

1. Dyes
2. Castings
3. Paint
4. Clock
5. Bottle
6. Pump
7. Automobile
8. Candy
9. Flour
10. Rails for R.R.
11. Coke
12. Underwear

Problem B

In manufacturing automobile tires, the product passes through various distinct operations which are very dissimilar. Many operations on the various materials at intermediate steps have no relation to the finished individual or unit tire. The operations are, roughly:

1. Raw rubber and various other components are "milled" into a compound which goes into stock as such for ageing. The formulas call for all components by weight.
2. Fabric bought by the pound in large rolls is impregnated with one of the previously described compounds by passing through the calenders and on completion is specified for use in the further operations by fixed sizes.
3. Other compounds are calendered into sheets for use in making tubes.
4. Machines with large knives called "bias cutters" cut the rubber impregnated fabric into strips exactly as used in the finished tires.
5. The tire builders shape the fabric and other necessary parts into the finished tire.

Questions

Assuming that an operation cost method is used, and eliminating other operations of tire manufacturing not described in this problem, on what basis would you handle:

(a) Cost of compound
(b) Cost of impregnated fabric
(c) Cost of bias cut strips
(d) Cost of finished tire

Chapter VI—Controlling Cost Records

Questions

1. Why are control accounts necessary?
2. Draft a set of journal entries showing the control of labor and

material. In each case indicate what and where the details supporting the controls are.

3. Should a single or several work in process accounts be kept? Why?
4. How is the control of burden handled?
5. Generally speaking, how are expense and burden accounts built up?
6. How do expense accounts differ from burden accounts?
7. Indicate the sources of data for entries in burden accounts.
8. Make clear the meaning of the words "analysis" and "control" when used in connection with control accounts.
9. Reproduce from memory a code of standing orders for electric power expense.
10. Draw up a comparative cost table that can be used in connection with any expense or burden account.
11. Classify control accounts according to function.
12. What class is the more important from a managerial standpoint?
13. Classify control accounts according to their degree of permanency. Give example.
14. Outline briefly the progress of cost data through cost accounts.

    Note: Be sure to study the chart at the end of the book in this connection.
15. Draw up skeleton ledger accounts of an expense, direct labor, direct material and burden account, respectively.

Problem

The bookkeeper of the Holden Mfg. Co. had the following items among others to post to his general ledger at the end of the month. What control accounts did he use?

New packing machine	$ 3,000.00
Repairs to boilers	1,800.00
Salary of superintendent's clerk	200.00
Received from J. Jones on account	700.00
Fabric for tires purchased	12,000.00
New steam gauge—replacement	120.00
Screws for product purchased	900.00
Direct labor pay-roll	1,400.00
Credit account defective goods sold	300.00
	$20,420.00

The control accounts on ledgers were: (1) Machinery and Equipment, (2) Steam Power, (3) Work in Process, (4) Raw Materials, (5) General Factory Expense, (6) Accounts Receivable.

Chapter VII—Mechanisms of Cost Control

Questions

1. Why is Chapter VII to be regarded as an index chapter?
2. What is the first prime requisite for an adequate cost system?
3. Classify orders, and state briefly the function of each class.
4. Why is the voucher record such an important pivotal record?
5. What is meant by temporary class control in connection with the use of a voucher record?
6. What is meant by an analysis sheet in connection with the use of a voucher record?
7. What are the advantages of using analysis sheets in connection with a voucher record?
8. List the major columns that should appear in a modern voucher register.
9. Discuss briefly the nature of the entries in each column and how the various columns are operated.
10. Draw up a sample journal entry illustrating how the data in the voucher register are distributed at the end of the month.
11. Discuss in detail the operation of the expense ledger account and the expense debit slip, bringing out their relation.
12. What are the advantages of this method of accounting?
13. State briefly the function of the chief original cost forms.
14. State briefly the function of the forms used to record the flow of material.
15. State briefly the function of the forms that are used in accounting for labor in the plant and in the pay-roll office.
16. How are transfers between control accounts accomplished?
17. What are some of the accumulation sheets that are used in obtaining data for journal entries made at the end of the month?
18. Make a list of statements that are compiled monthly and state briefly the function of each.

Problem

You are asked to enter the following transactions to the Vouchers Payable Register. Use the form shown in Chapter VII.

Voucher 1: For bill for various chemicals used in manufacturing product bought from Southern Chemical Co. Amount of invoice $1,340. Invoice charged to Account 1005, Raw Materials.

Voucher 2: For pay-roll for entire plant (the company carries a Pay-Roll account), amount $2,230.

Voucher 3: A bill from the General Supply Co. for some special parts for Dept. 1. Standing Order 3121, amount $225.

Voucher 4: For freight bills of C.R.R., total $1,020. The company's goods are all sold f.o.b. customer. The freight on outgoing shipments amounted to $200.

Incoming freight bills amounted to $820 of which $382 was to be recovered from vendors, the balance being on the shipment of chemicals in Voucher 1, bought f.o.b. purchaser's works.

Voucher 5: For coal purchased from Big Run Coal Co. in amount of $220. Charge to Account 1006, Coal.

Voucher 6: For a pair of new mixing tanks from the Blaine Tank Co., amount $3,250. Account 1009, Machinery and Equipment.

Voucher 7: For raw materials received from Northern Chemical Co., amount $3,850. Account 1005, Raw Materials.

Voucher 8: For various items of standard supplies from the Smith Co. Amount $3,280. Account 1003, General Stores.

Voucher 9: For invoice from the Expert Repair Co. for $620 for repairs of various descriptions during month, charged as follows:

Dept. 1—Standing Order	3121	$160.00
" 2— " "	3221	280.00
" 3— " "	3321	180.00

Voucher 10: For various items purchased from the City Sales Co. amounting to $1,040 and accounted as follows:

Dept. 1—Standing Order	3125	$120.00
" 2— " "	3223	380.00
Ad. Expense " "	10106	240.00
Selling " " "	12106	300.00

Voucher 11: For bill of C.R.R. for $200, being prepaid freight on shipments of goods sold on special terms of f.o.b. seller's works.

Enter the above on Voucher Register, making out proper analysis and expense slips.

Then make the necessary closing entry, closing out the voucher register totals.

Chapter VIII—Prevailing Methods of Costing the Product

Questions

1. Why is the establishment of the proper bases for figuring costs important?
2. What are the names of the prevailing methods of costing the product?
3. How can one determine what the prevailing method of costing is in a given concern?
4. Does one method of costing usually prevail throughout an entire plant? Why?
5. Discuss the main features of a job cost system.
6. Which is the most common method of costing?
   When is a job cost system unsuitable?
8. (a) What are the main features of a class cost system?
   (b) Give an example of a class cost system.
9. What are the points of similarity and dissimilarity between a job cost system and a class cost system?
10. (a) Outline the chief features of an operation cost system.
    (b) Give an example of such a system.
11. (a) Discuss the main characteristics of a process cost system?
    (b) Give an example of where such a system is applicable.
12. How does a process system differ from an operation system.

Problem A

In a mill manufacturing wire nails, the sizes, complicated by various types for each size, multiplies the items of product to a great number. Throughout all the items, however, the difference in types is accomplished by different dies in the same machine.

What type of cost system is indicated?

Problem B

In a certain chemical plant, the operations follow so closely one after the other, that there is no possibility of getting a physical check after each operation on the quantity produced.

An entire plant is set aside for the manufacture of a single chemical product. The raw material goes in at one end, and the finished product comes out at the other. The entire process takes 7 days, which means that at the end of each month, a varying quantity remains in process at the various operation points. What type of cost system would you suggest for this plant, and how would you take care of this fluctuating work in process inventory in your costs?

Problem C

You are asked to compile a cost sheet, showing all transactions and computations, to get the cost of the following order and to compute operation unit costs:

Use the following data:

Order 12001 for 60 pieces, Part A-908.

The plant has five departments, whose general burden rates are standardized at:

Dept.	1—45	cents	per	direct-labor	hour
"	2—60	"	"	"	"	"
"	3—90	"	"	"	"	"
"	4—30	"	"	"	"	"
"	5—50	"	"	"	"	"

The following machine burden super-rates are in effect:

In	Dept.	1—	Class	A—	Machines	20	cents	per	machine	hour
"	"		"	B—	"	12	"	"	"	"
"	"	2—	"	C—	"	42	"	"	"	"
			"	D—	"	27	"	"	"	"
			"	E—	"	35	"	"	"	"
"	"	3—	"	F—	"	82	"	"	"	"
			"	G—	"	125	"	"	"	"

There are no machine burden super-rates for Depts. 4 and 5, but simply the departmental rates.

The time cards turned in against this order are:

Dept. 1:
- Operation 300—Done on Class B Machines
  - 60 labor hours at 65 cents
  - 52 machine hours
  - 49 good pieces finished

Dept. 2:
- Operation 305—Done on Class D Machines
  - 80 labor hours at 50 cents
  - 85 machine hours
  - 48 good pieces finished

Dept. 3:
Operation 309—Done on Class G Machines
110 labor hours at 42 cents
82 machine hours
46 good pieces finished
Dept. 4:
Operation 318
6 labor hours at 70 cents
46 good pieces
Dept. 5:
Operation 320
6 labor hours at 75 cents
45 good pieces

The material used was: 50 brass castings at 34 cents each.

The scrap from the 5 defective castings weighed 2 pounds. Scrap value 15 cents per pound.

Get total order cost, operation unit costs, and costs per good piece.

Draw up proper form of cost sheet.

Chapter IX—Specifications of Product and Operations

Questions

1. Why are specifications of product and operations necessary?
2. Sketch roughly a specification sheet for a product.
3. Discuss briefly the important uses of specifications of product.
4. Explain in a few words the meaning of each item on a specification sheet of operations.
5. Summarize very briefly the objectives of specifications.

Chapter X—Orders and Symbols

Questions

1. Why is an adequate system of orders necessary to a modern plant?
2. Why are oral orders insufficient?
3. Classify orders and briefly state the function of each class.
4. Why should a production order cover but one item?

5. What information should a production order show?
6. What is the function of an identification and move card, and what information should it show?
7. What kind of costs are charged to standing orders?
8. Why are standing expense orders so-called?
9. Why should indirect costs be carefully analyzed?
10. Why is the identification of orders, accounts, departments and machines important?
11. What are the advantages of coding?
12. Outline briefly one method of assigning orders.
13. List some of the items in a code for administrative, sales and general office expenses.

Chapter XI—Purchase and Receiving Records

Questions

1. Into what principal classes can all purchases be grouped?
2. Define and explain the mechanism for purchasing and receiving.
3. Explain and show the importance of proper accounting at the source.
4. How should the inspection of incoming material be performed in relation to the receiving of material?

Problem

For each of the following items state where the requests for purchase should originate and by whom they should be approved.

1. Chemicals for manufacture
2. Repairs to electric power house
3. Invoice for advertising in magazine
4. Repairs to adding machine
5. Lumber for stock
6. Repairs to yard locomotive
   A new machine
   12 tons steel for manufacture
   New forms printed for sales department
10. New desks for general office
11. Overhauling of machine
12. Invoice for auditors
13. Blotters for advertising

14. New switch
15. Samples for customers

Chapter XII—Transportation Charges

Questions

1. What does transportation cover?
2. On what classes of goods are incoming transportation charges incurred?
3. On what classes are outgoing transportation charges incurred?
4. What are the five main divisions of all transportation charges, from the accounting viewpoint?
5. Explain the accounting of freight bills:
   (a) When they are to be deducted from payment of invoices.
   (b) When they are to be added to invoices.
   (c) When the charges are absorbed in cost of goods.
   (d) When they are for charges on delivery of sales.
   (e) When they are for charges of expense nature.

Problem A

A company bought goods on terms f.o.b. buyer's works. The goods were shipped freight collect. The amount of freight was $18.20. To what account should this freight be charged when the freight bill is paid?

Problem B

A company sells all goods f.o.b. seller's works. A sale was made to a company in a small town where there was no freight office and prepaid the freight. To what account should this freight bill be charged when paid?

Problem C

A bunch of freight bills amounting to $450 showed the following circumstances:

(a) Bills amounting to $200 were for goods bought from vendors, f.o.b. buyer's works.
(b) Bills amounting to $30 were for advertising supplies sent to a jobber.
(c) Bills amounting to $100 were for raw materials bought f.o.b. vendor's works.

(d) Bills amounting to $40 were for goods shipped customers on terms f.o.b. seller's works.

(e) Bills amounting to $20 were for goods returned by customers on account of their being defective.

(f) Bills amounting to $60 were for a machine sent away for repairs.

Give the proper accounting for each of the items described above.

Chapter XIII—Stock Record Accounting

Questions

1. Discuss the organization of the stores department in plants where a production control department is not maintained; and where there is a production control department.
2. Should storerooms from an organization standpoint be under the control of the purchasing agent?
3. Should stock records be under the control of the storekeeper?
4. Why are stock records essential to the proper costing of individual parts and assemblies?
5. In what different forms are stock records kept?
6. Name the sections of a modern stock record sheet.
7. (a) What is a running total column?
   (b) Why does a running total column obviate the need of a Balance column in a stock record?
8. What information may appear on the heading of a stock record sheet?
9. (a) What data does the Requirements column show?
   (b) From what sources are the data obtained?
10. (a) What information appears in the Appropriated columns?
    (b) How is this column operated?
11. What do the Ordered columns show?
12. How are the Received, Issued and Adjustment columns operated?
13. What data should appear on a material requisition?
14. Explain the procedure in filling out a requisition.
15. What are some points to be kept in mind in honoring requisitions?
16. Discuss the chief points in accounting for scrap.
17. What use is made of the material credit slip?

18. Explain the technique of a simple stock record.
19. Why is it important and absolutely necessary to pay attention to minimum and maximum stock limits?
20. What important points are involved in setting the minimum limit?
21. What important points are involved in determining the best quantities to order?

Problem A

Post to the stock record sheet shown in Figure 27 the following data:

Special Brass Casting,
Pattern 1308-1, used for type 13 machine. Carried in
Casting Stockroom, Section C, Shelf 3, Bin 32.

The castings are charged to Account 84, and are usually purchased from the American Foundries, Inc. It requires 10 days to get the first castings after placing of purchase order. They weigh 3½ pounds each.

The quantities used in previous years were:

1917	2,230	1919	2,541
1918	2,300	1920	1,972

The original maximum established March 18, 1917, was 700, and the minimum 300. These were kept until January 3, 1919, when they were changed to 820 and 300, respectively. On December 15, 1920, they were changed again to 700 and 200.

Requirements were shown to be:

87	for	Order	S–2081
190	"	"	S–2108
230	"	"	S–2112
145	"	"	S–2180

Purchase Order P–3805 was placed January 4, 1921, for 800.

The inventory of January 1, 1921, showed 250 on hand, which were priced at 85 cents each.

On January 15, 1921, there were 160 castings received on Purchase Order P–3805, which were invoiced at $117, plus transportation charges of $2.50 which were charged against the castings, they being bought f.o.b. seller.

Appropriations made previous to receipt of castings on Purchase Order P–3805 were as follows:

S–2081	86
S–2108	160

After castings were received, these additional appropriations were made:

S–2108	23
S–2112	122

The issued transactions were as follows:

Jan. 5, 1921—S–2081	86
Jan. 6, 1921—S–2108	160
Jan. 16, 1921—S–2108	23
Jan. 25, 1921—S–2112	122

Problem B

The following data appeared on a stock record sheet. You are asked to point out what is wrong and what should be done, considering the uses of all 5 columns.

The Requirement column showed these requirements:

Order 12108	5,000	pieces
" 12200	6,500	"
" 12506	15,600	"
12618	25,000	"
12702	4,500	"

The Appropriated column showed:

Order 12108	4,000	pieces
" 12200	6,500	"
" C-802	8,000	"
12506	2,500	

The Ordered column showed that on January 3, Purchase Order P–2956 was placed for 30,000 pieces.

The Received column showed that on February 1, 10,000 pieces were received on Order P–2910—Invoice $2,000, and on February 3, 5,000 pieces were received on Order P–2956—Invoice $750.

The Issued column showed that on February 2, 10,000 pieces

priced at 20 cents each, were issued, 4,000 on Order 12108 and 6,000 on Order 12200.

And on February 4, 3,000 pieces, priced at 20 cents each, were issued, 500 on Order 12200 and 2,500 on Order 12618.

The minimum quantity to be carried on hand was 75,000 pieces.

Problem C

On April 4, 14 special brass castings, Piece No. A–902, were scrapped on Order 2805. The drilling on them, done in Department 15, from which they were received, was defective, owing to the carelessness of a worker there. The castings were marked to be returned to "brass stores."

This company followed the practice of charging the total loss due to carelessness to the department held accountable for error. It was charged to Burden Cost account of the responsible department.

The order was to receive credit.

The material, labor and burden value of the order was carried in Work in Process account.

The company kept an account called "Brass Scrap," for all scrap brass castings.

The 14 castings referred to above weighed 24 pounds when they were returned to the storeroom. Their scrap value was 20 cents per pound.

The cost value of them up to time they were scrapped was $8.70, which was deducted from the total cost of the order.

Using the form of scrap ticket shown in Figure 30, you are asked to post a ticket showing the above case of the 14 scrapped castings. Make the necessary debit and credit entries to the proper accounts.

Chapter XIV—Securing Data of Material Consumption

Questions

1. Describe how most effectively and easily to secure data as to material on assembly orders?
2. Describe procedure of securing data on material:
   (a) Where used in quantities too small to measure
   (b) Where impractical to measure
   (c) Where used for different products
3. How would special material situations, such as in 2(b), be controlled ?

CHAPTER XV—METHODS OF PRICING MATERIAL REQUISITIONS

Questions

1. What two prime factors are important in connection with pricing requisitions?
2. What methods prevail in pricing requisitions?
3. Describe the principal points involved in pricing requisitions:
   (a) At actual cost
   (b) At average cost
   (c) At market price
   (d) At standard cost
   (e) At estimated cost
4. Explain the use of a Material Adjustment account:

Problem A

In a hardware specialty company, the following castings were on the stock records at inventory time:

Pattern A-901	2,282 Castings at 26 cents each
Pattern A-908	5,840 Castings at 13 cents each

During the month the following were received, f.o.b. seller:

Pattern A-901—	10,000—	Amount of invoice	$2,400.00
		" " freight	100.00
	3,000	" " invoice	630.00
		" " freight	30.00
Pattern A-908—	2,000—	Amount of invoice	180.00
		" " freight	10.00
	1,000	" " invoice	70.00
		" " freight	5.00

Illustrate how you would price each one of the following requisitions for castings, using the *lot method* of pricing:

Pattern A-901—	1st requisition for	2,000
	2nd " "	1,000
	3rd " "	12,000
Pattern A-908—	1st requisition for	5,000
	2nd " "	2,000
	3rd " "	950
	4th " "	725

Problem B

In a certain brass foundry, the stock records show the following on hand, the first of the month:

Copper	138,000 lb.	at 15 cents
Tin	20,000 "	" 62 "
Lead	25,000 "	" 7 "
Zinc	15,000 "	" 43 "

The control account covering the above is captioned Brass Metal Stores.

During the month, the metals received were as follows:

Copper	115,000 lb.	at 16 cents
Tin	50,000 "	" 58 "
Lead	30,000 "	" 6 "
Zinc	30,000 "	" 50 "

The metals consumed during the month by the melting department were:

Copper	150,000 lb.
Tin	9,000 "
Lead	10,000 "
Zinc	10,000 "

With the above data given, you are asked to price out the metals consumed during the month, using the average price method and explaining very carefully the method you use for arriving at the average.

Illustrate detail entries on stock records for each kind of metal, and also show the condition of the control account after the transactions are made.

Problem C

Use the same quantities and prices of metals given in Problem B and assume that this company is following the practice of charging its metals into Cost of Melt account at average *market prices* for the month in which they were consumed. The metal trade journals showed this month's market prices to be:

Copper	17 cents
Tin	63 "
Lead	7 "
Zinc	52

The company desires to know its profits or losses on metal, owing to rising or falling markets, as distinct from manufacturing profits or losses, this being very essential in order to gauge the effectiveness of the purchasing department.

How would you take care of this from the accounting viewpoint? Open up the proper accounts and show all journal entries necessary for these transactions, to clear the stores control account and show difference between *market* and actual costs.

Chapter XVI—How to Take Inventory

Questions

1. Describe how perpetual inventories are kept checked up.
2. What are the chief steps in taking inventory according to the "duplicate tag" method, so-called?
3. What subjects do inventory instructions deal with?
4. What is meant by the inventory period?
5. What is the personnel of the inventory committee?
6. Discuss somewhat in detail the special preparations made by departments primarily concerned with the taking of inventory.
7. Discuss in detail the listing of the inventory.
8. How are inventories of raw material supplies, work in process and finished product priced and valued?
9. Discuss the contents and use of inventory tags and sheets.

Chapter XVII—Advantages of Stock Records

Questions

1. Discuss in a general way how a system of stock records aids different departments.
2. What savings are made by prompt ordering of stock?
3. How is production aided by listing requirements?
4. How are deliveries facilitated by stock appropriations?
5. How does prompt ordering and urging help to maintain an even flow of production?
6. What are the advantages of keeping deliveries within contract limits?

7. How is improper accounting for receipts detected?
8. How is buying and economical consumption of material aided by stock records?
9. Discuss the other advantages of stock records with particular reference to each column of a modern stock record sheet.
10. Discuss the relations between the columns of a stock record sheet.
11. What are the advantages of carrying money values on stock records?

Chapter XVIII—Accounting for Labor in the Plant

Questions

1. What are the chief steps in accounting for labor?
2. (a) Which of these steps are taken in the plant?
   (b) Which in the office?
3. What are the four main objectives of labor accounting?
4. Name the chief forms used in labor accounting.
5. Explain briefly the function of each one of these forms.
6. (a) What information does the weekly in-and-out clock card show?
   (b) What use is made of weekly in-and-out clock cards?
7. State the different duties of the dispatch clerk.
8. Name the two principal kinds of time cards.
9. State in detail the data that are entered on the time cards used to record the cost of direct labor.
10. Describe the method of calculating factors.
11. How is the labor accounted for under the bonus and premium methods of wage payment?
12. What relation has the matter of inspecting to the accounting for direct labor?
13. What information appears on time cards for indirect work?
14. What is meant by the term "loaned worker"?
15. How is the time of loaned workers accounted for in the factory?
16. How does the accounting for "other department standing order labor" differ from "loaned labor"?
17. How is O.D.S.O. labor accounted for in the factory?
18. What are short operations?

19. Explain the method of accounting for short operations, citing an example.
20. Describe the routine of checking labor cards.
21. Who should keep the file of day and piece rates, and where should the rating of time cards be done?
22. Explain the procedure in extending labor cards.

Chapter XIX—Accounting for Labor on Pay-Rolls

Questions

1. For what three purposes are pay-rolls used?
2. What points should be kept in mind in turning over time cards to the pay-roll department?
3. What preparatory steps should be taken in regard to pay-roll sheets before labor costs are entered thereon?
4. Discuss the content and arrangement of a pay-roll sheet.
5. How is transfer or loaned labor accounted for in the pay-roll office?
6. Describe the accounting for direct labor by the pay-roll clerk.
7. What provision is made on the pay-roll sheet for showing the different classes of direct labor?
8. What is indirect labor?
9. How is it accounted for on pay-rolls?
10. How is O.D.S.O. labor handled in the pay-roll office?
11. How are the total columns filled out?
12. The accuracy of the pay records is safeguarded in two ways—what are they?
13. Describe the different steps in closing pay-rolls.
14. What procedure may be followed when pay-rolls are split?
15. How is the total of the pay-roll for each department ascertained?
16. From where is the information obtained that is necessary for the preparation of journal entries to effect the controls of labor?
17. Why is there usually an accrued pay-roll item among the liabilities on the monthly balance sheets?
18. Discuss in quite comprehensive manner the different steps in analyzing pay-rolls.
19. Discuss in detail the procedure in the pay-roll office of accounting for:

(a) Loaned workers
(b) O.D.S.O. labor

20. Where are the time cards for these two classes of labor filed?

Problem A

A certain manufacturing company employs 800 men throughout its 16 departments. The workers are all on a day-work basis, and because of this pay-rolls are now made up directly from in-and-out cards. This plant is engaged in a strictly jobbing business and makes over 1,000 products. Consequently, the workers are changing jobs sometimes three or four times a day in some departments.

The in-and-out cards are sorted by departments and separated as to direct and indirect labor for the producing departments. There are certain service departments, such as millwrights, carpenter shop, etc., that perform work for other departments. At present the time spent on other department work is classified as indirect labor in the department in which it is done.

Also, this plant loans workers between departments for 8 or 10 hours at the most. At present, the worker is given a new number for each time he is loaned to a department regardless of length of time.

Assume that you were called in the above company to advise them as to whether or not they were conducting their time-keeping and pay-roll functions properly as regards good cost accounting. What would be your decisions and how would you advise them to correct conditions if they needed corrections? Back up your statements with full arguments?

Problem B

Two of the operations connected with the manufacture of a certain product were "scouring" and "polishing." In one plant these operations were very short and of such a nature that there was no real basis for an operation cost, as pounds, or even pounds by classes. The product was so varied in style, and so many different styles were put through these operations during the day, that it was impossible to get time against each style. As some styles were not scoured or polished, the cost could not be considered as part of the burden.

It had to be considered as a direct labor cost against the various styles produced.

If you were confronted with this situation, in a plant using a job cost scheme, how would you get the operation cost of scouring and polishing of each job going through?

Chapter XX—Expense and Burden Accounts

Questions

1. What is the distinction between expense and burden accounts?
2. Into what three classes are expense accounts subdivided?
3. Describe what each of the above three classes includes.
4. Into what three classes are burden accounts subdivided?
5. Describe what each of the above three classes includes.
6. Describe the importance of expense and burden accounts as controlling accounts.

Chapter XXI—Distribution of Expense Accounts

Questions

1. Why is it wrong to distribute general expenses to burden accounts on the basis of *total direct labor costs?*
2. What basis is better than the direct-labor costs?
3. What are the bases of distribution for the following costs:

(a) Trucking
(b) Steam
(c) Electric Power
(d) Compressed Air
(e) Rent
(f) Taxes
(g) Depreciation
(h) Fire Insurance
(i) Liability and Compensation
(j) Telephone
(k) Drafting
(l) Stores

4. Into what segregated accounts should the old General Expense account, so-called, be split up?

Problem A

In a certain plant, the following items were all included in the general expense of the plant, and distributed to the departmental burdens on the basis of the direct-labor hours in each department. In this plant departmental burden was applied on the basis of direct-labor hours.

1. Electric Power Plant Cost
2. Rent
3. Depreciation
4. General Superintendent's office

5. General Office Expense
6. Trucking Expense
7. Compensation Insurance
8. Taxes

Which ones of the above should be distributed on their own basis, and what is the basis?

Which would you leave in general expense, and would you distribute these on the same basis as before?

Problem B

An engineering department with 10 draftsmen, a blue-print boy, two clerks and two stenographers was included by a plant in general expense.

This department was serving the various departments of the plant with designs of equipment and the sales department with designs of special product. From this it is evident that the time of the draftsman indicated a different method of distributing this expense. How would you do it?

Chapter XXII—Departmental Burden Rates and Their Application

Questions

1. Is burden as elusive as commonly imagined?
2. What have been the chief methods used in the evolution of burden?
3. Describe the technique of the fixed percentage method.
4. Describe the technique of the blanket-rate method.
5. Generally speaking, what is the modern method of handling burden?
6. What are the chief steps involved in treating burden under this modern method?
7. What is meant by a basis of distribution?
8. What is meant by predetermining burden?
9. What essential factors should be held in mind in predetermining burden rates?
10. What is normal production?
11. Explain its significance in connection with burden?
12. Why are predetermined rates necessary?

13. What is the general theory underlying the calculation and application of departmental burden rates?
14. What are the chief bases used in calculating and applying burden rates?
15. Discuss the different technical steps in the calculation and application of burden under each of the following methods:
    (a) Direct-labor hours
    (b) Direct-labor costs
    (c) Machine hours
16. What is meant by super-rate?
17. What burden costs are handled by means of it?
18. What is the difference between a departmental burden account and a burden credit account?
19. Why are both necessary for the proper control of burden?
20. What is a plant balance or over- and under-absorbed burden?
21. Briefly, how is this item treated?
22. Generally speaking, when should burden rates be revised?
23. What specific conditions make this advisable?

Problem A

A plant manufactures brass machine parts; steel forgings, rough and machined; and brass and iron castings, rough and machined. All of the output is made on special orders, large and small. In arriving at the costs, the manufacturer has applied a flat overhead per labor hour.

Assuming that the manufacturer has adequate means for keeping track of labor and materials by jobs, why would the plant costs obtained still be unreliable and what would be the first thing you would do in inaugurating a proper cost system?

Problem B

A manufacturing concern has a machine department, a lumber mill and an assembly department, and is using a blanket rate for its burden application. The articles that go through the lumber mill are never routed through the other departments, and vice versa.

The present blanket rate is based on the actual burden costs obtained when the plant was operating at about 50% of its capacity.

State what is wrong with the above method of applying burden? What would you recommend as a proper basis?

Problem C

For a certain department in a plant (where the machinery is such as not to warrant separate machine rates), the following data appeared on the books of the company:

Total Actual Burden for year	$80,000.00
Total Actual Direct Labor Hours for year	70,000 hours
Total Actual Direct Labor Pay-roll for year	$50,000.00

Analysis showed that this statement represented a condition of only 60% of capacity operation, that is, as to possible direct labor. In discussing the situation, the factory manager stated that the normal condition of operating should be 80% of capacity, and if this were reached the burden cost would increase only 10%.

Assume that the department was estimating on a large order of 50,000 pieces, which it was anxious to get.

Direct costs of filling the order would be:

Material	$42,000
Labor—1,500 hours at	55 cents
2,000 " "	60 "
5,000 " "	65 "

The manager has asked to have the estimate figured both on the percentage and on the direct-hour plan of burden distribution. Compute the cost per unit on each plan, advising which to use and why.

Problem D

In 1917 the X Glove Co. followed the practice of applying their overhead on the basis of prime cost (labor and material) to the respective orders for gloves. This percentage of overhead was a blanket percentage based on the previous year's cost figures.

During the latter part of 1917, the United States government entered into a contract with them for fur gloves on a cost-plus basis. This government contract brought the plant up to full operating capacity, as against only half-capacity the previous year, which gave the basis for the blanket overhead rate.

Also, in making these fur gloves for the government, the material cost was 70% of the total cost. Heretofore, as this factory was making ordinary kid gloves, the material had been only about 25%.

Assume that the United States government had sent you to this glove company in order to recommend the proper basis for calculation and applying the overhead, so that the government would not suffer under its cost-plus contract. What would be your criticisms of the existing methods, and your recommendations for the future?

Chapter XXIII—Advantages and Disadvantages of Different Methods of Applying Burden

Questions

1. What is the best basis of applying burden?
2. What other bases of applying burden are used?
3. What are the advantages and disadvantages of the following methods of applying burden:
    (a) Direct-labor hours
    (b) Direct-labor cost
    (c) Machine hours

Problem

A certain department was using a straight machine rate for two classes of machines. This ratio included both direct and indirect labor and all burden applied to the machines by various methods.

The machines required a varying number of men as the nature of work changed; sometimes two, three or four men. Obviously it became inaccurate to use a rate for the machine which did not reflect this difference in direct labor.

Over a considerable period of time the charges against the two classes of machines were

	Class A	Class B
Power	$ 50.00	$ 40.00
Direct Labor on Machines	4,200.00	3,100.00
Depreciation on Machines	350.00	182.00
Maintenance of Machines	1,100.00	94.00
No. machine hours operated	1,500 hours	1,120 hours
Direct labor hours applied	5,300 "	4,200 "
General Department Burden apportioned on basis of floor space occupied—or any other basis used for the old rates	$3,200.00	$2,310.00

From the above data, arrive at new rates for burden and machine hours where the costs will be more accurate than under the straight machine rates.

Chapter XXIV—Preparation of Journal Entries

Questions

1. Into what two main classes are journal entries divided?
2. Which is the preferable method of posting the entries from the voucher register?
3. Describe how requisitions for material are accumulated for journal entry.
4. Describe how expense debit slips are accumulated for journal entry.
5. How are scrap tickets entered to prepare data for journal entry?
6. Describe the general fundamental principle involved in distributing such fixed charges as depreciation, taxes, etc.
7. Why is proper and accurate journalizing an important feature of cost accounting?

Problem A

Upon the completion of the month, the following pay-roll analysis existed in a plant:

Dept.	Direct Labor	Indirect Labor	O.D.S.O.	Transfers	Total
1	$3,200.00	$2,500.00	$700.00	$200.00	$ 6,600.00
2	4,500.00	3,200.00	......	......	7,700.00
3	2,000.00	1,700.00	......	......	3,700.00
Total					$18,000.00

The plant operated separate accounts for department pay-roll, and separate department accounts for work in process, labor, material and burden.

The labor transfer record showed the transfer to be all indirect labor and to Dept. 2.

The O.D.S.O. transfer record showed all the O.D.S.O. labor as being done for Dept. 3, with the burden rate for Dept. 1 at 100% of the direct labor.

From the above given data, make out the necessary labor-distribution journal entries, covering the original pay-roll, the transfer record, and the O.D.S.O. record.

Problem B

At the end of the month, the two material accumulation sheets for requisitions, and the accumulation sheet for expense ledger charges, showed the following:

The total direct material requisitions passing through for the month amounted to $17,000. The company used but one Work in Process Material account for all direct material, it being difficult to effect further segregation.

The total indirect material requisitions of $7,000.00 showed this distribution:

Dept. 1—Burden	$1,000.00
" 2 "	2,200.00
" 3 "	2,400.00
" 4	1,050.00
" 5	350.00

The material represented on these requisitions came from:

Raw Materials	$12,000.00
Part Finished Stock	4,250.00
Steel Stores	3,000.00
Supply Stores	4,750.00

The expense ledger charges were distributed as follows:

Dept. 1	$1,550.00
" 3	500.00
" 4	1,925.00
5	350.00
Total	$4,325.00

With the above data given, prepare a journal entry for the distribution of material, both direct and indirect, and for the expense ledger charges.

Problem C

Make the *work in process burden* journal entry for a plant having departmental Work in Process accounts.

On the pay-roll summary sheet, direct-labor hours appeared as follows:

Dept. 1	11,080	Direct-Labor Hours
" 2	5,360	" " "
" 3	5,600	" " "
" 4	13,982	" " "

The burden rates per hour that were predetermined for these departments were:

$0.82	for	Dept.	1
1.75	"	"	2
1.00	"	"	3
0.78	"	"	4

Chapter XXV—Expense and Burden Statements

Questions

1. Distinguish between expense and burden accounts, citing examples.
2. Why are expense and burden details important?
3. How are the figures of expense and burden proved?
4. Mention the chief sections of expense and burden statements.
5. What is a "collating sheet"?
6. Discuss in detail how it is prepared.
7. How is it proved?
8. How are "apportioned expenses" handled?
9. How are expense and burden statements completed?
10. How are expenses and burdens compared?
11. Why is proper presentation of expenses and burdens so important?

Note: As the construction of expense and burden statements is so involved, the General Problem in Cost Accounting which follows is for the purpose of testing the student on his knowledge in this respect.

Chapter XXVI—Administration Expense

Questions

1. What does administration expense include?
2. How are salaries prorated to the various itemized accounts of the administrative expense?
3. Why is there less opportunity to reduce cost by knowing the administration expense than is the case with other expense accounts?

Chapter XXVII—Sale and Distribution Expense

Questions

1. Why are the costs of selling so important?
2. What is the best method of issuing comparative selling expense accounts; by dollars or some other method?
3. Is it correct practice to include freight out on sales as a selling cost?
4. Is cash discount taken by customers a selling expense?
5. Is there any advantage in prorating the general selling expense to branch selling expenses?
6. State the advantages gained from furnishing branch sales managers with statements comparing selling costs of all branches?

Chapter XXVIII—Financial Statements

Questions

1. What are the advantages of correct financial statements?
2. Should statements be voluminous? Give reasons.
3. What are some typical schedules that support the balance sheet?
4. What are the different kinds of balance sheets?
5. What are the broad classes of items in a profit and loss statement?
6. What schedules back up this statement?
7. Discuss the accounting for items in the financial section of the profit and loss statement.
8. What are the main sections in burden statements and expense statements, respectively?
9. Indicate by illustration how a balance sheet may be read.

Problem A

The following trial balance was taken from the general ledger of the company, January 31, 1921.

You are asked to make a proper balance sheet, listing as to current and fixed assets, liabilities, etc.

Also, make a profit and loss statement, proving the profit listed on the balance sheet.

Accounts	Debits	Credits
Accounts Payable—General Ledger		$ 483.24
Accrued Pay-Roll		2,748.53
Accounts Receivable	$ 5,785.17	
Administrative Expense	2,749.00	
Bills Payable		5,000.00
Bills Receivable	3,000.00	
Capital Stock		25,000.00
Cash on Hand and in Banks	5,007.15	
Cost of Sales	9,048.71	
Dividends Paid	2,500.00	
Discounts Given	125.40	
Discounts Taken		106.81
Freight out on Sales	324.36	
Good-Will	4,000.00	
Interest Paid	41.50	
Interest Received		25.00
Liberty Bonds	4,000.00	
Machinery and Equipment Owned	8,745.00	
Manufactured Stock	4,994.38	
Material in Process	6,190.88	
Prepaid Expenses	374.00	
Raw Materials	6,748.75	
Real Estate and Buildings	10,742,56	
Reserve for Depreciation		2,189.02
Sales		15,486.89
Selling Expense	1,574.29	
Surplus—December 31, 1920		21,821.17
Vouchers Payable		3,172.51
Burden Cost Account	3,256.06	
Burden Credit Account		3,174.04
Totals	$79,207.21	$79,207.21

Problem B

In the trial balance, listed in the previous problem, the burden cost total is shown as $3,056.64. The analysis of this burden cost is as follows:

Foremen and Assistants	$ 535.00
Storekeepers and Timekeepers	250.00
General Labor	400.00
Cleaning and Sweeping	275.06
Oiling and Shafting	50.00
Work on Account Shop Error	56.00

Shipping Expense	$ 234.00
Inventory Expense	16.74
Drills	18.34
Lights	8.40
Miscellaneous Expense	55.06
Trucking Expense	130.00
Liability Insurance	10.55
Power, Light and Heat	260.00
Depreciation	65.00
Bonus	480.00
Miscellaneous	174.30
Maintenance of Machinery	56.24
" " Tools	45.43
" " Dies and Jigs	25.50
" " Electrical Apparatus	47.30
" " Belting	52.74
" " Fixtures	10.40
Total	$3,256.06

The total direct or productive labor for the month is $3,174.04.

The predetermined burden rate, used on all costs, is 100% of the direct labor.

With the above data given, make up a burden statement, as you would wish to have it submitted.

Problem C

A large corporation has two large steam power plants within a quarter of a mile of each other. The equipment in each plant is practically the same. The boilers are the same type and the facilities for handling coal and ashes are practically the same.

When the first detailed monthly statements of the expenses of these two plants were presented to the general manager, he looked at each statement, compared the results and then discharged his chief power engineer. Why did he do this? The statements of the two power plants were as follows:

No. 1. Steam Power Plant

Labor—Firemen, Coal Passers, etc.	$ 4,116.71
Maintenance	284.95
Coal	7,209.81
Miscellaneous Supplies	32.14
	$11,643.61

No. 2. Steam Power Plant

Labor—Firemen, Coal Passers, etc.	$ 1,244.75
Maintenance	187.25
Coal	6,213.68
Miscellaneous Supplies	26.12
	$ 7,671.80

Chapter XXIX—Budgetary Control

Questions

1. What is meant by "budgetary control"?
2. What two factors enter into the preparation of budgets? Describe each.
3. What two factors effect the order of precedence in importance as between quotas of sales and the expense budgets?
4. Name the various important quotas and budgets to be set.
5. Describe the setting of standard budgets of burden for various speeds of operation.

Chapter XXX—Use of Cost Reports by Executives

Questions

1. Describe the great importance of proper presentation of cost figures?
2. Tell how an executive looks over the statements which are provided?
3. What importance attaches to attitude of the chief executive toward cost figures?
4. What is the importance to executives of comparisons of cost?
5. What is the function of a cost research department?
6. What is a most important spirit for the chief executive to cultivate in respect to costs?
7. From an executive standpoint, to what extent and how are costs of value:
   (a) In respect to setting selling prices?
   (b) In respect to selling policies?
8. Why is great care necessary in adding administrative and selling costs to manufacturing costs in arriving at the final costs?

Chapter XXXI—Use of Cost Reports by Department Heads

Questions

1. Why should costs be made known to the pivotal persons in an industrial enterprise?
2. Discuss in detail the preparation of a statement showing comparison of burdens.
3. Discuss in detail the uses that can be made of cost reports by foremen.
4. How are direct labor and direct material costs kept track of and reduced?

Problem A

The incoming orders indicate a slackening of the future business. The manager knows that future orders are below the capacity of the plant and that a safe policy is the best.

How should he proceed?

Problem B

A foreman finds his cost of handling material slowly creeping up in ratio to his production. The plant trucks all material with old-fashioned hand trucks. The volume of material is large. The floors are wooden and very old and rotten.

What should the foreman do?

Chapter XXXII—Defective Work Losses

Questions

1. (a) Generally speaking, what is the cause of defective work?
   (b) Give reasons to bring out the point.
2. Why are proper process and final inspection important?
3. What are some other methods of guarding against defective work?
4. Classify defective work losses.
5. What are some important points to be held in mind in deciding whether to salvage or scrap product?
6. Why should a department be charged with the cost of defective work for which it is responsible?
7. How are the causes of defective work analyzed?
8. When should defective work losses be treated as burden and when as direct costs?

Chapter XXXIII—Regulation of Idle-Equipment Delays

Questions

1. Why is the regulation of idle-equipment delays important?
2. Why should the causes of delays be treated at the source?
3. How and by whom is idle time accounted for?
4. What are the two classes of action required to correct causes of delays?
5. List the causes of idle machines and equipment and discuss each one of these in detail.
6. What data does an idle machine report show?

Chapter XXXIV—Joint and By-Product Costs

Questions

1. Define by-products.
2. Define joint products.
3. Describe the underlying principle of costing by-products.
4. Describe the general principle of costing joint products.
5. Describe the differences between prorating costs of joint products:
   (a) On analytical value
   (b) On weight basis
   (c) On market value
   (d) On standard ratio

Chapter XXXV—Interest as a Cost

Questions

1. State a practical approach to the interest problem?
2. State whether interest should be considered as a cost and why in respect to:
   (a) Buildings and Real Estate
   (b) Machinery
   (c) Fixture
   (d) Raw Materials

(e) Materials, Labor and Burden in Process
(f) Finished Goods
(g) Cash on Hand
(h) Accounts Receivable
(i) Assets not specified

GENERAL PROBLEM IN COST ACCOUNTING

By Henry Heaton Baily, C.P.A.
Asst. Professor of Accounting, University of Illinois

This problem is designed to bring into action all the fundamental movements involved in compiling the cost records for a month, the preparation of statements, and the closing of the books for the year.

The incidental or minor movements of filling out the various forms are taken care of by the various chapter problems. This problem is designed to impress on and test the student in the mechanism of establishing and operating the various control accounts which are so necessary to preserve the integrity of any cost methods in any business whatever. Irrespective of the exact design of books, forms, etc., the fundamental principles underlying the progressive control of accounts are fixed, and this problem is for the purpose of training the student in these principles.

PROBLEM

THE WESTERN MANUFACTURING COMPANY

1. The Western Manufacturing Co. has been in operation for some time. It is the policy of the company to have a trial balance taken and comparative statements prepared each month. The books are closed twice a year; June 30 and December 31.

2.

Trial Balance

of the Western Manufacturing Co., June 30, 19—

(This trial balance contains all adjustments and was taken just before the ledger was closed)

1. Cash	$ 13,826.86	
2. Accounts Receivable	41,892.93	
3. Notes Receivable	16,349.50	
4. Land	9,000.00	
5. Buildings	36,000.00	
6. Machinery and Equipment	70,045.18	
7. General Office Equipment	3,306.00	
8. Good-Will	25,000.00	
9. Prepaid Fire Insurance	1,720.00	
10. Freight to be Deducted	87.54	
11. Discount on Bonds Payable	837.50	
12. Interest Prepaid	82.14	
13. Vouchers Payable		$ 37,379.67
14. Notes Payable		14,700.00
15. Pay-Roll Accrued		6,210.74
16. Taxes Accrued		
17. Dividends Payable		
18. Interest Accrued on Bonds Payable		1,250.00
19. Bonds Payable, 6%		50,000.00
20. Capital Stock		200,000.00
21. Surplus		56,992.19
22. Reserve for Doubtful Accounts Receivable		4,104.69
23. Reserve for Depreciation on Buildings		5,750.00
24. Reserve for Depreciation of Machinery and Equipment		14,632.47
25. Reserve for Depreciation of General Office Equipment		617.78
26. Accrued Compensation Insurance		1,329.48
27. Materials	26,749.54	
28. Purchased Parts	21,657.10	
29. Supplies	5,871.16	
30. Finished Goods	71,354.27	
31. Miscellaneous Finished Goods	4,316.51	
32. Work in Process Material	19,347.11	
33. Work in Process Labor	15,628.46	
34. Work in Process Burden	9,876.58	
35. Department I Burden Account		
36. Department I Burden Credit Account		
37. Department II Burden Account		

38. Department II Burden Credit Account......		
39. Department III Burden Account............		
40. Department III Burden Credit Account......		
41. Cost of Sales (Regular).....................		
42. Cost of Miscellaneous Sales.................		
43. Sales.....................................		
44. Miscellaneous Sales........................		
45. Material Adjustment Account..............		
46. Shop Material Account....................	$ 18.64	
47. Discount Taken...........................		
48. Discount Given...........................		
49. Interest Cost............................		
50. Interest on Bonds Payable................		
51. Interest Income..........................		
52. Freight Out on Sales.....................		
53. Administration Expense...................		
54. Selling Expense..........................		
	$392,967.02	$392,967.02

3. TRIAL BALANCE

OF THE WESTERN MANUFACTURING CO., NOVEMBER 30, 19—.

(This trial balance reflects the condition of the ledger as it stands ready to receive the transactions of December. All entries for December are to be made, trial balance found and comparative statements prepared.)

1. Cash....................................$	23,112.90	
2. Accounts Receivable......................	57,102.18	
3. Notes Receivable.........................	20,347.00	
4. Land.....................................	9,000.00	
5. Buildings................................	36,000.00	
6. Machinery and Equipment..................	71,400.18	
7. General Office Equipment.................	3,416.00	
8. Good-Will................................	25,000.00	
9. Prepaid Fire Insurance...................	1,854.00	
10. Freight to be Deducted..................	121.04	
11. Discount on Bonds Payable...............	775.00	
12. Interest Prepaid........................		
13. Vouchers Payable........................		$ 43,116.25
14. Notes Payable...........................		15,770.00
15. Pay-Roll Accrued........................		9,629.54

16. Taxes Accrued		$ 700.00
17. Dividends Payable		10,000.00
18. Interest Accrued on Bonds Payable		1,000.00
19. Bonds Payable 6%		50,000.00
20. Capital Stock		200,000.00
21. Surplus		46,973.55
22. Reserve for Doubtful Accounts Receivable		4,032.45
23. Reserve for Depreciation on Buildings		6,500.00
24. Reserve for Depreciation of Machinery and Equipment		18,045.62
25. Reserve for Depreciation of General Office Equipment		784.18
26. Accrued Compensation Insurance		1,706.12
27. Materials	24,291.30	
28. Purchased Parts	22,429.98	
29. Supplies	4,729.64	
30. Finished Goods	79,845.71	
31. Miscellaneous Finished Goods	6,529.61	
32. Work in Process Material	22,979.42	
33. Work in Process Labor	17,629.78	
34. Work in Process Burden	11,891.28	
35. Department I Burden Account	45,015.13	
36. Department I Burden Credit Account		46,903.09
37. Department II Burden Account	20,348.71	
38. Department II Burden Credit Account		19,999.40
39. Department III Burden Account	30,917.55	
40. Department III Burden Credit Account		29,844.90
41. Cost of Sales (Regular)	397,216.74	
42. Cost of Miscellaneous Sales	24,617.50	
43. Sales		501,248.10
44. Miscellaneous Sales		31,217.64
45. Material Adjustment Account	19,228.60	
46. Shop Material Account	46.48	
47. Discount Taken		5,976.31
48. Discount Given	5,216.20	
49. Interest Cost	1,412.31	
50. Interest on Bonds Payable	1,312.50	
51. Interest Income		338.20
52. Freight Out on Sales	6,670.15	
53. Administration Expense	13,030.70	
54. Selling Expense	40,297.76	
	$1,043,785.35	$1,043,785.35

4. *Other Accounts.*—In addition to the accounts in the trial balance the following accounts appear in the ledger and are closed out regularly at the end of each month.

Department IV Expense Account. This account receives the charges for the electric power plant.

Department V Expense Account. This account receives the charges for the steam department.

Department VI Expense Account. This account is charged for the costs of the teaming department.

Department VII Expense Account. The expenses of the cost and production department are charged to this account.

Department VIII Expense Account. This account receives the charges for the general factory expenses.

O.D.S.O. Clearance Account.

Labor Transfer Account.

Expense Ledger Account.

Spoiled Work.

Scrap.

5. *Material Adjustment Account.*—Material and purchased parts requisitioned are charged to this account at cost price and credited to it at market price. When materials are returned to stores they are returned through this account and the above procedure is reversed. The account is closed at the end of each six months, and appears on the monthly statements as an adjustment of manufacturing profit.

6. *Shop Material Account.*—Material that is consumed in amounts too small to requisition in actual quantities used on each order is charged to this account and then distributed over the orders at a predetermined rate. At the end of the year the account is credited with the inventory of any of the material on hand, and the under- or over-absorbed balance closed to profit and loss, appearing in the "plant balances."

7. *Plant Balances.*—The under- and over-absorbed balances of burden accounts and such accounts as may be provided like the Shop Material account, appear individually on the trial balance. A subsidiary schedule is used to gather these balances together, and the net balance of all appears in the Profit and Loss account as an adjustment of the gross manufacturing profit. No ledger account called "plant balances" is required.

8. *Production Departments.*—Departments I, II and III are production departments and are on a direct labor hour basis. The predetermined or standard burden rates are respectively 60 cents, 75 cents and 56 cents per direct labor hour. Separate work in process accounts are not kept for each department, but separate accounts are provided for the material, labor and burden on goods in process.

9. *Labor.*—As the cost records deal with all costs for a full calendar month, and as all wages and salaries are paid every other week, the debits to the various cost accounts will automatically show a credit of accrued pay-roll in the Pay-roll account at the end of each month. This clears itself automatically when the pay-rolls are vouchered.

10. *Miscellaneous Sales.*—The miscellaneous sales are sales of by-products and scrap. By-products are manufactured along with the main product. The same accounts are used to record the cost of the by-product that are used to record the cost of the main product. Separate cost sheets are used for the by-products; the cost of the by-products is obtained from them, the debit is made to Miscellaneous Finished Goods account. Scrap is sold without any further work being done on it and the Scrap account is closed directly to the Miscellaneous Finished Goods account.

11. *Voucher Register.*—The voucher register contains columns showing the following totals for the month of December: Material and Supplies, $32,329.16; Labor $28,365.88; Expense Ledger $5,778.88; Freight to be Added $342.12; Freight to be Deducted $768.10; Freight out on Sales $874.18; and Miscellaneous Charges $15,442.12.

The analysis of the materials and supplies purchased showed that $18,921.60 was for purchased parts, $7,848.61 was for materials, and $5,558.95 was for supplies.

The miscellaneous charges consisted of a dividend of 5% which was declared on November 20, and made payable on December 20, the purchase of additional machinery for $672, the purchase of new office equipment for $170, the vouchering of a note for $3,400, of interest $120.12, a bill for fire insurance $1,080.

12. *Sales.*—The summary showed sales to the amount of $78,321.80 and miscellaneous sales amounting to $4,281.67. The cost of the sales were $61,215.70 and $3,438.41, respectively. In addition to the above, a charge of $342.12 was made to customers because of freight paid, and added to the sales invoice.

13. *Cash Receipts.*—At the end of December the various columns showed the following results: Cash Receipts (does not include the balance on December 1) $67,391.20; Accounts Receivable $65.645.99; Discounts Given $1,008.21; Miscellaneous Receipts $2,753.42. The items entered in the miscellaneous columns show a total of $118.42 received as interest, $125 received for the sale of machinery which was out of date, and $2,510 received in payment of notes due.

The machinery, which was sold December 29, cost $450; because of obsolescence it did not last the expected length of time. The reserve for the machinery to December 1 is $103.50. The reserve account does not provide for obsolescence. The machinery was purchased on January 3, nearly two years ago. It was used in Department II.

14. *Cash Payments.*—The totals of the columns in this book showed the following: Cash Paid $89,388.56; Voucher Payable $91,405.30; Freight to be Deducted $783.16; Discount Taken $1,233.58.

15. *Notes Receivable and Notes Payable.*—The Notes Receivable Book showed that notes received from customers totaled $4,820. The Notes Payable Book showed that notes amounting to $6,789.50 were issued in payment of vouchers due.

16. *Purchases Returned.*—Defective materials returned to vendors during the month amounted to $209.41. Purchased parts returned to vendors amounted to $368.29, both before payment of vouchers.

17. *Sales Returned.*—Customers returned goods which we sold them for $497.18, the goods costing us $388.11. Of the returned goods, $27.50 were miscellaneous sales, and they cost us $22.19. The remainder of the items was for regular sales.

18. *Pay-Roll Analysis.*

Dept.	Indirect Labor		Direct Labor		O.D.S.O. Labor		Transfer Labor		Total
	Hrs.	Amt.	Hrs.	Amt.	Hrs.	Amt.	Hrs.	Amt.	
I	4,539	$2,415.27	10,147	$8,241.18	218	$189 21	21	$16.20	$10,861.86
II	765	413 31	3,416	2,810 11	45	37 11	57	42.75	3,303.28
III	2,194	1,229 67	6,841	5,870 90	103	82 50	39	31.48	7,214.55
IV	1,087	574 20	–	–	–	–	–	–	574.20
V	1,173	651.64	–	–	–	–	–	–	651.64
VI	1,928	1,033 55	–	–	–	–	–	–	1,033.55
VII	–	1,591.30	–	–	–	–	–	–	1,591.30
VIII	–	1,233.16	–	–	–	–	–	–	1,233.16
Total		$9,142 10		$16,922 19		$308 82		$90.43	$26,463.54
Salaries of Officers									$ 1,200.00
Salaries in the General Office									915.00
Salaries of Salesmen									2,241.00
Salaries in Sales Department									812.00
Total									$31,631.54

The standing order numbers shown on the time cards which made up the above pay-roll showed distribution of the indirect time as follows:

Dept. I: The total of $2,415.27 was made up as follows: Order 3101–$450; 3102–$200; 3103–$460; 3104–$102; 3105–$450; 3106–$52; 3108–$82; 3121–$228; 3122–$140; 3123–$86.27; 3125–$48; 3126–$32; 3127–$54; 3128–$31.

Dept. II: The total of $413.31 was made up as follows: Order 3201–$200; 3202–$75; 3204–$30; 3205–$90.31; 3208–$18.

Dept. III: The total of $1,229.67 was made up as follows: Order 3301–$350; 3302–$100; 3303–$300; 3304–$75; 3305–$234.67; 3306–$22; 3308–$20; 3321–$13; 3322–$28; 3325–$24; 3326–$14; 3327–$31; 3328–$18.

Dept. IV: The total of $574.20 was made up as follows: Order 2101–$350; 2108–$224.20.

Dept. V: The total of $651.64 was made up as follows: Order 2201–$250; 2208–$401.64.

Dept. VI: The total of $1,033.35 was made up as follows: Order 2401–$200; 2402–$100; 2408–$513.55; 2421–$200; 2425–$20.

Dept. VII: The total of $1,591.30 was all charged to Order 1102.

Dept. VIII: The total of $1,233.16 was made up as follows: Order 1001–$500; 1002–$400; 1004–$48.16; 1008–$25; 1009–$220; 1024–$40.

Salaries of Officers to Order 10101.

Salaries of General Office to Order 10101.

Salaries of Salesmen to Order 12102.

Salaries of Sales Department to Order 12101.

19. *O.D.S.O. Labor.*—An analysis of the O.D.S.O. time cards showed the following:

Done by Departments

Done for Depts.	I		II		III	
	Hours	Amount	Hours	Amount	Hours	Amount
I	..	$.....	12	$ 9.60	16	$12.30
II	112	94.25	..	.....	70	58.55
III	82	75.46	33	27.51	..	.....
IV	..	.....	..	.....	14	9.80
V	15	12.75	..	.....	..	.....
VI	9	6.75	..	.....	3	1.85

Thus Dept. I did 112 O.D.S.O. hours for Dept. II at a cost of $94.25, 82 hours for Dept. III at a cost of $75.46, etc. The amounts given do not include any calculations for burden.

The charges to Dept. I were all charged by time slips to Standing Order 3121.

Charges to Dept. II were: Order 3221–$159.20; 3222–$52; 3223–$48.

Charges to Dept. III were: Order 3321–$102; 3322–$50; 3323–$24.92.

Charges to Dept. IV were all to Order 2127.

Charges to Dept. V were all to Order 2221.

Charges to Dept. VI were all to order 2421.

20. *Transfer Labor.*—An analysis of the time cards for the transfer labor is as follows:

Done for Depts.	Done by Departments: I		II		III	
	Hours	Amount	Hours	Amount	Hours	Amount
I Direct	..	$.....	10	$10.00	5	$ 5.00
I Indirect	..	.....	14	10.35	9	6.94
II Direct	..	.....	..	.....	10	10.00
II Indirect	6	4.20	..	.....	7	3.94
III Direct	5	5.00	..	.....	..	.....
III Indirect	5	3.50	14	9.05	..	
IV	..	.....	12	8.10	..	.....
V	..	.....	7	5.25	..	.....
VI	5	3.50	..	.....	8	5.60

When making the entries for compensation insurance and to close the expense accounts for Dept. VII and VIII, the above labor hours and labor cost should be taken into consideration.

The charges to Dept. I for indirect labor were all charged by time slips to Standing Order 3105. Charges to Dept. II were to Order 3205; charges to Dept. III to Order 3305; Dept. IV, to Order 2108; Dept. V, to Order 2208; Dept. VI, to Order 2408.

21. *Analysis of Requisitions for Materials and Supplies.*—Materials put into process on requisitions, cost price $12,284.60; market price $9,872.50. Of the $9,872.50 the amount charged to the Shop Material Account was $411.63, while the amount credited to this account was $432.13. Purchased parts put into process on requisitions, cost price $21,378.62; market price $18,462.39. Supplies requisitioned $4,909.60. (They are taken out at cost.) The supplies chargeable to the various burden and expense accounts are as follows: Dept. I, $477.42; Dept. II, $102.41; Dept. III, $311.51; Dept. IV, $394.18; Dept. V, $3,162.40;

Dept. VI, $78.29; Dept. VII, $95.20; Dept. VIII, $112.42; Administrative Expense, $113.70; Selling Expense, $62.07.

The standing order number shown on the requisitions which made up the above charges to Burden and Expense accounts showed distributions as follows:

Dept. I: The total of $477.42 was made up as follows: Order 3106–$22.42; 3121–$80; 3122–$68; 3123–$42; 3125–$30; 3126–$20; 3127–$42; 3128–$18; 3141–$75; 3142–$32; 3143–$28; 3146–$20.

Dept. II: The total of $102.41 was made up as follows: Order 3241–$62; 3242–$10; 3243–$10; 3246–$20.41.

Dept. III: The total of $311.51 was made up as follows: Order 3321–$50; 3322–$48; 3323–$38; 3325–$22; 3326–$17; 3327–$14; 3328–$32; 3341–$44; 3342–$12; 3346–$34.51.

Dept. IV: The total of $394.18 was made up as follows: Order 2121–$270; 2126–$38.18; 2127–$24; 2142–$15; 2143–$34; 2146–$13.

Dept. V: The total of $3162.40 was made up as follows: Order 2221–$122; 2224–$40; 2226–$22; 2228–$34; 2242–$22; 2243–$18; 2245–$2,892.40; 2246–$12.

Dept. VI: The total of $78.29 was made up as follows: Order 2443–$40; 2446–$38.29.

Dept. VII: The total material is charged to Order 1148.

Dept. VIII: The total of $112.42 was made up as follows: Order 1021–$17; 1025–$50; 1042–$20; 1048–$25.42.

Administrative Expense—The total is charged to Order 10105.

Selling Expense—The total is charged to Order 12105.

22. *Analysis of Expense Debit Slips.*—The charges were for the following departments: Dept. I, $82.68; Dept. II, $31.43; Dept. III, $69.84; Dept. IV, $48.52; Dept. V, $47.10; Dept. VI, $83.19; Dept. VII, $38.15; Dept. VIII, $41.67; Administrative Expense $60.11; Selling Expense $5,276.19.

The standing order numbers shown on the expense debit slips which make up the above charges to Burden and Expense accounts showed distribution as follows:

Dept. I: The total of $82.68 was made up as follows: Order 3121–$52.68; 3123–$30.

Dept. II: The total was charged to Order 3225.

Dept. III: The total of $69.84 was made up as follows: Order 3321–$40; 3322–$29.84.

Dept. IV: The total of $48.52 was made up as follows: Order 2121–$30; 2127–$18.52.

Dept. V: The total of $47.10 was made up as follows: Order 2221–$27.10; 2228–$20.

Dept. VI: The total was charged to Order 2421.

Dept. VII: The total of $38.15 was made up as follows: Order 1125–$25; 1148–$13.15.

Dept. VIII: The total was charged to Order 1025.

Administrative Expense—The total was charged to Order 10,106.

Selling Expense—The total of $5,276.19 was made up as follows: Order 12104–$462.13; 12106–$34.42; 12107–$25; 12108–$25; 12116–$4,729.64.

23. *Analysis of Material Returned to Stores from Productive Orders.*—Materials returned, $218.91 market value, $265 cost. Purchased parts returned, $428.70 market value, $492 cost. (No work was done on the items returned to stores.)

24. *Cost Sheets.*—An analysis of cost sheets completed during the month showed that in the finished goods the direct labor cost $19,248.11, and the materials and purchased parts cost $31,677.51, while in the miscellaneous finished goods the direct labor cost $2,218.21 and the material cost $2,524.64. The direct labor hours chargeable to finished goods in Dept. I amounted to 9,821, in Dept. II, 3,241, and in Dept. III, 6,636, while on miscellaneous finished goods Dept. I put in 1,008 direct labor hours, Dept. II, 342, and Dept. III, 633 direct labor hours.

25. *Scrap and By-Products.*—A summary of the scrap tickets for the month shows the following totals: Work in Process Material $119.61; Work in Process Labor $38.26; Work in Process Burden $28.11.

After inspection, a part of the work was put back in process. Cost of this work: Material $64.12; Labor $22.68; Burden $15.07. The amount charged to the Scrap account was $45.40.

The loss in material value, cost of the labor and burden lost on the work spoiled is charged to the burden accounts of the department in which the work is spoiled. Dept. I is to be charged with $15.15 (Order 3106), Dept. II with $10.29 (Order 3206), and Dept. III with $13.27 (Order 3306).

The Scrap account is closed to the Miscellaneous Finished Goods account.

26. *Apportioned Charges.*—Depreciation on all equipment is calculated at rate of 1% per month. The depreciation on General Office

Equipment is charged equally to the accounts for administrative and selling expenses.

The buildings are depreciated at the rate of 5% per year.

Fire insurance is $400 per month.

Taxes average $140 per month.

Compensation insurance is at the rate of 1% on wages paid in the eight departments. (In Depts. I, II and III adjustments must be made for the transfer labor; O.D.S.O. labor to be figured with originating department.)

27. *Summary Analysis of Apportioned Charges.*—(The numbers given are the percentages to be charged to each department, i.e., 35% of the depreciation on machinery and equipment is to be charged to Dept. I and 20% is to be charged to Dept. II.)

Charge to Dept.	Depreciation		Fire Insurance	Taxes
	On Machinery	On Bldgs.		
I	35	34	30	35
II	20	20	18	20
III	27	26	23	25
IV	6	6	10	7
V	8	10	15	8
VI	2	2	2	3
VII	1	1	1	1
VIII	1	1	1	1

28. *Distribution of Expense Accounts.*—Basis for distribution of expenses for Depts. IV-VIII inclusive. (The numbers given are the percentages of the given accounts to be charged to each department, thus 40% of the expenses of Dept. IV is to be charged to Dept. I and 10% is to be charged to Dept. II.)

Charge to Dept.	Expense Accounts Distributed		
	IV	V	VI
I	40	20	25
II	10	10	44
III	32	20	27
IV	..	37	..
V	..	..	..
VI	10	..	..
VII	3	5	1
VIII	3	5	3
Admin. Expense	1	1	..
Selling Expense	1	2	

The total of the expenses for Depts. VII and VIII should be distributed to Depts. I, II and III on the basis of total labor hours.

29. *Doubtful Accounts.*—It has been the policy of the company to set up a reserve for doubtful accounts equal to 1% of the net sales during the month.

30. *Other Adjustments.*—The bonds were issued February 1, 19—. They run for 10 years and were issued at 97. It has been the policy of the company to write off the discount monthly to the interest account. The interest is payable semi-annually.

Smith, Jones & Sons have gone into bankruptcy and during the month the last payment was received from them. The amount lost is $102.48.

The head of the sales department reports that during the month the salesmen earned commission amounting to $147.56. The item has not yet been vouchered. (Charge to Standing Order 12.103.)

INSTRUCTIONS COVERING SOLUTION OF PROBLEM

WORKING PAPERS NECESSARY:

1. Six-column paper for equivalent of ledger. First two columns for starting trial balance; second two columns for posting journal entries, and last two columns for extended trial balance ready to make out statements. If desired, ten columns can be used, the fourth two columns being for final closing entries and the fifth two columns for the extended trial balance after books are entirely closed for the year, or, the final closing may be on separate paper.
2. Journal paper for preparation of journal entries.
3. Statement paper with five columns for financial statements.
4. Collating sheets ruled up as shown in Chapter XXV for assembling burden and expense statements.
5. All papers should have margin at left for binding.
6. A clear explanation should be made of all entries on all working papers.

A—*Journal Entries*

A-1. Of voucher register.
 2. Of sales and sales cost (two entries).
 3. Of cash receipts.
 4. For clearing from the records the machinery sold. The management desires that the loss caused by the obsolescence be apportioned between past and present periods. Regard machines in service 2 full years.

5. Of cash payments.
6. Of notes received and issued (two entries).
7. Of purchases returned.
8. Of sales returned (two entries).
9. Of pay-roll entries.
10. For distributing tht O.D.S.O. labor and burden.
11. For distributing the transfer labor.
12. Of requisitions for material and supplies. (Remember the use of Material Adjustment account.)
13. For distributing expense ledger charges.
14. Of materials returned to stores (two entries, cost and market).
15. Of goods finished (two entries, one for each finished goods account).
16. Of spoiled work and scrap:
    (a) Of work spoiled.
    (b) Of work returned to shop.
    (c) Of scrap.
    (d) Of loss charged to burden accounts.
    (e) To close Scrap account.
17. Of depreciation entries covering machinery and equipment, buildings and general office equipment (one entry for each of the three).
18. Of insurance expired.
19. Of taxes accrued.
20. Of accrued compensation insurance. (See note under paragraph 20.)
21. To distribute Dept. V Expense account.
22. To distribute Dept. IV Expense account.
23. To distribute Dept. VI Expense account.
24. To distribute Dept. VII Expense account. (See note under paragraph 20.)
25. To distribute Dept. VIII Expense account. (See note under paragraph 20.)
26. To charge the Work in Process Burden with the proper amount.
27. To set up reserve for bad accounts.
28. To take care of the necessary adjustments called for in paragraph 30.

B—*Posting to Trial Balance*

B–1. Copy the trial balance for November on a working sheet.

In copying this balance extra lines should be allowed for posting the various journal entries for December transactions. The burden and expense accounts, of course, require the most space, and should have at least six lines allowed for even small figures used in posting.

2. Post the entries for December to the third and fourth columns of the working sheet.
3. Prepare trial balance for December in fifth and six columns.

C—*Statements and Closing*

NOTE: See column arrangements given at end of problem.

C-1. Prepare Comparative Balance Sheet for the months of June, November and December, giving columns for increase and decrease of December over June and December over November.

2. Prepare supporting schedules for the various items in the balance sheet requiring same for December.
3. Prepare comparative to date Profit and Loss statements for November and December, and Profit and Loss for month of December.
4. Prepare schedule of plant balances. (Shop Material Account has no inventory.)
5. Prepare Burden statements for Depts. I, II and III for December, showing credit at standard burden rates and the under- or over-absorbed balances in each.
6. Prepare expense statements for Dept. IV, V, VI, VII, and VIII for December, showing distribution of same.
7. Prepare administrative and selling expense statements for December which show the detail of these items in Profit and Loss statement.
8. Prepare the compound journal entries for closing the books for the period.
9. Post the closing entries and prepare trial balance of accounts as ready for new period.

D—*Classification of Accounts*

D-1. Prepare a classification of accounts to take the place of the Numbering System given in the trial balances of June and November. Make any necessary changes in the arrangement of the accounts.

E—*Arrangement of Work*

E-1. Arrange the work in logical order; put it in folder.

Arrangements of Columns for Statements

For Balance Sheet and Balance Sheet Schedules

Accounts	June 30	Dec. 31	Nov. 30	Dec. 31 as to	
				June 30	Nov. 30

For Profit and Loss Account and Plant Balances

Accounts		Dec. 31	Nov. 30	Month of Dec.	

For Burden and Expense Statements

Accounts		Month of Dec.			

Note: Ordinarily the headings for these statements would be as in text. But as this problem deals with but one month, only one column is necessary.

INDEX

A

B

F

G

I

P

T

U

V

W

Spotted something that isn't quite right?

Let us know and we'll fix it for future reprints. And as a thank you for your diligence, we'll send you a free Sothis book of your choice.

publisher@sothis.press

This page intentionally left blank

Except of course for that line above. And this one.
And whilst we have your attention, perhaps you'd
like to follow us on Instagram @sothis.press. Go on.

Made in United States
Orlando, FL
07 November 2026

90337482R00335